D1701802

Bhagavad Gītā

Home Study Course

(Text in Sanskrit with transliteration, word-to-word and verse meaning, along with an elaborate commentary in English based on Śaṅkara-bhāṣyam)

Volume 5

Chapter 6

Summary of Chapters 1-6

Chapter 7

Swami Dayananda Saraswati
Arsha Vidya

Arsha Vidya
Research and Publication Trust
Chennai

Published by :

Arsha Vidya Research and Publication Trust
4 'Srinidhi' Apts 3rd Floor
Sir Desika Road Mylapore
Chennai 600 004 INDIA
Tel : 044 2499 7023
Telefax : 2499 7131
Email : avrandpt@gmail.com
Website: www.avrpt.com

© Swami Dayananda Saraswati
Arsha Vidya

All Rights Reserved.
No part of this book may be reproduced or transmitted in any form or by any means, electronic or mechanical, including photocopying, recording, or by any information storage and retrieval system, without written permission from the author and the publisher.

ISBN : 978-93-80049-34-2

ISBN : 978-93-80049-39-7 (Set of 9 Volumes)

New Edition & Format	: July	2011	Copies : 1200
1st Reprint	: July	2012	Copies : 1000

Design & Layout :
Graaphic Design

Printed at :
Sudarsan Graphics
27, Neelakanta Mehta Street
T. Nagar, Chennai 600 017
Email : info@sudarsan.com

Preface

I am very happy that the 'Bhagavad Gītā Home Study Course' will now be available in nine compact volumes so that one can carry a given volume while travelling. As I said in my foreword for the last edition, I want the readers to be aware that these books do not constitute another set of books on the *Bhagavadgītā*. They are different in that they are edited transcript-pages of classroom discussions; they are presented to the reader as a program for self-study. If this is borne in mind, while reading, one can enjoy the same attitude of a student in the classroom, making oneself available to the whole process of unfoldment of the content of the words of Bhagavān. The study will then prove to be as rewarding as directly listening to the teacher. This attitude would prove to be *ātma-kṛpā*. Once this *kṛpā* is there, the other two, *śāstra-kṛpā* and *īśvara-kṛpā* would follow.

The enormous job of patient editing of the pages, thousands of them, and presenting them, retaining the original words and content without any compromise, was done by Dr. Martha Doherty. These books have created a number of committed students of the *Bhagavadgītā,* thanks to Martha's invaluable contribution to the teaching tradition of Vedanta. I also congratulate the staff of our Publication division ably led by Ms. K. Chandra, a dedicated student of Vedanta.

Swami Dayananda Saraswati
Arsha Vidya
June 19 2011

Key to Transliteration and Pronunciation of Sanskrit Letters

Sanskrit is a highly phonetic language and hence accuracy in articulation of the letters is important. For those unfamiliar with the *Devanāgari* script, the international transliteration is a guide to the proper pronunciation of Sanskrit letters.

अ	*a*	*(but)*
आ	*ā*	*(father)*
इ	*i*	*(it)*
ई	*ī*	*(beat)*
उ	*u*	*(full)*
ऊ	*ū*	*(pool)*
ऋ	*ṛ*	*(rhythm)*
ॠ	*ṝ*	*(marine)*
ऌ	*ḷ*	*(revelry)*
ए	*e*	*(play)*
ऐ	*ai*	*(aisle)*
ओ	*o*	*(go)*
औ	*au*	*(loud)*
क	*ka*	*(seek)* 1
ख	*kha*	*(blockhead)**1
ग	*ga*	*(get)* 1
घ	*gha*	*(log hut)**1
ङ	*ṅa*	*(sing)* 1
च	*ca*	*(chunk)* 2
छ	*cha*	*(catch him)**2
ज	*ja*	*(jump)* 2
झ	*jha*	*(hedgehog)**2
ञ	*ña*	*(bunch)* 2
ट	*ṭa*	*(true)**3
ठ	*ṭha*	*(anthill)**3
ड	*ḍa*	*(drum)**3
ढ	*ḍha*	*(godhead)**3
ण	*ṇa*	*(under)**3
त	*ta*	*(path)**4
थ	*tha*	*(thunder)**4
द	*da*	*(that)**4
ध	*dha*	*(breathe)**4
न	*na*	*(nut)**4
प	*pa*	*(put)* 5
फ	*pha*	*(loophole)**5
ब	*ba*	*(bin)* 5
भ	*bha*	*(abhor)**5
म	*ma*	*(much)* 5
य	*ya*	*(loyal)*
र	*ra*	*(red)*
ल	*la*	*(luck)*
व	*va*	*(vase)*
श	*śa*	*(sure)*
ष	*ṣa*	*(shun)*
स	*sa*	*(so)*
ह	*ha*	*(hum)*

ं	*ṁ*	*anusvāra*	(nasalisation of preceding vowel)
ः	*ḥ*	*visarga*	(aspiration of preceding vowel)
*			No exact English equivalents for these letters

1.	Guttural	–	Pronounced from throat
2.	Palatal	–	Pronounced from palate
3.	Lingual	–	Pronounced from cerebrum
4.	Dental	–	Pronounced from teeth
5.	Labial	–	Pronounced from lips

The 5th letter of each of the above class – called nasals – are also pronounced nasally.

Contents

Chapter 6

Introduction 1

Verses 1&2

The external means – karma-yoga – to introduce the internal means, dhyāna-yoga 4

Karma to be done 6

Conformity to dharma 7

The value of values 8

Values require alertness 9

Renunciation of the two-fold activities 10

Verse 3

Kṛṣṇa points out how karma-yoga is a means for dhyāna-yoga 13

Meditation does not involve the will 14

Complete detachment comes only through knowledge 15

Verse 4

One whose mind is not disturbed by anything attains liberation 16

Only the doer performs action 17

Verses 5&6

The self alone is one's benefactor and one's enemy 20

Understanding the fundamental problem 21

Helping yourself 22

Do not look down upon yourself 23

The three powers at our disposal 26

Your mind is with you wherever you go 28

Verse 7

Kṛṣṇa discusses the person who is a friend to oneself 29

The nature of tranquillity 31

Why criticism is difficult to handle 32

Verse 8

A wise person's attitude with reference to all objects in the world 34

Jñāna and vijñāna 35

The need to convert jñāna into vijñāna 37

One who has enough – alaṁ buddhi 38

The wise person is not swayed by anything external or internal 39

How qualifications become spontaneous virtues 40

The only security is knowing one is secure in oneself 41

Insecurity is due to one's subjective values 42

Gold represents all desirable objects including relationships 44

Verse 9

Kṛṣṇa describes the wise person's attitude towards different types of people 47

Suhṛd and mitra 48

Ari 49

Udāsīna and madhyastha 49

Dveṣya and bandhu 51

Sādhus and pāpas 51

A wise person never condemns another person 55

The fear of being judged 56

The wise person is the most exalted among yogīs 58

Verse 10

May the yogī always connect the mind to the object of meditation 60

Meditation does not require an accomplice 61

Meditation requires freedom from longing 64

What it means to be free of possessions 65

Meditation requires a discipline 66

Verse 11&12

Where to sit and with what to sit in meditation 67

Find a quiet corner to meditate 69

The significance of the materials of the traditional āsana 71

The purpose of meditation 73

Meditation is both prayerful and contemplative 74

Verse 13&14

Sitting posture, object of meditation and the nature of the meditator 77

The emphasis throughout the Gītā is on the meditator 81

The source of fear 82

The one who is free from fear is a vigatabhī 83

The need for two types of vākyas 85

Kṛṣṇa as Parameśvara - the Lord 86

Meditation on Parameśvara 88

The meditator is mat-para 89

Verse 15

The ultimate end gained as a result of dhyāna-yoga – meditation 91

The meaning of śānti 92

Svarūpa śānti – the śānti that is oneself 95

Verse 16

The discipline of eating and sleeping required for meditation 96

The discipline of sleep 99

Verse 17

Dhyāna yoga is for the one who follows a life of discipline 100

'Spiritual' obsessions 101

One needs a sense of proportion in one's activities 102

One decides for oneself what is proper 103
The knowledge that destroys sorrow 104

Verse 18

The mind – through knowledge – sees the contemplator and the contemplated as ātmā 107
The result of knowledge is freedom from binding desires 108
The definition of an accomplished person 110

Verse 19

An oft quoted illustration to describe the mind of the accomplished person 112

Verse 20

The mind – mastered by dhyāna-yoga – abides in oneself 116

Verse 21

The sukha that is yourself 117
The difference between recognition and experience 123
Experience always has an end 124
Discipline implies certain mastery of the mind 126
Thought is you 127

Verses 22&23

The yoga that Kṛṣṇa talks about is more a disassociation than association 128
Mokṣa is a matter of understanding – not of memory 130

There is no better gain than self-knowledge 131
The resolution of seeking 134
Another definition for yoga 135
What is joined together can also fall apart 136
Ignorance makes the impossible possible 141
There is only ātmā 141
Erroneous notions cannot be surrendered 143
Self-knowledge is the only pursuit that solves the problem 145

Verse 24&25

Kṛṣṇa talks of yoga in the sense of viyoga 146
The basis of all desires 148
Withdrawing the sense organs 149
Definition of ātmā 151
The knower-known-knowledge are one 153
Nothing is separate from existence 154
Redirecting the mind to the very basis of thoughts is dhyāna 155
No will is required in contemplation 157

Verse 26

The mind needs to be dealt with 159
The mind itself is not a problem 160

Verse 27

One reaches the most exalted happiness as a result of meditation 161

Verse 28

Resolving the difference between the subject and the object 164

Atyanta sukha is not experiential 167

No effort is required to gain svarūpa sukha 168

The vision of the śāstra 170

Ātmā is eternally present 172

There is only one track – jñāna 173

Verse 29

Seeing the sameness that is in everything 174

Contemplation is the appreciation of what is being said here 176

The resolution of all beings into the self by knowledge 181

Verse 30

The one who sees me in everything is not remote from me 185

The result of the vision 188

Verse 31

The yogī – recognising me in all beings – abides in me 190

Īśvara is not remote from oneself	192
Self-knowledge is immediate knowledge	194
Verse 32	
Wrong action is not possible for the wise person	195
The basis of dharma	197
Ego is ignorance-based	198
A second interpretation of the verse	200
Fullness depends on nothing	202
All human beings must follow the order of dharma	204
Verses 33&34	
The nature of Arjuna's problem is very clear	205
Arjuna says - mind is agitation	208
The mind is dṛḍha – it keeps one under its control	210
Arjuna's problem is universal	213
Verses 35&36	
The mind is mastered by practice and objectivity	214
Acceptance is the first step	215
Caring for the child within	218
Practice and usefulness of japa	219
Vairāgya – objectivity	221
We seek acceptance from others because of superimposition	222
The superimposition is not deliberate	224
Neutralising the superimposition	225

Seeing things as they are 226

Vairāgya is nothing but one's emotional growth 229

Verses 37-39

Arjuna presents another problem that is purely imagined 233

Verse 40

Kṛṣṇa answers – anyone who performs good actions never comes to a bad end 243

Changing the course of karma 246

Verses 41-44

What happens to the yoga-bhraṣṭa 248

The person can be born into a family of yogīs 253

A seeker can be born anywhere 256

The connection with the past is by means of the intellect 260

There is no going back once self-enquiry has begun 263

Verse 45

The ultimate result of this pursuit 263

To be a seeker is no ordinary accomplishment 265

An end that never ends 266

Verse 46

Kṛṣṇa tells Arjuna to be a yogī 266

Scholarship alone does not give one the vision 267

Verse 47

The exalted yogī is one who has the sameness of vision 270

There are not two yogīs here 271

Summary of chapters 1-6 273

Arjuna's predicament 274

Arjuna's lot is everyone's lot 276

Regaining the kingdom was no longer important 277

'Tat Tvam Asi' is Vedanta 280

Two-fold lifestyle 282

Kṛṣṇa as Īśvara 284

Renouncing the doer 285

There is no choice really speaking 287

Karma-yoga and then sannyāsa is the order 288

Meditation 289

The basis of Arjuna's fear 290

Chapter 7

Introduction 292

Verse 1

Unfoldment to tat pada begins 293

In seeking Parameśvara - the end and the means are the same 295

Verse 2

Vijñāna is distinguished from jñāna 296

Praise of knowledge – knowing one thing everything is as well-known 298

Verse 3

This knowledge is rare in terms of its result 301

This knowledge is rare in terms of its difficulty to gain 302

Among thousands – one given person seeks ātmā 303

Among the seekers – one given person knows the reality 304

The two-fold cause of creation 306

Svarūpa-prakṛti 306

Svabhāva-prakṛti 307

Verse 4

Prakṛti is divided in an eight-fold way 308

Prakriyā – a teaching model 309

Sṛṣṭi-prakriyā – analysis of creation in Chāndogyopaniṣad 310

Avasthā-traya prakriyā – analysis of the three states of experience in the Māṇḍūkyopaniṣad 311

Pañca-kośa-prakriyā – analysis of the five levels of experience of oneself in the Taittirīyopaniṣad 312

Tanmātra-prakriyā – a type of sṛṣṭi-prakriyā 313

Verse 5

What has been described so far is aparā
(svabhāva) prakṛti 315

My real nature – parā-prakṛti – sustains everything 316

Verse 6

I am the cause for the projection
and resolution of creation 318

Definition of the cause – the maker and the material 321

Two types of lakṣaṇas:

Svarūpa-lakṣaṇa 322

Taṭastha-lakṣaṇa 323

Satya must be understood to understand mithyā 324

Two types of material cause: 324

Vivarta-upādāna-kāraṇa 325

Pariṇāmi-upādāna-kāraṇa – māyā 327

Verse 7

Everything has its being in me – like the beads
in a string 328

Verses 8-12

Everything is non-separate from me 332

Verse 13

People get deluded by modifications
of the three guṇas 348

Verse 14

Māyā is difficult to overcome but those who seek me cross this māyā 351

Māyā is mohinī – the one who deludes 354

Some erroneous interpretations of such verses 356

Prapatti 357

Resolution of the seeming duality 359

Verse 15

The people who do not seek Īśvara at all 360

Verse 16

Four types of devotees: 364

Ārtaḥ 365

Arthārthī 366

Jijñāsuḥ 366

Jñānī 368

Verse 17

The jñānī is eka-bhakta – always united to Īśvara 370

The jñānī is distinguished 372

Verse 18

All devotees are exalted but the wise person is myself alone 374

The jñānī is not different from Bhagavān 376

Verse 19

The jñānī is again praised 377

Everything is Vāsudeva 378

It is difficult to find a mahātmā who has this knowledge 381

Verse 20

Desires rob one's discrimination 381

Verse 21

In whichever form people worship me – in that form I bless them 385

Verse 22

I make their śraddhā more firm by giving the result 387

Verse 23

For those of limited discrimination – the result is limited 391

Verse 24

Lack of discrimination denies recognition of Īśvara 397

Gaining Parameśvara is sulabha – easy 402

Verse 25

Covered by māyā – not everyone recognises Bhagavān 405

The original mistake is not corrected 409

Uniqueness of ignorance of ātmā 410

Uniqueness of knowledge of ātmā 410

Verse 26

When Īśvara is not known 415

The truth of Īśvara 418

Īśvara is aparokṣa 420

Verse 27

People are totally deluded due to delusion of the opposites 422

Delusion obstructs even the desire for knowledge 425

Verses 28-30

Released from the delusion of opposites – people of good actions reach me 426

Dṛḍha-vratāḥ are people with firm vows and commitment 429

Takng refuge in me one gains freedom from death 430

The wise know Brahman as not separate from themselves 435

They also understand karma in its entirety 437

Knowledge of Īśvara as both efficient and material cause 441

Even at the time of death, their knowledge stands firm 444

Alphabetical index of verses (9 Volumes) 448

Chapter 6

ध्यान-योगः

Dhyāna-yogaḥ
Topic of meditation

Introduction

The topic of the sixth chapter is meditation, *dhyāna*. *Dhyāna* means the act of meditation. So, *dhyāna* is a *sādhana,* a means for gaining *mokṣa*.

We have seen that *sādhana* is two-fold – *bahiraṅga-sādhana,* implying *karma,* and *antaraṅga-sādhana,* which is where *dhyāna* comes in. *Karma* becomes a *yoga* because it helps you gain the preparedness of mind, *antaḥ-karaṇa-śuddhi,* that enables you gain the knowledge that is *mokṣa*. *Karma-yoga* is an external means, *bahiraṅga-sādhana,* whereas *dhyāna* is purely internal, *antaraṅga-sādhana*.

Meditation is an action born purely of the mind. In fact, every action is born in the mind, but it does not necessarily remain in the mind. The act of speaking, for example, is born of the mind. The words are formed in the mind and are then expressed through the organ of speech. Although different forms of action emanate from the mind alone, they do not always stop there. They may manifest through the various means of expression. But in *dhyāna,* the activity is born of mind and remains in the mind; therefore, it is purely a mental action, *mānasa-vyāpāra,* an activity that is a *sādhana,* a means, a *yoga*.

Any worry is also a mental activity. But, can a person who worries constantly say, 'I am doing meditation?' No, he cannot say that. *Dhyāna* is a mental activity in which the subject matter is predetermined. It is an activity whose subject matter is *saguṇa-brahma* – *saguṇa-brahma-viṣaya-mānasa-vyāpāra*. This is one definiton of meditation.

Saguṇa-brahma means limitless Brahman, *satya-jñāna-ananta-brahma* as Īśvara, the cause of the world. *Saguṇa-brahma* is the object for the mental activity called meditation. Now, suppose I think of *saguṇa-brahma* for half-a-minute every morning at nine o' clock and then again at twelve o'clock for another half-a-minute. Is this *dhyāna?* It is a mental activity, no doubt; I think of the Lord and then the thought goes away. But, even though this thinking occurs in the mind and resolves there, it is not *dhyāna*. Therefore, the mental activity, *mānasa-vyāpāra* called *dhyāna,* is defined still further as a mental activity where all the thoughts other than those concerning the chosen object are removed, *vijātīya-pratyaya-rahita*, and only those concerning the chosen object flow for a length of time, *sajātīya-pratyaya-pravāha*. Then there is *dhyāna*.

The word '*jāti*' means 'species.' Here, *vijātīya* refers to external objects, objects other than the one chosen for meditation. *Pratyaya* is a thought, *vṛtti*, and *vijātīya-pratyaya* is a thought other than the one chosen, that is, other than *saguṇa-brahma*. *Rahita* means 'without.' When there are no thoughts other than *saguṇa-brahma*, all of them having been removed, there is a flow, *pravāha*, of the chosen *vṛtti*, the chosen thought; there is a *sajātīya-pratyaya-pravāha*.

When the *vijātīya*s are removed and the *sajātīya*s are allowed to flow for a length of time, then the ongoing mental activity is called meditation, *dhyāna*. Therefore, *dhyāna* is definitely an action on the part of the mind, a mental activity, *mānasa-karma,* the object of meditation being *saguṇa-brahma*. It is therefore a *saguṇa-brahma-viṣaya-mānasa-karma*. This definition of the act of doing *dhyāna* is given in one compound that is given here, which defines it completely – *vijātīya-vṛtti-rahita-sajātīya-vṛtti-pravāha-rūpa-saguṇa-brahma-viṣaya-mānasa-vyāpāraḥ*.

Another aspect of *dhyāna* that you must know is that when the mind moves away from the object of meditation, it should be brought back to the object of meditation. This 'bringing it back' is a part of the definition, *lakṣaṇa*, of *dhyāna*. It is not going away from *dhyāna,* as you may think. Many times people say to me, ' Swamiji, when I meditate, my mind goes away!' Going away is not a distraction to meditation; it is a part of meditation. In fact, thinking that it is a problem is the problem. When the mind goes, you simply bring it back. Bringing the mind back is a part of the definition of *dhyāna*. The mind running away is definitely a characteristic of *dhyāna* and when it does you bring it back. If the mind does not run away at all, it is called *samādhi*.

When the *vijātīya-vṛtti*s come, we turn away from them and return to the object of meditation, the *saguṇa-brahma,* the *iṣṭa-devatā*. This is one definition of *dhyāna*. The other is the mental activity involved when the object of meditation is Brahman with no attributes – *nirguṇa-brahma-viṣaya-mānasa-vyāpāra* – wherein *saguṇa-brahma* is substituted by *nirguṇa-brahma*. This mental activity is called *nididhyāsana*, contemplation.

Both *dhyāna* and *nididhyāsana* are *mānasa-vyāpāras*, mental activities. In the former, there is *saguṇa-brahma* and in the latter, there is *nirguṇa-brahma,* meaning *svarūpa-dhyāna,* contemplating on the truth of Brahman. In this *nididhyāsana,* you contemplate on certain words or statements such as, 'I am the whole, *ahaṁ pūrṇaḥ,* my nature is nothing other than existence-consciousness-limitlessness, *ahaṁ satya-jñāna-ananta-svarūpaḥ.*' This contemplation implies thought because, you bring up a word and you see its meaning. Therefore, there is *mānasa-vyāpāra,* mental activity, but, at the same time, it is different that the mental activity involved in *saguṇa-brahma-viṣaya-mānasa-vyāpāra,* which is why it is called contemplation rather than meditation.

The topic of contemplation is naturally preceded by all types of meditation or internal means, *antaraṅga-sādhana,* for gaining *mokṣa*. Therefore, any prayerful meditation, which is *saguṇa-brahma-viṣaya-mānasa-vyāpāra,* and *nididhyāsana,* which takes the form of a quiet contemplation, should be taken as *dhyāna*. The *dhyāna* discussed in the sixth chaper, immediately after Kṛṣṇa talked about *sannyāsa,* is mainly the second type of *dhyāna,* that is *nididhyāsana,* which we shall see as we proceed.

Verses 1&2

The external means – karma-yoga – to introduce the internal means, dhyāna-yoga

श्रीभगवानुवाच ।
अनाश्रितः कर्मफलं कार्यं कर्म करोति यः ।
स संन्यासी च योगी च न निरग्निर्नचाक्रियः ॥ १ ॥

śrībhagavān uvāca
anāśritaḥ karmaphalaṁ kāryaṁ karma karoti yaḥ
sa sannyāsī ca yogī ca na niragnirnacākriyaḥ (1)

śrībhagavān – Lord Kṛṣṇa; *uvāca* – said;
yaḥ – the one who; *karmaphalam* – result of action; *anāśritaḥ* – not driven by ends in view; *kāryam* – that is to be done; *karma* – action; *karoti* – performs; *saḥ* – he (or she); *sannyāsī* – renunciate; *ca* – and also; *yogī* – *yogī* (the one who has contemplative mind); *ca* – and; *na* – is not; *niragniḥ* – the one who has renounced all fire rituals; *na* – not; *ca* – and; *akriyaḥ* – one who does not perform any other action

Śrī Bhagavān said:

The one who performs action that is to be done, not driven by ends in view, he is a *sannyāsin* and a *yogī* as well, and not just the *sannyāsī* who has renounced all fire rituals and who does not perform any other action.

A means, *sādhana*, to an end, *sādhya*, can be with reference to anything. There are even means for gaining imprisonment, such as breaking the law. However, when what is to be accomplished is freedom from bondage, freedom from *saṁsāra*, the *sādhana* is two-fold, external and internal, as we have seen. Performing *karma* as *yoga*, called *karma-yoga*, is the external means, *bahiraṅga-sādhana*. Both the internal and external means are meant to prepare the mind, *antaḥ-karaṇa*, for knowledge, *mokṣa*.

Generally speaking, one can say that meditation gives you steadiness of mind, *citta-naiścalya*. The mind is always in a state of flux, *cala*; that which is free from this *calatva*, the state of being in a flux, is called *niścala*. Steadiness of mind, also referred to as composure, is therefore, called *naiścalya*, the nature of being *niścala*, which is the result of *antaraṅga-sādhana* called *dhyāna*, meditation.

Meditation is for *antaḥ-karaṇa-naiścalya*, steadiness of the mind, and *karma-yoga* is for *antaḥ-karaṇa-śuddhi*, purification of the mind, by freeing oneself from one's *rāga-dveṣa*s. Both these *sādhana*s are for *mokṣa*.

Leading up to the topic of *dhyāna* which Kṛṣṇa introduced in the last three verses of the previous chapter, he again talks about *karma-yoga* in the first two verses of this chapter. *Karma-yoga* was also discussed in the second, third, fourth and fifth chapters and is mentioned throughout the *Gītā* as a means for gaining *mokṣa*. Here, Kṛṣṇa uses the external means, *karma-yoga*, to introduce the internal means, *dhyāna*, meditation.

Karma to be done

In this verse, *karma* refers to any type of action that is to be done. How does the person under discussion perform this action? Without depending on the result or various ends of the action, the person does what is to be done. For this person, *karma-phala* alone is not the principal criterion for performing action.

Whereas, for a *karmī*, the personal likes and dislikes are the only factors that determine what he has to do. No other criterion is taken into account by the person because he has *rāga-dveṣa*s that must be fulfilled. The person is a go-getter, always busy trying to accomplish or acquire something. And, in the process of fulfilling the *rāga-dveṣa*s, the person does not care about *dharma* and *adharma*, right and wrong, since these are not the governing factors.

*Rāga-dveṣa*s being the only criterion for performing action, the *karmī* is one who is completely dependent on the result of action, *karma-phala-āśritaḥ*. And these are the very tendencies that the *karma-yogī* has to give up; otherwise, he is still a *karmī*.

A *karma-yogī* is not a person who has no *rāga-dveṣa*s. He is someone who has *rāga-dveṣa*s but gives them up, meaning that he does not go by them. Instead of going by 'I must get this and I must not get that,' the *karma-yogī* goes by what is to be done. In other words, he gives up the desires for this and that and performs whatever action that is to be done according to *dharma* and *adharma*, not going by his or her *rāga-dveṣa*s. In this way, one's *rāga-dveṣa*s are given up to an extent and those that remain are pursued and fulfilled according to *dharma*.

Conformity to dharma

In fulfilling any desire, there is choice involved in both the means and the ends. The choices themselves are determined by one's *rāga-dveṣa*s, which need not necessarily conform to right and wrong. Sometimes one's *rāga-dveṣa*s will conform to right and wrong, but more often they may not. What, then, is a person to do? This will depend on whether he is a *karma-yogī*. If the person is not a *karma-yogī*, he will not care about the means and ends but will simply say, 'I want this; therefore, I will get it!' Such a person is a *karmī*, one who follows whatever means that are necessary to accomplish his chosen end.

The approach of a *karma-yogī* is different, often implying some renunciation on one's part, the main criterion being conformity with *dharma* and *adharma*. The *karma-yogī* renounces his or her *rāga-dveṣas* and does whatever is to be done without being guided by likes and dislikes. When a person says, 'This is to be done, therefore I do it whether[1] I like it,' it means that the person is renouncing certain *rāga-dveṣas*, the results of actions, and is a kind of *sannyāsī*. This is why Kṛṣṇa says here that such a person is both a *sannyāsī* and a *karma-yogī*. The *karma-yogī* is not a complete *sannyāsī*, but has the quality of a *sannyāsī* in terms of his or her renunciation of *rāga-dveṣas*.

The value of values

Anything that anyone wants is very important to that person. Someone may say, 'I am unhappy,' and go after certain pleasures. Here, again, the value of these pleasures is not adequately understood. Their limitations are not known and, therefore, they are over-valued. At the same time, the universal values, also not being fully understood by the person, are under-valued; they are de-valued. It means that, while we have knowledge of values, we have no education with reference to them. The value of the values not being known, we do not have adequate knowledge of the values and this situation creates conflict.

Upon analysis of the value structure, we see that if the value of all the values is not known, the universal values

---

[1] Whether or not is a common expression but the correct usage is only 'whether' without being followed by 'or not'. Whether one likes this, grammatically this is right (Author).

naturally remain under-valued and the things which people have a value for, like money and power, have an exaggerated value. However, when such 'values' are clearly understood, they no longer have full value for us. Until then, they rule–power rules, money rules, name and fame rule, influence rules. So they rule the roost of your heart!

Values require alertness

To understand the value structure well and to see the limitations of what you value, you need to live an alert life, a life of *karma-yoga*. Because the *rāga-dveṣa*s are still alive in the *karma-yogī*, what he values will have a hold over the person. Thus, the *karma-yogī* has to sacrifice his or her *rāga-dveṣa*s. The person may not be able to use the most convenient means available anymore, because his or her commitment now is to a life of *karma-yoga* for the sake of *mokṣa*.

The *karma-yogī* has a desire for knowledge, which implies purification of the mind, *antaḥ-karaṇa-śuddhi*. If nothing else, one wants to be a mature person and, to accomplish that, the person will definitely have to sacrifice something. The cause of conflict, *vikṣepa-hetu*, is what has to be sacrificed here. The person gives up the seeds of conflict, the cause for conflict, meaning one gives up doing wrong actions.

Conflict begins even before doing a wrong action, 'Should I do it or should I not?' In fact, there is always conflict before doing, while doing, and after doing! Before doing, there is the conflict of whether to do it. While doing, you have to look to both sides, especially if you are stealing something. And after doing, there is conflict – when the police come looking for you!

However, if you perform action in accordance with *dharma*, you sacrifice your *rāga-dveṣa*s. Then what happens? Before doing, there may be conflict because you have to make a choice in order to avoid doing wrong. Doing the right thing is not always spontaneous because if there is a choice to be made on your part, there is conflict. However, once you have done the right thing, there is no conflict. So, the *karma-yogī* may start with a conflict but does not end with conflict.

In this way, both the *sannyāsī* and the *karma-yogī* are free from the spell of *rāga-dveṣa*s. Therefore, Kṛṣṇa tells Arjuna that, by doing what is to be done without depending on one's likes and dislikes, a person is both a *sannyāsī* and a *yogī*.

Renunciation of the two-fold activities

Kṛṣṇa then goes on to describe what this person is not, *na niragniḥ na ca akriyaḥ*. These two expressions refer to the two-fold activities given up by the person who takes to a life of *sannyāsa*, *vaidika-karma*, scripturally enjoined activities, and *laukika-karma*, all other activities. Before becoming a *sannyāsī*, the person performed certain daily and occasional Vedic rituals, *nitya-naimittika karma*s. All Vedic rituals imply fire, *agni*, and because a *sannyāsī* no longer performs fire rituals, the person is referred to in this verse as *niragni*.[2] The *sannyāsī* gives up all other activities – all forms of worship, familial duties, and business. In other words, he has no more roles to play – as son or daughter, as a parent, as a friend, as a citizen. Thus, the person is also referred to here as *akriya*, one who has given up

---

[2] *agniḥ na vidyate yasya saḥ niragniḥ*

all activities. When a person has given up scripturally enjoined and worldly activities as part of the ritual of *sannyāsa*, he is called a *sannyāsī*.

'Why did you become a *sannyāsī*?' is a very interesting question that people often ask a Swami. Each Swami has his or her own story, and if the story is not a very pleasant one, the Swami is not likely to answer the question. Nevertheless, there is always a reason. The person may have lost his business and had nowhere to go. A person can even become a *sannyāsī* by mail these days, I am told. The point here is that if a person takes to a life of *sannyāsa* by choice, it does not mean that his or her *rāga-dveṣa*s are gone. If nothing else, the person may have the desire to save people by teaching them without really knowing what it is all about! Often, such people will say, 'I have a burning desire to save the people, to serve the people.' So the question must be asked – is this really a desire to save people or to save oneself? Surely, to save the people one should first save oneself. What service can one give when one requires all the services! Some people are so full of *rāga-dveṣa*s that they are unable to understand even this simple fact. Therefore, taking *sannyāsa* does not mean that a person becomes a *sannyāsī* in the true sense of the word.

Further, Kṛṣṇa says:

यं संन्यासमिति प्राहुर्योगं तं विद्धि पाण्डव ।
न ह्यसंन्यस्तसङ्कल्पो योगी भवति कश्चन ॥ २ ॥

yaṁ sannyāsam iti prāhuryogaṁ taṁ viddhi pāṇḍava
na hyasannyastasaṅkalpo yogī bhavati kaścana (2)

pāṇḍava – O son of Pāṇḍu (Arjuna)!; *yam* – that which; *sannyāsam iti* – as renunciation; *prāhuḥ* – they say; *tam* – that; *yogam* – as *karma-yoga*; *viddhi* – know; *hi* – because; *kaścana* – any one; *asannyasta-saṅkalpaḥ* – who has not given up desires (for limited results like heaven, etc.); *yogī* – *karma-yogī; na bhavati* – does not become

> What they say as renunciation, know that to be *karma-yoga*, Pāṇḍava (Arjuna)! because, anyone who has not given up desires (for limited results like heaven, etc.) does not become a *karma-yogī.*

The person who becomes a *karma-yogī* has given up all *saṅkalpa*s. *Saṅkalpa*s are those which provide the impetus for all desires – the desire to earn money, to enhance the status of his or her family, to earn *puṇya.* Although the *karma-yogī* has given up all *saṅkalpa*s, he continues to perform action for the purification of mind. If only the activities are given up and not the *saṅkalpa*s, the person is neither a *karma-yogī* nor a *sannyāsī.*

How does a *karma-yogī* renounce all his or her *saṅkalpa*s? By giving up only those *rāga-dveṣa*s that are opposed to *dharma* and *adharma*. Whereas the *paramārtha sannyāsī*, the real *sannyāsī*, gives up totally the *rāga-dveṣa*s and *karma*. How does the *sannyāsī* do this? He does this by giving up the notion of doership through knowledge.

In this verse, Kṛṣṇa uses the word '*sannyāsī*' to mean the person who has taken *sannyāsa* to pursue knowledge. Because both the *karma-yogī* and the *sannyāsī* give up all *saṅkalpa*s, he equates the two here. Since both the *sannyāsī* and the *karma-yogī* have to give up *saṅkalpa*s, *yogī* is a kind of *sannyāsī.*

The topic of renunciation in terms of *karma-yoga* was also discussed by Kṛṣṇa at the beginning of the fifth chapter as an introduction to his discussion on *sannyāsa,* real *sannyāsa.* Here, the topic is meditation, *dhyāna-yoga,* for which you also require *karma-yoga.* So, Kṛṣṇa is praising *karma-yoga* as opposed to mere *sannyāsa,* which is simply giving up of action.

Even though meditation is something that one can do by one's will, it is not effective unless the mind is ready for it. The mind's capacity to stay with itself or with the object of meditation is what we call *dhyāna-yoga. Karma-yoga* is the means for preparing the mind and is, therefore, a means for *dhyāna-yoga.* So, there is a connection between *karma-yoga* and *dhyāna-yoga,* the external and internal means for *mokṣa.*

Verse 3

Kṛṣṇa points out how karma-yoga is a means for dhyāna-yoga

आरुरुक्षोर्मुनेर्योगं कर्म कारणमुच्यते ।
योगारूढस्य तस्यैव शमः कारणमुच्यते ॥ ३ ॥

ārurukṣormuneryogaṁ karma kāraṇam ucyate
yogārūḍhasya tasyaiva śamaḥ kāraṇam ucyate (3)

yogam– (the contemplative disposition of the) *yoga,* (meditation); *ārurukṣoḥ muneḥ* – for the discriminating person who is desirous of attaining; *karma* – *karma-yoga; kāraṇam* – means; *ucyate* – is said; *yoga-ārūḍhasya* – for the person who has (already) attained (this) *yoga; tasya* – for him (or her); *śamaḥ* – total renunciation; *eva* – alone; *kāraṇam* – means; *ucyate* – is said

> For the discriminating person who is desirous of attaining (the contemplative disposition of the) *yoga* (of meditation), *karma-yoga* is said to be the means. For the person who has (already) attained (this) *yoga*, total renunciation alone is said to be the means.

Āruruksu refers to one who wants to climb or mount something, for which there is a method. For instance, a person who wants to mount a horse, which is not easy to do, must have a method. Similarly, there are those who are desirous of mounting the horse of *yoga* – *yoga*, here meaning *dhyāna-yoga*, meditation. And what is the means, *kāraṇa*, for doing so? *Karma-yoga* alone is the means because you have to take care of the reasons for the problems that are created in your mind.

What are the reasons, the causes, for your problems? Your *rāga-dveṣa*s are the causes; they have to be taken care of. For one who is desirous of gaining a mind that is not under the spell of *rāga-dveṣas, karma-yoga* is the means.

Meditation does not involve the will

A meditative or contemplative disposition is not created by your will, although you can will yourself to sit in meditation. Such a disposition happens when you are ready for it and that readiness is what is meant by preparedness of the mind. Gaining this preparedness is not given over to the hands of time, but is created by living a life of *karma-yoga*.

We see that the external means, *karma-yoga*, for gaining *mokṣa* is not unconnected to the inner means, *dhyāna-yoga*.

In fact, it is very much connected; it is a part of the whole thing. *Karma-yoga* becomes the *sādhana*, the means, for the person who wishes to mount the horse of *dhyāna-yoga*, the capacity to contemplate. Once this capacity is gained by living a life of *karma-yoga*, the person is called *yoga-ārūḍha*. Only then, *śama*, *sannyāsa*, giving up of all actions, takes place.

Karma-yoga itself does not make a person a *yoga-ārūḍha*. By living a life of *karma-yoga*, the person first becomes contemplative; then, he develops a complete dispassion, detachment towards all activities that makes one a *yoga-ārūḍha*.

Complete detachment comes only through knowledge

Śama here means complete withdrawal, total renunciation of activities. And, since this can only happen through knowledge, knowledge is the means. Therefore, as a *sādhana* for gaining *mokṣa*, knowledge is equated to renunciation, *sannyāsa*, and which is why a *jñānī*, a wise person, is called *yoga-ārūḍha* in this verse.

The *yoga-ārūḍha* did not become wise by *karma-yoga*; he is wise because of *jñāna*, knowledge. So, the direct means for becoming wise is given here as *sannyāsa*, which is nothing but *jñāna*. On this particular point, this verse is often misinterpreted even though Śaṅkara, in his commentary, has made its meaning very clear that only by knowledge can one be free of all activities; there is no other way. In order to be a *yoga-ārūḍha*, a complete renunciation of all *karma*s should take place. This is not a withdrawal from activity, strictly speaking, but a renunciation of activity in terms of knowledge, knowing that one is not the doer. Therefore, total renunciation, *śama*, is to be taken as knowledge.

When does this person become *yoga-ārūḍha*? Kṛṣṇa's answer to this question is in the next verse.

Verse 4

One whose mind is not disturbed by anything attains liberation

यदा हि नेन्द्रियार्थेषु न कर्मस्वनुषज्जते ।
सर्वसङ्कल्पसंन्यासी योगारूढस्तदोच्यते ॥ ४ ॥

yadā hi nendriyārtheṣu na karmasvanuṣajjate
sarvasaṅkalpasannyāsī yogārūḍhastadocyate (4)

yadā – when; *hi* – indeed; *na* – neither; *indriya-artheṣu* – with reference to sense objects; *na karmasu* – nor with reference to actions; *anuṣajjate* – is attached; *tadā* – then; *sarva-saṅkalpa-sannyāsī* – one who has renounced the cause of all desires; *yoga-ārūḍhaḥ* – one who has attained liberation; *ucyate* – is said

> When one is attached neither to sense objects nor to actions, then that person is said to be one who has attained liberation, one who has renounced the cause of all desires.

The person described here is one whose mind is not disturbed by anything. Such a mind enjoys dispassion and contentment; it is a resolved mind. With reference to sense objects, *indriya-artheṣu*, and with reference to actions, *karmasu*, there is no attachment whatsoever.

All actions, *karmas*, come under two types, as we have seen previously, *vaidika-karma* and *laukika-karma*. With reference to both these *karmas*, this person no longer thinks of himself or herself as a doer. In other words, the person does not have *kartavya-buddhi*, a mind that thinks in terms of, 'This must be done by me, doing which I am going to better my lot.'

Only the doer performs action

A *karma-yogī*, on the other hand, has this *kartavya-buddhi*, the attitude that, something is to be done by me and therefore, I do it. This attitude itself is *karma-yoga*. Here, however, Kṛṣṇa is talking about a *yoga-ārūḍha*, one for whom doership no longer applies. In fact, the Veda does not address such a person at all; it addresses only the doer, the *kartā*. It is similar to you calling someone by name, 'Hey! John, please come here.' Only the person whose name is John will come. Similarly, the Veda addresses you, saying, 'O *kartā*, doer, do this action and you will get this result.' Who will respond to this call? Only the doer, the one who has the *kartavya-buddhi*, the one who thinks, I am the doer.

So, the person who takes *ātmā* as the doer will respond. Whereas, the person who recognises that he or she is not the doer will not respond at all. This is what is meant here by the statement, *karmasu na anuṣajjate*. With reference to *karmas*, there is no attachment because the *kartavya-buddhi* is not there for the person. When there is no *kartavya-buddhi*, the person is not attached to or bound by the sense objects or actions because they do not invoke the particular thought that makes the person think that he or she will be different because of it. For such a person, there is nothing to be done.

In his commentary to this verse, Śaṅkara uses the compound, *nitya-naimittika-kāmya-pratiṣiddha*, to refer to the various types of action that people generally do. As we have seen before, *nitya-karma*s are the Vedic rituals that are to be done daily and *naimittika-karma*s are those that are to be done occasionally. There are also *vaidika-karma*s to fulfil desires such as desire for progeny, health, wealth, heaven and so on. These actions are called *kāmya-karmas*. *Pratiṣiddha-karma*s are the ones prohibited by the scriptures. The point being made here is that, whether the action is scripturally enjoined or worldly in nature, there is no *kartavya buddhi*, 'this is to be done by me,' for the wise person because being full, he or she is not attached in any way to sense objects or the results of action.

Thus, the person is a *sarva-saṅkalpa-sannyāsī*, *saṅkalpa*, referring to the notion, 'I am the doer, *kartā*, I am the enjoyer, *bhoktā*.' Free of these notions of doership and enjoyership, the person does not think that this is to be done or gained by me so that I will be different or I will liberate the whole world, I will save the world, which is the greatest fantasy of them all. Such grandiose ideas are simply erroneous notions about oneself, none of which the *sarva-saṅkalpa-sannyāsī* has.

A person can only be a *sarva-saṅkalpa-sannyāsī* when he or she does not have the notion of doership, *kartṛtva*. If this notion is there, then *kāma*, desire, will also be there. And wherever there is *kāma*, there is *karma*, action. This is the action that has to be made into *yoga*. As long as the *kartṛtva* is there, the person is a *karma yogī*. When the *kartṛtva* is no longer there, there is nothing more to be accomplished by performing action and whatever the person does is due to *prārabdha* alone. This is why Kṛṣṇa said earlier that, in all the three worlds, there was nothing not yet accomplished that had to be accomplished by him, even though he was still engaged in action.[3]

Karma itself is not what binds you; it has no inherent hook that hooks you to it. It is the notion that you will become something or accomplish something by performing action that binds you to action. 'I will become someone, I will become greater, I will be more secure' are all notions, fancies, *saṅkalpa*s, and the person who is free from all *saṅkalpa*s is called a *sarva-saṅkalpa-sannyāsī*.

Please do not conclude that you should become a *sarva-saṅkalpa-sannyāsī*. *Sarva-saṅkalpa-sannyāsa* is not an ideal; it is to be understood. It is freedom from *saṅkalpa*s, a freedom that comes from knowing that the self is free from doership and enjoyership. The person who knows this is a wise person, a *yoga-ārūḍha*, a *jñānī*.

Kṛṣṇa is actually talking about *sarva-karma-sannyāsa* in this verse. Giving up all actions imply giving up all desires since you cannot give up all actions unless you give up the desires that prompt them. And you cannot give up the desires unless you know, 'I am the whole.' Knowing this, the doership is gone; only then is the renunciation of all desires possible. So, this giving up of desires, passion, and activity is nothing but the discovery that the self, *ātmā*, is the whole.

Therefore, what should you do?

---

[3] *Gītā* 3. 22

Verses 5&6

The self alone is one's benefactor and one's enemy

उद्धरेदात्मनात्मानं नात्मानमवसादयेत्।
आत्मैव ह्यात्मनो बन्धुरात्मैव रिपुरात्मनः ॥ ५ ॥

uddhared ātmanātmānaṁ nātmānam avasādayet
ātmaiva hyātmano bandhurātmaiva ripurātmanaḥ (5)

ātmanā – by oneself; *ātmānam* – oneself; *uddharet* – may one lift; *ātmānam* – oneself; *na avasādayet* – may one not destroy; *hi* – for; *ātmā eva* – the self alone; *ātmanaḥ bandhuḥ* – is one's benefactor; *ātmā eva* – the self alone; *ātmanaḥ ripuḥ* – is one's enemy

> May one lift oneself by oneself, may one not destroy oneself. For, the self alone is one's benefactor (and) the self alone is one's enemy.

This verse makes it very clear that you have to save yourself, that you should not destroy yourself or allow yourself to be destroyed. Why, because *ātmā*, oneself, is a great helper, a great benefactor for you. In other words, you are your own benefactor. And who is the beneficiary? You. Therefore, you are both the beneficiary and the benefactor. Kṛṣṇa goes on to say that you are also your own enemy. It means you can become a great friend, a benefactor, or an enemy to yourself.

A person who is a *yoga-ārūḍha, sarva-saṅkalpa-sannyāsī*, has saved himself or herself totally from all that is undesirable. In other words, from the life of *saṁsāra*, just as one saves oneself from drowning by pulling oneself out of the water. In fact, all of a person's activities are meant only to save oneself. The person wants to become secure, to be free of all problems, including loss of money, power, loss of health, old age, and death, which means he or she wants to save oneself from insecurity. Thus, everyone is busy working for his or her own safety. Whether we call it self-safety, self-security, or self welfare, there is no question that the pursuit is 'self-ish'– for the self alone.

Understanding the fundamental problem

Seeking an alternative lifestyle is not what is implied here. Rather, the person is seeking answers to some very fundamental questions. Certain questions arise in the person, however vague they may be, which tend to disturb the usual activities that people naturally absorb themselves in. The questions themselves give a direction to one's life until the person comes to understand that he or she is under the spell of likes and dislikes, *rāga-dveṣa*s, to use the language of the *Gītā*. One begins to recognise that the natural pursuit, *svabhāvika-pravṛtti,* that everyone engages in, is out of these likes and dislikes, 'I like it, I want it. Therefore, I do it.' These responses arise from *rāga-dveṣa*s alone.

Within this particular sphere of reality, everything becomes right – anger is legitimate, sorrow is legitimate, pain is legitimate. This is where we get confused. Where anger is legitimate, it is legitimate to get angry. Therefore, if someone says you should not get angry, you get angrier. Even if you do not get angry, you run into problems! Once you accept the legitimacy, you can move ahead without disturbing your natural activity.

But, when you begin questioning the activity itself, you question the very life you are living. Only when you really question, when the flame of enquiry is proper, can you come to understand the fundamental problem.

There is a mature way and also an immature way of approaching this problem. And, in the light of what we discover, there is something that can be called a prayerful life, a life of enlightened prayer, not blind prayer. There is a prayerful attitude or disposition, which is *karma-yoga*. *Karma-yoga* implies the acceptance or appreciation of Īśvara, the Lord, and living a prayerful life. This is what brings about the capacity to be contemplative, meditative. Such a life creates this kind of a disposition naturally, a disposition in which knowledge of *ātmā*, oneself, takes care of itself. So, it is very clear that because of *karma-yoga* one can gain *jñāna*, knowledge.

Helping yourself

In this verse, the word '*ātmā*' refers to you, the individual, who, by nature, is already in the ocean of *saṁsāra*. You did not suddenly slip into this *saṁsāra*; you were born into it, along with it. And how do you get out of it? By your own will, *ātmanā*, you turn yourself about; you question yourself and your values. By questioning yourself, you re-estimate the whole value structure and whatever there is about it that is confusing.

All problems are primarily due to improper priorities. Therefore, we have to reorganise our value structure and, in the process, our priorities will become proper. This enquiry, *vicāra*, into one's value structure is done by oneself alone, *ātmanā eva*; it is an enquiry into right and wrong, what one is to do and not to do. Because of this *vicāra*, your vision undergoes a cognitive change. This is one stage of the enquiry.

The next stage of enquiry is also done by you. By your own enquiry, you appreciate your helplessness in certain situations. This itself brings about a prayerful attitude on your part. A given situation raises certain doubts in you; later, there is an appreciation of Īśvara and then there is prayer. This makes a person a *vaśī*, one whose body, mind, and senses are together, all of which is done by one's own efforts alone.

Going to a teacher to gain the knowledge is also done by you and implies an effort on your part. In all of these ways, you pull yourself up. This is why Kṛṣṇa says here that one's benefactor is no one else but oneself, *ātmā eva ātmanaḥ bandhuḥ*.

Do not look down upon yourself

To have been born a *saṁsārī* itself is destructive. If your mind is not in order, if your value structure is confused, then your entire life and the lives of those around you will be confused. Thus, Kṛṣṇa also says that you are your own enemy. When your own mind, *ātmā*, your own will, is abused, or when it is not used at all, then it naturally becomes your enemy; it stands against you, it destroys you. Your mind is where all the notions, 'this or that will save me,' originate. These ideas are indicative of a will that has been fooled, by itself and by others, because you allow yourself to be fooled. It means that the final fool is you alone. 'Because I am a fool, I can be fooled! I allow myself to be fooled; therefore, I am my own enemy.

What is the use of blaming anyone? I myself am an enemy to myself,' *ātmā eva ātmanaḥ ripuḥ*.

Therefore, Kṛṣṇa says, 'May one not destroy oneself, *ātmānaṁ na ava sādayet*.' May you make use of the will and change, which does not happen without your undergoing some kind of inner revolution. This inner revolution is a quiet revolution; it is not the creation of many conflicting ideas. Rather, a quiet, inner revolution takes place in one's way of looking at things, in one's understanding. Therefore, 'do not look down upon yourself,' is another way of taking the expression, *ātmānaṁ na avasādayet*, because to do so, is to destroy yourself.

In this process, you may sometimes have to mother the child within you and thus take care of it. If you had been neglected as a child, then you have probably picked up some problems along the way. And who has to care for this 'child'? Who is the friend to this 'child'? You alone, as an adult, have to mother the 'child' within. This is what Kṛṣṇa was trying to convey when he said here, 'May one lift oneself up, *ātmānaṁ uddharet*.'

The verse can be taken in an absolute sense in that, at every level, one can say, 'May one not destroy oneself, *ātmānaṁ na avasādayet*; may one lift oneself up, *ātmanā ātmānaṁ uddharet*.' Since one has to take care of oneself at every level, in the final analysis, there is no other force, nothing external to yourself, that can help you. Oneself means one's own body mind-sense-complex, *kārya-karaṇa-saṅghāta*. This *kārya-karaṇa-saṅghāta*, along with the will, is both the friend and enemy of the *ātmā*.

In other words, you can be either your own benefactor or your own enemy.

This means that to become free of this *saṁsāra*, another person cannot become a *bandhu*, a benefactor, for you. Only you can do what is to be done. To grow or to mature within the *saṁsāra*, another person may be helpful to you, but to get out of *saṁsāra*, you have to release yourself. In fact, where *mokṣa* is concerned, the very person who was previously your benefactor could very well become an obstruction to you. *Bandhu* implies affection and friendship, which can also be binding, even though such qualities may be quite helpful to your emotional growth. Therefore, in the final analysis, in terms of gaining *mokṣa*, you are the only one who can be a friend to yourself. And unless you become a friend to yourself, you become inimical, an enemy to yourself.

Further, Kṛṣṇa continues:

बन्धुरात्मात्मनस्तस्य येनात्मैवात्मना जितः ।
अनात्मनस्तु शत्रुत्वे वर्तेतात्मैव शत्रुवत् ॥ ६ ॥

bandhurātmātmanastasya yenātmaivātmanā jitaḥ
anātmanastu śatrutve vartetātmaiva śatruvat (6)

yena – by whom; *ātmanā eva* – by oneself alone; *ātmā* – oneself; *jitaḥ* – has been mastered; *tasya* – for that person (self); *ātmā* – the self; *ātmanaḥ* – of oneself; *bandhuḥ* – friend; *tu* – whereas; *anātmanaḥ* – for the self who has not mastered oneself; *ātmā* – the self; *eva* – alone; *śatruvat* – like an enemy; *śatrutve* – in the status of an enemy; *varteta* – would remain

For that (self) who has mastered oneself by oneself, the self alone is a friend of oneself. Whereas, for the self who has not mastered oneself, the self alone would remain in the status of an enemy, like an enemy.

Tasya here refers to the *ātmā,* oneself, discussed in the previous verse, for that self, the self is a friend. When? When the self has been won over, *jitaḥ*. And what self is being discussed here? What *ātmā* can be won over? It cannot be *sat-cit-ānanda-ātmā*. Because one can only win over something that one can objectify. And the only object in which one has the 'I'-notion, *ātma-buddhi,* is the *kārya-kāraṇa-saṅghāta,* the body-mind-sense complex. It is this complex that is in one's hands and has to be mastered. Won over by whom? By oneself, *ātmanā,* meaning by one's own enquiry, discipline, will and effort.

The three powers at our disposal

The one who has mastered the body-mind-sense complex is called a *vaśī* and is a friend to oneself. The body-mind-sense complex serves this person with the three-fold powers, *śakti*s, it is endowed with – *jñāna-śakti,* the power to think, explore, know, and remember; *icchā-śakti,* the power to desire, to will; and *kriyā-śakti,* the power to act, to make or do. These three powers are at the disposal of one who is a *vaśī,* who has mastery over the entire *kārya-karaṇa-saṅghāta.*

When you have mastery over the body, mind, and senses, then all their powers are with you. Therefore, the *kārya-karaṇa-saṅghāta* becomes a benefactor for gaining that which is desirable; it can take you anywhere, to *brahma-loka* or even to *mokṣa*, to Brahman. This is the maximum it can do because you cannot become greater than Brahman. You are already Brahman, in fact. As one who has mastery over the body-mind-sense complex, you are endowed with the powers, you require to recognise this fact.

Because you can gain *puṇya* by following a life of *dharma*, the *kārya-karaṇa-saṅghāta* again becomes a *bandhu*. And for gaining *mokṣa*, it also becomes a benefactor to you. So, the same *kārya-karaṇa-saṅghāta*, the body-mind-sense complex, is a benefactor to you all the way - provided, of course, it is won over by you.

Now, suppose this body-mind-sense complex is not won over by you but, instead, is holding you hostage. Then what happens? The body-mind-sense complex cannot become a *bandhu* for you. Instead, you are a *bandhu* for the body, mind, and senses. In this way, the same *ātmā*, *kārya-karaṇa-saṅghāta*, becomes *ripu*, an enemy, one who creates obstructions for you, one who puts the proverbial spokes in your wheels.

The person who does not have *ātmā*, oneself, in his or her own hands is called *anātmā* in this verse. This is the person for whom the *kārya-karaṇa-saṅghāta* remains as an enemy alone, meaning that the self plays the role of an enemy. Kṛṣṇa makes it very clear that there is no enemy other than oneself alone.

Generally, we point a finger at someone other than ourselves and declare that person an enemy. This is done by everyone to some degree or other. And, if no one is available locally, Satan or some other planet will be accused! Everyone feels persecuted by someone or something. Always, there is some imagined fear in people that makes them point at someone as an enemy. By doing this, of course, you are giving the other person a handle with which he or she can disturb you.

No one can disturb you unless you allow them to. Nevertheless, people do have this persecution problem to some extent and they suffer from it. In fact, whenever you point out an enemy with your index finger, your accusing finger, there are three remaining fingers that point back towards yourself. These three fingers, therefore, are said to stand for the physical body, mind, and senses, the *kārya-karaṇa-saṅghāta* that is *ātmā*, oneself, the only enemy, there is. In this way, then, *ātmā* occupies the place of the enemy. Just like an external enemy, it is inimical to you.

Your mind is with you wherever you go

When you analyse your complaints, you find that they are mental, meaning they are of the mind. You allow yourself to be affected by the world and then, afterwards, you call the world bad and renounce it. You want to renounce this world you have labelled 'bad' and go to a world that you have imagined to be 'good,' which is called fantasy. But, when you go to this 'good world,' you find it is as bad as the one you left behind! Why? Because you carry your mind, the enemy, with you; you do not leave it behind.

The same mind that interpreted the world as bad is not given up and, with that mind, you move to the so called good world. So, the mind is carried with you wherever you go. Even if you go to heaven, you will find problems there because the same mind goes with you, it is carried forward and carried over! And having this same mind, the complaining mind, you always find enough reason to complain, whatever the place or the circumstances. This is what Kṛṣṇa means when he says that one is indeed like an enemy for oneself.

When you carry such a mind with you, mind that is always interpreting given situations according to its own notions, even your *guru*, considered to be a great *bandhu*, benefactor, cannot help you. What can any *guru* do if the person is always thinking, 'My *guru* does not care about me. I don't think he considers me a good student,' and so on. You make such conclusions because of that same mind alone. Finally speaking, you are the only *bandhu* there is.

Verse 7

Kṛṣṇa discusses the person who is a friend to oneself

जितात्मनः प्रशान्तस्य परमात्मा समाहितः ।
शीतोष्णसुखदुःखेषु तथा मानापमानयोः ॥ ७ ॥

jitātmanaḥ praśāntasya paramātmā samāhitaḥ
śītoṣṇasukhaduḥkheṣu tathā mānāpamānayoḥ (7)

śīta-uṣṇa-sukha-duḥkheṣu – with reference to heat and cold, pleasure and pain; *tathā* – so too; *māna-apamānayoḥ* – with reference to praise and criticism; *jita-ātmanaḥ* – for the one who has mastery over oneself; *praśāntasya* – for the one whose mind is tranquil; *ātmā* – the mind; *paraṁ samāhitaḥ* – is always in a state of composure

> For the one who has mastery over oneself, whose mind is tranquil with reference to heat and cold, pleasure and pain, and praise and criticism, the mind is always in a state of composure.

This verse can be looked at in two ways, depending on whether the word *param* is placed with *samāhitaḥ* or *ātmā*. First we shall look at it as *ātmā* (mind) *param samāhitaḥ*. And then we shall look at it as *paramātmā samāhitaḥ*, as Śaṅkara does in his commentary.

We have already seen the meaning *of jita-ātmā*, one whose body, mind, and senses are mastered. To have mastery over your mind means that you are not carried away by its various moods. In other words, moods should be left to grammar, that is, imperative mood, potential mood, subjunctive mood, and so on. For one who has mastered the mind, there are no other moods than these!

People are generally subject to moods – in the morning there is one mood, in the evening there is another mood, and in between there are so many more. When the moods of the mind are understood properly, you are not carried away by the mind. This is not to say that you should not have moods. To even suggest such a thing puts you in a bad mood! Please do not think that I say you should not have moods. Have your moods, by all means, and understand them so that you will not be carried away by them. Then, you are the master of the moods; they are not the master of you. If you can gain the space necessary to come out on top of the mood, then, the mood does not take you as its hostage. This is what is meant by *jita-ātmā*, one who has mastered his or her moods.

The nature of tranquillity

Naturally, such a person will be one whose mind is tranquil, *praśānta*. Why? Because he or she is *jitātmā*, one who is not carried away by the moods of the mind. For the one who is *jitātmā* and *praśānta*, there is no situation that can disturb the person. The mind is always in one's hand, meaning that it is always composed, *paraṁ-samāhita*; it never loses itself in any situation.

When everything is going well, when the food you want is right there, when the music is just right, when the people you want to talk to are readily available, it is not difficult for the mind to be composed. In this verse, however, we are talking about a person whose mind is always composed, *paraṁ-samāhita*, in all situations. The compound here, *śīta-uṣṇa-sukha-duḥkheṣu*, stands for all situations, all the opposites. *Śīta* means cold, not simply pleasantly cold but so cold that you cannot stand it. Similarly, *uṣṇa* means unpleasantly hot. Thus, the cold and the heat referred to here is not all that comfortable.

Then, there are situations that give people some kind of *sukha*, comfort, happiness, pleasure, and other situations that give *duḥkha*, discomfort, unhappiness and sorrow. In all of these constantly changing situations, one who has mastery over the mind, remains always composed. For such a person, there is no question of *duḥkha* coming because, for *duḥkha* to come, one's composure must already be gone. The point being made here is that all those situations that generally bring about *sukha* or *duḥkha* for people create no disturbance whatsoever in the mind of the person whose mind is always composed.

This verse also points out one more set of opposites – *māna,* praise, and *apamāna,* censure or shame. These two are given special mention here because they are very difficult to deal with. Even praise can be hard to handle sometimes because, when someone praises you, you may think the person is going to ask you for something; therefore you are afraid. You can handle the praise alright, but if it is just a preamble to something else, you do not hear it because you are waiting for what is to come.

Censure is always difficult to handle. Suppose someone says that he can handle criticism very well. And if another person counters that by saying 'No! You cannot,' this in itself is enough for the person to feel offended. It is because he cannot handle censure even though he thought he could. Another example of taking things personally and getting offended is, when you are doing a particular job and someone tells you that you are not to do that job, you are to do another. Immediately, you are inclined to take it personally.

Why criticism is difficult to handle

Criticism is very difficult to take because it is personalised; it touches some painful part of you. This problem comes from one's childhood. If parents constantly criticise their child, the criticism becomes a problem for the child. It creates a vulnerable area, a raw, sensitive area, and any subsequent criticism causes the pain to come out. This is the aspect of criticism that makes it so difficult to handle.

The person discussed in this verse is one who has taken care of these problems through proper understanding.

Without proper understanding, new philosophies may be created, which are nothing but superimpositions upon the pain, sorrow, and other problems. To simply conclude that you should not subject yourself to censure does not work. You have to work on gaining mastery over your mind because these opposites – cold and heat, pleasure and pain, praise and censure – are all disturbing elements for people.

What Kṛṣṇa is saying here is that these pairs of opposites do disturb you; therefore make sure that they do not disturb you. To say, 'I should not be disturbed,' is a superimposition upon you, the one who is disturbed and, in fact, is nothing but confusion. People who preach that you should not be disturbed, never help anyone because whatever they say becomes superimposed on the old pain that is already there. It becomes a superimposed philosophy – a list of 'do-s and don'ts,' 'should-s and should-not-s.' The old pain that is inside simply becomes confused by the new superimposed philosophy, thereby adding to the confusion that was already there. Instead of the new philosophy helping, it becomes a problem.

So we need to understand very clearly what this verse is trying to say – in all situations, the person's mind, *ātmā*, is always in a state of great composure, *paraṁ-samāhitaḥ*, and we have to work for such composure, which does not imply the superimposition of ideas.

The verse can also be taken as how Śaṅkara took it. The person whose *kārya-karaṇa-saṅghāta* is mastered is called a *jitātmā*, and because his mind is tranquil, he is also called *praśānta* in this verse. For such a person, *paramātmā,* Brahman, becomes the *ātmā*. In other words, the person who has the knowledge recognises *sat-cit-ānanda-ātmā, paramātmā,* as one's own *ātmā*. And such a person is one who is always the same, *samāhita*, even when the situations change.

Verse 8

A wise person's attitude with reference to all objects in the world

ज्ञानविज्ञानतृप्तात्मा कूटस्थो विजितेन्द्रियः ।
युक्त इत्युच्यते योगी समलोष्टाश्मकाञ्चनः ॥ ८ ॥

jñānavijñānatṛptātmā kūṭastho vijitendriyaḥ
yukta ityucyate yogī samaloṣṭāśmakāñcanaḥ (8)

jñāna-vijñāna-tṛpta-ātmā – one whose mind is content in the knowledge of the self; *kūṭasthaḥ* – one who remains unchanged; *vijitendriyaḥ* – one who has mastered the sense organs and organs of action; *sama-loṣṭa-aśma-kāñcanaḥ* – one for whom a clump of earth, a stone, and gold are the same; *yuktaḥ* – a composed person; *yogī iti* – as a *yogī*; *ucyate* – is referred to

> One whose mind is content in the knowledge of the self, who remains unchanged, who has mastered the sense organs and organs of action, for whom a clump of earth, a stone, and gold are the same, this composed person is referred to as a *yogī*.

Kṛṣṇa uses the word '*yogī*' in three ways throughout the *Gītā*. He talks about the *karma-yogī* as a *yogī*. He also refers to the person who is committed to *dhyāna*, to a life of meditation, a life of *sannyāsa* as a *yogī*. He calls the *jñānī* a *yogī* as well. In these three contexts, then, we find the word *yogī* is used.

In this verse, *yogī* means *jñānī*, a person of knowledge. By using the word in this way here, Kṛṣṇa is pointing out the flow, the order, involved in gaining the knowledge that is *mokṣa*. Before taking up the topic of meditation, Kṛṣṇa says that one must lift oneself up and not destroy oneself,[4] that one who knows oneself is steadfast in the fact of all opposites,[5] and that one who wants to attain this knowledge must commit himself or herself to a life of *karma-yoga*.[6] Having said all this, Kṛṣṇa is now discussing the *yoga-ārūḍha*, one who has mounted the horse of *yoga*, in other words, the person of wisdom.

Jñāna and vijñāna

This wise person is called *jñāna-vijñāna-tṛpta-ātmā* here. Both *jñāna* and *vijñāna* mean knowledge, but when they appear together, *vijñāna* is *viśeṣa-jñāna*, specific or particular knowledge, and is something more than *jñāna*. Since both words mean knowledge when they appear together there is a connection between the two, which is purely contextual. When they appear together, as they do in this compound describing a wise person, *jñāna* is to be understood as something a little less than *vijñāna*. Śaṅkara makes it clear by defining *jñāna* as that particular knowledge conveyed by the meaning of the words of the *śāstra*.

---

4 *uddharedātmānaṁ nātmānamavasādayet* (*Gītā* 6.5)

5 *jitātmanaḥ praśāntasya paramātmā samāhitaḥ, śītoṣṇasukhaduḥkheṣu tathā mānāpamānayoḥ* (*Gītā* 6.7)

6 *āruruksormuneryogaṁ karma kāraṇamucyate* (*Gītā* 6.3)

And explaining *vijñāna* he says that it refers to totally assimilated and owned up *jñāna*, that is, *aparokṣa-jñāna* without any *pratibandhaka*s,[7] inhibiting factors.

Between a person and the knowledge he has, there is a certain distance. For instance, when I tell you that the *śāstra* says *ātmā* is Brahman, the statement itself is very clear to you, which is a kind of knowledge. Yet you have to realise it, you have to recognise the fact. So, there is a stage where knowledge is in the form of some insight imbued with *śraddhā*, or a faith pending discovery, the possibility of the self being Brahman is established. At the same time, what the *śāstra* says is also established, meaning that there is no confusion about whether the *śāstra* is talking about the difference between the individual, the Lord, and the world or the non-difference between them.

The knowledge, *jñāna*, contained in the *śāstra* is converted into *vijñāna*, for which there is analysis, *manana*, and contemplation, *nididhyāsana*. This conversion is not necessary, however, if the person is an *adhikārī*, one whose mind is properly prepared for the knowledge. Because the person has *viveka* and *vairāgya*, discrimination and dispassion, one recognises the fact immediately upon receiving the knowledge. There are no problems obstructing the person's understanding because of one's maturity. This maturity is marked by a mind that does not concern itself with the past or the future. This is the sanest kind of mind one can have and is the mind that a *sannyāsī* enjoys.

---

7 ज्ञानं शास्त्रोक्तपदार्थानां परिज्ञानं विज्ञानं तु शास्त्रतः ज्ञातानां तथैव स्वानुभवकरणम् (शङ्कर भाष्यम्)

A psychiatrist, who travelled and met people from all over the world, wrote a book in which he said that the mind of a *sannyāsī* is the sanest mind. I think this is due to the *sannyāsī*'s freedom from concern for the morrow. Having no money or possessions and wanting none, a *sannyāsī* is not concerned with maintaining or protecting anything. If you do not have money and you want money, you are a poor person, and being poor is your problem. On the other hand, if you have money, others may think that you have no problems regarding money. But you have the problem of protecting what you have. Thus, both the rich and the poor have problems. Whereas, the person who does not care what he or she has is the sanest person, a *sannyāsī*, one who is oneself alone. If such a person listens to the *śāstra*, there is no conversion necessary. Any doubt that may arise is taken care of in the *śravaṇa-manana* process, and then it is over; the knowledge is gained.

The need to convert jñāna into vijñāna

Generally, a person is not a complete *adhikārī*. While the desire to be liberated, *mumukṣutva*, and the desire for knowledge, *jijñāsā*, may be there, the person has to convert his or her *jñāna* into *vijñāna* by *manana, nididhyāsana*, and anything else that may be required. In this process, the *jñāna* that one has about *ātmā* becomes *vijñāna*, immediate knowledge of the self, *aparokṣa-jñāna*. The *śāstra* does not give you indirect knowledge, *parokṣa-jñāna*. It says, '*tat tvam asi*, you are Brahman,' and it is a fact. Because the *śāstra*'s vision is a fact, this knowledge has to be as true as the fact. You cannot have indirect knowledge here. At most, *parokṣa-jñāna* can refer to the insight a person has with reference to *ātmā* being Brahman, as opposed to *vijñāna*, the truth of that knowledge.

The *śraddhā* you have about *ātmā*, 'I,' being Brahman, the whole, helps you do the *manana* and *nididhyāsana* that converts the *jñāna* into *vijñāna*. This process of conversion is called *svānubhava-karaṇa*, meaning *aparokṣī-karaṇa* – converting it to immediate knowledge. *Anubhava* means immediate knowledge. And the word '*svānubhava*' with reference to this knowledge means that whatever has been revealed about the self is no more an insight or a possibility, no more an article of faith but immediate knowledge. There is a sure recognition, the immediate knowledge of the fact that 'I am Brahman.' And this sure knowledge is *vijñāna*.

One who has enough – alaṁ buddhi

Through *jñāna* and *vijñāna*, a person is *tṛpta*, a beautiful Sanskrit word defined by Śaṅkara as *sañjāta-alam-pratyaya*, one who has a sense of satisfaction, completeness in oneself. *Alam* means adequate or enough. *Sañjāta-alam-pratyaya* means the one in whom this recognition that, 'it is enough or there is nothing wanting in me' has been born due to the knowledge that he is *sat-cit-ānanda-ātmā*.

This person is always happy, satisfied with whatever comes. And how does one become *sañjāta-alam-pratyaya*? Only by *jñāna* and *vijñāna*, wherein the self is no more found to be inadequate. The person is freed from all the notions previously held about the self. In its own essential glory, the self is *pūrṇa*, fullness, meaning that there is nothing that is separate from the self and the one for whom *ātmā* is *pūrṇa-ātmā*. Thus, a person who is *sañjāta-alam-pratyaya* is called *tṛpta* here.

The word *ātmā* in this compound, *jñāna-vijñāna-tṛpta-ātmā*, means the mind, *antaḥ-karaṇa*. So, *tṛpta* is one whose mind says, *alam*, an attitude born of *jñāna* and *vijñāna*, insight and *śraddhā*. This attitude is born of *jñāna* that has been converted into immediate knowledge of oneself, *vijñāna*. The definition of a wise person, *jñāna-vijñāna-tṛpta-ātmā*, also reveals the nature of the knowledge itself. This is the advantage of Sanskrit compounds. Not only do they name a person, they also serve as definitions.

The wise person is not swayed by anything external or internal

The wise person is also described here in this verse as *kūṭastha*, one who remains like an anvil, the solid iron block upon which the blacksmiths of yesteryear hammered red hot iron bits into different shapes. Knives used to be made this way. The point here is that, for all the hammering that went on, the anvil itself never changed. Since the iron bits had to change, the block on which they were changing could not change. Therefore, a person who does not change and allows all possible changes to take place is called *kūṭastha*. The person, like the *ātmā*, is not moved by anything.

In his commentary to this verse, Śaṅkara defined *kūṭastha* as *aprakampya*, one who is not swayed by any situation, internally or externally, because one is *jñāna-vijñāna-tṛpta-ātmā*. This person has gone through the necessary disciplines and has gained the knowledge of *ātmā* as fullness, without which all problems exist. Having gained this knowledge, there is nothing inside or outside to disturb the person. Such a person is strong and unshaken, *aprakampya*.

How qualifications become spontaneous virtues

The beauty of a person is not in one's nose or hair colour; it is in the strength, gentleness, and compassion of the person. Compassion is the readiness to share one's time, mind, wisdom, wealth and so on. This readiness to share is strength. Only a truly rich person can share in this way. Therefore, this compassion is the beauty and also the strength of the person.

Compassion is not something that one melts into, although it sometimes looks as though, out of sheer compassion, people liquefy themselves to the extent that they begin to cry at the plight of another. But this is not compassion; nor does it help anyone. If someone requires help from you and you become liquefied in the process, of what help is that? Now you require help from yet another person, who may also get liquefied in the process! We need solid people who have the compassion called strength, the compassion that requires inner satisfaction. Such a person is a *tṛpta*.

Please understand that we are not setting up ideals for ourselves. Rather, there is a condition that is to be understood wherein the sense organs, meaning the mind and all its fancies, are always mastered. It means that the eyes do not ask, 'Come on, take me to see something,' and the ears do not say, 'I am tired of listening to Vedanta; take me to listen to some music.' It is the unmastered mind with its fancies that makes one go after the sense objects. With reference to fancies, then, the person described here is *vijita-indriya,* what the person wants to do is done and what one does not want to do is not done. Because the *vijita-indriya* has this composure, or wisdom, the person is also called *yuktaḥ*. What were previously *sādhana*s for him as a *mumukṣu* are now the natural spontaneous virtues of a wise person. This is the person Kṛṣṇa calls a *yogī* here.

The only security is knowing one is secure in oneself

Further, the person is *sama-loṣṭa-aśma-kāñcana,*[8] one for whom *loṣṭa,* a clod of earth, *aśma,* a stone, and *kāñcana*, gold, are one and the same, *sama*, equal. It does not mean that the person sees all three as clod of earth or as stone or as gold. Equal, *sama,* is purely in terms of the person's response to these objects in particular, and to all objects in general. For the *sama-loṣṭa-aśma-kāñcana*, there is no security in any of them. For such a person, there is no more security in a precious stone or gold than there is in a clod of earth or a simple rock. Any one of the three is as good as the other two. Even though the person understands what gold is and its value, one knows that it does not give security and that one's only security is oneself alone.

So, the description of a wise person, *sama-loṣṭa-aśma-kāñcana*, is purely with reference to security. The only security there is, is to know oneself as the truth of everything, without which nothing exists. When this vision is clear, the person is secure and, because he or she is secure, the person requires no security whatsoever. This being the case, what would one's

---

[8] लोष्टः च अश्म च काञ्चनं च लोष्टाश्मकाञ्चनानि। लोष्टाश्मकाञ्चनानि समानि यस्य सः समलोष्टाश्मकाञ्चनः।

vision be towards the so called securities of gold and the like? Of course, there would be an objective understanding of gold as gold, earth as earth, stone as stone, and their respective values based on their availability to society. Gold is definitely more valuable than stone because the gold is buried under the earth and stone is not. If this situation were reversed, stone would definitely be considered to be more precious than gold and stone ornaments would be everywhere!

Essentially, the only difference between a rock and gold is an objective difference. Gold has a particular atomic weight and is a rare, highly malleable, shiny metal not subject to corrosion. Because of these particular qualities, which are its nature, gold had a value even before it was converted into the base for the monetary system, a value that was heightened by its being thousands of feet down under the ground. But, regardless of how greedy or gold hungry a person is, no one will eat gold. Everyone knows that gold, even in the form of biscuits, is metal and is, therefore, not edible. This is what is meant by the objective value of an object.

Insecurity is due to one's subjective values

It is the subjective value, thinking gold is security, that makes a person crazy. But does gold always give you security? For instance, I ask you to watch over a bundle of gold ornaments for me, valued at several hundred thousand dollars, while I am away. At first, you may agree, until you find that you cannot sleep! You keep waking up to see if the gold is still there. Whereas, if I ask you to keep an old vacuum cleaner for me, which weighs much more than the gold, you will not lose any sleep.

Even though there is a lot more metal in the vacuum cleaner than there is in the gold, it is not a problem because it does not have the same value as gold. Therefore, does gold give you security or insecurity?

Similarly, if you are walking on the street with no money, there is no problem, whereas if you are carrying money, you feel very insecure and look around to see if any muggers are around. In fact, your very look will signal such people. Muggers are not unintelligent; we are the unintelligent ones. When you have money, it is more intelligent not to look around as though you were expecting to be robbed. The point to note in all of this is that, money is not security in spite of what you may think. And, because it is not security, money can make you more insecure.

Money does have an objective value. It has buying power which can provide you with certain comforts. But, if you see more in money, if you think that it will make you secure, then the value you have for it is purely subjective.

Everything is subject to change; it is always in a flux. The self alone remains changeless and that self is me. I am the only one who is secure; everything else is ever changing – my mind is constantly changing and so are my thoughts and the objects of thought. Whatever 'changes' is time bound; it has a beginning and an end. The only thing that remains untouched and comes out unscathed in all of this is 'I,' the self.

If the knowledge of this 'I' is clear, if you have this vision of yourself as secure, then you are a free person. You are a *jñāna-vijñāna-tṛpta-ātmā*. You are one who requires nothing to be free; you simply look out and see the world as it is. The world that you see is a simple world because you do not project all your nonsense onto it. The world remains as it is and you are a secure, free person. And why does this freedom seem so difficult to gain? Perhaps it is simple; in fact, it is yourself. Because people always look for something big, this freedom, this security, seems difficult to gain.

The self, being infinite, is not something that is produced. Since it is not produced, it cannot be gained through effort. As long as you look for something that can be produced by your efforts, you will always miss out. In areas where you need to grow, effort certainly has its place and involves alertness, among other things. Whereas, here, fundamentally speaking, you are already secure.

Gold represents all desirable objects including relationships

There is a story told about a *guru* by his disciples. It seems that one *śiṣya*, wanting to test the *guru*'s *vairāgya*, dispassion, placed a gold coin under his pillow. When the saint placed his head on the pillow, he found that he could not sleep. He tried everything, but still he could not fall asleep, so great was his *vairāgya*. The *śiṣya*, who was watching all this, realised his mistake, and prostrating to the *guru*, admitted what he had done. He then removed the gold coin and the *guru* fell asleep.

On hearing this story, one can question, whether the *guru* really had great *vairāgya*. Suppose one placed the gold coin under the pillow of the person for whom gold was everything.

This person also would not be able to sleep, fearing that someone would take the coin. Or, if the person did sleep and woke up to find the coin was gone, he or she would not sleep again until the thief had been found and the coin recovered. So, we have a person who loses sleep because of the absence of the gold and another person who loses sleep because of its presence. Who is greater, tell me? Since both are hooked to the gold, how can it be said that one is greater or lesser than the other?

In the *guru*'s room there may be a variety of metals – a copper vessel, a metal plate, and iron nails to hold his cot together, doorknobs, and locks. These metals do not affect the person, whereas gold does. What does it mean? Does the problem belong to the gold or to the person? Gold itself does not do anything; it is just what it is, metal with its own objective value, like any other metal. It is Bhagavān's creation. Therefore, to a god-inspired person, how can gold be any different than copper or iron, which is also Bhagavān's creation?

Are we to take the story to mean that the *guru* has a problem or that the *śiṣya* has a problem? It is usually better to give the benefit of doubt to the *guru* and take the problem to be the *śiṣya*'s problem. Why? Because, sometimes, when *śiṣya*s praise their *guru*, the praise may actually belittle the *guru* without the *śiṣya*s intending to do so. In this particular story, the *śiṣya*'s vision was that, not being able to sleep proved the greatness of the *guru*'s *vairāgya*. But, all it did was demonstrate the *śiṣya*'s lack of understanding of *vairāgya*. Because *vairāgya* may not have been properly understood, the benefit of doubt should go to the *mahātmā*, not to the *śiṣya* or those who wrote about him. In other words, we assume that the limitation belongs to the writer, not to the *mahātmā* whom we do not know at all. If the person was a *mahātmā* he would not have lost sleep over a piece of gold because, as a *mahātmā*, the person is *sama-loṣṭa-aśma-kāñcana*. Whether the object is *loṣṭa*, a lump of earth, *aśma*, a rock, or *kāñcana*, gold, the person's vision is that each object is the same in the sense that one's security does not lie outside oneself.

This applies not only to gold but to everything. The gold, *kāñcana*, is simply an *upalakṣaṇa*, meaning that it stands for everything else of the same category. It even stands for the notion that God is there and will protect me. Since God alone is there, where is the question of him protecting me? He will protect himself, which is me. The security of one who is *sama-loṣṭa-aśma-kāñcana* does not depend upon anything. To everything, whether it is a lump of earth, a rock, or a piece of gold, the person responds equally, meaning indifferently.

Since no one has any great response towards a rock or a clump of earth, why are they brought in here? Simply to show that the wise person's attitude towards gold is the same as one's attitude towards a pebble or a clump of earth. Just as the clump of earth or pebble does not enhance the person's security, neither does the gold. Generally, gold imbues people with a false sense of security, but, in fact, an insecure person does not become secure because of gold.

In the past, the value of gold was purely in terms of its usefulness in ornaments. Now, it is used in many ways, even in electronics, and has a bullion value as well. Currency, on the other hand, loses its value, its buying power, due to inflation, whereas gold retains its value. Therefore, people have a love for gold and retain their money in the form of gold.

Gold has both an intrinsic value and a man made value in that it does give you a sense of security. This sense of security is false because it does not make you secure. The insecure person does not become secure just because one has some bars or bricks of gold. The insecure is always insecure. To have bricks of gold simply means that you are attracting thieves and all those other people who would never visit you otherwise. The point being made is that you commonly look upon gold as providing a sense of security, whereas the wise person looks to oneself alone for security. In fact, the wise person is the only secure person on earth because he or she does not require gold or anything else in the world in order to be secure.

Verse 9

Kṛṣṇa describes the wise person's attitude towards different types of people

सुहृन्मित्रार्युदासीनमध्यस्थद्वेष्यबन्धुषु ।
साधुष्वपि च पापेषु समबुद्धिर्विशिष्यते ॥ ९ ॥

suhṛnmitrāryudāsīnamadhyasthadveṣyabandhuṣu
sādhuṣvapi ca pāpeṣu samabuddhirviśiṣyate (9)

suhṛnmitrāryudāsīna-madhyastha-dveṣya-bandhuṣu – with reference to a benefactor, a friend, an enemy, an acquaintance, an arbitrator, a person who evokes dislike, and a relative; *sādhuṣu* – towards good people; *api* – even; *ca* – and; *pāpeṣu* – with reference to sinners; *sama-buddhiḥ* – one whose vision is the same; *viśiṣyate* – is the most exalted

> The one whose vision is the same with reference to a benefactor, a friend, an enemy, an acquaintance, an arbitrator, a person who evokes dislike, a relative, good people and even towards sinners, he (or she) is the most exalted.

The compound that forms the first line of this verse is so long that Śaṅkara thinks it necessary to confirm that it was one word, a *samasta-padam*. This compound, *suhṛd-mitra-ari-udāsīna-dveṣya-bandhuṣu*, describes various types of people. There are also two other kinds of people described in the verse, the good people and the sinners. With reference to all of them, *sādhuṣvapi ca pāpeṣu*, the wise person's vision or attitude is equal or the same. That is, he is a *sama-buddhiḥ*. Such a person is the most exalted among all people, *sa viśiṣyate*. One by one, let us look at the types of people Kṛṣṇa mentions and Śaṅkara's definitions of them.

Suhṛd and mitra

According to Śaṅkara's definition, a *suhṛd* is a benefactor, one who extends a helping hand without expecting anything in return.[9] Generally, help is extended out of friendship or because some return is expected. But a *suhṛd* is one who helps

---

9 प्रत्युपकारम् अनपेक्ष्य एव उपकर्ता सुहृत् ।
pratyupakāram anapekṣya eva upakartā suhṛt

without expecting any help in return, a rare person indeed. The next type of person mentioned is *mitra,* a friendly person or a person with whom you share certain understanding or friendship.

Ari

There is also the *ari,* an enemy, *śatru,* one who is inimical towards you. Why would a wise person consider anyone as an enemy, you might ask? Enemies are not necessarily created; sometimes they are just there, especially for a person who is always happy with oneself. That the person is always happy is often enough to make other people inimical.

There are so many reasons for others to be inimical towards you. That you have a longer nose and another person wants to have a similar nose can be reason enough! The other person may have a flat nose, and, according to that person, you have a good nose. So, he or she may become inimical towards you without you having done anything to the person. Therefore, an enemy is possible in the society, even for a wise person.

Some people may become inimical towards a wise person because of their own beliefs. They may think that a person teaching Vedanta, for example, is Satan himself, simply because he or she is saying that everything is Brahman. Such people may become very hostile towards a wise person and are therefore described as enemies here.

Udāsīna and madhyastha

Udāsīna is one with whom you have a nodding acquaintance. This is the person you often see at the bus stop, or at the gas station every time you go for gas, or in the elevator every other day. You simply nod to each other and go about your business. Another type of person mentioned in this verse is *madyastha*, one who arbitrates. If two people are fighting, the person previously mentioned, *udāsīna*, remains neutral and joins neither side; this person just watches and, at the most, may thank the two who are fighting for the thrill he or she got from watching the fight. Whereas, the *madhyastha* is an arbitrator who is interested in each of the contenders; therefore, whatever the *madhyastha* says is acceptable to both of them.

An arbitrator is always appointed based on the confidence that both people have about the person's ability to arbitrate objectively and not take sides. Switzerland, for example, often plays this role in world affairs. When there is a conflict between two countries that has resulted in the closing of one or both embassies, Switzerland is sometimes asked to take over as an arbitrator because it is one country that remains totally neutral. That the Swiss have gained considerably in terms of certain monetary benefits from its neutral status is a result of having lived smartly in this way.

A *madhyastha* is one who does not join any group or either side of a conflict. A person can be neutral, *udāsīna*, or desirous of the happiness of all, *hitaiṣī*. If you are a *hitaiṣī*, you try to bring about an understanding between people so that everyone can be happy, and the person who does this is called an arbitrator, a mediator, *madhyastha*, the literal meaning for which is 'one who is in between.'

People are the society.

The types of people mentioned here are people we find in every society. There is no society, in fact; there are only people. 'Society' is not an entity unto itself; it is made up of people, all of whom are referred to in this verse. Any society includes all these types of people. Whenever there is a dispute or fight between people, there are both friends and enemies. There are also those who want to bring about an understanding and others who simply stand by and watch.

Dveṣya and bandhu

Another type of person mentioned in this long compound is the *dveṣya*, one who deserves to be disliked because of his or her actions. The *dveṣya* is someone who is not at all likeable, according to you, because of what the person is or did. Such a person becomes eligible for your dislike. Then, there are one's relatives, *bandhus*–father, mother, brother, sister, uncle, aunt, and so on, the people whose opinions really affect you. Because you want them to have a good opinion of you, they can control and manipulate you emotionally and psychologically.

Sādhus and pāpas

Finally, Kṛṣṇa mentions two more types of people, *sādhus* and *pāpas*.[10] A person who follows very closely what is enjoined in the *dharma-śāstra* is called a *sādhu* here and one who does

[10] *pāpa* here means a sinner, *a pāpī*. The word *pāpa* means sin and the one who has sin is also called a *pāpa* – *pāpam asya asti iti pāpaḥ*

not is called *pāpa* or a *pāpī*. The *sādhu* is found in every society; he or she is the person who follows what is right and avoids what is wrong.

The opposite type of person is also found in every society, those who always transgress the norms laid down by the *śāstra*. What is not to be done, according to the *śāstra* and the society, is done and what is to be done is not done. These actions are called *pāpa*s and the person performing them is a *pāpī*.

The *śāstra* does not specifically say that you should not take drugs because a drug problem was not there at that time. Simply because the *śāstra* does not say not to do something is no reason to do it. If you say you do not take alcohol because the *śāstra* specifically says it is not to be taken, but you do take heroin, you should not think you are conforming to the *śāstra*. If people had been taking drugs in those days as they are today, the *śāstra* would have certainly included drugs, along with alcohol, as substances to be avoided. The mention of alcohol in the *śāstra* is an *upalakṣaṇa*, meaning that it stands for all substances that are harmful to you.

People rebel because of inner pressure.

People love to rebel against statements such as, '*surāṁ na pibet*, may you not drink alcohol.' Anything that is not to be done, they want to do. Rebellion is due to some internal pressure. It may start with some sense of adventure, which is also due to some inner pressure. This is not to say that conformists are good people. Some people are good simply because they are incapable of being bad due to dullness or fear.

Such people may even want to be bad, but their fear prevents them from doing what they really want to do. Whereas, for people who conform as a result of their knowledge and understanding, life is very pleasant; their conformity is a willing conformity in which there is no internal pressure and therefore, no problem.

To rebel means there is pressure inside the person and that pressure itself is the problem. The rebellious nature is not the problem, the pressure behind the rebellious nature is the problem. We are all rebels, really speaking. I am also a rebel, which is why I became a Swami. I may not be a rebel in the eyes of the society in which I was raised, but certainly in my mother's eyes, I am one. Which mother wants her son to become a Swami? No Indian mother wants it. Only when the neighbour's son becomes a Swami it is alright! All Indian mothers prostrate to such a person and give *bhikṣā* and *dakṣiṇa*, as long as it is someone else's son! Therefore, to be a Swami, one has to be a rebel.

Rebellion can be due to some inner pressure or because there is some understanding, some vision. More often than not, however, a rebellious nature is because of some problem inside caused by one's upbringing or whatever. Due to this internal pressure, people do what is not to be done – from picking pockets to acting as dons of Mafia groups, with so many others in between. Looters come in many shapes and sizes, including the very dignified corporate looters, those who manage never to get exposed. The word *pāpī* here covers all types of wrongdoers in every society.

We do not relate to people but to definition and categories under which we put them.

Thus, Kṛṣṇa began with *suhṛd* and ended with *pāpī*, with everyone else in the world being covered in between. And how are you to deal with all of them? Kṛṣṇa says here, in so many words, that you must always deal with them without differentiating between them. Instead, what you tend to do is bracket these various types of people and then deal with them. You do not look at a person as the person is. You look at the person according to a particular category or definition you have applied to him or her. Only then do you relate to the person. But this is not relating at all. When you look at people according to definitions or categories under which you have put them, you are relating to definitions, not to the people.

People relate to people very rarely. You define people and relate only to your definitions. No one can fulfil a definition. For example, no one can fulfil the definition of an enemy. What does it mean to define someone as your enemy? To what part of you is the person an enemy? You are made up of so many parts. Is the person an enemy to your nose? To your legs? To your hands? To your mind? To your soul? To what is the person an enemy? From this you can see that no one really fulfils any definition; yet, you deal with people based on your definitions.

When you deal with people according to your definitions, you meet only your definition – your definition of friend, enemy, or whatever; you do not meet the person. It means you are stuck with yourself, with your own definitions. Therefore, you live in an imagined world. And this problem will only go when your front is gone.

You have a front for yourself. You want to protect yourself, because you have your own insecurities, your own pains and so on. Therefore, there is always a shield, a mask, through which you face the world. But the person being discussed here, the *jñāna-tṛpta-ātmā*, has no such problem. By knowledge, this person is completely free, totally satisfied with oneself. What front has such a person got? None, whatsoever; all fronts are gone, and what remains is a simple person with a mind and senses. This is why the person is called *sama-buddhi* here.

A wise person never condemns another person

The *sama-buddhi* is not a dull, dumb person who cannot tell the difference between a *suhṛd* and a *pāpī*. He or she recognises a *suhṛd* as *suhṛd* and a *pāpī* as a *pāpī*. The point being made here is that *sama-buddhi* does not condemn the person as a *pāpī*. Indeed, there is no such person as a *pāpī*; there is only a person who has done those actions that are *pāpa*s. Therefore, you meet people as they are, take them as they are, and respond to them, deal with them. This particular vision, this capacity to take people as they are, definitely implies certain freedom on your part and enables a new type of dynamic relationship, a true relationship, to take place.

For instance, a man who has money goes to a party will search out his own class or a little higher class of people and talk only to them. Everyone does this in one way or the other.

You may come across someone who is informed, a scholarly person, and run away, simply because he or she is a scholar. Because you feel uneasy in this person's presence, you find it more comfortable to be away. You may either run away from those who are moneyed and proud, or you may seek them out.

This is not the same thing as being careful about your choice of friends. A friend is one with whom you can share and be free. Therefore, there is some validity in choosing your friends carefully. But we are not talking about empirical life here; we are talking about a wise person, a *jñāna-tṛpta-ātmā*. How does such a person respond to all these different kinds of people? With reference to them all, this person is one of equal vision, *sama-buddhi*, regardless of their social status, profession, astrological sign, or whatever. The wise person does not bother about what a person was or is, what one did or is doing, whether one is a *sādhu* or a *pāpī*, whether one is a follower of the *śāstra*, or one who goes against the *śāstra*. Instead, the wise person takes people as they are because he or she is a free person; in other words, a non-judging person.

The fear of being judged

People are always afraid of being judged. Otherwise, why do they feel shy when asked to talk in front of others? Even those who have had the experience of talking publicly remain a little shy. Why? Because they are afraid of what other people think. In fact, we spend most of our lives thinking about what others think. Now, I ask, what do you think? What do you think about yourself? You are what you think about yourself and you think wrongly. This is the thinking we are trying to correct, not other people's thinking.

Others think you are an individual, a *jīva*. Are you accepting that? Who cares about what others think? What you think about yourself is what requires correction. Let others think what they think; that is their problem, not yours. Always thinking about what others think is a common problem. It is not just your problem or someone else's problem; it is the problem of the whole of humanity. You are not controlled by other people, you are controlled by your own thinking, your own fear about what others think.

You think that people are thinking about you, even though they have their own problems and have no time to think about you. In fact, they think only about themselves. Yet, you allow yourself to be controlled by your own thought of what others think. You think society is controlling you when, in fact, society does not control anyone. The only controlling factor here is your own thinking of what society thinks.

The wise person, on the other hand, is not subjectively involved in any of this; he or she is totally non-judgmental towards everyone. This is not to say that you should look at others in terms of whether they are non-judgmental. It would simply be making a new judgement! So, may you not be judgmental towards yourself and towards others too.

Empirically, being non-judgmental has a value and, for a wise person it is very natural. In fact, the quality of being non-judgmental is to be accomplished before wisdom. Therefore, we say, do not judge yourself on the basis of your mind, that is, on the basis of your mental condition. This is the basis of all judgement – judgement of your qualifications, your skills, your physical body and its status in terms of age, weight, colour, hair and so on. Not only do we judge ourselves this way, but we judge others also. This is all false, absolutely false, which is why correction takes time.

In every area, there is a mistake, an error. Our whole perception of ourselves and the world is wrong. Therefore, a total revolution has to take place. First, we put things in order empirically and, then, we say these are all judgements and the self is not to be judged according to anything. The self is something that has to be recognised. Such recognition is knowing, not judging.

Knowing is simply recognising the nature of the self as it is. The whole vision, therefore, is a deconditioning programme. We have hypnotised ourselves into believing certain things about ourselves, and that self-hypnosis has to be removed by de-hypnosis. This de-hypnotising process culminates in the recognition that 'I am limitless, fullness, *ahaṁ pūrṇaḥ, sat-cit ānanda-ātmā.*'

The wise person is the most exalted among yogīs

Because this *jñāna-vijñāna-tṛpta-ātmā*, this *sama-buddhi,* does not sit in judgement, he or she attains the status of being the most exalted, *viśiṣyate*, among the *yogī*s. The expression, 'the most exalted,' has to be understood in this context here.

Among those who are not yet wise, there are different degrees of insight and understanding, whereas among those who are wise, there is no such difference. Thus, we cannot really compare the wise person being discussed here, the *jñāna-vijñāna-tṛpta-ātmā,* with others. In terms of *sama-buddhi,* however, Kṛṣṇa uses a word as some kind of descriptive paradigm for the *jñāna-vijñāna-tṛpta-ātmā,* some comparison can be made. Thus, it is said here that the one whose *buddhi* is of equal nature with reference to all these people, *sama-buddhi* is the most exalted, *viśiṣyate.*

Another interpretation is also possible. In Śaṅkara's time all manuscripts were hand written on palm leaves. Śaṅkara may have seen the word *viśiṣyate* as *vimucyate* or he may have had a manuscript that actually said *vimucyate,* meaning the person whose vision is equal with reference to different kinds of people is liberated. Since one who is liberated is the most exalted among *yogī*s, the meaning is the same.

This verse and the one before it point out what is gained by this knowledge. The person is said to be the most exalted, the most accomplished, among *yogī*s and is called *brahma-niṣṭha,* one who has the knowledge of *ātmā* as Brahman. How to gain this great result is the subject matter of this chapter.

To gain the status of a *sama-buddhi,* to gain freedom from insecurity, otherwise called *mokṣa,* one should follow the two-fold *sādhana* of *karma-yoga* and *dhyāna yoga.* We have already seen that *karma-yoga* implies one's attitude with reference to action. *Dhyāna-yoga,* meditation is pointed out in the next verse.

Verse 10

May the yogī always connect the mind to the object of meditation

योगी युञ्जीत सततमात्मानं रहसि स्थितः ।
एकाकी यतचित्तात्मा निराशीरपरिग्रहः ॥ १० ॥

yogī yuñjīta satatam ātmānaṁ rahasi sthitaḥ
ekākī yatacittātmā nirāśīraparigrahaḥ (10)

satatam – constantly; *rahasi* – in a quiet place; *sthitaḥ* – remaining; *ekākī* – being alone; *yatacittātmā* – one whose body and mind are relaxed; *nirāśiḥ* – one who is free from longing; *aparigrahaḥ* – one who is free from possessions; *yogī* – the meditator; *ātmānam* – his (or her) mind; *yuñjīta* – may unite (with the object of meditation)

> May the meditator, whose body and mind are relaxed, who is free from longing and possessions, remaining alone in a quiet place, constantly unite his (or her) mind (with the object of meditation).

In this verse, the word '*yogī*' is qualified by several other words and this *yogī* constantly meditates upon the self. *Yogī* means meditator, *dhyātā*, the one who does the *dhyāna*. And the advice given is *yuñjīta*, may one absorb the mind, unite the mind, commit the mind to the object of meditation. In other words, may one meditate upon the object of meditation, which is mentioned later.

This is the general advice given by Kṛṣṇa. May the *yogī* always, *satatam*, connect his or her mind to the object of meditation.

Although *satatam* means 'always' and can even mean 'eternal,' the context determines its actual meaning. Here, *satatam* means that the person should meditate as often as possible or as long as possible.

Meditation does not require an accomplice

Where should this meditation take place? In a secret place, *rahasi*, meaning a quiet place, which in Śaṅkara's time was a hilltop, *giri*, or a cave, *guha*. Thus, Śaṅkara explains Kṛṣṇa's words, *rahasi-sthitaḥ*, as *giri-guhādau-sthitaḥ* meaning the one who meditates remaining on a hill or in a cave. Because you may take along some other people when you go to a quiet place, Kṛṣṇa says that the *yogī*, the meditator, is one who remains alone, *yogī ekākī*, or as Śaṅkara puts it, without an accomplice, *asahāya*. In meditation you do not require an accomplice. It is not a job to be done that requires the help of others, no sidekick or understudy is needed.

To do meditation, you do not need anyone, not even a friend. It is your own job, a quiet job with yourself where you are your own friend, just as we saw earlier in the chapter.[11] Your *bandhu*, friend, is yourself.

Śaṅkara uses the word *asahāya*, meaning without any *sahāya*, accomplice, because he takes the word *ekākī* to refer to a *sannyāsī*, *sannyāsa* being synonymous with *jñāna* for him. *Sahāya* can also mean *bhāryā*, wife, whom the *yogī*, being a

---

[11] *Gītā* 6.5

sannyāsī, naturally leaves behind. These kinds of mandates were meant as simple rules, not absolute rules. Therefore, we can take the spirit of them and edit or adopt them as necessary. Even so, how can you go to a quiet place, far away from home, wife, and children, unless you take to a life of *sannyāsa*?

If you are not a *sannyāsī*, you have to remain at home and perform your duties. Then the person who remains at home, who does not go away and leave all the people behind, is a *gṛhastha*, *gṛha* meaning 'home.' Married people are called *gṛhastha*s whether they live in a house or a van. The word *gṛhastha*, like all words, is born of the tradition itself. Even if a man does not always remain in the house because he has a job, he is at home in the sense that he has certain duties to perform. Unless he renounces these duties, he remains at home and is called a *gṛhastha*.

We have seen that the status of *gṛhastha*, house-holder, is one of the four stages, *āśrama*, of a person's life. First, the person is a *brahmacārī* and then a *gṛhastha*, which is important because this stage prepares one for the third and fourth stages, *vānaprastha* and *sannyāsa*. Once a person becomes a *sannyāsī* he or she leaves home and is no more a *gṛhastha*. So, *gṛhastha*, which literally means, 'one who remains at home,' is from the standpoint of *sannyāsa* alone. For instance, when a man leaves home as a *sannyāsī*, there is no sense of divorce implied in terms of his marriage. He is not renouncing his wife in order to be free to remarry, which is not renunciation at all; it is simply frustration. Rather, it is growing out of, a maturing, because of which the marriage has served its purpose. Neither person requires the other; they are both *sannyāsī*s. So he walks away and she remains where she is, protected no doubt, but also living like a *sādhu*, the home having become an *āśrama*.

The word *gṛhastha* itself has its basis in *sannyāsa, sannyāsa* being the ultimate goal of the *gṛhastha*. *Sannyāsa* is not a choice; it is the ultimate goal. A person who is alone, who remains in a quiet place, and who has the attributes of a *yogī* can meditate constantly, whereas a person who has a home and family cannot. It is impossible. Therefore, Śaṅkara says that Kṛṣṇa is talking about a *sannyāsī* here. First, he had talked about the *karma-yogī*, and now he is talking about the *dhyāna-yogī*, the *sannyāsī*, one who lives a life of meditation.

This *dhyāna-yogī* is further described by Kṛṣṇa as *yata-citta-ātmā*. *Citta* means memory, but here it refers more generally to the *antaḥ-karaṇa*, the mind, which includes memory, usually the predominant factor that disturbs you in meditation. Because your mind continues to operate in meditation, when as sound comes, you are definitely going to hear it. This is why you withdraw the sense organs to the extent possible, for example, closing the eyes, so that you can be absorbed with the object of meditation. What, then, is left to disturb you? *Citta*, memory, memories from the past. Therefore, *citta* is mentioned here.

Since *citta* stands for the mind in the compound, *yata-citta-ātmā*, the word *ātmā* in this compound is taken to mean *deha*, the physical body, and *yata* refers to both the body and mind being brought under one's mastery. The body is totally relaxed and the mind is absorbed. Whatever problems there may be, they are taken care of, which is all a part of meditation. Thus, *yatacittātmā* is both a name for the *yogī* and a qualification. Whenever a disturbance comes, the body is kept relaxed, and whenever a memory comes, the mind is brought back again to the object of meditation, all of which Kṛṣṇa discusses later.

Meditation requires freedom from longing

Further, if you have to sit in meditation, you have to be a person who is free from longings, *nirāśīḥ*. To sit in meditation means that there should be no pressure from inside; otherwise, you cannot sit. This inner pressure is longing, and *nirāśīḥ*, refers to the one for whom all longings are gone. If you simply close your eyes, and if longings are there in your mind, you will not even be able to keep your eyes closed, let alone sit quietly. And, in no time at all, you will feel the fuming and fretting inside. Just by closing the eyes, all the longings well up. At least with the eyes open, your mind is arrested by the objects you see because there is something going on and that gives you a direction. But if the eyes are closed, then the whole world is within you and the longings will create so much disturbance that you cannot remain sitting.

Whereas the *nirāśīḥ* is dispassionate, free from longing, is relatively satisfied with himself or herself and is therefore, a cheerful person. Because the meditator is a person who has been living the life of *karma-yoga*, Kṛṣṇa mentions these particular qualifications here, which, according to Śaṅkara's definition of *sannyāsa*, are the qualities of a *sannyāsī*.

What it means to be free of possessions

Finally, Kṛṣṇa describes the *dhyāna-yogī* as *aparigraha,* one who is free from possessions. *Parigraha* means hoarding or gathering, which can be a big problem. In fact, it is a disease that everyone has, to some extent. Because it is so difficult for people to give up things, they keep on gathering. Even if you give them away, you go on gathering more. This capacity to give things up is to be always retained so that you are the boss. The person who is alert to this fact is called *aparigraha* here.

Śaṅkara himself questions how the word *aparigraha* could apply to a *sannyāsī,* one who is supposed to be free from gathering things. But even a *sannyāsī* has the tendency to gather. A person may be alone in terms of other people, but in terms of possessions, he or she may not be *aparigraha.* Therefore, this gathering tendency has to be kept away by continually giving things away.

Aparigraha is a very interesting word here. Not only does it mean to be free from gathering things, but also from the longing to gather. The tendency to gather various objects is a common trait of the *saṁsārī,* and an old habit. Because this habit may still be there, and also because things do have a tendency to gather, the *sannyāsī* has to constantly maintain the status of being an *aparigraha.*

After this Kṛṣṇa goes on to say that, all the necessary qualifications being there, may you unite your mind to the object of meditation, *ātmānaṁ yuñjīta;* in other words, may you meditate. Although Kṛṣṇa's advice may look as though it is directed to a *sannyāsī*, it is really for anyone because everyone is *ekākī*, in fact. Even though you may be married and have a family, you are *ekākī*, one who is alone, at least when you close your eyes. Freeing yourself from all duties and roles, you become *ekākī*. Whereas, if you think of the father you are, the mother you are, or the daughter or son you are, then you are not *ekākī*. It is as though all these people, all these roles, are inside of you. Therefore, to just be yourself, *ekākī*, you drop the roles and their problems when you meditate. You strip yourself to be the simple person you are, whatever that person may be, the one who is meditating, the one called *ekākī, dhyāyī, yogī*.

Meditation requires a discipline

The next section of this chapter deals with what has to be done by the person striving for meditation in terms of discipline, *niyama*, beginning with where and how to sit, *āsana*. In this section, Kṛṣṇa discusses the eating habits, *āhāra*, of the meditator, saying that one who does not eat at all will have no *yoga*, nor will the one who eats too much. In fact, both of them may have *roga*, disease, instead. Discipline in terms of other activities, *vihāra* that are conducive to *yoga*, to meditation, are also mentioned by Kṛṣṇa in this section.

Meditation itself is a means for the steadiness and clarity of mind that leads to knowledge. But to live a life of meditation also requires a discipline, which is considered to be a secondary means or *sādhana* for meditation. The remainder of this section of chapter six is devoted to the accomplishment of this *yoga*, the discipline and its results.

Verses 11&12

Where to sit and with what to sit in meditation

शुचौ देशे प्रतिष्ठाप्य स्थिरमासनमात्मनः ।
नात्युच्छ्रितं नातिनीचं चैलाजिनकुशोत्तरम् ॥ ११ ॥

तत्रैकाग्रं मनः कृत्वा यतचित्तेन्द्रियक्रियः ।
उपविश्यासने युञ्ज्याद्योगमात्मविशुद्धये ॥ १२ ॥

śucau deśe pratiṣṭhāpya sthiramāsanamātmanaḥ
nātyucchritaṁ nātinīcaṁ cailājinakuśottaram (11)

tatraikāgraṁ manaḥ kṛtvā yatacittendriyakriyaḥ
upaviśyāsane yuñjyād yogam ātmaviśuddhaye (12)

śucau – in a clean; *deśe* – place; *sthiram* – firm; *na atyucchritam* – not too high; *na atinīcam* – not too low; *caila-ajina-kuśa-uttaram* – a piece of soft cloth, a skin and a grass mat layered in (reverse) order; *āsanam* – seat; *ātmanaḥ* – one's; *pratiṣṭhāpya* – having arranged; *tatra* – there; *āsane* – on the seat; *upaviśya* – sitting; *manaḥ* – mind; *ekāgram* – one pointed (absorbed in the object of meditation); *kṛtvā* – making; *yata-citta-indriya-kriyaḥ* – one who has mastered the mind and the senses; *ātma-viśuddhaye* – for the purification of the mind; *yogam* – meditation; *yuñjyāt* – practice

Having arranged one's seat (made of) a piece of soft cloth, a skin, and a grass mat layered in (reverse) order, in a clean place, firm, not too high (and) not too low…

… sitting there on the seat, making one's mind one pointed (absorbed in the object of meditation), may the one who has mastered the mind and senses practice meditation for the purification of the mind;

In these verses, the word *āsana*[12] is used for the actual seat upon which the meditator should sit. How you sit is also called *āsana,* which Kṛṣṇa discusses later. The words, *śucau deśe,* describe the place where one sits, meaning that it should be a clean place. You cannot sit in a garage, for instance, simply because you bought a house that has a garage and you do not have a car to park in it.

The place of meditation must be clean. For every action, everything you want to do, you require an appropriate place. And meditation is no exception. It requires a place that is inspiring; if not inspiring, at least clean. So, Kṛṣṇa says *śucau deśe.* In his commentary of this verse, Śaṅkara adds that the place should also be quiet, *vivikta.*

A riverside, a mountain, or some wooded area is considered to be clean and quiet because there is usually no one there and the natural surroundings tend to be inspiring. For a place to be inspiring, meaning conducive to meditation, there should be nothing to draw your attention away from meditation and a clean, quiet place meets this requirement. In such places, people can observe nature and spend time with themselves. They need not be always meditating, but they can be meditative while watching.

This does not mean that you must say, 'I have to meditate and therefore, I have to find a mountain or a riverside.'

---

12 *āste asmin iti āsanam* – that on which one sits is called *āsana,* a seat.

By your own action you can make the place clean. Wherever you are, you can make that a place where you can sit quietly. Does this mean that you have to drive away the people who may be there? No, you need not do that; nor can you do it if the people are a part of your life. How, then, you might ask, are you going to meditate?

Find a quiet corner to meditate

You can find a time, early in the morning perhaps, before others get up, to do meditation. When everyone is sleeping and you are the only one interested in meditation, this is a good time to do it. If others in the house were interested in meditation and also wanted to do it early in the morning, it could be a problem. So, by getting up a little earlier, you have a quiet place. Some quiet corner is always available. Or, if your home is always noisy, you can go to a nearby park or some other quiet place.

When Kṛṣṇa says here that one should arrange his or her own *āsana,* he does not mean it in a possessive sense. It is not that you have a particular seat upon which you must sit every day; this is not the emphasis here. Rather, your *āsana,* seat of meditation, is in terms of what is most conducive to meditation. For example, the seat should be positioned firmly, meaning that it should not wobble. The seat may be a bench, a plank, or whatever, but it should be firm, *sthira.* It should not be too high, *na atyucchrita,* a seat from which you could fall, nor too low, *na atinīca,* meaning that you should not sit directly on the ground lest you be bothered by insects and the dampness.

Because the body has a tendency to become very relaxed in meditation, and may even fall asleep, the fear of falling will be there if the *āsana* is too high. Instead of meditating, you will be afraid and then distracted by the thought that you should not be afraid. Similarly, if you sit directly on the ground there may be a fear of being bitten by creepy, crawly creatures, a real concern for those who inhabited the jungle areas of India.

Na atyucchrita and *na atinīca* can also be taken in another way. Some people think that if they want to meditate they should go to the higher altitudes, *atyucchrita*, or into a cave below the ground, *atinīca*. Here, Kṛṣṇa advises against both locations. Meditation may seem to be very successful at the higher altitudes, like in Gangotri at about 10,000 feet, because the person who meditates will have no disturbance in his or her mind. But this is because the mind cannot think due to lack of oxygen. We meditate with a thinking mind, not an incapacitated mind.

Therefore, to incapacitate the mind by going to high altitudes is not an accomplishment; in fact, you do not even know what is going on. Arranging one's *āsana* in too low a place is also a problem for the same reason. There may be no sounds to disturb you in a cave dug into the ground, but, again, there is the problem of the mind not being able to think because the oxygen supply is extremely limited in such places. Therefore, Kṛṣṇa says here that the seat of meditation should not be too high, *na atyucchrita*, nor too low, *na atinīca* – in other words, neither on a mountain top nor under the ground.

The significance of the materials of the traditional āsana

Kṛṣṇa mentions one final thing about the *āsana* itself – *caila ajina kuśa uttaram. Caila* means a soft cloth; *ajina* is a skin such as a deer or tiger skin used by the ancient sages, and *kuśa* is a grass mat. The word *uttara* completes the compound by referring to the order in which these three materials are to be placed, one over the other. When three materials are given, one needs to know what should be over what because it can be done in several ways.

For instance, if you arrange your *āsana* by first placing a soft cloth on the ground or floor, on top of which you put the skin and then the grass mat, you will not be able to sit there because to sit on a mat made of grass is a problem, I assure you. Śaṅkara confirmed here that the order to be followed is the other way around *viparīta* – with the *kuśa* on the bottom, then the *ajina*, on top of which is the soft cloth. Only then is the *āsana* called *caila-ajina kuśa-uttara.*

All this had to be said because meditation should not be done on the damp ground. In those days, all dwellings had mud floors and the benches or seats were made out of clay. If a person were to sit in meditation on such an *āsana* without these three layers of material, after three months their minds may have bent in the right direction, but their legs would be unable to bend at all, the knees having a tendency to develop arthritis when exposed to dampness. So, to avoid the dampness, the *kuśa* was recommended, on top of which was placed a furred skin, like a deerskin, to make the *āsana* warm.

Finally, to avoid irritation from the furred skin, a piece of soft cloth was placed on the top of it.

This does not mean that you must find a deer in order to arrange your *āsana* for meditation. This was simply what was done at that particular time. The skin of a deer was often chosen because the deer is one animal that is considered to be very clean since it will not touch anything that any other tongue has touched. In the Indian religious culture also, this is a very common custom. No one takes a bite of something and then shares it with another person. Only in certain instances will people eat what has already been touched by the tongue of another.

Food that has been offered to the Lord can be eaten, which is not a problem anyway because the Lord has not actually touched it with his tongue. Similarly, food offered to one's forefathers through the *brāhmaṇa*s who perform the ritual called *śrāddha*, is also eaten. The forefathers are invoked in the *brāhmaṇa*s and then the food is eaten by the *brāhmaṇa*s. Again, the forefathers have not actually touched on the food. Finally, a wife will eat from the same plate as her husband after he has eaten and a *śiṣya* will do the same after the *guru* has eaten. These are the exceptions to eating food that has been touched by others.

I actually tested this trait in deer when I was in a deer park one day. I gave the deer some bananas and they ate them. Then, I put my tongue on another banana and gave it to one of the deer. It sniffed at the banana and walked away. Whether an American deer would be so careful about what it eats, I do not know!

It seems to be the nature of the deer. Besides being clean, the deer has enough fur for the skin to be very soft.

There was also a rule about the skin that was to be used for one's *āsana*. It was not to be one that someone gave you or one that had been taken from a deer that had been killed. Some hunters would sometimes kill a deer and try to give the skin to a *sādhu*. Therefore, the *sādhu* had to hunt for a dead dear and ensure that it had died naturally.

The purpose of meditation

Having arranged your seat of meditation, what are you to do? The verb here is *yuñjyāt*, meaning 'May one practice.' And what are you to practice? Meditation, *yoga*. Why? For steadiness and purification of the mind alone, *ātma viśuddhaye*, not for anything else. Gaining knowledge of *ātmā* is accomplished only by enquiry, *vicāra*, which requires *ātma-viśuddhi*. The obstructions in the mind that prevent this knowledge from taking place have to be removed. This removal of the obstructions in the mind, *antaḥ-karaṇa-pratibandhaka-nivṛtti*, is done through *dhyāna*, meditation. Therefore, Kṛṣṇa says here, 'May one practice meditation for purification of the mind, *yuñjyāt yogam ātma viśuddhaye*.'

Sitting on the *āsana* described earlier, may there be absorption, *samādhāna*, into the object of meditation. How is this to be done? By making the mind single-pointed, *ekāgraṁ manaḥkṛtvā*. *Agra* means what is in front and refers here to what is to be meditated on, that being one thing alone, *eka*. Thus, Kṛṣṇa is saying to bring the mind to the object of meditation and let it be absorbed there.

The person who does meditation is described once again as *yata-citta-indriya-kriya*, one who has- mastery over the mind, senses, and their various activities. Because we tend to take this qualification lightly, it is repeated over and over again. And, since it has been repeated so often, we should take it seriously. This means that the senses, which are usually directed outward, are withdrawn along with all other activities of the mind. And the person who does this is called *yata-citta-indriya-kriya*. Being such a person, may he or she meditate, *yogaṁ yuñjyāt*.

Why should the person meditate? For the purification of the mind, *ātma viśuddhaye*. In this context, *ātmā* refers to the *antaḥ-karaṇa*, the mind, and not *sat-cit-ānanda-ātmā*, as *sat-cit-ānanda-ātmā* is already *viśuddha* and needs no purification.

Viśuddhi can also be taken in a different sense. To be free from the hold of *rāga-dveṣa*s is *śuddhi*. *Viśuddhi* can also be in terms of old memories, *kaṣāya*s, that come up unexpectedly in contemplation when the mind is quiet. These memories lie under the surface and are like the decaying organic matter that lies under the water, producing certain gases that bubble up to the surface. A pond can be quiet and clean one minute, but then, if you keep watching, you will suddenly see something coming up – blub.. blub.. blub. Why do the bubbles come up? Because there is something underneath.

Meditation is both prayerful and contemplative

The mind is quietened by meditation, which can be either contemplative meditation or purely prayerful meditation. Prayerful meditation is on Brahman with qualities, *saguṇa-*

brahma, whereas contemplative meditation is on Brahman without qualities, *nirguṇa-brahma*. Here, the words are such that you can take them to mean both *saguṇa-brahma* and *nirguṇa-brahma* meditation, as you will see later when the object of meditation, *dhyeya*, is discussed. In fact, meditation includes both because you start with a prayerful meditation and end with contemplative meditation.

When certain peace, *śānti*, is gained, the mind is composed, tranquil, and in that tranquil mind, various thoughts may occur. These thoughts are to be understood as *kaṣāya*s, memories that may pop up in a quiet mind at any time without any seeming connection or relevancy. When you understand meditation properly, your thoughts will not frighten you. You need not think you are disturbed; you just let the thoughts bubble up and remain a witness.

Generally, when these thoughts come, you take them as yourself. But here, in the seat of meditation, because you have certain composure, it is possible for you to discover a distance between yourself and these bubbles of thoughts. So, you are neither disturbed by them, nor do you need to try to avoid them. Just be an observer, a *sākṣī*; understand the thoughts as they are and do not be afraid of them. Let them rise, and watch them go away like so many bubbles on the surface of a quiet pond. This is what Kṛṣṇa means here when he said that for purifying the mind, may one practice meditation, *ātma-viśuddhaye-yogaṁ-yuñjyāt*.

Prayer can bring about *ātma-viśuddhi* because it brings about certain change on your part – a glad acceptance of what has gone before, or what has happened in your life.

Usually we spend our lives fighting against this! This glad acceptance of the past requires an intimate acceptance on your part, a prayerful acceptance of what has already happened. Therefore, prayerful meditation takes care of your *rāga-dveṣa*s in terms of the past – what I would have liked to have happened, what I should have done, what should not have happened to me and so on, all the things that usually bother a person. This is also called *ātma-viśuddhi*. And again, the release of various *kaṣāya*s – *saṁskāra*s, impressions, that are deep within the person, those unassimilated, undigested, hurtful experiences that are stored in the form of memories – is called *ātma-viśuddhi*.

Identifying myself with my thoughts or the physical body, thinking that anything that happens to the body happens to me, is an obstruction, *pratibandhaka*, a great impurity, *aśuddhi*, for the one who desires liberation. This identification has to be removed. Anything that has to be removed, that is unclean, is called *aśuddhi*. To eliminate *aśuddhi*, contemplation is helpful. Contemplation is not for *ātma-jñāna*; it is for *ātma-viśuddhi* alone.

Since *ātma-jñāna* is *vṛtti-jñāna*, it can only take place by the operation of a *pramāṇa*. *Pramāṇa-vicāra* alone produces *vṛtti-jñāna* and destroys self-ignorance. And, for this *vṛtti-jñāna* to take place, the various *pratibandhaka*s that are there, due to *rāga-dveṣa*s, *kaṣāya*s, or *viparīta bhāvana*s, have to be removed, and this removal is taken care of by *dhyāna*, meditation.

Saying that *pramāṇa vicāra* alone produces knowledge does not mean that you give meditation or prayer a lesser place. There is no lesser place, in fact. Because meditation is for *ātma-viśuddhi*, it occupies an important position in the life of a seeker. Thus, Kṛṣṇa says, 'May one do meditation, *yogaṁ yuñjyāt*.'

This is an important point to note because it is commonly thought that Vedanta is only a theory and it is *dhyāna*, the practice of meditation, that produces the knowledge. This is not true. *Dhyāna* is for *ātma-viśuddhi*, not for *ātma-jñāna*, even though ultimately it enables *ātma-jñāna* to take place. The knowledge itself depends entirely upon *antaḥ-karaṇa-viśuddhi*, because it depends on a mind that is fit for the knowledge. In making the mind fit for knowledge, *dhyāna* is important. Although there is a certain order involved here in terms of *dhyāna* being necessary for the first step of preparing the mind, *dhyāna* itself does not produce knowledge. The *vṛtti-jñāna* produced by *pramāṇa-vicāra* alone produces knowledge.

Having described the *āsana* and what is to take place while in the seat of meditation, Kṛṣṇa then talks about how one is to sit.

Verses 13&14

Sitting posture, object of meditation and the nature of the meditator

समं कायशिरोग्रीवं धारयन्नचलं स्थिरः ।
संप्रेक्ष्य नासिकाग्रं स्वं दिशश्चानवलोकयन् ॥ १३ ॥

प्रशान्तात्मा विगतभीर्ब्रह्मचारिव्रते स्थितः ।
मनः संयम्य मच्चित्तो युक्त आसीत मत्परः ॥ १४ ॥

samaṁ kāyaśirogrīvaṁ dhārayannacalaṁ sthiraḥ
samprekṣya nāsikāgraṁ svaṁ diśaścānavalokayan (13)

praśāntātmā vigatabhīrbrahmacārivrate sthitaḥ
manaḥ saṁyamya maccitto yukta āsīta matparaḥ (14)

kāya-śiro-grīvam – body, head and neck; *samam* – in one straight line; *acalam* – without moving; *dhārayan* – holding; *sthiraḥ* (*san*) – (being) firm; *svaṁ nāsikāgram* – the tip of one's nose; *samprekṣya* – (as though) looking at; *diśaḥ ca* – and directions; *anavalokayan* – not looking; *praśānta-ātmā* – one whose mind is tranquil; *vigata-bhīḥ* – one who is free from fear; *brahmacārivrate sthitaḥ* (*san*) – (being) established in one's committment to the life of a *brahmacārī*; *manaḥ* – mind; *saṁyamya* – withdrawing from everything else; *mat-cittaḥ* – thinking of me; *mat-paraḥ* – having me as the ultimate goal; *yuktaḥ* – *yogī* (meditator); *āsīta* – may he (or she) sit

> Holding oneself firm without moving, keeping the body, head, and neck in one straight line, (as though) looking at the tip of one's nose (for eye position) and not looking in all directions...
>
> ...being the one whose mind is tranquil, who is free from fear, established in one's commitment to the life of a *brahmacārī*, may (that) meditator sit thinking of me, having me as the ultimate goal, while withdrawing the mind from everything else.

To hold the body, head, and neck in one straight line means not to bend them in any way. In other words, you should sit erect for meditation. But, even though the body, head, and neck are vertical, you may sway or rock a little; therefore, Kṛṣṇa adds the word *acalam,* meaning that the body is to be kept still, and also *sthira,* meaning that you should be very firm in your seat. This means that, prior to meditation, the legs and feet are placed in such a way that they do not require any kind of change. Thus, there is both stillness and firmness in your seat of meditation.

Does one really meditate on the tip of one's nose?

The posture described in this verse brings out a certain attitude or disposition in the person that is conducive to meditation. This posture includes your gaze also. The expression, 'looking at the tip of the nose, *samprekṣya nāsikāgram,*' is sometimes misunderstood to mean that you should meditate on the tip of the nose. There are even two schools of thought on this, one saying you should meditate on the spot between the eyebrows, and the other saying that you should meditate on the tip of the nose itself. Because it could be literally taken and therefore, misunderstood, Śaṅkara explains what Kṛṣṇa means by this expression in his commentary of this verse.

In explaining the gaze, Kṛṣṇa says, '*samprekṣya nāsikāgram,* looking at the tip of one's nose.' It does not mean that you must sit cross-eyed. Rather, given the position of the eyes as they look out, they naturally fall or converge upon a particular point and that is where they are to remain. It means you neither look up nor down; you look 'as though' at the tip of your nose. Therefore, looking at one's nose is not what is being enjoined here by the expression, *samprekṣya nāsikāgram;* it simply addresses where the gaze should fall. This is explained by Śaṅkara as follows. He says that there is the word, *iva* here. The word, *samprekṣya,* looking, should be understood as 'as though looking, *darśanaṁ kṛtvā iva.*' The eyes are not closed in fact; they just look out in such a way that they do not look directly at any particular object, which is another way of avoiding distractions.

Śaṅkara questions what would happen if the person were asked to look at the tip of the nose. Looking at the tip of the nose, where would the person's absorption be? At the tip of the nose, of course, which is not what is desired here at all. In contemplation, the mind is to be absorbed in *ātmā* alone and, for this, your mind must be available. If you are busy looking at the tip of the nose, how are you going to make use of the mind to contemplate upon *ātmā*? Therefore, the object of meditation, *dhyeya*, is not the tip of the nose but something entirely different, as we shall see.

Śaṅkara also clarifies Kṛṣṇa's words, *diśaḥ anavalokayan*, as meaning 'not looking in any particular direction.' When you are sitting in meditation, it is possible to look to the left, to the right, to the front, and to the back, as well as up or down. Kṛṣṇa already covered the possibility of looking up and down here by saying, '*samaṁ kāya śiro grīvaṁ dhārayan*, keeping the body, head, and neck in one straight line.' Since you can also look to the left and right, why not meditate that way? Because you will develop a pain in the neck. So, to avoid such discomforts, the position for meditation was established.

Sitting outwardly in meditation is one thing, but there is also another sitting involved, an inner sitting. This inner sitting is what is meant by 'meditation' and is what is referred to by the words *mat-cittaḥ* and *mat-paraḥ*.

Having already talked about the place of meditation, the seat itself, and the sitting posture, Kṛṣṇa points out the object of meditation and also the nature of the meditator here. In fact, there are not many verses in the *Gītā* that talk about meditation as such, whereas the meditator is talked about a lot. If you look at the entire *Gītā*, you will find only one or two other sentences on meditation itself.[13]

The emphasis throughout the Gītā is on the meditator

Who is the one who meditates is what makes the difference between a successful meditation and an unsuccessful one, a mere act of meditation. The present verse also talks a lot about the meditator, referring to the person as *praśānta-ātmā*, one for whom *ātmā*, the mind, the *antaḥ-karaṇa*, has gained certain degree of tranquillity.

Kṛṣṇa talks about the real *śānti* later, the *śānti* that is gained as a result of meditation and knowledge. In this verse, however, because the person being discussed is a *mumukṣu*, a seeker, the *śānti* talked about is relative, and refers to the degree of tranquillity one has gained by living a life of *karma-yoga*. We know this by the context since, in the previous verses, Kṛṣṇa had been talking about the meditator and what he or she had accomplished thus far, all of which is conveyed here by describing the person as *praśānta-ātmā*. *Praśānta-ātmā* is one who has lived a life of *karma-yoga,* who has taken care of his or her *rāga-dveṣa*s and is therefore, no longer pressurised by them.

Such a person is free from fear, *vigata-bhī*. There are many varieties of fear. The fear of death, for example, is said to be a

---

[13] *Gītā 6.25*

very common fear for some people in the seat of meditation. When the body is as relaxed as it is in meditation, we generally go to sleep and there is no fear because there is nobody to be afraid of. But when the body is relaxed and you do not go to sleep, there may be a feeling of going out of the body, which may give rise to the fear of death if what is happening is not properly understood. The physical relaxation itself is as though you are going out of this body. Then, the entire internal defence system sends out an alarm and the person experiences fear.

The source of fear

No matter how old you are, there is a fear in giving up the body even though you know you have to give it up one day. However, what is involved here is the dissolution of the doer, the *kartā*. This means the very subject, the meditator is resolved, which is a kind of suicide. And because the person does not want to dissolve oneself, there is fear. In fact, there is no dissolution; there is only resolution. The resolving of the *ahaṅkāra* is also false because the *ahaṅkāra* is *ātmā*, but *ātmā* is not *ahaṅkāra*. In contemplation, the *ahaṅkāra*, the meditator, naturally resolves into *ātmā*.

The meditator is *ātmā*, the meditated is *ātmā*, and the attempt is called meditation. If the attempt is successful, the meditator is gone, having resolved into *ātmā*. Therefore, the means and the end become one and the same. The meditator resolves into the very object of meditation as one attempts meditation. This is the situation that some people are afraid of because they feel as though they are being decimated or destroyed. Thus, some people see fear where there is no fear at all. They feel as though something is going to disappear and they retain it. In fact, the retention of the *ahaṅkāra* is the only source of fear there is, the *ahaṅkāra* itself being the source of fear.

If the *ahaṅkāra* does not want to quit, naturally there will be some fear. This fear, then, is due to *avicāra*, lack of enquiry alone. A person who enquires is free from fear and is called *vigata-bhī* here.

The one who is free from fear is a vigatabhī

Vigatabhī can also be taken as a person who is not afraid of tomorrow, a very common fear. People often ask, 'If I keep on meditating, what will happen to me? Suppose I go into *samādhi* and I don't come out. What will happen then? Or, suppose I get enlightened, then what will happen to me? How will I behave? How will I hold a job?' Because the person being described in this verse is a *sannyāsī*, this fear of tomorrow is not possible. But a meditator need not always be a *sannyāsī*; therefore, one may have all these fears.

I read once that a woman approached Swami Vivekananda after a talk he had given and asked, 'Did you say that the ego is to be destroyed?' 'Yes,' he replied. 'But if my ego is destroyed, who will run the house?' she asked. 'Who will do the dishes?' This kind of problem arises because of the use of the word 'destruction.' Destruction of the ego has to be properly understood. The ego is not really destroyed. It remains even for the person who is qualified to talk about it. But it is an enlightened ego. The 'I' is independent of the I thought, whereas the I thought is not independent of 'I.' Thus, the

I thought is already nullified. It is only a shadow 'I.' It is not the 'I' itself.

The problem is only in the 'I.' If the I thought is taken at one time as 'I,' and at other times as I thought, then 'I' become a yo-yo – now up, now down, now *sukhī,* now *duḥkhī.* Because the person identifies with the conditions of one's mind, the person is subject to *saṁsāra.* To be free of this identification is often described as the destruction of the ego, but if it is not explained in this way, all kinds of problems and fears are possible. However, for the person discussed here, *vigatabhī,* there is no fear of tomorrow or of anything else.

The *vigatabhī* can also be called *brahmacāri-vrate sthitaḥ,* one who remains with the vows or the commitment of a *brahmacārī.* And what is that commitment that implies living the life of a *brahmacārī*? Śaṅkara defines it in terms of service to the teacher, *guru-śuśruṣā,* eating happily whatever food comes one's way as alms, etc., *bhikṣā-anna-bhuktyādi.* A person with this kind of commitment does not bother about tomorrow and is called a *brahmacārī.* Since Kṛṣṇa is talking about meditation, the context in which the word *brahmacārī* is used here also implies an emphasis on the study of the *śāstra*; therefore it is assumed that the meditator has done a lot of *śravaṇa* and *manana.*

How to live a life of a *brahmacārī* is also mentioned in this verse. One must withdraw from the various forms of thinking that takes place in the mind, *manaḥ saṁyama.* And, because one cannot withdraw from them unless one applies the mind to the *dhyeya,* the object of meditation, Kṛṣṇa says here, 'Thinking of me, may the meditator sit, *mat-citto yukta āsīta.*'

Mat-citta means one whose mind is in me, Parameśvara, *mayi parameśvara cittaṁ yasya*. The 'me,' of course, is Kṛṣṇa as Parameśvara. Parameśvara has two meanings and is a common expression throughout the *śāstra*. It can mean either the Lord as the cause of the world, *jagat-kāraṇa*, or the Lord in his essential form, Brahman, *paramātmā*. *Paramātmā* is used because the *jīva*, the individual who thinks, 'I am the *jīva*,' is equated to Parameśvara, even though there seems to be a difference between the two. In reality, there is no difference.

The need for two types of vākyas

The resolution of the seeming difference is Kṛṣṇa's *upadeśa* and the teaching of Vedanta. Thus, the *jīva*'s predication as Parameśvara, the Lord, is the *upadeśa*, for which there are two types of statements, *vākyas*, in the *vedānta-śāstra*. One kind of *vākya* reveals the nature of *ātmā*, Parameśvara, and the other reveals the non-difference between *jīva* and Parameśvara.

The nature of *ātmā* is revealed either by saying that *satya-jñāna-ananta* is Brahman or by saying that *sat-cit-ānanda* is *ātmā*. It is the same revelation in that both are one and the same. The words that reveal the nature of the self or the *paramātmā* by implication are always the same. But there is also the equation between *jīva* and Īśvara, the equation itself being the *upadeśa*, the teaching. So, there are these two types of *vākyas* – *vastu svarūpa-para-vākya*, a statement revealing the nature of *ātmā*, and *ekatva-para-vākya*, a statement revealing the identity between the individual and the Lord, such as, You are that Brahman, *tat tvam asi*, or I am Brahman, *ahaṁ brahma asmi*.

How is an identity between the *jīva* and Īśvara possible? It is because both Parameśvara and the the *jīva* are *sat-cit-ānanda*. The *svarūpa* of *ātmā* being *sat-cit-ānanda*, this *jīva-īśvara-aikya-vākya*, the equation stating that the *jīva* and Īśvara are one and the same, is valid. If the *svarūpa* of *ātmā* were not *sat-cit-ānanda*, the equation would have no validity at all. Therefore, both types of *vākya*s are important. The *jīva-īśvara-aikya-vākya* can be understood only when the *vākya*s revealing the nature of *ātmā* are available. If such *vākya*s were not there, the equation *vākya* would be meaningless. The *jīva* would be a *jīva* and Īśvara would be Īśvara.

When we say that the wave is ocean, the water itself must be understood. Only then the *vākya* talking about the identity of wave and ocean will be meaningful. If someone says to a wave that thinks it is a wave, 'Hey, you are the ocean!' the statement will only be understood by the wave if it has the knowledge that *satya* is water. Because of the seeming difference, *upādhī*, one is called 'wave' and the other is called 'ocean.' In fact, there is no 'one' or the 'other.' There is only one – water. Therefore, together, both types of *vākya*s do the job.

Kṛṣṇa as Parameśvara - the Lord

Here, Kṛṣṇa uses the first person singular, 'me,' in the sense of Parameśvara, the Lord. Whether or not the historical Kṛṣṇa is the Lord is not our concern. We are talking about Kṛṣṇa who is the Lord because he talks as Īśvara. Because the word Kṛṣṇa indicates Parameśvara alone, whenever Kṛṣṇa uses the word *aham*, the first person singular, Parameśvara is to be understood.

Whether there was such a person as Kṛṣṇa who danced and played beautiful music on the flute is besides the point. These accounts are stories designed to create certain appreciation of the historical person who walked along the banks of the Yamuna as an *avatāra*.

Any wise person can use the word *aham* in the same way. There are such *vākya*s in the *śāstra* in fact, 'I was Manu, *ahaṁ manuḥ abhavam*,' 'I am the Sun,' 'I am everything,' are statements that any wise person can make. What happened before, what is here and now, and what is going to come later are all *puruṣa*, *ātmā*, alone, there being nothing separate from this *puruṣa*. And who is the *puruṣa*? The one who knows the *puruṣa* as oneself as, 'That I am, *so'ham*,' becomes free from all mortality, *sa iha amṛto bhavati*. He or she is *ātmā*.

There is only one *puruṣa* and that is *ātmā*; thus the *puruṣa* is the one who is everywhere, but available only in the heart. 'That which is within my heart is *ātmā*' is an expression that anyone can say; Kṛṣṇa is not the only one who can say it. The point being made here is that Kṛṣṇa always presents himself either in the sense of Parameśvara, the cause of the world, or pure *paramātmā*. Either way it is one and the same.

The word Parameśvara here can be taken as *saguṇa-brahma*, meaning Īśvara, the Lord, *sṛṣṭi-kartā*, the one who creates, *sthiti-kartā*, the one who sustains the creation, and *laya-kartā*, the one who resolves the creation into himself. In this way, Parameśvara is the *kartā* and performs these three jobs simultaneously. All three activities are going on at the same time. At this second, an object is born; as it is born, it is; and as it is, it is gone.

It is cyclic and therefore, we do not know which is first, second, or third – is-born-gone; gone-born-is; gone-is-born; or born-is-gone. Nor does it matter because all three occur simultaneously.

Since the whole creation is in time, it is called *mithyā,* time itself being *mithyā*. Is this present second, this micro-second, pico-second, etc., born or is it gone? It is born and, as it is born, it is going. Going, it is born, which means there is no 'birth.' This is the nature of time and everything is in time, which is *mithyā*.

Meditation on Parameśvara

The nature of time is nothing but the trick of the *māyāvī,* another name for the great magician, Īśvara, who is the agent, *kartā,* of *sṛṣṭi, sthiti,* and *laya*. If you absorb your mind in this Parameśvara, it is called *saguṇa-brahma-dhyāna*. To do this, you meditate on the virtues of Parameśvara. Thus, for you, Parameśvara is one who is all-compassion, mercy, *ānanda*. Or, Parameśvara is *sṛṣṭi-sthiti-laya-kartā,* the one who is the creator, sustainer, and resolver of everything. In this way, any one virtue can be taken in its absolute sense and meditated upon. Or, the meditation can be in the form of a simple prayer, '*Parameśvarāya namaḥ,* unto that Lord my salutations.'

The word '*mat*' in the compound, *mat-citta* can also mean, Parameśvara, the cause of everything, *paraṁ-brahma*. And that Brahman is *satya-jñāna-ananta-brahma, ātmā*. Here, the one whose mind is contemplating upon the *svarūpa* of the *ātmā,* pure consciousness, is called *mat-citta*. With reference to this *caitanya-ātmā* there are other revealing words that reveal the *svarūpa* of *ātmā* upon which you contemplate. With the help of these words, you contemplate upon the meaning and this contemplation is called meditation.

The meditator is mat-para

The person being discussed in this verse is also called *mat-para,* another word that describes the person in terms of the object of meditation. People meditate for many reasons. For instance, a person who meditates in order to lower one's blood pressure may be a blood-pressure-*para* but one is definitely not *mat-para.* There is another person who meditates for one hundred percent spiritual success, while another does for material success. This only proves that meditation is not properly understood. Meditation is not a technique; meditation is life. Therefore, Kṛṣṇa refers to the meditator as *mat-para,* one for whom the Lord, Parameśvara is everything. The mind of such a person will stay with the object of meditation because there is nothing other than Parameśvara, *paramātmā* to be gained, which is everything. Kṛṣṇa says that the one for whom *paramātmā* alone is to be accomplished is called *mat-para.*

Śaṅkara adds here that such a person is very careful in terms of the objects that he or she desires. For example, the person does not think of a particular woman or man as the ultimate end, *para.* Instead, one has another *para,* that is, one's mind is committed to Īśvara, the Lord, as the ultimate end. The *svarūpa* of Īśvara, the *paramātmā,* as the ultimate end, *para,* is called *parama-pada* and the person who has this as the only pursuit is called *mat-para.*

The expression 'ultimate end' can give rise to another problem if its meaning is not properly understood. 'Ultimate end' does not mean, 'Ultimately, I will reach that; in the meantime, I have other ends to reach.' Thus, 'ultimate end' is not to be interpreted here as an end to be gained later in time, like after retirement. The ultimate end is the predominant end, meaning there is no other end. All other 'so called' ends subserve this ultimate end. Everything one does is for the ultimate end alone; one even eats to gain this end alone as Kṛṣṇa says later.

The study of Sanskrit also serves the same purpose. The study of Sanskrit is not so that you may become a Sanskrit scholar. You study whatever is to be studied as a discipline, as a means to gain access into what is being taught in the *vedānta-śāstra*. The 'ultimate end' here is not to champion the cause of Īśvara in any way, although there are self appointed champions who say they want to propagate Īśvara. Surely, Īśvara does not need any such help. By the very definition of Īśvara, he should be able to achieve whatever he wants to accomplish. He does not want you to champion him at all. If he wants to accomplish something, he can accomplish it without you. Your commitment is only to understand what Īśvara is.

Īśvara, *paramātmā*, is the only end for the meditator, the *dhyāna-yoga*. Kṛṣṇa speaking as Īśvara, says that his or her mind is lost in me; he is *mat-citta*. In the mind of this person who is *mat-citta,* the predominant object is Īśvara. Also, by calling the person, *mat-para*, Kṛṣṇa conveys the fact that Īśvara is to be accomplished; in fact, Īśvara is the only end to be accomplished for this person. Both these words, *mat-citta* and *mat-para* indicate the person's exact understanding of what he or she wants to accomplish, to know.

Verse 15

The ultimate end gained as a result of dhyāna-yoga - meditation

युञ्जन्नेवं सदात्मानं योगी नियतमानसः ।
शान्तिं निर्वाणपरमां मत्संस्थामधिगच्छति ॥ १५ ॥

yuñjannevaṁ sadātmānaṁ yogī niyatamānasaḥ
śāntiṁ nirvāṇaparamāṁ matsaṁsthām adhigacchati (15)

evam – in this manner; *sadā* – always; *ātmānam* – the mind; *yuñjan* – connecting; *niyatamānasaḥ* – the one whose mind is mastered; *yogī* – the meditator; *nirvāṇaparamām* – that which is the ultimate liberation; *matsaṁsthām* – that which is centred on me; *śāntim* – the peace; *adhigacchati* – gains

> Always connecting the mind in this manner, the meditator, the one whose mind is mastered, gains the peace, which is centred on me (which is in the form of an absorption in me), which is the ultimate liberation.

Here, the word '*sadā,* always,' may raise the question – when does the meditator have time for other activities such as eating, bathing, and sleeping? *Sadā* here simply indicates that the person does not waste time, using whatever time is available for this particular pursuit. *Ātmā* here, refers to the mind that is always connected in this manner, *yuñjan evaṁ sadā ātmānaṁ*, meaning in all the ways already described, starting from finding the place and preparing the seat, etc., *śucau deśe… caila ajina kuśottaram.*[14] The mind is connected, absorbed, in Brahman, which is Parameśvara, *paramātmā*, the *svarūpa* of *ātmā*.

How does one connect the mind to the *svarūpa* of *ātmā*? Through contemplative words, *śabda,* which is why words are so important. Through a word you can connect yourself to *ātmā*. And what kind of words? In contemplation we make use of revealing words, words that reveal the *svarūpa* of *ātmā* and thereby connect the mind to *ātmā*. *Yuñjan* means 'meditating or connecting,'connecting the mind, the *antaḥ-karaṇa*, to the object of meditation, which in fact is the act of meditating.

In this verse, the person is again described as one who has mastered the mind, whose mind is tranquil, absorbed, *niyata-mānasa*. And what does this *niyata-mānasa-yogī* gain? Meditating, the person comes to understand properly what is being said. All that is taught becomes clear because there are no obstructions for the person. Therefore, the teaching becomes real and he or she gains *śānti–śāntim adhigacchati.*

The meaning of śānti

Śānti usually means peace. Does this mean that after doing meditation, all you will get out of it is the same peace that can be gained from a tranquiliser or a shot of something? No, this

---

[14] *Gītā* 6.11

śānti is not that kind of peace; it is *mat-saṁsthā* and *nirvāṇa-paramā*. In his commentary, Śaṅkara defined *śānti* as *uparati, uparati*, meaning resolution or *sarva-karma-sannyāsa*, wherein doership and enjoyership are renounced as discussed at length previously. *Nirvāṇa* means *mokṣa*. Therefore, this is a *śānti* that has its basis in *mokṣa*. It is *mokṣa-śānti* itself.

And what is this *mokṣa-śānti*? There are three types of *śānti*. One *śānti* is where there is no thinking whatsoever, which can be induced so that the frequency of thinking is cut down. Another *śānti* is when you enjoy a *śānti* along with certain capacity to manage an active mind. This is important because you need the mind in order to think.

The first *śānti*, which is freedom from thinking, can only be temporary and requires a lot of inducements. This *śānti* is that which is there between two thoughts or between two spells of agitation. Whereas the second *śānti* is there when there is certain distance between yourself and the mind, whatever be the situation. And because of this you are able to manage your affairs with certain composure.

The third *śānti* is *mokṣa*, wherein the mind becomes a privilege. Whatever the mind is, it is me, but I am not the mind. This knowledge is the freedom, total freedom. I do not control the mind. I do not take the mind somewhere. Rather, wherever the mind goes, the person always has this knowledge. Then, the person is truly a devotee because, wherever the mind is, there the Lord is for this person.

To express this knowledge based devotion, there are many stories. One such story is about a great devotee of Lord Śiva.

One day he came and found a *sādhu* sleeping with his feet placed on a *liṅga*. For anyone to do such a thing, let alone a *sādhu*, is a desecration. Therefore, the devotee shouted angrily at the *sādhu*, 'Wake up! How dare you to put your feet on the *liṅga*!' To this, the *sādhu* replied, 'I am very old. I am tired and sleepy. I have no strength to move my feet. Therefore, please put my feet wherever you want. I cannot lift them.' Then the devotee picked up the *sādhu*'s feet and moved them away from the *liṅga*. But to his surprise, another *liṅga* appeared under the *sādhu*'s feet. Confused, he moved the *sādhu*'s feet again. But wherever he placed them, yet another *liṅga* appeared in that very place! Then he understood that there is no place where the Lord is not. In other words, there is no place to put one's feet that is not the Lord.

Similarly, wherever the mind goes, it remains in the Lord's presence. There is no question of getting the mind out of or into anything here. To make this point, a seeker in the *Bṛhadāraṇyakopaniṣad* said, 'It is as though the mind has gone away and, therefore, I am as though meditating.'[15] For the 'as though' gone away mind, 'as though' meditation is good enough. And, when the 'as though' becomes clear to you, then the mind does not go away and therefore, does not require any meditation. This is the *śānti* called *nirvāṇa-paramā śānti*, *mokṣa*, the *śānti* that is one's *svarūpa*, in which there is no coming and going, no degrees or variations, and for which no comparison to anything is possible.

---

[15] *dhyāyati iva lelāyati iva (Bṛhadāraṇyakopaniṣad 4.3.7)*

Svarūpa śānti – the śānti that is oneself

Because this *śānti* is identical with oneself, Kṛṣṇa describes it as *mat-saṁsthā*, meaning *mat-adhīnā*, that which always obtains in the *paramātmā* because *paramātmā* does not move at anytime, it is *kūṭastha*, immutable, it does not get involved with anything, and does not stand opposed to anything either. If there is opposition, there is some rub or resistance, which is *aśānti*. *Śānti* is identical with *paramātmā* in that it is not opposed to thought, it is not opposed to the world, it is not opposed to knowledge, it is not opposed to ignorance, it is not opposed to anything. At the same time, it lends itself to everything. Thus, the meditator gains this *śānti*, freedom or liberation, *mat-adhīnāṁ śāntim adhigacchati*.

Nirvāṇa-paramā-śānti does not depend upon the condition of the mind, whereas the *śānti* that depends on one's mental state is always subject to becoming disturbed. Here, *ātmā* is called *śānta* because it is a description, a *lakṣaṇa*, revealing the nature of *ātmā*. This must be clearly understood. *Śānti* is not something that sticks to *ātmā* as an attribute, like the 'blue' of a blue pot.

An attribute, *viśeṣaṇa*, distinguishes an object from all other objects belonging to the same species. Otherwise, attributes are not required. For example, if all pots were blue, you would not need to use the word 'blue.' Attributes by definition can be perceived. When we say *ātmā* is *śānta*, the *śānti* in *ātmā* is not something that is perceivable but the word itself points out the nature of *ātmā*. Therefore, it is a *lakṣaṇa*, not an attribute of *ātmā*.

The conditions of the mind like agitation are superimpositions on *ātmā*, which is *caitanya*, consciousness, that which obtains in all conditions and is independent, free of all conditions. Words like *śānta* negate the superimposition, revealing the *svarūpa* of *ātmā* as independent of *aśānti* that is superimposed upon *ātmā*, when we say *ātmā* is *aśānta*.

Therefore, this *śānti* is not a conditional *śānti*; it is *svarūpa-śānti*. Because it is not conditional, it is called *svarūpa*. *Ātmā* is free from any form of *vṛtti*, thought, even though *vṛtti*s are not free from *ātmā*. When the *vṛtti*s happen and there is an appreciation of *ātmā* as *ahaṁ śāntaḥ*, the *vṛtti*s do not disturb the *śānta-ātmā*. This is what is meant by *nirvāṇa-paramā-śānti*, that is purely in the form of knowledge, recognition.

The one who recognises oneself as *paramātmā* and understands the *svarūpa-śānti* of *paramātmā*, is said to have gained this because he or she has gained the knowledge. Such a person is called *yogī* here, not in terms of the eight-fold *yoga* called *aṣṭāṅga-yoga*, but purely in terms of knowledge alone.

In the next verse, Kṛṣṇa points out certain other conditions that make a life of contemplation possible.

Verse 16

The discipline of eating and sleeping required for meditation

नात्यश्नतस्तु योगोऽस्ति न चैकान्तमनश्नतः ।
न चातिस्वप्नशीलस्य जाग्रतो नैव चार्जुन ॥ १६ ॥

nātyaśnatastu yogo'sti na caikāntam anasnataḥ
na cātisvapnaśīlasya jāgrato naiva cārjuna (16)

arjuna – O Arjuna!; *atyaśnataḥ* – for one who eats too much; *tu* – indeed; *yogaḥ na asti* – meditation is not; *ca* – and; *na ekāntam anaśnataḥ* – not for one who does not eat at all; *ca* – and; *na atisvapnaśīlasya* – not for one who sleeps too much; *ca* – and; *eva* – indeed; *na jāgrataḥ* – not for one who is always awake

Meditation is not for one who eats too much or for one who does not eat at all; nor indeed, Arjuna! (it is) for one who sleeps too much or who is always awake.

Here, Kṛṣṇa mentions the discipline with reference to eating required for meditation. He does not go into details but makes the point that the extremes in terms of the quantity of food eaten are not conducive to meditation. Later, he also talks in a general way about what one should and should not eat from the standpoint of the *sāttvika*, *rājasika*, and *tāmasika* aspects of food.

Only certain quantity of food is acceptable to a person. Beyond that one should not eat if one wants to meditate. Kṛṣṇa says here that for the one who overeats or for the one who hardly eats, there will be no meditation, no *yoga*, even though there may be *bhoga*, enjoyment, at least for the time being. And, if there is too much *bhoga*, *roga*, disease, may follow just as it may for the one who eats too little. *Yoga* is the opposite of *bhoga* and *roga*. For the one who is a *bhogī* or *rogī*, a life of meditation and contemplation is not possible, *yogaḥ nāsti*. Here 'meditation' refers to *saguṇa-brahma-dhyāna* and 'contemplation' refers to *nirguṇa-brahma-dhyāna*, as discussed earlier.

In his commentary of this verse, Śaṅkara quotes from the Veda,[16] 'Indeed the food that is acceptable to oneself (in quantity and quality) will protect, nourish; it will not destroy (the person). The food that is more destroys; that which is less does not protect.' Food eaten in the proper quantities will not bring about the diseases that destroy a person who habitually over-eats. No specific amount of food is prescribed; one eats only to one's own known limit.

Similarly, if one does not take enough food, the food eaten will not nourish the person. It will not destroy the person, but it will not provide the necessary nourishment either. Thus one who overeats, *atyaśnat*, and one who undereats, *anaśnat*, will not be fit for meditation. The *yogī* discussed here is a person who neither over-eats nor under-eats. He or she eats only what the stomach allows.

Śaṅkara quotes a *vākya* concerning the quantity of food to be taken, '*ardham aśanasya savyañjanasya tṛtīyam udakasya ca vāyoḥ sañcaraṇārthaṁ tu caturtham avaśeṣayet*, half the stomach is for solid food, the third quarter is for water or other liquids, and the fourth quarter is to be left empty so that there is enough space for the churning that takes place during the digestive process.' For those who cross these boundaries, there will be no meditation.

---

[16] यदु ह वा आत्म संमितम् अन्नं तदवति तन्न हिनस्ति यद् भूयो हिनस्ति तद्यत्कनीयो न तदवति (शतपथ ब्राह्मण)

yadu ha vā ātma-sammitam annaṁ tadavati tanna hinasti yad bhūyo hinasti tat kanīyo na tadavati (*Śatapatha-brāhmaṇa*)

Naturally, a person who does not eat enough will be tired and will not be able to sit for meditation and a person who eats too much will be sleepy, which is also a problem. So, there has to be certain measure applied to the food that one eats. But please do not ask, 'Swamiji, how do I know when I have filled half the stomach?' When you feel like having another helping, don't – just stop eating, that's all.

The discipline of sleep

Equally important to the discipline required in terms of the amount of food one eats is the discipline in terms of the amount of sleep one gets. There are people who sleep so much that, even when they are awake, they are sleepy. This over sleeping goes along with over-eating and a lack of exercise. *Atisvapnaśilasya yogaḥ nāsti*, for one who over-sleeps there is no meditation. Nor is there meditation for the person who deprives his or her sleep to meditate. Having heard that 4:00 AM in the morning is the best time to meditate, if a person goes to bed at midnight, and gets up at 4:00 AM to meditate, the meditation becomes sleep in no time.

In the past, when there was no electricity and people went to bed as soon as it was dark, getting up at 4:00 AM was natural. But now, the situation is quite different. In fact, there are people who wake up, go to work, and live their lives after dark! So, for the one who does not get adequate sleep, who is awake all the time, *jāgrat*, there is no *yoga* because, having so little sleep, the person will be sleepy all the time.

The unfortunate thing here is that both types of people, those who sleep too much and those who sleep too little, end up sleeping. So, Kṛṣṇa says here, there is no *yoga*, no contemplative life, for either of them. How, then, is this *yoga* to take place and for whom? The answer is given in the next verse.

Verse 17

Dhyāna yoga is for the one who follows a life of discipline

युक्ताहारविहारस्य युक्तचेष्टस्य कर्मसु ।
युक्तस्वप्नावबोधस्य योगो भवति दुःखहा ॥ १७ ॥

yuktāhāravihārasya yuktaceṣṭasya karmasu
yuktasvapnāvabodhasya yogo bhavati duḥkhahā (17)

yukta-āhāra-vihārasya – for one who is moderate in eating and other activities; *karmasu* – with reference to one's duties; *yukta-ceṣṭasya* – for one who is mindful in all activities; *yukta-svapna-avabodhasya* – for one who is moderate in terms of sleeping and waking hours; *duḥkhahā* – the destroyer of sorrow; *yogaḥ* – meditation; *bhavati* – becomes

> For one who is moderate in eating and other activities, who is mindful in all activities, (and) to one's sleeping and waking hours, (for such a person) meditation becomes the destroyer of sorrow.

Again, this verse names the person and describes the qualifications required for meditation in the same compound. *Yukta* here means 'proper' in terms of having a sense of proportion in all of one's activities.

The person is described here as *yukta-āhāra-vihāra*, one whose eating and other activities are proper; *yukta-ceṣṭa*, one whose activities are proper, and *yukta-svapna-avabodha*, one whose sleeping and waking hours are properly apportioned. In other words, this person follows a life of discipline, which in itself is *yoga*, a *yoga* that destroys the sorrow of *saṁsāra* – *yogo bhavati duḥkhahā*.

In his commentary to this verse, Śaṅkara explains the compound *yukta-āhāra-vihāra*. He says, anything taken in by you is called *āhāra* – *āhrīyate iti āhāraḥ*, which in the present context means food, *anna*. *Vihāra* refers to your moving around in terms of activities, like walking, running, and so on. Therefore, the person for whom both of these, *āhāra* and *vihāra*, are proper, meaning that they are done with the proper sense of proportion, is called *yukta-āhāra-vihāra*. In other words, they are not allowed to become obsessions, which is always possible, especially in terms of food.

'Spiritual' obsessions

Spending your whole time in planning meals, for example, is definitely an obsession. *Āhāra*, food, can take up your entire life; it even becomes a religion for many people. Whereas, for others, some form of exercise becomes a religion. You may eat only junk food and be obsessed with getting it out of your system by doing aerobics for hours every day. In this way, aerobics too becomes a religion. Whole lifetimes are spent exercising. For what? There are people who exercise so much and are so tired afterwards that all they do is eat and go to sleep, only to repeat the same cycle again the next day. No activity should be given this kind of time. Therefore, Kṛṣṇa says here, whatever the activity, it should be *yukta*; there should be a sense of proportion. Otherwise, *āhāra* can get you and *vihāra* can also get you.

What you eat and how much you eat can become an obsession and, for a spiritual seeker, eating can become a 'spiritual' obsession. Such a person thinks that eating properly is being spiritual, whereas, in fact, eating properly is a matter of health, nothing else. A demon can eat properly and still accomplish all his demonic activities in a disciplined way. A thief may follow a proper diet and exercise daily, but still continues to commit crimes. Therefore, *yukta* is a very important word here, meaning the one who has a sense of proportion in all things.

One who is *yukta-ceṣṭa*, with reference to all activities, *karmasu*, is one who does not waste his or her time fuming and fretting because there is a lot to be done. This person performs each activity deliberately, consciously, one by one. In this way, everything gets done efficiently and in the proper order. *Ceṣṭā* refers to any movement, including those of the hands and legs. The *yukta-ceṣṭa*, therefore, is also a person who does not waste the movements of his or her limbs while performing various activities.

One needs a sense of proportion in one's activities

You know what happens if you want to do too many things at the same time. The end result is that nothing gets done. You want to do a particular thing and suddenly you remember something else. So, you leave what you are doing and go to the other activity. Then you remember something else and off you go again. Some people cannot even take a bath, without becoming distracted by other things they want to do at the same time. These people are *ayukta-ceṣṭa*s, whereas a *yukta-ceṣṭa* does each thing that is to be done deliberately and consciously. Even the hand movements of the person are done consciously. In fact, this is what the life of a Zen master is all about. Watching his or her every movement, watching what the hands are doing and where they go becomes a form of meditation for the person.

However, you need not go that far, the point being that a sense of proportion in all activities is necessary so that nothing becomes an obsession. There is nothing to be gained from an obsession, but there is something to be gained from being conscious about what you do. What is gained is a sense of alertness. *Yukta* means that you are conscious about what you do and you do what is to be done. In this way, there is an inner leisure that enables you to gain knowledge.

One decides for oneself what is proper

The person discussed in this verse is also called *yukta-svapna-avabodha,* one for whom there is a sense of proportion with reference to sleep, *svapna,* and waking hours, *avabodha.* Again, please do not ask me how many hours you should sleep. What is proper for one person is not proper for another because the amount of sleep required depends on several factors such as how many hours you slept as a child and your constitution. Sleep for as many hours as you require.

The amount of time you sleep can be altered a little, perhaps by half an hour or forty-five minutes. But changing the time you sleep by any more than this is likely to affect your whole day. You will walk around like a zombie and be completely useless. Therefore, follow what your constitution tells you. It knows what it needs and it tells you. And, if it does not get enough sleep, it tells you that also. If, for example, you find yourself always feeling drowsy, this may indicate that you require more sleep.

We must understand that the word *yukta* is used very cautiously here because there is no set rule that applies to everyone all the time. Each person must decide for himself or herself. It is not correct to assume that everyone should sleep a certain number of hours. There are people who require only five hours sleep and others who require six, seven, or eight hours. It all depends on the individual's constitution. Therefore, for the person who has a sense of proportion with reference to waking and sleep, *yukta-svapna-avabodhasya,* there is *yoga, yogaḥ bhavati.*

The knowledge that destroys sorrow

And what kind of *yoga* is it? Knowledge alone, the knowledge that destroys sorrow, *duḥkhahā,* by shifting the entire vision of the person who is subject to sorrow. This shift in vision is in terms of self-understanding, self-knowledge, seeing one's *svarūpa* as free from sorrow. By negating the doership, the sorrow is taken care of. Thus, the destruction of sorrow is purely in terms of knowledge, *jñāna,* and this knowledge is called *yoga* here.

In his commentary to this verse, Śaṅkara emphasises that *duḥkha* refers to all kinds of sorrow, *sarva-saṁsāra-duḥkha*. You may say, 'Swamiji, my life is all right, but the people around me are a problem.' It means that your life is not all right. Therefore, commit your life to the pursuit of the knowledge that will destroy sorrow. Do not commit yourself to anything else, not to over-eating or under-eating, sleeping too much or too little, or to exercising a lot or not at all.

One must have discipline in one's life but in proper proportions. *Yogāsana*s and *prāṇāyāma*, for example, are useful because they are disciplines. But it does not mean that one should commit one's life solely to the practice of *yogāsana*s and *prāṇāyāma*. Nor does it mean that one should neglect such disciplines. In fact, a meditative life includes *yogāsana*s and *prāṇāyāma*. Every seeker follows certain discipline based on *aṣṭāṅga-yoga*. The point being made here is that whatever discipline is followed must be kept in proper proportion, meaning that there is neither neglect nor over-enthusiasm. Everything is to be in moderation and one should not become a faddist, a very common tendency in some people – whatever they take up becomes a religion for them. Because there is something to know, rather than to do, one should not become a faddist, Kṛṣṇa is saying here.

A person who is not too inactive, *karmasu-yukta-ceṣṭa*, one who is moderate in terms of what is eaten and who does not sleep too much or too little, one who looks after the body properly without becoming obsessive about it, usually enjoys the necessary health to enable him or her gain self-knowledge.

The human body, *śarīra*, was defined by Kālidāsa as the basic means, *sādhana*, for gaining *mokṣa*, health being a basic requirement.[17] Therefore, whatever one must do to maintain proper health, one does, which implies eating, sleeping, and exercising properly. In other words, one should not be negligent about these basic requirements.

When will I gain the vision?

Two questions may now arise – What is to be gained by all this and how long will it take? Living a life of discipline, coupled with meditation and contemplation, when can it be said that the person is accomplished? *Saṁsārīs* always ask this question of 'when?' Before they make a commitment, naturally they want to know if such a lengthy, seemingly arduous pursuit is really worth the time and trouble! But here we say, having gained yourself, you do not gain anything, knowing which is the greatest freedom there is.

All right, you may say, this freedom that implies total self-acceptance and the vision that I am the whole seems to be very desirable. But when will I gain this vision? How long will it take? I want to do it quickly so that I can pick up the threads of my life and continue. Again, we say, this is life. There is no when or anything; there is just life. There is no life other than this; everything subserves this. Whether you do one thing or the other, a pursuit like this does not go away from you; it is always right there with you. You have enough material with you to be with yourself, no matter wherever you are, whatever

---

[17] *śarīram ādyaṁ khalu dharmasādhanam*

you are doing. There is a growing clarity about this knowledge, which takes its own time; but it does not matter because it is pleasant all the way.

Only when something is unpleasant does one come up with the question, 'How long do I have to do this?' The pursuit of self-knowledge is not a prison sentence! It is pleasant all the way because it is *ātma-vidyā*, knowledge of oneself, a knowledge that tells you how wonderful you are. No religion does this. Religions usually tell you how terrible you are and that you have to be saved. Whereas, this knowledge tells you that you are already saved. Because there is no problem here, the question of 'when' does not arise. What must be addressed, however, is the condition of the person who has this knowledge, as we shall see in the next verse.

Verse 18

The mind – through knowledge – sees the contemplator and the contemplated as ātmā

यदा विनियतं चित्तमात्मन्येवावतिष्ठते ।
निःस्पृहः सर्वकामेभ्यो युक्त इत्युच्यते तदा ॥ १८ ॥

yadā viniyataṁ cittam ātmanyevāvatiṣṭhate
niḥspṛhaḥ sarvakāmebhyo yukta ityucyate tadā (18)

yadā – when; *viniyatam cittam* – the mind has gained a certain composure; *ātmani eva* – in the self alone; *avatiṣṭhate* – remains; *tadā* – then; *sarva-kāmebhyaḥ* – for all the objects (of desire); *niḥspṛhaḥ* – one who is free from longing; *yuktaḥ iti* – as one who is accomplished; *ucyate* – the person is said (to be)

When the mind has gained a certain composure (and) remains in the self alone, when one is free from longing for all the objects (of desire), then (the person) is said (to be) one who is accomplished.

The word '*viniyata*' is defined by Śaṅkara here as *ekāgratā*, meaning that the mind, *citta*, has the capacity to remain single-pointedly on the object of contemplation alone without getting distracted. In such a mind, both the object of contemplation and the meditator, the contemplator, become one and the same, there being no separation whatsoever between the two. The mind has gained certain mastery, a contemplative disposition, composure by itself, in itself, through the disciplines that have already been mentioned as qualifications for gaining such a mind. And this mind abides in *ātmā* alone, *tasmin ātmani eva avatiṣṭhate*, which means that there is no separation between the mind and *ātmā*.

For the person discussed here, there is no *ātmā* to be contemplated upon because both the contemplator and the contemplated are *ātmā*. Previously, there was 'as though' contemplation, whereas now, there is no necessity for 'as though' contemplation because the self remains in the self alone.

The result of knowledge is freedom from binding desires

How does this contemplator's mind abide in *sat-cit-ānanda ātmā*? How is it located there? Is it like two objects, one sitting upon the other? No, the mind abides in *ātmā* purely in the form of knowledge, clarity. In other words, the meaning of the word 'I' is no more a matter for conjecture and mistaken notions for the person. It is not something that one has to contemplate upon in order to understand it further. This capacity of the mind to remain in *ātmā* is the meaning of the expression, *ātmani eva avatiṣṭhate.*

Having given up all one's concerns and anxieties about the various things that are external to oneself, the person is awake to *ātmā*, meaning that the mind always remains or abides in *ātmā* and therefore, is never separated from *ātmā*. For one who has gained this clarity of knowledge about *ātmā*, there is freedom from the longing for all objects of desire; one is *niḥspṛhaḥ sarva kāmebhyaḥ*. This freedom is not something that must be gained separately but is a natural condition of having gained the knowledge itself.

We have already seen that the word *kāma* has two meanings – the desire itself and the object of desire. The thought process wherein you want to gain an object is called *kāma* and that which you desire is also called *kāma*. Because *kāma* is used throughout the *Gītā* in this two-fold sense, we have to see the context in which it is used to understand its meaning. Here, it means object of desire.

What are the objects of desire? They can be both *dṛṣṭa*, seen, whatever you can accomplish now, and *adṛṣṭa*, unseen, something that is not seen by you, like *puṇya*. *Puṇya* is desirable to you because it brings you something desirable later. *Puṇya* is like currency. You cannot enjoy it in and of itself, but it has a buying power; it can buy objects that you can enjoy. Thus, *puṇya* is an intermediary goal, achieving which you are qualifying yourself, empowering yourself, to accomplish various ends such as comfortable situations, wealth, power and so on. Because these ends are not seen now, they are *adṛṣṭa*.

Kāma, then can be for either *dṛṣṭa* or *adṛṣṭa*, that which is the result of *puṇya*, which itself is *adṛṣṭa*. Suppose a man performs a particular fire ritual for the purpose of gaining something here in this world. The ritual itself does not produce the object since what he wants out of the ritual is not the fire! Rather, by performing the ritual, he gains certain grace of *puṇya*, which removes all the obstacles to his effort to gain what he wants. This is what is called *adṛṣṭa*. Naturally, then, there is a desire, *kāma*, for *adṛṣṭa* as well as *dṛṣṭa*.

The definition of an accomplished person

The person discussed here is free from the longing for all objects of desire, both *dṛṣṭa* and *adṛṣṭa* – *niḥspṛhaḥ sarva kāmebhyaḥ*. The longing for objects, known and unknown, visible and invisible, has gone away. Therefore, the person is said to be one who is accomplished, *yuktaḥ ityucyate*, meaning that the person's contemplation has become successful.

What does it mean to call someone as accomplished? How can being with oneself cause all the longings to go away? The reason one longs for objects is due to not knowing oneself. Therefore, when this self-knowledge has been gained, when the mind abides in the self alone, the person is fulfilled and happy. One knows that *ātmā* does not require any improvement for one's security or perfection. Because there is no lack in *ātmā*, the sense of lack is not there for the person. The nature of *ātmā* being *pūrṇa,* full, the whole, there is nothing to improve it; therefore, the person has no longings whatsoever.

For a person who recognises the nature, *svarūpa,* of oneself, desires are born of fullness, and not out of a sense of lack. In fact, the desires of such a person are privileges, having a mind that has a great capacity to desire. Whereas, for the *ajñānī,* one who does not have knowledge of the self, there is a sense of want centred on 'I.' It is not that the mind is lacking in something. For example, when you say the body lacks, the lack is centred on 'I,' which you identify with the body. The body naturally has its limitations and in that sense it can be said to lack. That the body lacks is not the problem; that I lack is the problem, born of the non-recognition of the *svarūpa,* the nature, of 'I.'

All desires stem from this sense of lack centred on 'I' alone. These are the desires that are binding in nature because their fulfilment is the basis upon which I think I am going to discover some sense of security in myself, some kind of satisfaction from myself. This is why fulfilling my desires become my main purpose in life. But, sooner or later, I discover that desires have a knack of breeding like rabbits; I either give up and become a hobo or go crazy. The point here is that desires born of my sense of lack are endless and, having discovered this fact, my enquiry begins. Therefore, I ask, 'Who am I? 'Am I really seeking something?' 'Why I am seeking?' 'Am I seeking something other than myself or am I seeking myself?'

In fact, I am seeking myself, the problem being that I have a sense of lack centred on myself and I want to be free from this lack.

This is all I want. If I am a person whose nature is stuck with a sense of lack, then I can never get rid of it. But now and then I see myself free from this sense of lack. Whenever I open my eyes and see something so beautiful that I also open my mouth and say, 'Ah!' I find myself free from any sense of lack. There is a heaven inside me. Whenever I laugh, it is all heaven. Because I have these two versions of myself, one with the sense of lack and one without it, a very valid doubt arises in me. I begin to think that, I am confused about myself, perhaps my conclusions are wrong. This doubt marks the beginning of my enquiry.

The person discussed in this verse has come to know the self by means of such an enquiry, accompanied by whatever disciplines those were necessary to prepare the mind so that the knowledge could take place. The mind of this person has no more doubts and is totally awake with reference to *ātmā*. There is no more guesswork or vagueness and the person is naturally free from all longing and attachments.

Verse 19

An oft quoted illustration to describe the mind of the accomplished person

यथा दीपो निवातस्थो नेङ्गते सोपमा स्मृता ।
योगिनो यतचित्तस्य युञ्जतो योगमात्मनः ॥ १९ ॥

yathā dīpo nivātastho neṅgate sopamā smṛtā
yogino yatacittasya yuñjato yogam ātmanaḥ (19)

yathā – just as ; *nivātasthaḥ* – protected from the wind; *dīpaḥ* – lamp; *na iṅgate* – does not tremble; *ātmanaḥ yogam* – contemplation of the self; *yuñjataḥ* – of one who practices; *yoginaḥ* – of the meditator; *yatacittasya* – for the composed mind; *sā* – this; *upamā* – illustration; *smṛtā* – is cited

> A lamp, protected from the wind, does not tremble. This illustration is cited for the composed mind of the meditator who practices contemplation of the self.

An illustration cannot give you the knowledge of the object of illustration, but it can bring one's understanding of it a little closer. To say, 'A water buffalo is like a water buffalo,' is not an illustration because your understanding of 'water buffalo' is not brought any closer to the object 'water buffalo' than it was before the statement was made. Whereas the statement, 'A water buffalo is like a huge cow,' gives you a clearer understanding of what a water buffalo is; it belongs to the cow family and it is huge. When you actually see a water buffalo, you will then know exactly how it differs from a cow. This statement is an illustration, *upamā*.

Similarly, here, the people who have contemplated upon *ātmā*, who know *ātmā*, have likened the mind of a wise person to a flame that is protected from the wind. They say this mind does not tremble. It does not mean that it awakens in any way, but, like the flame, there is a continuous flow of light. In fact, a flame is not really a flame; if you could reduce the speed at which the flame rises, you would find that it is moving all the time. The point being made here is that, in spite of this movement, the flame does not shake at all. Similarly, the well-mastered mind of the *yogī*, the wise person, has a continuous flow of *vṛttis*, thoughts, but it does not tremble for any reason. It does not tremble out of fear, agitation or anything else, meaning that it is never swayed by any situations that confront the person. And only those who know the mind of a *yogī* can cite such an illustration, *upamā*.

An illustration is needed to understand what the mind of a wise person is.

An illustration must be known to both the person citing it and the person to whom it is being cited. And it should be close to that which is to be conveyed. Why was an illustration cited here by those who know the mind of a wise person? Because the one being addressed cannot, at this point in time, envision the mind of such a person, just as a child cannot possibly envision the problems of an adult not yet understanding the adult aspects of life. Suppose a child hears his father saying, 'Oh, no! The stocks have gone down.' He sees that his father is unhappy, his mother is unhappy, and everyone around is unhappy, but the child does not understand why the adults are crying. All he wants is one more toy. This is because there are two different minds here altogether. Only when the child becomes an adult will he understand.

An adult mind can be stifled by the child's mind that he or she has carried over into adult mind, but, until a child becomes an adult, his or her mind will have only a child's problems. Even if a person who is twenty five years old still wants balloons, dolls, and marbles, the person has no real problem, although the other people around may naturally think otherwise. The problem only comes when one is an adult with a child inside craving for all kinds of security and attention. Such a person cannot relate well to another adult who is an adult all the way, meaning a person with a mature mind, a mind that does not pose a problem for the person, for whom the mind is only an instrument. This mature mind is the one that is likened here to a flame for those who cannot envision such a mind.

Something that can be seen or envisioned does not require an illustration. If it is available, it can be shown to the person. For example, I can say, 'This is a crystal.' Since I am showing it to you, I need not tell you that crystal is like glass. Because the crystal is available, an illustration is not required. Whereas, if you do not know what a bison is, but you know what a buffalo is, I can tell you that a bison is like a buffalo. Because there is an approximation between the two, your understanding of a bison is a little closer than it was. Similarly, the flame is an illustration to help you understand what the mind of a wise person is like, cited by people who know what it is all about.

In this verse, the words, *yogaṁ yuñjataḥ*, can be taken to refer either to a person who is following Patañjali's eight-fold *yoga* called *aṣṭāṅga-yoga* or a person who contemplates upon *ātmā*. *Yoga* itself is the practice, which means that the person attempts to unite his or her mind with the desirable *ātmā* – *yuñjataḥ yogaṁ ātmanaḥ*. Śaṅkara defined *yuñjat* here as one who practices this *yoga*, this contemplation, uniting the mind with *ātmā*, which Kṛṣṇa discusses further in the next four verses.

Verse 20

The mind – mastered by dhyāna-yoga – abides in oneself

यत्रोपरमते चित्तं निरुद्धं योगसेवया ।
यत्र चैवात्मनात्मानं पश्यन्नात्मनि तुष्यति ॥ २० ॥

yatroparamate cittaṁ niruddhaṁ yogasevayā
yatra caivātmanātmānaṁ paśyannātmani tuṣyati (20)

yatra – when ; *yoga-sevayā* – by the practice of meditation; *niruddham* – mastered; *cittam* – mind; *uparamate* – abides (in *ātmā*); *yatra* – when; *ca* – and; *ātmanā* – by oneself; *ātmānam* – oneself; *paśyan* – seeing; *ātmani* – in oneself; *eva* – alone; *tuṣyati* – one rejoices

> When the mind, mastered by the practice of meditation, abides (in *ātmā*) and when, seeing oneself by oneself alone, one rejoices in oneself...

Ātmā in the word *ātmānam* refers to *sat-cit-ānanda-ātmā*, meaning that one sees oneself as Brahman. With what does one see *ātmā* as Brahman? By the mind, *ātmanā*, by the *vṛtti*, the thought. Recognising oneself as Brahman, one rejoices in *ātmā*, *ātmani tuṣyati*. Thus, there are four case endings here for *ātmā*–the second case, accusative, *ātmānam* – meaning oneself; the third case, instrumental, *ātmanā* – meaning by oneself; and the seventh case, locative, *ātmani* – meaning in oneself. And who rejoices? The *yogī*, the self, *ātmā*, the first case, nominative, the agent of rejoicing. Thus, seeing oneself by oneself, one rejoices in oneself – *ātmanā ātmānaṁ paśyan ātmani tuṣyati*. The person rejoices in the *ātmā*, the nature of *ātmā* being *ānanda*, free from any sense of lack. We will see the implications of this verse in the discussion of the next verse.

Verse 21

The sukha that is yourself

सुखमात्यन्तिकं यत्तद्बुद्धिग्राह्यमतीन्द्रियम् ।
वेत्ति यत्र न चैवायं स्थितश्चलति तत्त्वतः ॥ २१ ॥

sukham ātyantikaṁ yattad buddhigrāhyam atīndriyam
vetti yatra na caivāyaṁ sthitaścalati tattvataḥ (21)

yat tat – that which (is); *ātyantikam* – absolute; *buddhi-grāhyam* – recognised by the intellect; *atīndriyam* – beyond sense perception; *sukham* – happiness; *yatra* – when; *ayaṁ vetti* – one recognises; *ca* – and; *sthitaḥ* – being rooted (there in); *tattvataḥ* – from the truth of oneself; *na eva calati* – one never moves away

...(and when) one recognises this absolute happiness, which is known by the intellect, which is beyond sense perception and when, being rooted (therein) one never moves away from the truth of oneself...

The *vṛtti*, thought, by which one recognises an object, and the object of the *vṛtti* are identical. That is, in order to recognise the object, the *vṛtti* must necessarily have the object in itself. If I have to recognise a pot, *ghaṭa*, the *vṛtti* must assume the very form of the pot. Therefore, the *vṛtti* is called *ghaṭa-vṛtti*. By the *ghaṭa-vṛtti* alone, I recognise the object *ghaṭa*, pot.

For the recognition of *ātmā* also, there must be a *vṛtti*. This *vṛtti* is created by the *śāstra* and it destroys self-ignorance.

And this *vṛtti* is brought back by the contemplator in *nididhyāsana*. In the recognition of the *svarūpa* of the self, the *vṛtti* assumes the very *svarūpa* of *ātmā,* without objectifying it. This is not similar to knowing an object such as the pot. In the recognition of the *svarūpa* of the *ātmā* there is only one operation involved, whereas in the objectification of a pot, there are two operations.

One operation is the *vṛtti* assuming the form of the pot and the second operation is the recognition of that *vṛtti,* thereby recognising the pot. One is the objectification of the object, by the *vṛtti,* and the other is the recognition of the *vṛtti*. The objectifying *vṛtti* is recognised by another *vṛtti,* which is the *draṣṭa,* the seer. I become the seer, the knower of the pot. Therefore, this I-thought, *ahaṁ vṛtti,* assuming the status of the knower, recognises an object through a *vṛtti,* the *ghaṭa vṛtti,* and says, 'This is a pot, *ayaṁ ghaṭaḥ*.'

Any piece of knowledge – where there is this peculiar connection, *ātma-anātma sambandha,* between the self, the knower, and the object that is objectified by that knower – takes place by these two operations. That is, the object is objectified by the *vṛtti* and you cognise the *vṛtti,* which is why you can say, 'This is a pot.' However, you cannot say, 'This is *ātmā*.' Who is there to say it? You are the one who has to say it. If it were to be so, then, the self, *ātmā,* would become an object of the self who is objectifying it. Therefore, it would become *anātmā,* not *ātmā,* just like any other object of your knowledge.

Naturally, when Kṛṣṇa said, 'seeing *ātmā,*' in the last verse, some difference was definitely implied. The difference is that in the number of operations involved. Seeing *ātmā* implies only one operation; there is no second operation at all as there is when one sees an object. Only the first operation is there, the *vṛtti* that objectifies *ātmā*, that assumes the very form of *ātmā*. If I say *ātmā* is pure consciousness, *kevala-caitanya*, *śuddha-caitanya*, and the recognition of this fact takes place, the recognition implies that the *vṛtti* assumes the very form of consciousness and there is no other object involved. That particular form destroys the ignorance with reference to the *svarūpa* of the *ātmā* and then disappears. This is the only operation that takes place, meaning that there is no second operation in the form of the recognition, 'This is *ātmā*' as there is in the cognition of other objects.

The one operation that takes place is only with reference to one's confusion about oneself, the self-ignorance that was there; that ignorance is destroyed by the *vṛtti*. This is what happens in self-knowledge, in knowing the self, more of which we shall see later.

What does a wise person have to rejoice over?

Generally, a person rejoices only when he or she has something to rejoice over other than knowing *ātmā*. Some revelling situation is usually there for any rejoicing to take place. But what is there for the person being discussed in this verse to rejoice over? It is the recognition of the absolute happiness that is one's own nature, a recognition by the intellect that is beyond sense perception, *sukhaṁ ātyantikaṁ yattad buddhi-grāhyam atīndriyam*.

Śaṅkara explains in his commentary that *ātyantika-sukha* is happiness, which is absolute, a happiness that is the nature of oneself, *svarūpa-sukha*. This means that it has nothing to do with the *vṛtti*, in reality. It is a particular *vṛtti*, no doubt, but it is not born out of a particular condition external to oneself. The word, *ātmānam*, mentioned in the previous verse is converted here into *ātyantika-sukha*. Seeing the self is recognising the self as *sukha-svarūpa*, one whose nature is absolute happiness, *ātyantika-sukha*. And this recognition takes place in the intellect, in the *buddhi* alone. At the same time, this *sukha* is beyond sense perception, *atīndriya*.

Ātyantika-sukha or *ātma-sukha* is something quite different from the pleasure you pick up because of a sense object or a situation, *viṣaya-sukha*. Both *ātma-sukha* and *viṣaya-sukha* are recognised by the *buddhi*. There is no nasal *sukha* or other *sukha* that is not recognised by the *buddhi*. A *sukha* born out of hearing something pleasant, for example, is always inside, not outside. There is also a *sukha* born of having solved a problem or a riddle for yourself, the kind of happiness that causes you to say 'Eureka!' born of some recognition or a piece of knowledge. This is called *vidyā-sukha*. There is a clarity there, which, to use the language of the *Gītā*, increases your *sattva* disposition. This heightened *sattva* makes the mind more composed, gives rise to a *śānta-antaḥ-karaṇa*. Because knowledge and *sattva* go together, there is *sukha*. So, whenever you pick up a piece of knowledge, no matter how simple or complex, there is some *sukha*, which we call *vidyā-sukha*. But the *sukha* that one picks up by a piece of knowledge is still a relative *sukha* because it is subject to change. A challenge is met successfully, *sukha* is discovered, and then it is gone. If the *sukha* was the result of having unravelled a few knots in a tangled ball of wool, you pick up the yarn again and begin unravelling more to gain some more *sukha*.

There is also *viṣaya-sukha*, a *sukha* born of fulfilling a desire for a particular object and the experience thereof. An object of desire brings about *sukha* in different degrees. Just the sight of it brings about certain *sukha* and owning it or experiencing it brings about some more *sukha*. So, there are levels or degrees of *viṣaya-sukha*. Everyone has this kind of *sukha*, even a cat or a dog, whereas *vidyā-sukha* is only for human beings. *Vidyā-sukha* includes any accomplishment and *viṣaya-sukha* implies a situational gain in terms of a desire fulfilled.

There is also *sukha* born of *yoga* which includes prayer and meditation. *Prāṇāyāma*, etc., can also bring about some *sukha*. There are three kinds of *sukha–viṣaya-sukha*, *vidyā-sukha*, and *yoga-sukha*. *Vidyā-sukha* and *viṣaya-sukha* are experienced by everyone, whereas *yoga-sukha* is experienced by a disciplined person, a *karma-yogī*, a prayerful person, a devotee. Because of the person's maturity, there is some *sukha* in the seat of meditation. Discipline, health, and so on also bring about *sukha*, a satisfaction, all of which is implied by *yoga-sukha*.

The fourth *sukha*, called *turīya-sukha*, does not depend on any gain, accomplishment, or anything. It is not born out of any particular piece of knowledge that you discover nor any object that you gain. It is just the recognition of yourself alone because of which there is a *sukha*. This *sukha* is the *sukha* mentioned by Kṛṣṇa in this verse, *ātyantika-sukha*, absolute *sukha*, this is also recognised by the intellect, *buddhi-grāhya*, and is beyond sense perception, *atīndriya*.

This is where people sometimes commit mistakes. *Atīndriya-sukha* means that the *sukha* is not due to sense perception. At the same time, every *sukha* is *buddhi-grāhya*, recognised by the intellect. *Viṣaya-sukha, vidyā-sukha,* and *yoga-sukha* are also *buddhi-grāhya* but not *atīndriya*, whereas this absolute *sukha* is *buddhi-grāhya* and also *atīndriya,* meaning that it is not due to any external situation or internal condition. *Yoga-sukha* also is not born of an external situation, but it is born of an internal situation, while *viṣaya-sukha* is born of external situations. But the *sukha* that Kṛṣṇa is talking about here is not born of anything. It is you.

People naturally want to know what this *sukha* is born of, how can it be brought into being. The concept of *sukha* being 'born' is due to ignorance; it is a *saṁsārī*'s approach – an approach of the ignorant, the non-discriminating person. Therefore, we have to be very careful here. Absolute *sukha* is *buddhi-grāhya* and, at the same time, *atīndriya*, which means it has nothing to do with sense perception or anything. It is oneself.

When the person, the meditator, the seeker, comes to recognise the *ātma-svarūpa, yatra vetti,* what happens? He or she does not slip away from the truth, the truth of *ātmā* as absolute happiness, *ātyantikaṁ sukham – tattvataḥ na calati.* Here, *tattva* means the *svarūpa*, the essential nature of a thing, as expressed by the suffix 'ness.' There is no appropriate word in English for *svarūpa*. Here, *tattva* is the truth, the *svarūpa* of *ātmā*, which is *ātyantika-sukha-svarūpa*, which is free from any form of limitation, *pūrṇa svarūpa*. From this, the person never moves away, *na eva calati*.

The difference between recognition and experience

This recognition marks the difference between ordinary *yoga*, meaning *aṣṭāṅga-yoga*, and what we are talking about here. You must know this well and not confuse this recognition with the *samādhi* of *aṣṭāṅga-yoga*. *Aṣṭāṅga-yoga* is a discipline which has its own place in preparing the mind for knowledge to take place. For this reason, you should not think of it as useless or anything. *Aṣṭāṅga-yoga* is a great discipline, but if it is not understood as such, there can naturally be confusion between it and the knowledge of oneself, *ātma-jñāna*, which is the ultimate end, the freedom that everyone seeks.

The *samādhi* that *aṣṭāṅga-yoga* talks about is in terms of experience. In fact, if, as a *saṁsārī*, you have to accomplish anything in this world, that is in the world of *saṁsāra, samādhi,* is the greatest accomplishment experientially. In this sense, *aṣṭāṅga-yoga* has the last word in terms of *nirvikalpa-samādhi*, a state of absorption wherein there is no second thing at all. The knower, known, and the instrument of knowledge, all three of them, coalesce into one experience lasting for a length of time. Although it does not take away the *saṁsāra*, it is definitely the last word in *saṁsāra*.

Nirvikalpa-samādhi is the opposite of deep sleep. In deep sleep there is *nirvikalpa* alright, meaning that the knower-known-knowledge division is not there. But, in the *nirvikalpa-samādhi* the mind is awake, unlike in deep sleep where the mind is sleeping. In both cases, there is *ajñāna,* the difference being that when the mind is asleep there is no *vṛtti,* whereas in *nirvikalpa-samādhi,* the mind is awake, meaning there is *vṛtti.* Therefore, the greatest thing you can have in life is *nirvikalpa-samādhi,* which is why it is also the greatest hooker. It baits people because it is the last thing that you can think of accomplishing in *saṁsāra,* in your life here in this world.

Experience always has an end

But *nirvikalpa-samādhi* has an end; it is something you come out of. All that is needed is for someone to drop something in front of you or to start a vacuum cleaner in the next house. As soon as you become aware of the sound, you are not only out of *nirvikalpa-samādhi,* you may be into anger as well! Why? This is because, *nirvikalpa-samādhi* is something that does not last forever; you will come out of it in time. And, once you are out of it, it becomes a past experience that you then talk to others about, 'Swamiji, yesterday I had the most wonderful thing happen to me!' Even the language used to describe the experience is different. But as soon as the thoughts come, or someone begins hammering, or a child begins to cry, or a bug creeps up your leg, real or imagined, it is gone; you have come out of *nirvikalpa-samādhi.*

There are those who will tell you that once you experience *nirvikalpa-samādhi* and you come out of that experience, the world will be different. They also say that you experience the *ātmā* in *nirvikalpa-samādhi*. How can this be? All that happened was that the knower-known-knowledge difference coalesced. All differences disappeared, a desirable experience, no doubt. It is *buddhi-grāhya*, recognised by the intellect, and it is also *atīndriya*, beyond sense perception. But how has this experience changed the state of your vision? In fact, you may become very sad. Before you knew *ātmā*, you were only sad if you lost money, power, some hair, or a relationship. Now, having known the *ātmā*, you have a new item which can be lost and be a cause for sadness – yourself. Previously, you lost things but retained yourself, but now you have experienced a much greater loss – the loss of yourself.

So, practitioners of *samādhi* may have some sadness if *samādhi* does not come, and sadness even when it comes, because it does not last. Even if it lasts for some time, there is sadness because it ends. All that you can say is that, 'I was eternal for half an hour!' For that period of time, the division between the knower, known, and knowledge that is usually there went away; time itself went away. For half an hour you were free from time, which means you were timeless, eternal. And, after half an hour, you become what? Non-eternal. Even if you have *samādhi* for two days, you become non-eternal. In this way, it is no different than being in a coma for two days and then coming out of it. While in the coma, there was no division whatsoever and the person also did not know what was happening. Therefore, the length of time that you are in *nirvikalpa-samādhi* has no meaning.

Discipline implies certain mastery of the mind

As a discipline, however, *nirvikalpa-samādhi* is great because, when you gather such an experience, it indicates that you have some mastery. Otherwise, you would not have been able to have the experience of *nirvikalpa-samādhi*. Because certain mastery is involved, *nirvikalpa-samādhi* is considered to be the height of experience that you can gain. It is like a prize, the end for those who want to gain experience. To say that it indicates a *sāttvika-vṛtti* on your part is fine, but to say that after you come out of *nirvikalpa-samādhi*, you will see the world entirely differently is not correct because, how you see the world depends purely on your vision of reality. Having experienced *nirvikalpa-samādhi*, you have to interpret that experience. And to interpret the experience, you must have a *pramāṇa*, a means of knowledge.

Again, we come back to *pramāṇa* because you do not interpret an experience in any other way than by what you know. All interpretations depend entirely upon your knowledge, which is dependent on the *pramāṇa* available to you. The *pramāṇa*s that you have, perception, inference, and so on, operate by maintaining a duality – duality of *kartā*, the doer; *karma*, the object of doing; *kriyā*, the act of doing; *karaṇa*, the instrument of doing, etc. All these are collectively called as *kāraka*s. Retaining the duality alone, your *pramāṇa*s, the various means of knowledge, operate.

Perception, *pratyakṣa*, and inference, *anumāna*, do not swallow the *kāraka*s. Only the *āgama*, the teaching, swallows them. It says that you are not the knower, *pramātā*; you are the very essence of the knower, knowledge, and the object of knowledge, all three of them being one and the same. In this way, the *āgama* resolves the division, which is exactly what this verse is saying.

Thought is you

Knowing *ātmā*, not moving from the truth of *ātmā* there is no knower-known-knowledge division for the person. Nor is there any question about when you are going to get out of yourself, because both thought and the object of thought are you, *ātmā*.

There is no way of getting out of yourself because, with thought, you are and without thought, you are. Whether you are with the world or without the world, it is you all the time. Because the statement '*tattvataḥ na calati,*' in the verse under study, implies *jñāna*, knowledge, the word *yoga* is not to be taken in its usual sense. It is more *viyoga* than *yoga*, as Kṛṣṇa explains a little later. Previously, due to ignorance there was association, *saṁyoga*, with *duḥkha*, sorrow, taking it to be oneself, which was the problem. *Yoga* means joining, association, and *viyoga* means dissociation from the association. Previously, the person was in association with the body, mind, and senses, which was not a simple association because the person actually took the body-mind-sense complex to be oneself. Then, the person dissociated himself or herself from sorrow by knowledge, which does not imply *aṣṭāṅga-yoga*.

In order to remove any confusion here, Kṛṣṇa first says, *tattvataḥ na calati*, and then re-defines the word *yoga* in one sentence later in keeping with what he is teaching.

Verses 22&23

The yoga that Kṛṣṇa talks about is more a disassociation than association

यं लब्ध्वा चापरं लाभं मन्यते नाधिकं ततः ।
यस्मिन् स्थितो न दुःखेन गुरुणापि विचाल्यते ॥ २२ ॥

तं विद्याद् दुःखसंयोगवियोगं योगसंज्ञितम् ।
स निश्चयेन योक्तव्यो योगोऽनिर्विण्णचेतसा ॥ २३ ॥

yaṁ labdhvā cāparaṁ lābhaṁ manyate nādhikaṁ tataḥ
yasmin sthito na duḥkhena guruṇāpi vicālyate (22)

taṁ vidyād duḥkhasaṁyogaviyogaṁ yogasaṁjñitam
sa niścayena yoktavyo-yogo'nirviṇṇacetasā (23)

ca – and; *labdhvā* – having gained which; *tataḥ adhikam* – better than that; *aparam* – other; *lābham* – gain; *na manyate* – does not think; *yasmin* – in which; *sthitaḥ* – established; *guruṇā api duḥkhena* – even by a great sorrow; *na vicālyate* – is not affected; *tam* – that; *duḥkha-saṁyoga-viyogam* – dissociation from association with sorrow; *yoga-saṁjñitam* – called by the name of *yoga*; *vidyāt* – may one know; *anirviṇṇa-cetasā* – with the mind that is not discouraged; *saḥ yogaḥ* – that *yoga*; *niścayena* – with clarity of purpose; *yoktavyaḥ* – should be pursued

> ...and, having gained which, one does not think there is any other better gain than that, established in which, one is not affected even by a great sorrow (sorrowful event)...

> ...may one know that dissociation from association with sorrow, to be what is called as *yoga*. That *yoga* should be pursued with clarity of purpose with a mind that is not discouraged.

The person being discussed here does not slip away from the truth of oneself, *ātma-tattva*, because *ātmā* is not some place he or she went to and can return from. When it is said that you go to the abode of *ātmā* and rejoice there, some location comes to mind and the question then becomes, for how long? All kinds of imaginations are possible. You may think it is like going somewhere as a guest, staying as long as you are entertained, and then, afterwards, coming back. However, when it is clear that remaining with *ātmā* is in terms of knowledge of the *svarūpa* of *ātmā*, conveyed here by the expression, *tattvataḥ na calati*, then there is no question of ever being away from it because remaining does not depend even on memory.

People sometimes ask, 'Swamiji, suppose I forget the *ātmā*?' You can forget the words I use to point out the *ātmā*, but you cannot forget the meaning of those words once you have understood it. The meaning of the words is *ātmā*. You can forget *sat-cit-ānanda*, but if *sat* is understood by you, *cit* is understood by you, and *ānanda* is understood by you, how can you forget? The words themselves are only the *lakṣaṇa* of *ātmā*, for revealing the nature of *ātmā*; therefore, they can be forgotten. But the meaning is you. How can you forget yourself? You cannot because knowing yourself is not something that is memory based. Even if you lose your memory in an accident or whatever, it is the same.

Mokṣa is a matter of understanding – not of memory

People often pose this question, 'Swamiji, suppose a *jñānī*, a man who already has self-knowledge, has a car accident and loses the use of all his brain cells. His head is smashed up, he remembers nothing, not even his own name. Isn't his knowledge of *ātmā* also gone?' No, his knowledge is not gone because there was no 'his' knowledge. There was only 'This self is Brahman, *ayam ātmā brahma*.' Recognising this fact, he was already liberated. There is only one *mokṣa* and that takes place while living, *jīvan-mukti*. *Mokṣa* is a matter of understanding, not of memory. And once you gain this knowledge, understanding, there is no moving away.

Then, the question may come, 'Swamiji, suppose I do gain *ātmā*. Then what should I do?' Previously, you had many adventures and now you are thinking about having an *ātmā* adventure. Naturally, you want to know what your next adventure will be after *ātmā* has been gained. You have been to the Caribbean, to Hawaii, you have scaled mountains, skied the slopes, and you have learned how to roller-skate. All these adventures being over, you say, 'Let me do some *ātmā* adventure; let me see what it is all about,' because there are people who keep talking about it. Wanting to cover everything, you come to *ātmā*.

This wanting to cover everything is a different attitude than that of a *mumukṣu*. Unlike the *mumukṣu*, this person does not want anyone to know more about anything than he or she knows. Perhaps the person had heard the word *ātmā* or Brahman at some dinner party and he or she wants to know what it is all about so as not to appear ignorant in this particular area. Suppose, in the process of finding out, this person gets caught in this particular pursuit and gets this *ātmā-jñāna, ātmā,* now being covered, what would the person do next, is the question.

Some people really think like this. They say they have tried this and that and they have tried Vedanta also! This verse is for such people. The word 'gain' is used here with this kind of person in view, the one who always wants to cover all areas. The word, 'gaining,' *labdhvā,* means 'knowing,' *jñātvā*. The *jñāna* itself is the gain here because it is *sukha*. This gain is in terms of human ends, *puruṣārtha*s, what people go after. Gaining *ātmā,* the person does not think, *na manyate,* that there is anything other, *apara,* that is better than *ātmā, tataḥ adhikaḥ,* to gain.

There is no better gain than self-knowledge

Why is there no better gain, *lābha*? Because a gain is something that should make you better. If you gain something that makes you worse, it is not a gain; it is a problem. You thought you bought a gain, but instead you bought a problem, just like when you buy a property, the property itself is a great gain, but the litigation against it is the problem. And because you do not know how to get out of the problem, the property is not really a gain; it is only a problem gained.

Gain, then, means that you must feel that you are better off than you were before. If you gain *ātmā,* its *svarūpa* being *ātyantika-sukha,* a *sukha* that is not dependent upon anything because *ātmā* is everything, it is *pūrṇa*, what gain is greater than that? How are you going to better it? By what are you going to better it? Therefore, the person discussed in this verse does not even think there can be another gain. He or she does not say, 'Okay, I have seen *ātmā*. Now let me look for something else.' There is no something else; something else is also *ātmā*.

Even if this is accepted, the question may then be asked. Suppose the person does not come out of this gain and go after something else, there being nothing else, what happens if some great tragedy occurs to him or her? Will the person's *ānanda* not be disturbed? No, remaining in that, *yasmin sthitaḥ*, meaning knowledge of *ātmā*, the person is not affected even by some colossal tragedy, *duḥkhena guruṇā api na vicālyate*. The word '*guru*' has many meanings. Here it means big or heavy, and is the opposite of *laghu*, meaning easy, simple, lightweight.

One may be able to endure a great deal of pain or sorrow without being affected, but suppose a great tragedy happens? Will this person not come out of that *ātmā* in which he or she remains and go somewhere else? No. The person remains in *ātmā*. To come out of *ātmā* and go somewhere else is not possible because somewhere else is also *ātmā*. Therefore, whatever the *duḥkha*, the person remains in *ātmā*, confirming what Kṛṣṇa had said previously when he said *tattvataḥ na eva calati*, the person never moves away. Here, he says that this person is not shaken, not affected by any situation because for this person, all situations are also not other than *ātmā*.

The *yoga* Kṛṣṇa is talking about here, is a *yoga* that is more a dissociation than association. In verse 20, '*yoga*' referred to the practice of contemplation, the object of which is *ātmā*, seeing which one rejoices in oneself – *yatra uparamate cittaṁ niruddhaṁ yoga sevayā, yatra ca eva ātmanā ātmānaṁ paśyan ātmani tuṣyati.* This *yoga* is called *jñāna-yoga* because *ātmā* is seen with the mind with the help of knowledge. And, in the wake of this self-knowledge, naturally there is self-rejoicing because self-seeking is no longer there. There is freedom from seeking.

In verse 21, the nature of *ātmā* was said to be absolute happiness, recognised by the intellect and yet beyond sense perception, *sukham ātyantikaṁ yat tad buddhi-grāhyam atīndriyam,* knowing which one remains in oneself, never moving away from the truth of oneself, *vetti yatra na ca eva ayaṁ sthitaḥ calati tattvataḥ.* The truth of oneself is absolute happiness, *ānanda,* whereas all other happiness always depends upon a mental condition. Ordinary enjoyments, *bhoga*s, depend upon one's external and mental condition. Some external object must be available in a situation and in a form that is desirable.

Even if the external situation is available, you may not be in the mood for it. Therefore, it has to wait for you to be in a better mood. You may have bought a particular tape of music that you generally love, but not today. The music has to wait for you to enjoy it until you are in the mood for it. This is because the *sukha* that is born of an external condition depends upon two situations, the external condition itself and a conducive internal, mental, condition. Whereas the *svarūpa-sukha* that we are talking about does not depend upon either. Rather, it is born out of the recognition of the self being free from any sense of limitation.

Kṛṣṇa then points out that the person who recognises this *svarūpa-sukha* never comes out of it because there is nothing better to be gained – *yaṁ labdhvā ca aparaṁ lābhaṁ manyate na adhikaṁ tataḥ*. This gain in the form of self-knowledge is also called *yoga*. It is not a challenge that, once achieved and no longer holding your interest, has to be followed by another challenge. Looking for greater and greater challenges is based on the desire to prove oneself, to prove that one exists, for which one has to do something adventurous, something different, something new, something challenging. Only then does one feel alive and not like an old piece of furniture. This feeling is what keeps people going, in fact. Because they have to live within themselves, a challenge can become so important that they sacrifice everything for it. If a person does not feel that he or she is a 'somebody,' naturally the person has to create some challenge in order to feel, 'I exist, I am somebody,' and so on.

The resolution of seeking

Having gained *ātmā*, then, would I still have to create new challenges for myself? No, because gaining *ātmā* is a gain, gaining which there is no better gain. The person does not move from the truth of oneself, *tattvataḥ na calati*, meaning that creating challenges is resolved. This resolution is the gain, in fact.

All seeking can be reduced to self-confusion. Therefore, the resolving of the self-confusion is the resolving of the very seeking itself. In this resolution, the seeker and the sought become one and the same, which was what Kṛṣṇa meant in verse 22, when he said, 'And, having gained that *ātmā*, one does not think that there is any other better gain – *yaṁ labdhvā ca aparaṁ lābhaṁ manyate na adhikaṁ tataḥ* .'

If a big tragedy should occur, what happens to the person? Kṛṣṇa covers that too. He says, 'firmly established in that *ātmā*, he (or she) is not disturbed even by great sorrow, *yasmin sthitaḥ duḥkhena guruṇā api na vicālyate*.' Therefore, there is no question of getting out of *ātmā*. No external situation is going to affect the person, nor will the person become tired of oneself and get out. Moving away from something can take place either by slipping away from it, or by withdrawing from it, or by something else coming and disturbing you. But fullness cannot be disturbed in any way. Neither the world nor anything else can disturb fullness. Fullness accommodates every event that can take place in one's life. Also, fullness is not something that one can get out of because it is oneself.

Therefore, knowing all that has been discussed in the previous three verses, there is no coming back from the *sukha* that is *ātmā*. The gain of it, the joy of it, the fullness of it, the freedom of it, all that has been pointed out, is called *yoga*. *Yoga-saṁjñitam*, Kṛṣṇa says. Thus, he gave us a new way of looking at the word '*yoga*.'

Another definition for yoga

The root *yuj*, from which the word '*yoga*' is derived, has two meanings, *yojana* and *nirodha*. *Yojana* means connecting or uniting two things. When two things are put together it is *yoga*. Whereas, *nirodha* means control, stopping, mastering, which is how Patañjali defined *yoga* in the second *sūtra* of the *yoga-śāstra* – *yogaḥ citta-vṛtti-nirodhaḥ,* meaning '*yoga* is the mastery of one's thinking processes,' indicating that *yoga* is a discipline by itself. Since both meanings for the word '*yoga*' are used in the *Gītā,* we have to see from the context whether the word is used in the sense of union or control.

Here, originally there seems to be union of the mind with *ātmā*. The mind contemplates upon *ātmā*; therefore, *ātmā* becomes the *dhyeya,* the object of contemplation. The mind is the one that becomes united with the object of contemplation, *ātmā,* and the attempt to unite the two is called *yoga,* which is the sense we generally get from the word '*yoga*'. It implies two different things coming together, just as two people come together in marriage, a connection, *sambandha,* or whatever the nature of the connection may be.

What is joined together can also fall apart

Whenever two things come together, there is a tendency for them to fall apart also. Therefore, they have to be kept together somehow. If two people are involved, the tendency is for them to move away from each other, each one going off in opposite directions. Similarly, two pieces of material tied together will stay together only as long as that which binds them lasts. Once the binding factor wears out, the two pieces of material will fall apart.

Here, too, the mind can move away from *ātmā* if it is attracted by some external object. It can be disturbed by a *vṛtti,* thought, for which there is an object, for which you are given senses, etc. And if your senses do not operate, your memory is always there. Your memory is good enough to provide you with the whole world! Because of memory, the mind will never find itself wanting in terms of objects to think about. Therefore, the sense of connection between the mind and *ātmā,* conveyed by the word '*yoga*' makes it seem that the mind, contemplating on *ātmā,* will come away from *ātmā.* Because the word '*yoga*' has this intrinsic problem, Kṛṣṇa redefines it here in an opposite sense. This redefinition is called *viparīta-lakṣaṇa,* meaning that the word is used in its limited sense and then the limitations are knocked off by redefining it. In fact, because words have to be used, the whole teaching is like this. A particular word is used and then its limitations are knocked off to reveal its absolute sense which is *ātmā.*

Yoga – Dissociation from association.

Until now, Kṛṣṇa uses the word '*yoga*' in its limited sense. And, here, he knocks off the limitations. In fact, he knocks off the very word itself by presenting *yoga* in a different way. He defines *yoga* as *saṁyoga-viyoga. Saṁyoga* has the same meaning as *yoga*, union, the prefix '*sam*' 'conveying the sense of being very well united. When the prefix '*sam*' is replaced with the prefix '*vi*' the resultant word is *viyoga* which conveys exactly the opposite meaning – that of dissociation. *Saṁyoga* means association, and wherever there is association, there can be dissociation, which is the meaning of *viyoga*. In either case, the word '*yoga*' remains, one prefix being replaced by the other to create the opposite meaning.

For this reason, prefixes, *upasarga*s, are very important in Sanskrit. In English also, prefixes can be used in this way, as in 'declinable' and 'indeclinable,' for example, where a negative prefix is used to arrive at the opposite meaning of the word. Similarly, the prefix '*vi*' added to '*yoga*' points out the negative aspect or the absence of *yoga*. In this way, Kṛṣṇa is saying that the *yoga* we are talking about here is more a dissociation than an association.

All that was said before in terms of *yoga* – how to sit, how to live one's life, and so on – the disciplines that were advised earlier, are for the sake of which *yoga*? For the *yoga* being discussed here in the previous three verses. May one know that, *taṁ vidyāt*. May one know that *yoga* as what? As *duḥkha saṁyoga-viyoga*, as the dissociation from the association with sorrow. This is what Kṛṣṇa calls '*yoga*' here and this is the *yoga* that is to be known, *yoga saṁjñitam taṁ vidyāt*.

Association with *duḥkha* means association with pain, with sorrow. Anything undesirable is connected with *duḥkha* – there is *duḥkhena saṁyogaḥ*. And this union or association with *duḥkha* is no ordinary association; it is a very well-entrenched association. Because this association with sorrow is not ordinary, Kṛṣṇa uses the word '*saṁyoga*' here. No one wants to have *duḥkha*, but the *yoga* with it, the union with it, is so complete that, although you want to get out of it, you cannot. Even though no one wants sorrow, everyone is subject to it. Since we do not want to be sad, why do we become sad? It is not that we want to get into a state of sadness, but then there is *yoga* with sadness and that *yoga* seems to be *saṁyoga*, a connection that is very difficult to pull out of. In fact, we cannot pull out; there is no way of pulling out.

Sorrow is well-entrenched because it is the *duḥkhī* who wants to pull out of *duḥkha*.

People have been trying to pull out of *duḥkha-saṁyoga* but are not able to. Why not? Because it is the *duḥkhī*, the sad person, who wants to pull out of *duḥkha*. The very person who wants to pull out of *duḥkha* has created the *duḥkhī* by taking himself or herself to be limited and therefore, there is association with sorrow. Being associated with *duḥkha*, how can he or she pull out?

'I am a human being, I am a mortal, I am a man, I am a *brāhmaṇa* or a *kṣatriya*, I am young, I am old, I am only this much,'– for the *duḥkhī*, the one associated with sorrow, this is exactly what 'I' is. The person thinks of himself or herself as limited, small, a *saṁsārī*, one who is subject to pain and sorrow. The *aham*, the ego, by its very standing, is doomed. Its very standing is on *duḥkha*, on a sense of limitation. In fact, it is nothing but the sense of limitation. Therefore, all I have to do to be sad is to remember myself!

I just need to remind myself of how limited I am. What happens sometimes is that I forget myself because the *saṁsāra* has so many fascinating objects that can take my attention away from myself for the time being. That is when I forget myself, when I laugh and pick up those gleaming moments of joy. Then, afterwards, I come back to remember myself. And that is enough to make me sad!

Whenever I forget myself I am fine and, whenever I remember myself, I feel sad because of the 'I' that I am. Therefore, *duḥkha-saṁyoga* is my self-identity. Because I identify with the body-mind-sense complex, which is limited, I take myself to be limited and I say, 'This is me.' If this is me, then of course I am *duḥkhī*. Fortunately, however, this is not me.

When you say, 'This is me,' then you want to get rid of yourself. But how can you get rid of yourself? Wherever you go, you are there very much. This is why, wherever you go, you carry your *duḥkha* with you. You do not even need a situation to cause you *duḥkha*; you just go and it will be there with you. Furthermore, you will contribute your *duḥkha* to others, even if you go to a place where everyone is laughing. Sitting in a corner, you will create *duḥkha* in that place because you have brought *duḥkha* with you. This is the nature of a *saṁsārī*. It is not something unique to a given person. Every *saṁsārī*, wherever he or she goes, is going to create *duḥkha* in that place, because he or she is a *duḥkhī*. This is *saṁyoga*, the union between *ātmā* and *anātmā* – *ātmā-anātma- saṁyoga*.

The word, '*duḥkhī*' reveals an 'I,' a person. And that person is separate from what causes the person sorrow, *duḥkha*. The person is what we call *ātmā* and what causes the person *duḥkha* is *anātmā*. And between this person, *ātmā*, and *anātmā*, there is *saṁyoga*. How did the person get this *saṁyoga*? *Ātmā*, as we have seen, is pure *caitanya*, consciousness. Its nature is consciousness. It does not have any kind of attribute. If *ātmā* had any attribute, it would stick there always and you would not be able to know anything new. The nature of *ātmā*, consciousness, then, does not have any particular attribute. This being so, how consciousness has *saṁyoga*? How is that, between *ātmā* and *anātmā* there is *saṁyoga*?

Ignorance makes the impossible possible

Consciousness has no *saṁyoga*, in fact. *Saṁyoga* is possible because of ignorance, *avidyā*. By definition, ignorance is capable of making the impossible possible. *Avidyā* is capable of doing anything; it can even make a snake out of a rope and mirage water out of a desert. Ignorance can do all these things because, there is lack of knowledge. This means that the connection between *ātmā* and *anātmā, ātma-anātma-sambandha,* is brought about purely by *aviveka,* lack of discriminative knowledge. Therefore, that there is *duḥkha-saṁyoga* is established.

When *duḥkha-saṁyoga* is established, and I understand this *saṁyoga*, then, the next step is to find the way to withdraw from this *duḥkha*. But, because the connection itself is born of *avidyā*, there is no physical withdrawal possible. The association with *duḥkha* being born of a lack of discrimination, dissociation from the association that Kṛṣṇa refers to here as *duḥkha-saṁyoga-viyoga* can only be by knowledge. Association with *duḥkha* is due to a self-loss, a self-confusion, and therefore, a self, not-self identity. That is resolved by discriminative knowledge. In other words, I have to know that *ātmā* is *ātmā* and *anātmā* is *anātmā*, but that *ātmā* is not *anātmā*. Therefore, there is nothing separate from me.

There is only ātmā

If *ātmā* and *anātmā* were two separate entities enjoying the same reality, then there could be no *mokṣa*. Any enquiry would just bring in one more item because of which one would feel separate. *Ātmā* would be one entity sitting somewhere and the many *anātmā*s would be something different. Again, I would have the same problem, but I would be extending it to include the separate entity called *ātmā*.

Unfortunately, or fortunately, *anātmā* is never separate from *ātmā* at any time. No thought can exist apart from consciousness that is *ātmā*. While one depends upon the other, the other does not depend upon it. *Viyoga* means seeing *ātmā* as distinct from *ātmā*. Now you have a situation wherein *duḥkha saṁyoga* itself is not there, unless you take the thought or any other *anātmā* as 'I.' This is because *anātmā* is not distinct from *ātmā*. This is the *yoga* of *duḥkha-saṁyoga-viyoga*, which is more a dissociation than an association, the binding material could go away, but since it is a dissociation, there is no possibility of the mind coming away from *ātmā*.

Whatever you are bound to can go away, which is what happens with any happiness that depends on time and various other conditions. When the conditions change, any experience, whatever it is, is gone. Therefore, anything experiential is definitely dependent upon or associated with conditions, and it will go away. But if it is not experiential, if it is more a dissociation from your false association, it will not go away. This dissociation is what is called dissociation by knowledge, *jñānena viyogaḥ*. There is nothing physical about it. Because *anātmā* is *ātmā*. You cannot pull *ātmā* away from *anātmā*. Nor is there any necessity to do so because *ātmā* is in no way involved with *anātmā*. This recognition, this knowledge, which is more a dissociation than an association, is what Kṛṣṇa calls *yoga* here – May one know that dissociation from the association with sorrow is *yoga* – *taṁ duḥkha-saṁyoga-viyogaṁ yogaṁ vidyāt.*'

If an association with someone or something is a legal association, then you can only become dissociated from it legally. And if the association is physical, the dissociation will also be physical. If two physical objects are brought together, they can be separated by removing whatever binding factor that closed the physical distance between them in the first place. Here, the binding factor between *ātmā* and *anātmā* is *avidyā*, ignorance. The binding factor being *avidyā*, what removes the association is *vidyā*, knowledge.

That *yoga*, *duḥkha-saṁyoga-viyoga*, from which there is no question of loss, beyond which there is nothing greater, which is an end in itself, which is yourself, is not an association. It is more a withdrawal from *duḥkha*, and therefore, it is easy, just as it is easier to drop something than to lift it. The only problem here is that the dropping happens to be the dropping of ignorance, dropping all one's false notions about oneself, which is not easy to do. It is not just a matter of surrendering them unto the Lord, as some would have us think.

Erroneous notions cannot be surrendered

It has been said that in the present age, *Kali Yuga*, devotion is the easiest path. You simply surrender to the Lord and he will take care of everything. But what do you surrender? Whom do you surrender? Since everything belongs to the Lord, who are you to surrender anything? This is like my taking your coat and then telling you that I am surrendering it to you.

There is no surrendering here. Then what are you going to surrender? And where does it go? Whatever is surrendered does not go anywhere. It all just remains there as it is.

If you surrender something to the Lord and he says, 'Thank you,' picks it up, and goes away, then you may have surrendered something. But he does not pick up anything; therefore you do not surrender anything. And who is it that surrenders? 'Myself,' you say. But how are you going to surrender yourself? This only means that you want to surrender, perhaps because you think your ego is a little bloated and needs to be kept in check by performing acts of surrender. But who is this 'I' that has to surrender? I cannot surrender the 'I.' There has to be another 'I' to surrender this 'I.'

The 'I' that wants to surrender is the *ahaṅkāra,* the ego. It is a false entity; it is not *aham,* 'I,' *ātmā.* The *ahaṅkāra* is a notion and it cannot go away unless you falsify it. This falsification of the ego is what is called *jñāna,* knowledge, and surrender as well. The *yoga* discussed here is also the same. That is the *yoga* that has to be undertaken – *sa yogaḥ niścayena yoktavyaḥ,* meaning that it definitely has to be practised by you.

Dropping notions about oneself is difficult because ignorance is involved. At the same time, it is easy because all you have to do is destroy the ignorance. The destruction of ignorance is only difficult if your mind is not prepared. Trying to make a two year old child understand that one plus one is two does not work because the child's mind is not yet prepared, whereas, once the child has undergone the necessary preparation, it is very easy.

Self-knowledge is the only pursuit that solves the problem

Similarly, if you are already cheerful, it is easy for you to understand that you are Brahman, that you are the whole. *Saṁsāra* can give you this preparation; it can make you a fairly cheerful person, if you live very intelligently. But, *saṁsāra* also gives you *duḥkha* and, if you come to Vedanta to remove this *duḥkha,* Vedanta will just become another pain in your neck. Vedanta is meant for a cheerful person because, to understand you are *ānanda*, you have to be fairly cheerful. So, Vedanta is not an answer for the ordinary sorrows of *saṁsāra,* which is why there is *karma-yoga*, which includes *aṣṭāṅga-yoga* and other such disciplines.

Nor does one have to have all the qualifications – *viveka, vairāgya, śama-dama,* etc., and *mumukṣutva* in full measure. Such people exist only on paper. Living a life of *karma-yoga* means living a religious life, not a secular life. A prayerful life prepares the mind for the knowledge that is Vedanta. In the wake of this knowledge, all the notions about oneself get dropped. Therefore, it is easy and it is difficult. And it has to be done, *yoktavyaḥ*. Even if it is difficult, one better goes for it because there is nothing more appealing, more inspiring. And, if it is easy, where is the difficulty? One goes for it also. There is nothing more attractive or more purposeful because the whole pursuit is for oneself and is the only one that solves the problem.

How is this knowledge to be pursued? *Niścayena*, by understanding what is real and what is unreal, by knowing with certainty that this clarity is to be gained by me by *viveka,* discrimination. Further, Kṛṣṇa says, '*anirviṇṇa-cetasā,*' by a mind, *cetasā,* that is not dejected, frustrated, tired, *anirviṇṇa,* by a mind that is not indifferent, afflicted, or discouraged.' Can you understand all this without becoming discouraged? Of course you can because it is more a dissociation, *viyoga,* from sorrow. Therefore, there is nothing to discourage you on any score. There is nothing greater either, so, what is there to be discouraged about? Even if it were discouraging, there is nothing else available, so, what are you going to do? So, without being discouraged, *anirviṇṇa-cetasā,* and with a singleness of purpose, *niścayena,* this *yoga* should be undertaken by you, *yogaḥ yoktavyaḥ*

In fact, we are always trying to get rid of sorrow, to drop *duḥkha-saṁyoga*. We are constantly searching for *duḥkha-saṁyoga-viyoga*. This is the *yoga* that gets rid of the sorrow. Thus, Bhagavān uses the word '*yoga*' here in the sense of *viyoga.*

Verses 24&25

Kṛṣṇa talks of yoga in the sense of viyoga

सङ्कल्पप्रभवान्कामांस्त्यक्त्वा सर्वानशेषतः ।
मनसैवेन्द्रियग्रामं विनियम्य समन्ततः ॥ २४ ॥

शनैः शनैरुपरमेद् बुद्ध्या धृतिगृहीतया ।
आत्मसंस्थं मनः कृत्वा न किञ्चिदपि चिन्तयेत् ॥ २५ ॥

saṅkalpaprabhavān kāmāṁstyaktvā sarvān aśeṣataḥ
manasaivendriyagrāmaṁ viniyamya samantataḥ (24)

śanaiḥ śanairuparamed buddhyā dhṛtigṛhītayā
ātmasaṁsthaṁ manaḥ kṛtvā na kiñcid api cintayet (25)

saṅkalpa-prabhavān – born of thought; *sarvān* – all; *kāmān* – desires; *aśeṣataḥ* – totally; *tyaktvā* – giving up; *manasā* – by the mind; *eva* – alone; *samantataḥ* – completely; *indriya-grāmam* – the group of sense organs and organs of actions; *viniyamya* – withdrawing; *dhṛtigṛhītayā* – endowed with perseverance; *buddhyā* – with the intellect; *śanaiḥ śanaiḥ* – slowly; *uparamet* – may one resolve (the mind); *ātma-saṁsthaṁ manaḥ kṛtvā* – making the mind abide in the self; *kiñcit api* – anything else; *na cintayet* – may one not think of

> Giving up totally all desires, which are born of thought, completely withdrawing the group of sense organs and organs of action by the mind alone...

> ...with the intellect endowed with perseverance, may one slowly resolve the mind (in *ātmā*). Making the mind abide in the self, may one not think of anything else.

In verse 23, we saw that *yoga*, which means 'union,' was defined as dissociation, *viyoga*, from one's association *saṁyoga* with *duḥkha*. In other words, in the present context, the union is more a dissociation than an association – dissociation from *duḥkha* meaning dissociation from one's identification with the body-mind-sense complex, *kārya-karaṇa-saṅghāta*. Dissociation from this identification, which takes place by knowledge alone, is called *yoga* –*Yoga-saṁjñitam*. This is the *yoga* that has to be pursued, *sa yogaḥ yoktavyaḥ*, Kṛṣṇa says.

Kṛṣṇa also says that this *yoga* can be pursued without the mind being afflicted by any sense of despair or discouragement, *anirviṇṇa-cetasā*. This is because it is more a dissociation than association. The pursuit of knowledge is not like climbing Mount Everest; it is more like dropping a rock that you are holding in your hand. Because it is more dropping than climbing, it is not as difficult as you might think. It is simply a question of dissociating yourself from your own identity of being only so much. Thus, there is no cause for despair.

Having summarised what he had said so far, Kṛṣṇa begins to discuss the same topic again. Why because this *yoga* is something that needs to be pursued for, there are problems that tend to arise; therefore, Kṛṣṇa emphasises certain points again and again. In the verse under study, he presents the same topic in a slightly different form, repeating two statements made several times before.

The basis of all desires

First, there is the complete giving up of that from which all desires are born, '*saṅkalpaprabhavān sarvān kāmān aśeṣataḥ tyaktvā*.' We have seen how *kāma* can refer to either a desire itself or to the object of desire. Here, *kāma* means the desire for objects, the source of which is *saṅkalpa*. From *saṅkalpa* alone, desire is born. *Saṅkalpa* is a thought such as, 'May this be for me, may this come to me,' etc., which immediately turns into a desire. This source of all desire, *saṅkalpa* is what is given up totally, *aśeṣataḥ*. Therefore, renunciation here is in terms of the *saṅkalpa*, the basis of the desire, and not for the desire itself.

Saṅkalpa is a simple thought. But because that thought is capable of becoming a desire, *saṅkalpa* is said to be the root of all desire. Desire is that which the mind returns to over and over again. *Saṅkalpa* comes and then goes away, but once it becomes a desire, the desire has to be fulfilled. Therefore, *saṅkalpa* is what has to be dealt with and it is dealt with by analysing the thought itself. For instance, the thought, 'May this come to me,' is analysed. By this particular enquiry, *vicāra, saṅkalpa,* is dealt with.

The desires themselves need not be dealt with. *Saṅkalpa* alone is the problem and therefore, it needs to be dealt with. If you deal with the *saṅkalpa,* 'May I have this or that,' desires are not a problem at all. They become only fancies because they are not backed up by *saṅkalpa*s. The backing up of a desire is only from your *saṅkalpa,* 'May I have this,' which slowly becomes, 'I should have this.' Once this *saṅkalpa* has turned into 'I should have this,' then you have had it! Therefore, the *saṅkalpa* is to be analysed.

Withdrawing the sense organs

Kṛṣṇa also repeats here that the group of senses are to be completely withdrawn by the mind alone, *manasā eva,* meaning by a mind endowed with discrimination. The common meaning for *grāma* is village, which does not work here. Therefore, we go for its other meaning, *jāta,* group, meaning the group of sense organs and organs of action, *indriyāṇi. Indriya-grāmaṁ-viniyamya* means putting these *indriyā*s in their place, which is to withdraw them from their respective fields of activity. Again, here we have a piece of advice to be followed with reference to the mind while sitting in meditation. And that is, seated in meditation, let the mind be brought back to the object of meditation. Kṛṣṇa talks about this later.

Withdrawing the sense organs or putting them in their places means that they do not go towards their various sense objects because the *saṅkalpa*s have been taken care of. Because they are withdrawn from activities, this withdrawal is described here as total, *samantataḥ*. What is said in verse 24, is intended to cover all that was said before about how to sit in meditation, the posture, the gaze, etc., and is completed in verse 25.

Dhṛti means firmness and also *dhairya*, courage, which imply care and wisdom as well. Here, *dhṛti-gṛhīta* means the *buddhi* is endowed with courage, firmness, and wisdom, meaning discrimination, *viveka*. With this kind of *buddhi*, the mind is made to abide in *ātmā*, which we shall come back to later.

The use of repetition in this verse, '*śanaiḥ śanaiḥ*,' meaning 'slowly, slowly,' is typical of Sanskrit. And what does one do slowly, slowly? May one resolve, *uparamet*, the mind, meaning oneself, in this particular way, by making the mind abide in *ātmā*, without thinking of anything else – *ātma-saṁsthaṁ manaḥ kṛtvā na kiñcit api cintayet*, thinking only of *ātmā*, the object of meditation.

In this verse, two things need to be understood – what are this courage and discrimination that are required and what does it mean to place the mind in *ātmā*, the object of meditation, *dhyeya-viṣaya*. What kind of placing is involved here? Is the mind to be placed in *ātmā* like one places an orange in a basket? Or is the mind to be placed on top of *ātmā* perhaps? If *ātma-saṁsthaṁ manaḥ kṛtvā* is not properly understood, making the mind abide in *ātmā* becomes a very big problem. But once *ātma-saṁsthaṁ manaḥ kṛtvā* is clearly understood, there is no problem and *dhṛti* also becomes clear.

Definition of ātmā

In the expression, '*ātma-saṁsthaṁ manaḥ kṛtvā*,' what does *ātmā* mean? It is that wherein another thing is not heard, *yatra anyat na śruṇoti*, as the *Chāndogya-śruti* points out. It is that wherein another thing is not seen, *yatra anyat na paśyati*, wherein another thing is not known, *yatra na anyat vijānāti*.[18] The *śruti* also reveals *ātmā* as one that is free from all attributes, *nirviśeṣa*, and that is purely in the form of *caitanya*, consciousness, *cinmātra-svarūpa eva*.

Then, again, *ātmā* is presented as *draṣṭā na tu dṛśyam*, the seer but not the seen; *śrotā na tu śrutam*, the hearer but not the heard; *vijñātā na tu vijñeyam*, the knower but not the known; *mantā na tu mantavyam*, the thinker but not the thought. This is how the nature of *ātmā* is defined by the *śāstra*.

Given this definition of *ātmā*, how can I place the mind upon *ātmā*? How can I even think about *ātmā*? To think of *ātmā* means that *ātmā* becomes the object of my thought, which contradicts what the *śruti* says. Therefore, I cannot think of *ātmā*, which is why it is said in the *Taittirīyopaniṣad* that, having not gained *ātmā*, all the words come back, along with the mind –*yato vāco nivartante aprāpya manasā saha*. It is as though the mind and the words join forces and go after, only to return without

---

[18] *Chāndogyopaniṣad* 7.24.1

it, having found it too tough a nut to crack. Unfortunately, this is how *ātmā* is sometimes presented.

How can *ātmā* become an object of one's meditation?

So, how is one to place the mind upon *ātmā*? How can *ātmā* become an object of one's meditation? There is no way of placing the mind upon *ātmā* because the mind is *ātmā*. It is not that one takes the mind to *ātmā* and, having had the mind sitting upon it for some time, *ātmā* eventually yields because of the mind's pressure and so on. Some translations have taken this verse to mean this way and therefore, can be very misleading.

In the expression, '*ātmā eva idaṁ sarvam,*' *ātmā*, oneself, is defined as 'all this is *ātmā* alone.' '*Idaṁ sarvam*' implies the *jñātā*, knower; *jñāna*, the knowledge; and *jñeya*, the object of knowledge. *Sarva*, meaning 'all,' means all three with nothing left out. Within this *sarva* is the *draṣṭā*, *dṛśya*, and *darśana* – seer, the object seen, and seeing; *śrota*, *śruta* and *śravaṇa* – the hearer, the object heard, and hearing, and so on, all of which come under *jñātā*, *jñāna* and *jñeya*, knower, knowledge, and that which is known.

Any object that is there is *jñeya*, an object to be known alone. Even what is unknown is known and is, therefore, included under *jñeya*. Thus, we deal with these three – *jñātā*, *jñāna*, and *jñeya* alone. *Jñātā*, the knower, is non-separate from *ātmā* because *jñātā* is *ātmā*. Although we may clearly see the fact that the *jñātā* is *ātmā*, we still think of *jñāna* as belonging to *ātmā*, saying, 'This knowledge belongs to me. This is my knowledge.' I have the knowledge of a particular object, a tree. The tree is the object of knowledge and the *vṛtti*, the knowledge itself, belongs to me. Therefore, I take myself to be different from this knowledge whose object is the tree.

The knower-known-knowledge are one

This notion is nullified here by recasting it into an entirely different mould altogether. And what is this mould? *jñātā, jñāna, jñeya* – all three are made into one *ātmā*. Everything is myself alone, *ātmā eva idaṁ sarvam*. *Jñātā* is *ātmā*, *jñāna* is *ātmā*, and *jñeya* is also *ātmā*.

The example that is always used here is the dream. In dream, there is a knower of the dream, there is a known dream world, and there is knowledge of the dream itself. These three are nothing but one light, *jyotiḥ*, one consciousness, *caitanya*. Consciousness alone is the knower, known, and the knowledge in dream. All three of them are nothing but one *caitanya ātmā* alone.

In terms of the dream, this is very clear to you. Getting up, you understand that the dream knower, the dream known, and the dream knowledge all resolve into you again. Therefore, *jñātā* is nothing but consciousness, knowledge is nothing but consciousness, and *jñeya* is also nothing but consciousness.

Defined in this way, we understand that consciousness is as though qualified or limited by the status of being a knower, *jñātṛ-avacinna-caitanya*. We can refer to this as knower consciousness, knowledge consciousness, and known consciousness, there being no knower, knowledge, or known apart from consciousness. Can a known object ever be separate from consciousness? It cannot. When the known object is, consciousness is. When the known object is not, consciousness still is. You can destroy the object, but you cannot destroy the is-ness.

Nothing is separate from existence

With reference to the nature of existence, there is a two-fold argument, one in terms of existence itself and the other in terms of knowledge. In terms of existence, no object is apart from what is existent. For instance, when you say, 'The table is or the chair is,' the 'is-ness' that is there is qualified by the object, the name and form, *nāma-rūpa*, called table or chair. Further, if you analyse what a chair is, you find that the chair does not have any existence of its own; only the wood out of which the chair is made has an existence. And, if you analyse the wood, you find that it also has no existence; only the pulp from which the wood is made has existence. Similarly, the particles that form the pulp has existence, whereas the pulp does not. If you keep on shifting in this way, you find that existence always remains.

Only that which is self-existent can be called existence, *satya*, which is nothing but consciousness, *caitanya*. Consciousness alone is self-evident and everything else is evident to the self. Anything that you come to know, you question, is all for the knower, the person who is using the *pramāṇas*, the various means of knowledge, to ascertain the validity or the veracity of a particular object or statement of proof. Whereas, the existence of the very knower requires no proof. The knower must be a self-evident person. But who is this knower?

There is a part of the knower that is known to me. I know that I am the seer of the pot, *ghaṭa-draṣṭa*, for which there is a thought aspect, an adjective, *viśeṣa*, for the consciousness that is 'I.' The thought aspect is an adjective and the substantive is nothing but *ātmā*, consciousness. Therefore, for the knower there is consciousness, for the knowledge of course consciousness is present, and for the known also consciousness, the self-existent aspect of consciousness, is present. All three, knower, known, and knowledge, are non-separate from the presence of consciousness. Appreciation of this fact is what is meant here by *ātma-saṁsthaṁ manaḥ kṛtvā*.

Redirecting the mind to the very basis of thought is dhyāna

This appreciation enables you to see the mind, whereas, previously, the mind was always engaged in thinking about one thing or the other. The mind will still think about a variety of things, but now your attention is not upon what you see because you turn it away from the thoughts themselves and direct it to the very basis of the thoughts. This turning the attention is what is called *dhyāna*, contemplation. You turn your attention from the object of thought, whatever it may be, to the basis of thought.

The basis of thought is consciousness, whereas the object of thought can be anything, for example, a tree. The object of a tree thought is the tree and the basis of the thought is consciousness. Therefore, the tree thought is not separate from consciousness, the tree is not separate from consciousness, and the knower of the tree thought is not separate from consciousness, all three being nothing but consciousness, *ātmā*.

This very appreciation is also a thought. And what does this thought do? It simply destroys the ignorance that the three are separate and then it resolves. By not thinking of anything else but the oneness of all three, it resolves. Therefore, Kṛṣṇa says here, 'May one not think of anything else, *na kiñcit api cintayet*.' In fact, there is nothing else because everything is *ātmā*.

The point being made here, of course, is not to move away from the appreciation of *ātmā* as non-separate from everything else because if you think of something else, this appreciation will go. You can also appreciate that this object is a tree and that you are someone who is looking at the tree, which is true. But, then, the tree, the thought of the tree, and the *ātmā,* the one who looks at the tree, are one and the same. Turning your attention to the basis of these three is the appreciation, the contemplation, being referred to in this verse.

In order not to think of anything else, you require *dhṛti,* wisdom, which is gained by exposing the *buddhi* to the teaching. Only with the insight gained, with the help of the knowledge alone, can you practice this contemplation. *Dhṛti* also implies courage here because contemplation requires a steadiness, firmness, or commitment in order to understand that the knower-known-knowledge are one and the same, given that your orientation has always been that they are separate.

Because the orientation that they are one is against your experience, there will naturally be some obstruction in appreciating this fact. Until it becomes clear, you can assume that there is some obstacle, which will be taken care of by seeing the fact. Therefore, you do not worry about the obstacles; you simply keep on attempting to see, for which courage, firmness, and commitment are necessary.

To emphasise this point, Śaṅkara defined, *śanaiḥ śanaiḥ*, slowly, slowly, here as, *na sahasā*, meaning 'not immediately.' When he said, *ātma-saṁsthaṁ manaḥ kṛtvā*, it does not mean that you immediately turn your mind to some object called *ātmā*. *Ātmā* is not something you can put the mind into or on; the mind itself is *ātmā*. There is no job to be done here; there is simply an appreciation. Therefore, certain inner care is involved, wherein a contemplative atmosphere is created. In this atmosphere, recognition takes place for which no will whatsoever is involved. 'Slowly, slowly,' during the period of time in which contemplation takes place, you take to *ātmā*.

No will is required in contemplation

In meditation, will is only with reference to sitting and other preparations. Once these are taken care of, the will does not do anything. In fact, will is the problem and therefore, has to be surrendered to the contemplation itself. The contemplation takes over your will, so to speak. The mind becomes as though possessed. You, as a person, the contemplator, are possessed by that very contemplativeness. Therefore, no will is required here.

What do you require to appreciate something beautiful? None; the very will gets resolved in the appreciation of that which is beautiful, which is inspiring. What will is there when you love something? Whatever will there is, just resolves.

Similarly, in contemplation, you do not push your will in order to gain *ātmā*. You do not grind your teeth, roll up your sleeves, sit in your seat of meditation, and say, 'Today I am going to get that *ātmā*.' There is no such thing. It is not like wanting to do something or gain something that the world has to offer. If you want to do a particular job, for example, you can assert your will and get it done, but you cannot sit down, crush your eyelids together tightly, and say that you are going to get the *ātmā*. All that you will get is a headache! A person who tries to gain *ātmā* by using his or her will, will not gain *ātmā* because the person is *ātmā*.

So, first you create contemplativeness, which is taken care of by your exposure to the teaching. You must know what you are aiming at, conveyed here by *ātma-saṁsthaṁ manaḥ kṛtvā na kiñcit api cintayet*. Let the appreciation of *ātmā* take place in the mind, either by contemplating on the non-separation of knower-known-knowledge or by taking a particular expression such as '*satya-svarūpo'ham*, I am the truth of everything,' and meditating upon it. This is a contemplation that is in keeping with the teaching.

Nothing new, no new knowledge, is created here. Rather, your mind is brought to focus on what is already understood, again and again. This is the meaning of the expressions in this verse – *ātma-saṁsthaṁ manaḥ kṛtvā na kiñcit api cintayet*. Having said this much, Kṛṣṇa adds a little more.

Verse 26

The mind needs to be dealt with

यतो यतो निश्चरति मनश्चञ्चलमस्थिरम् ।
ततस्ततो नियम्यैतदात्मन्येव वशं नयेत् ॥ २६ ॥

yato yato niścarati manaścañcalam asthiram
tatastato niyamyaitad ātmanyeva vaśaṁ nayet (26)

cañcalam – always in a state of flux; *asthiram* – unsteady; *manaḥ* – the mind; *yataḥ yataḥ* – for whatever (reason); *niścarati* – goes away; *tataḥ tataḥ* – from that; *etat* – it (the mind); *niyamya* – bringing back; *ātmani* – with reference to the self; *eva* – alone; *vaśam* – into one's own hands; *nayet* – may one bring

For whatever reason the unsteady mind, always in a state of flux, goes away, bringing it back from that, with reference to the self alone, may one bring (the mind) into one's own hands.

Here, the mind is being dealt with, because it is the mind that is to be placed in *ātmā,* and it is the mind that has to contemplate upon *ātmā*. And also it is the mind, *manas,* that goes away, *niścarati*. For the mind, Kṛṣṇa uses two words, *cañcala* and *asthira*.

Cañcala means that the mind is always in a state of flux. This is in fact the nature of the mind. It is how the mind is made and it is good that it is made so. Otherwise, you would become stuck in one thought. The mind being *cañcala,* is also *asthira,* meaning that it is not at all steady. Always being in a state of flux, the mind is not steady, not firm. So, both the words, *cañcala* and *asthira,* qualify each other – being in flux, the mind is not steady, *cañcalatvāt asthiram*, and being unsteady, the mind is in flux, *asthiratvāt cañcalam*.

The mind itself is not a problem

Kṛṣṇa further describes the mind here by saying that it goes out, *niścarati*. That it goes out is not a problem; it is natural. Because the mind's nature is *cañcala* and *asthira*, it goes away from the chosen object of meditation for whatever reason, *yataḥ yataḥ*. You hear something, the sound of a bird perhaps, and you go along with the sound. You recognise it as the warble of a particular bird, and then you try to identify the kind of bird and so on. Or someone says something and off the mind goes. You do not even need the outside world for the mind to go away; there is a whole world right in your head. Is this not why you have gathered so many lifetime experiences, so that you can sit back and enjoy thinking about them? Even from inside then, all the birds warble; all the people you have ever known do this and that. Therefore, you have enough reasons for the mind to behave as it does.

For whatever reason the mind goes away from the object of meditation, and from that reason, from that situation, disciplining it, *niyamya*, you bring it back. Here, Śaṅkara gives an excellent piece of advice on how to do this. You do not try to pull it back; rather, you look at the very object to which the mind went. Let that itself be your object of attention for the time being. And what do you find? Does it exist independent of consciousness, *ātmā*? Does it continue to exist if you question it in this way? No, you find that it becomes *mithyā* and you get back to *satya*, the truth of it, which is yourself.

The entire Veda talks about the subject, object, action, instruments of action, and so on. And then, in the last chapter, it says that all that was said so far is not true, it is all *mithyā*. By looking into the thought that took you away, the very object that took you away from the object of meditation, the thought itself, along with its object, is converted into *mithyā*, simply by seeing the truth of it. Therefore, Kṛṣṇa says that, you should bring the mind back into your own hands, *vaśaṁ nayet*. As it moves away from you, may you bring it back to the object of meditation, meaning may you return to the contemplation of *ātmā*.

No force is used here. You just look at whatever took your mind away, thereby converting the object of distraction into object of meditation. In other words, your attention is turned from the distraction to the very *vastu* itself, to consciousness. Therefore, you have no problem. What object is going to distract you? By the strength of this practice of meditation, *dhyāna-yoga*, the mind resolves in *ātmā*. There is no question of distraction or false identity for the person. The mind remains as mind alone and, therefore, does not pose any problem.

Verse 27

One reaches the most exalted happiness as a result of meditation

प्रशान्तमनसं ह्येनं योगिनं सुखमुत्तमम् ।
उपैति शान्तरजसं ब्रह्मभूतमकल्मषम् ॥ २७ ॥

praśāntamanasaṁ hyenaṁ yoginaṁ sukham uttamam
upaiti śāntarajasaṁ brahmabhūtam akalmaṣam (27)

praśānta-manasam – one whose mind is tranquil; *śānta-rajasam* – one whose impurities have resolved; *akalmaṣam* – one whose life is free from defects; *brahmabhūtam* – one who has become Brahman; *enam* – this; *yoginam* – meditator; *hi* – indeed; *uttamam* – the most exalted; *sukham* – happiness; *upaiti* – reaches

> Indeed, the most exalted happiness reaches this meditator whose mind is tranquil, whose impurities have all resolved, whose life is free from all defects, who has become Brahman (through knowledge).

Here, Kṛṣṇa says that *uttama-sukha,* the most exalted happiness, reaches the person as a result of contemplation. This *sukha* is such that it cannot be compared with any happiness or joy that you know. It is a fullness, *pūrṇatva,* that is the very *svarūpa* of *ātmā.*

In any moment of joy or happiness, the seeker-sought difference is resolved, there being nothing but *ātmā,* even though there is an object or situation involved. Take music, for example. The music is there, the person enjoying the music is there, and the appreciation of the music in the form of thoughts, *vṛtttis*, is also there. In this music *sukha,* the division, the differences between the knower, knowledge and known is resolved; they experientially coalesce into one whole experience, called *sukha.* And what makes the experience whole? *Ātmā* whose nature is oneness, consciousness, makes it *sukha.*

Sukha is a word that you already know; therefore it can be used as a definition, a *lakṣaṇa,* to point out the *svarūpa* of *ātmā* as the wholeness, the limitlessness that stands undivided between an object and you. This undivided whole that is you, *ātmā*, is pointed out here by the word *sukha*. Therefore, it cannot be ordinary *sukha*, the *sukha* you know in moments of joy. It is not comparable to anything you know because it is *ātyantika-sukha*, absolute *sukha*, *uttama*, ultimate *sukha*, a *sukha* that is the very nature of *ātmā*, *svarūpa-sukha*.

Who qualifies for absolute *sukha*?

For whom does this *uttama-sukha* reach? The person who meditates upon *ātmā* described here as *praśānta-manas*, *śānta-rajas*, *brahma-bhūta* and *akalmaṣa*. Again, as we have seen before, these words describe the person and, at the same time, reveal the results of practising *dhyāna-yoga* and the qualifications required by a person before the knowledge can be gained.

A person who is *praśānta-manas* is one whose mind is resolved, tranquil, for whom the mind poses no problem. Therefore, this *uttama-sukha* reaches him or her. The person is also *śānta-rajas*, one for whom all the impurities, *rajas*, are resolved. Śaṅkara defines such impurity as the fascination for things that are totally false, *mohādi-kleśa*, based on one's *rāga*s and *dveśa*s. Whereas the person being described here is one who is no longer in the hands of *rāga*s and *dveśa*s, which is why he or she is *akalmaṣa*.

Kalmaṣa means a defect in terms of *adharma*, *pāpa*. Therefore, one whose pursuits in life are not improper is referred to as *akalmaṣa*. Such a person can become *brahma-bhūta*, one who has the *niścaya*, the definite knowledge that Brahman is everything, *idaṁ sarvaṁ brahmaiva*. And, because Brahman is everything,

I am that Brahman, *tat brahma aham asmi*. Brahman being everything, I am everything, *aham idaṁ sarvam*. Knowing this, the person is *brahma-bhūta*. And this *brahma-bhūta*, who is *akalmaṣa, śānta-rajas,* and *praśānta-manas*, gains *uttama-sukha, ānanda*, it being the *svarūpa* of *ātmā*. Because of the knowledge of *ātmā*, this *sukha* as though reaches the person.

In this particular verse, *uttama-sukha* is the subject of the sentence and the person it reaches is the object. Generally, you think of *uttama-sukha, ānanda*, as something that must be gained, but here it is said that it reaches you, which is a different thing altogether. You become the object and *ānanda* becomes the subject, the agent of the action of reaching. Now a question may arise – does *ānanda* reach me or do I reach *ānanda*? In fact, either way is correct, as we shall see in the next verse.

Verse 28

Resolving the difference between the subject and the object

युञ्जन्नेवं सदात्मानं योगी विगतकल्मषः ।
सुखेन ब्रह्मसंस्पर्शमत्यन्तं सुखमश्नुते ॥ २८ ॥

yuñjannevaṁ sadātmānaṁ yogī vigatakalmaṣaḥ
sukhena brahmasaṁsparśam atyantaṁ sukham aśnute (28)

evam – in this manner; *sadā* – always; *ātmānam* – the mind; *yuñjan* – uniting; *vigata-kalmaṣaḥ* – free from the conflicts born of *adharma; yogī* – the meditator; *sukhena* – easily; *brahma-saṁsparśam* – (born of) contact with (recognition of) Brahman; *atyantam* – absolute; *sukham* – happiness; *aśnute* – gains

The meditator, free from the conflicts born of *adharma*, always uniting the mind with the object of contemplation in this manner, easily gains absolute happiness (born of) contact with (recognition of) Brahman.

In the previous verse, the *kartā*, the subject, was *uttama-sukha* and the object, *karma*, was the *yogī*, the meditator, who receives the *sukha*. Whereas, in this verse, the *kartā* is the *yogī* and the object gained is *atyanta-sukha*, *atyanta* being a synonym for *uttama* to complete the metre. Why does Kṛṣṇa say that this *sukha* reaches the *yogī* in one verse and that the *yogī* gains it in the next? Does this mean there is some confusion about who is the *kartā*, and who is the *karma*? No. In fact, he expresses the result of contemplation in both senses in order to resolve whatever confusion there may be.

By saying *uttama-sukha* reaches the *yogī*, the *yogī* becomes an object. Now, does it mean that *ānanda* comes and overwhelms the person? If so, there is a problem. It means that the meditator is drowned in *ānanda*. In other words, the *ānanda* got the person! When you look at it this way, you seem to be an object, which is not so. You are the only subject in the world; therefore, you cannot be the object. To make this clear, Kṛṣṇa also puts it the other way, saying that the *yogī* gains *ānanda*, *uttama-sukha*, which means that the difference between *kartā* and *karma* is not there.

There is really no difference between *kartā* and *karma*, just as there is no difference between a river and the ocean at the point where the river reaches the ocean. You cannot tell whether the ocean receives the river or the river reaches the ocean. In the confluence of river and ocean, you will find that the river is salty for miles. Therefore, it looks as though the ocean is entering the river. Who is the *kartā* then? Who is the *karma*? You do not know. Sometimes you say the river reaches the ocean and at other times you say the ocean reaches the river.

Similarly, here, the *kartā,* the one who gains *ānanda,* does not see an *ānanda* other than himself or herself. Therefore, the subject and the object are one and the same, *kartā eva karma.* This is unlike any other thing; it is the knowledge of oneself. Thus, these two verses are to be read together.

In the present verse, *ātmānam yuñjan* means connecting or uniting the mind. The word '*evam,* in this manner,' indicates what the mind is to be connected to, meaning that it is united with the knowledge that *ātmā* alone is indeed everything, *aham eva idaṁ sarvam.* And, uniting the mind with the object of contemplation, the meditator gains *atyanta-sukha, uttama-sukha.*

The person is called a *yogī* here to indicate that his or her contemplation is successful. The *yogī,* the meditator, is one who is free of all obstacles. Again, this person is further described as one who is free from *adharma,* from *puṇya* and *pāpa, vigata-kalmaṣa,* because how one lives one's life is very important to the success of one's meditation. A successful meditator is one whose daily life is free from *adharma.* Living according to ethical values renders the person free from obstacles, in the form of conflicts. A *vigata-kalmaṣa* is one whose life is free from the conflicts born of *adharma.* And that *vigata-kalmaṣa,* that *yogī,* gains *atyanta-sukha.*

Atyanta sukha is not experiential

As has already been said, *atyanta-sukha* is a *sukha* that is not comparable to the degrees of *sukha* that you gather. This is where people make mistakes and talk about eternal bliss, and so on. This *sukha* is not eternal bliss; it is your nature, *svarūpa.*

To refer to *svarūpa-sukha* as bliss means that it is experiential. Then comes the question, what is eternal bliss and how can I get it? If it is something that you gain and that only lasts for a period of time, how can you call it eternal bliss? If it is something experiential, there is no *jñāna,* knowledge, there. Then what is this *atyanta-sukha*? The verse itself defines it as *brahma-saṁsparśa-atyanta-sukha,* a *sukha* born of recognising Brahman.

Whenever you touch something pleasant, the *sukha* you get is called *sparśa-sukha.* Does it mean that by contacting, by hugging Brahman, you will gain *atyanta-sukha*? No. Brahman is not an object available for hugging. Brahman is a word used by the *śāstra* for revealing oneself as the whole. Because of the knowledge that is, there is *sukha, brahma saṁsparśa-sukha,* born of the contact of Brahman, meaning the recognition of the self as Brahman. This *sukha* belongs to Brahman; it is the very nature of Brahman, in fact. Therefore, it is called *svarūpa-sukha.*

Svarūpa-sukha is not a *sukha* that is experiential. It is the *sukha* that is recognised as the nature, *svarūpa,* of every form of *sukha.* In any form of *sukha* that you get, the *sukha* is because of *svarūpa-sukha,* the wholeness that is the nature of Brahman. Born out of the knowledge that the self is Brahman, the meditator is said to gain this *svarūpa-sukha.*

In his commentary to this verse, Śaṅkara says that *atyanta-sukha* is that which does not come to an end. If this *sukha* were bliss, it would come to an end because any experience has a limit. Therefore, bliss is a finite *sukha*, not *atyanta-sukha* that transcends all limits, the limits of time or degrees. Such limits do not exist for the *sukha* that is one's very nature because *svarūpa-sukha* can never be experiential *sukha*.

For *sukha* to be experiential, there must be a particular condition of the mind and that condition will always change because it is within time. Since it is within time, experiential *sukha* is non-eternal. But, in every *sukha*, there is a *svarūpa*, a truth, and that truth is the nature of *ātmā*, which is free from any form of limitation. This limitlessness, wholeness, *pūrṇatva*, implied by the non-separation of the knower from all that is known, the firm understanding that, '*sarvam aham asmi*,' is the *svarūpa-sukha*, referred to in these two verses as *uttama-sukha* and *atyanta-sukha*. And, being the very *svarūpa* of *ātmā*, it cannot come to an end. As long as *ātmā* is there, *sukha* is there, and *ātmā*, being beyond time, is eternal.

No effort is required to gain svarūpa-sukha

How is this *sukha* gained? We always ask this question because, generally, the more you do in the world, the more you gain. More you work on something, greater is the result. This being a rule very well-known to you, how much should you do to gain infinite *sukha*? Infinite *karma*? No. The logic that you have for finite situations in this finite world does not work here. In fact, if *karma* were infinite, you could not even blink because blinking, like any action, is finite. Therefore, if you had to do infinite *karma*, you would do no *karma* at all!

In fact, no *karma* is involved in gaining *atyanta-sukha*, as Kṛṣṇa indicates here by the word '*sukhena*,' meaning 'easily,' without tears, without sweat, because this *sukha* is you. The self is Brahman and *atyanta-sukha* is born out of the recognition of this fact. Naturally, it is gained easily, *sukhena*.

Generally, in order to gain *sukha*, you have to do something that almost always involves some *duḥkha* also. For example, if you see a man packing and you ask him where he is going, he may say, 'I am going to Hawaii.' When you ask him why, he will say, 'To get some *sukha*.' On the way to the airport, he runs into a traffic jam and becomes upset – *duḥkha*. On arriving at the airport, there are more problems – more *duḥkha*. At the Hawaii airport, he finds that his baggage did not come – *duḥkha*. Even at the hotel, there is *duḥkha* for him because the travel agency did not book a room for him as arranged. All the way there is *duḥkha*, and for what? Just to gain a little *sukha*, to get some sun. And everyday he is there, it rains! On the day the sky clears, he has to catch a plane; his holiday is over.

This is called *alpa-sukha*, so much effort, so much invested, and so much *duḥkha* just for a little *sukha*. Whereas, here, how much effort is required, how much *duḥkha* is there, for *atyanta-sukha*? All the way it is pleasant. Pleasantly, *sukhena*, the person discovers. The very enquiry is pleasant because the *śāstra* says you are the whole. It does not say that you are an idiot or a sinner and so on. It says that you are everything and that not seeing it is idiocy. Therefore, listening to the *śāstra* is very pleasant indeed. No one else tells you that you are everything, that you are the whole. Only the *śāstra* accepts you totally. The prophets and great *gurus* do not accept you. Your father and mother, having their own ends to accomplish through you, do not accept you. Parents always want their children to be something other than what they are. Thus, no one accepts you totally except the *śāstra.*

The vision of the śāstra

No theology accepts you either. Every theology condemns you and then tells you that it will save you. Everyone wants to save you, it seems; everyone wants to be a saviour to others. All religions and theologies are meant only for this purpose because, in their eyes, you are condemned, whereas the *śāstra* says, '*tat tvam asi,* you are that.' It does not say, '*tat tvam bhaviṣyasi,* you will become that.' When the *śāstra* says, '*tat tvam asi,*' it is total, absolutely total. It is not even a matter of acceptance; it just points out that you are the whole. Because this is its vision, the *śāstra* could not condemn you, even if it wanted to.

You are the only *satya* that is in the creation; there is nothing else, everything else being *anātmā,* dependent upon the *ātmā* alone. You are the only one who is self-existent, *svataḥ siddhaḥ,* and everything else is dependent upon the self-evident being that you are. Therefore, you are always totally accepted by the *śāstra,* at the beginning and at the end also. In the beginning, *śāstra* says *mokṣa,* liberation, is yourself, *mokṣa* being in the form of knowledge of *ātmā* alone. The very starting point is that you are already free, even though you do not know it. Therefore, the subject matter of the *śāstra* is something that is already established, *siddha-viṣaya,* and gaining this knowledge is a gain of something that is already gained, *prāptasya prāptiḥ,* not the gain of something not yet gained, *na tu aprāptasya prāptiḥ*. To begin this way is very pleasant indeed and the journey itself is also pleasant.

Other kinds of *sukha* require effort and may not always be pleasant. Even going to heaven requires a lot of effort, according to the *śāstra*. You have to spend a lot of time performing the rituals properly, for which a lot of tears have to be shed, literally, since you have to sit before a fire to perform the rituals. Suppose, after having shed all these tears, you go to heaven, you gain heaven *sukha*. How long will you enjoy this *sukha*? Heaven *sukha* is also comparative *sukha,* heaven being just another place in which you cannot stay forever. There comes a time when you have to leave. Therefore, *sukha* that you gain in heaven is *anitya-sukha,* non-eternal *sukha,* that requires a lot of effort to gain.

Here, there is no effort; it is all *sukha*. It may seem a little silly or overly simplistic, but that is how it is. When you do a right about turn, your entire logic also reverses. Generally, all your desires are for *anātmā,* not for *ātmā*. Even heaven, *svarga,* is *anātmā,* not you. Whenever you say, 'I am going to reach somewhere or gain something,' the object to be gained or reached is *anātmā,* like heaven, money, or anything that you want.

All the *anātmā*s are for *ātmā* alone. To gain *sukha* is for *ātmā,* for your happiness, welfare, an experience of something that you want, you want to go here or there–all of which are *anātmā* for the sake of *ātmā*. Thus, there is always this connection between *ātmā* and *anātmā*. And as long as the connection is a desirable one, there is some kind of *sukha*, but it is always *anitya*, non-eternal.

It is this *anātmā-icchā*, desire for *anātmā*, that you give up and, in its place, you choose *ātma-icchā*. *Anātma-icchā* and *ātma-icchā* are opposites and are, therefore, two different things. *Ātma-icchā* is the right about turn, wherein you have a desire for the very *ātmā* itself. Being a right about turn, the logic that was applicable to *anātma-icchā* is not applicable at all to *ātma-icchā, ātmā* being accomplished already. *Ātmā* is; you are not going to create a new *ātmā*.

Ātmā is eternally present

Nor are you going to polish the *ātmā*. It is not that *ātmā* is covered and needs to be cleaned up so that its original colour will shine through. *Ātmā* is never coloured; it is always self-shining, *nitya-prasiddha*. Because it is eternally present, it is never covered by anything. The only covering possible, if the word is to be used at all, is ignorance. And ignorance is not something that is scraped off; ignorance just goes in the wake of knowledge, which is why Kṛṣṇa says that, without effort, the meditator gains the *sukha* that is his or her nature.

Sukha that is born out of contact with *anātmā* is *anitya*, non-eternal, whereas *sukha* born out of the knowledge of Brahman is *nitya*, eternal. *Ātmā* contacting Brahman means yourself contacting Brahman in terms of recognising Brahman.

Thus, *saṁsparśa* is used here only to point out that this is not like any other *sparśa*, meaning 'contact' the context here being that the recognition that *ātmā* is Brahman takes place, because of which one gains *nitya-sukha* without any effort.

In this verse, it is said that the *jīva* recognises and gains the *sukha* and in the previous verse it was said that the *sukha* reaches the *jīva*. Kṛṣṇa explains it in this way because the *jīva* is *sukha-svarūpa*. There is no *kartṛ-karma* difference because there is no *kartā* and no *karma*; there is only *ātmā*. Nor is there any reaching. There is only the dropping of ignorance and error, which is why it can be explained either as *sukha* reaching the person or the person reaching *sukha*. *Ānanda* approaching the *yogī* and the *yogī* gaining *ānanda* are one and the same.

There is only one track – jñāna

In all of this, you must be very clear that *yoga* is not something independent of knowledge. There is no *yoga* track by which you come to gain this *sukha*. Nor is there a *karma* track, *bhakti* track, or any other track, each track leading to the goal. There is only the track of *jñāna*. Here in this chapter, *yoga* is *dhyāna*, the track of *jñāna* consists of knowledge alone. To pursue knowledge, you can follow all kinds of *yoga* – *aṣṭāṅga-yoga*, *karma-yoga*, and so on. These disciplines will definitely be useful because you have to become a *vigata-kalmaṣa*. Therefore, you have to live a life of *dharma*, which implies certain attitude called *karma-yoga*. This attitude includes *bhakti*, prayer, etc., all of which are useful for gaining *jñāna*.

In this pursuit you use whatever is required, but the track is one and the same. There is no other track. Since this is how it is, what else can you do? *Ātmā* is Brahman and the problem is one of ignorance. Thus, the only track open to us is knowledge. The knowledge of the oneness of Brahman is the end result of the practice of contemplation. Therefore, let there be no confusion about there being any other track. The *yoga* discussed in the *Gītā* has its results in *jñāna* alone. It begins with *jñāna* and ends with *jñāna*.

Before contemplation, *nididhyāasana*, there is *śravaṇa*, listening to the vision of the *śāstra* that says *ātmā* and Brahman are one. Therefore, *nididhyāasana* is to make this vision clear of any obstacle.

Verse 29

Seeing the sameness that is in everything

सर्वभूतस्थमात्मानं सर्वभूतानि चात्मनि ।
ईक्षते योगयुक्तात्मा सर्वत्र समदर्शनः ॥ २९ ॥

sarvabhūtastham ātmānaṁ sarvabhūtāni cātmani
īkṣate yogayuktātmā sarvatra samadarśanaḥ (29)

yogayuktātmā – one whose mind is resolved by this contemplation; *sarvatra* – everywhere; *samadarśanaḥ* – one who has the vision of sameness; *ātmānam* – the self; *sarva-bhūtastham* – abiding in all beings; *sarva-bhūtāni* – all beings; *ca* – and; *ātmani* – in the self; *īkṣate* – sees

> One whose mind is resolved by this contemplation, who has the vision of sameness everywhere, sees the self abiding in all beings and all beings in the self.

Here, Kṛṣṇa says that the *yogī*, the meditator, sees the self, *ātmānam īkṣate*, meaning that he or she knows the self. And what self does this person see? Everyone knows oneself as a person having a history, a biography, which is identical with the physical body and the experiences one has had.

This body is connected to some other bodies and therefore, there is a brother, sister, son, daughter, or someone else. Generally, then, this self that is known is connected to a given physical body, as a person who abides in that body.

Whereas, the *yogī* being discussed in this verse recognises himself or herself as the self that abides in all beings, *sarva-bhūtastham ātmānaṁ paśyati*. And it is not just that; all the beings have their being in himself or herself alone, *sarva-bhūtāni ca ātmani*. Thus, *ātmā* runs through everything and, at the same time, everything is in *ātmā*. And who is it that sees this? *Yoga-yukta-ātmā,* one whose mind is resolved by contemplation, who has achieved success in this contemplation.

Such a person is also *sarvatra sama-darśanaḥ*, one who sees the sameness, *sama* that is *ātmā*, in everything. In other words, there is an appreciation, a vision, of that which is always the same in all beings. In all beings, in everything, there is something without any special attribute, *nirviśeṣa*, and there is something peculiar to each, *viśeṣa*. We see this *nirviśeṣa* and *viśeṣa* in different types of golden ornaments – chains, bangles, rings, and so on. In all of them there is one thing that is *nirviśeṣa* – gold; while the particular form such as chain, etc., is *viśeṣa*.

Although gold is also an attribute, this example illustrates the point being made here. With reference to all these chains, bangles, and rings, there is something common in all of them, something *nirviśeṣa*, something that is the truth, *satya*, of all of them – gold. There are many *viśeṣa*s, that is, all the various names and forms, *nāma-rūpa*. The attributes, chain, bangle, ring, and so on, have their existence in the *satya*, gold.

Similarly, all *nāma-rūpa*s have their basis, their truth, existence, *satya*, in *ātmā*, that is, Brahman and that Brahman I am. The one who knows the *nirviśeṣa*, that is free from attributes, the *satya* in everything, *sarvatra*, that which lends its existence to all names and forms, is called *sarvatra sama-darśanaḥ*. Wherever the person looks, he or she sees Brahman.

Contemplation is the appreciation of what is being said here

There is no real looking implied here. What is meant is that, for this person, there is no ignorance about the self. The vision of the person is that the self is in all beings and all beings are in the self. This vision, the vision of Vedanta, described in its entirety in this verse and the next two verses, is what is referred to as the knowledge. In fact, these three verses lend themselves to contemplation because contemplation is primarily the appreciation of what is being said here.

The meaning of the word 'I,' is not exactly as you understand it to be. It is not this physical body-mind-sense complex. When you say, 'This is my body, mind, senses,' you become someone who abides in the body-mind-sense complex. For this, you require no special knowledge; in fact, it is very common for people to take themselves in this way. And, not only do you take yourself to be someone who abides in the body-mind-sense complex, you also take the body, mind, and senses to be yours, which is why you say, 'This is my body, my mind, my senses.'

Similarly, when you say, 'I am fat,' the body itself becomes the 'I.' When you say, 'I am restless,' the mind becomes the 'I,' and when you say, 'I am tired,' the *prāṇa* becomes the 'I.' This makes it possible for us to have two situations here – either the physical body itself is *ātmā* or *ātmā* abides in the body. Both are being negated here. The *ātmā* that you talk about is the *ātmā* that abides in all beings, *sarvabhūtastha,* not just in one *bhūta,* in one body.

How do you appreciate this *sarva-bhūtastha-ātmā*?

Since *ātmā* never becomes an object, you cannot see it like you can see the string that runs through different beads,thereby holding them together. Because you can see both the beads and the string, you can say that the string is *sarva-bhūtastha,* the beads being all the *bhūta*s. The string is not just in one bead; it runs through all the beads. Even if the beads are of different shapes, colours, and value, all of them are run through by one string. Here, both the beads and the string are objects. Both of them are *anātmā.*

Although this illustration is used to explain *sarva-bhūtastha-ātmā,* like any illustration, it is subject to defect. The defect here is that both the beads and the string are *anātmā.* As an object perceived by you, the string is *anātmā,* and so are the beads. Even if the string is not seen by you because the beads are strung so closely together, you can infer that the string is there. Thus, the string is an object inferred by you. Whether an object is perceived or inferred, either way it is an object known by you and is, therefore, *anātmā*.

But, here, how does the one who recognises the *ātmā* in all beings, recognise it? You recognise the various beings, but if you recognise in all of them one *ātmā*, *ātmā*, becomes an object of recognition. *Ātmā* can never be recognised as an object. How is this statement, *sarva-bhūtastham ātmānaṁ īkṣate*, to be understood?

Ātmā is only one and that is 'I.' There is no other *ātmā* because everything else is *anātmā*. If you define *ātmā* as one thing referred to as the first person 'I,' then everything that is evident to this *ātmā* becomes *anātmā*. Therefore, is there not some difficulty here? How are you to recognise *ātmā* in all these *anātmā*?

This problem arises because the *ātmā* that you recognise as yourself is not only in your physical body. It is not in any one physical body alone. When you associate it with one body, it becomes *ahaṅkāra*, the 'I' notion. It becomes the *jīva*, the individual. Then you go one step further and recognise the *jīva* as pure *caitanya*, pure consciousness, alone. Then everything else in the world, all the beings, all the minds, etc., have their being in that consciousness, which has no particular location.

If consciousness had a location, then it would be located only in living beings. In other words, consciousness would be here in one living being and at another place in another living being.

Then how would you recognise the one that is present in all these beings? Between two beads you can see or infer there is string; this is how you know that the string obtains in space also. But if consciousness had a particular location, how could you recognise it? There is no way to recognise consciousness, *ātmā*, except by understanding that it has no location. It is not located anywhere.

Location itself is always in terms of spatial enquiry. The very concept of location is based upon the various forms that you see abiding in space. You see one object existing in 'place P,' another object existing in 'place P1,' and between them there is space. Therefore, you say, 'This object is located here and that object is located there.' The location for two objects not being the same, you ask where particular objects are located or from where a certain person comes, and so on.

A physical body definitely has a location; it has to be located. Even concepts have their own location. And, if you analyse the location of all these, you will find that they exist within the framework of time and space alone. All concepts, time space concepts and objects within time space concepts, exist where? That in which they are located is *ātmā*, consciousness, called *sarva-bhūtastha-ātmā*, the self or the truth of all beings.

Time and space also have their existence in *ātmā*.

Why? Because *ātmā* is not located in any one particular place. To understand this is to have an appreciation of *nirviśeṣa-caitanya*, attribute-free consciousness, which is the *svarūpa*, the nature, of *ātmā*. *Nirviśeṣa-caitanya* is not located in time or space because time and space are not absolutes existing parallel to *ātmā*. Time and space have their existence in the being that is *caitanya*. Consciousness, *cit*, is the being, the existence, *sat* – *sat is cit, cit is sat*. And in this *sat-cit-ātmā*, all beings have their existence.

Consciousness has no particular location in living beings because, wherever there is a mind, consciousness is manifest there and where there is no mind, consciousness is not manifest. There is nothing more to it than this. Therefore, manifest consciousness is seen as though it is a conscious being. A thought, certain response on the part of the person, is manifest and from this you may say that the person has consciousness. But, this is not the way to look at it. The object of such an inference is *anātmā*. Whatever you infer is *anātmā* alone.

Caitanya has no location whatsoever; in *caitanya* everything is located. If this is understood, then wherever there is a being, the being has its being in the self. The self is the basis, *adhiṣṭhāna*, for all beings. All beings have their *adhiṣṭhāna*, their basis, in the self alone. Therefore, the self runs through any being that you think about and that being is sustained, vivified, by this same self alone. In this way, *ātmā* becomes the *adhiṣṭhāna*, the basis, for any *bhūta*. Being limitless, *ātmā* is not bound by time or space. And, in this limitless consciousness alone, all beings have their being, their existence. Each one of them has its *adhiṣṭhāna*, its basis, in *ātmā* and therefore, in 'I,' *aham*. *Aham*, *ātmā*, is not the self of any one being; it is the self that abides in all beings – *sarva-bhūtastha-ātmā*.

The resolution of all beings into the self by knowledge

The other statement in this verse, '*sarva-bhūtāni ca ātmani īkṣate*' is also important. It means 'and (the meditator) sees all beings in the self.' How? This is what is meant by resolution. To understand this, let us look at the different types of resolution or dissolution, called *laya* or *pralaya*.

One type of *laya* is *nitya-laya*, the resolution that takes place daily when you go to sleep. Everything is resolved into yourself – your projections, your experiences, the world and all its beings, resolve into yourself alone in sleep. This is called *nitya-laya*, daily dissolution.

Then there is *mahā-pralaya*, cosmic dissolution, referred to by the expression, '*sṛṣṭi-sthiti-pralaya*, creation-sustenance-dissolution' of the world itself. This type of *laya* is like deep sleep but with reference to the total, the cosmos, rather than to a given individual. Nothing is really lost in these two types of dissolution since everything is merely in its unmanifest condition and when it manifests again it is just as it was before. When you come back from sleep, you are as you were before and everything else also comes back in the same form. Similarly, after *mahā-pralaya*, the creation also comes back exactly as it was before and can therefore, be considered an extension of the deep sleep condition alone. Because these manifest and unmanifest conditions form a cycle, nothing is really lost.

From a manifest condition to an unmanifest condition is called *pralaya*, dissolution or resolution; and from the unmanifest condition to a manifest condition is called *sṛṣṭi*, creation. And the continual change that the manifest form undergoes is called *sthiti*, sustenance, wherein the same manifestation seems to appear but with certain changes. *Sthiti* is not a stationary condition; it is time bound and always changing. Everything is always in a state of flux, but still recognisable.

Even though constantly changing, you recognise the mountain, the sun, moon to be the same. Meeting an old friend after ten years, you recognise the person in spite of the changes that have taken place in each of you. If, moment to moment, things were to change in such a drastic way that you could not recognise them at all, there would be continuous dissolution, *pralaya*, and no *sthiti* at all. Continuous dissolution and continuous creation is meaningless. There is a recognisable *sthiti*, sustenance, in spite of the changes taking place.

The sun itself is imploding all the time and thus is not exactly the same sun that you just saw a minute before. It may run out, too. In the same way, nothing remains the same; everything is constantly changing. There is creation, *sṛṣṭi*, constant change within itself, *sthiti*, and dissolution, *pralaya*. This *sṛṣṭi-sthiti-pralaya* cycle is nothing but the manifestation and unmanifestation of consciousness, *ātmā*.

A third type of *pralaya* is called *atyanta-pralaya*, total dissolution, and is what we call *mokṣa*. *Atyanta-pralaya* or *mokṣa* does not involve any kind of disappearance. You look at the same object and resolve it in the appreciation of its cause, the truth of the object, *satya-vastu*. For example, when you see a thousand pots born of clay, you resolve all of these objects by appreciating clay as the *satya* of every pot. Then there is *mahā-atyanta-pralaya*.

When all names and forms, with their various distinct features, go into a state of unmanifest condition, it is called either *laya* or *pralaya*. It means that it is either *nitya-laya* or *mahā-pralaya*. Whereas here, without changing any object, things are as they are, but at the same time, they are envisioned by you as non-separate from the cause, *brahma-ātmā*. This particular vision is unfolded in this verse by the words, *sarva-bhūtāni ca ātmani īkṣate*.

Vedanta reveals the cause, *kāraṇa*, of everything as *satya* and the effect, *kārya*, as *mithyā*. This particular analysis is therefore called *kāraṇa-kārya vāda*, cause-effect analysis. In fact, there is no real *kāraṇa* or *kārya* because one of them becomes *mithyā*. This means that the status of being a *kāraṇa* is also incidental. Everything that is here is *satya-brahma* alone. Knowing this, you look at the world, the same world, with a different *buddhi*. You look at it as the *puruṣa*, 'I,' the cause. Therefore, the entire creation is only in terms of subtle and gross bodies, *sūkṣma* and *sthūla śarīras*. These alone are created, whereas *ātmā*, being timeless, is not created. Uncreated, *ātmā* is the truth of everything, *satya-vastu*, the basis, *adhiṣṭhāna*, of any creation that may be there. *Ātmā* is the very basis for the vision implied by the words in this verse, *sarva-bhūtastham ātmānaṁ sarva-bhūtāni ca ātmani īkṣate*.

Here, a problem can arise. Wherever there is *adhiṣṭhāna*, a confusion is possible between the basis, *āśraya*, and the based, *āśrita*.

For instance, when I say, 'On the rope is a snake' or 'On the gold is a chain,' you may think that the snake is actually lying on the rope or the chain is actually sitting on top of the gold. It would mean that the rope and the snake, or that the gold and the chain are two different things, when in fact they are not. It is just a way of describing something wherein there are apparently two objects, but, in fact, there is only one. When you talk about the snake on the rope, or the chain on the gold, one object is the *adhiṣṭhāna*, the basis, and the other is something that is based, dependent on the *adhiṣṭhāna*, basis.

We see that the basis-based relationship generally implies two different things. Here too, *jagat*, the world, all the beings, *sarva-bhūtāni*, are based upon *ātmā*, and this is called *sarva-bhūtastha ātmā*, the *ātmā* that is the *adhiṣṭhāna* for all beings. Even so, this is not a basis-based relationship. Such a division is not there because all the *bhūta*s are non-separate from *ātmā*, which is why Kṛṣṇa says here, *sarva-bhūtāni ātmani īkṣate*. The person, the *sarvatra-sama-darśī*, the one who sees the *sama, ātmā,* in everything recognises all beings as non-separate from the *paramātmā*, just as he or she sees the clay in the pots and the gold in the chains.

Seeing all beings, time, space, everything, in *ātmā* is called *atyanta-pralaya*, a dissolution of the difference between objects and their cause. *Atyanta-pralaya* is not the dissolution of the world; it is the dissolution of the difference between the world and its *kāraṇa*, a difference born out of *ajñāna*, ignorance. This difference, division, is resolved in the vision that, whatever that is here is non-separate from *ātmā* that is Brahman.

Verse 30

The one who sees me in everything is not remote from me

योो मां पश्यति सर्वत्र सर्वं च मयि पश्यति ।
तस्याहं न प्रणश्यामि स च मे न प्रणश्यति ॥ ३० ॥

yo māṁ paśyati sarvatra sarvaṁ ca mayi paśyati
tasyāhaṁ na praṇaśyāmi sa ca me na praṇaśyati (30)

yaḥ – the one who; *mām* – me; *sarvatra* – everywhere (in all beings); *paśyati* – sees; *mayi* – in me; *ca* – and; *sarvam* – everything (all beings); *paśyati* – sees; *tasya* – for him (or her); *aham* – I; *na praṇaśyāmi* – am not remote; *saḥ* – he (or she); *ca* – and; *me* – (from) me; *na praṇaśyati* – is not remote

The one who sees me in all beings and sees all beings in me, for him (or her) I am not remote and he (or she) is not remote from me.

The vision of *ātmā* given in the previous verse is re-stated, using a different language, in the first line of this verse. The earlier expression, '*sarva-bhūtastham ātmānam*' is put into the first person here, the one who recognises me in all beings, *yaḥ māṁ paśyati sarvatra.*

'Me' does not refer to Kṛṣṇa, the person occupying the driver's seat of Arjuna's chariot. Seated in the chariot, the person, Kṛṣṇa seems to have a definite location, and, yet, when talking to Arjuna, he refers to himself as one who is everywhere, *sarva-bhūtastha ātmā.* Wherever there is a *bhūta*, a being, it has its being in me alone. This 'me' is *ātmā.*

By replacing the words *sarva bhūtastha ātmānam* with *mām,* meaning Īśvara, Kṛṣṇa quietly brings out the non-difference between Īśvara and the individual, *jīva*. The one who sees me, Īśvara, in all beings, meaning as the *adhiṣṭhāna,* the basis, of all beings, knows oneself to be that same Īśvara, *paramātmā,* being non-separate from *ātmā*.

Kṛṣṇa also says here that everything is in me alone, *sarvaṁ ca mayi eva*. I am the *kāraṇa,* the cause, for everything. I am the *adhiṣṭhāna* for everything, the basis for everything. So, the person being discussed here recognises himself or herself in all beings and all beings in the self alone.

The only difference between this verse and the previous verse, then, is that the word *ātmā* has been replaced by the first person, *mām,* 'me.' Between the 'me' in the present verse and *ātmā* in the previous verse, there is no difference whatsoever. One who sees *ātmā* in everything and everything in *ātmā* recognises Īśvara, 'me,' in everything and everything in 'me.' I am the one who is the basis of all beings and in me all the beings have their being, their existence.

Between Īśvara, Kṛṣṇa and *jīva*, the individual, there is no difference whatsoever. Is there another Īśvara? Since Īśvara is everything, how can he be separate from consciousness, *caitanya,* that is the *ātmā*? If *caitanya-ātmā* is limitless, that is, Brahman, then, there is no way another being called Īśvara can be standing separately somewhere. If this were the case, Īśvara would become just another guy! Then there would be a difference between *jīva* and Īśvara that could never be resolved.

There are various contentions in terms of Īśvara, the Lord, and the individual, which have to be analysed to see if there is any truth in them. Suppose you say, as some do, that the Lord is everywhere and I am a fraction of that Lord. Does it mean that all these fractions together make the Lord? If not, what does it mean? Which is the fraction, please tell me. Is your physical body the fraction? Is your mind the fraction? Or is *ātmā-caitanya* the fraction? And, in all of this, what is dependent on what? What is the reality of what?

What is the reality of this physical body, this mind, and so on? When you analyse them all, you find only one existence, and the *svarūpa* of this *satya* is nothing but *paraṁ-brahma*, which is *caitanya-ātmā*. When the *śāstra* talks of Īśvara, it is from one particular standpoint. All that is there is Parameśvara alone; *jīva* is also just a standpoint. Only from a particular standpoint is there a difference between *jīva* and Īśvara – from the standpoint of the *upādhi*, there is *jīva* and there is Īśvara. The resolution of the two takes place only in the appreciation of the essential *paramātmā*, the *satya-vastu*.

Therefore, when the Lord says, '*aham īśvaraḥ*, I am the Lord,' and the *jīva* says, '*ahaṁ jīvaḥ*, I am an individual,' the *aham* is common and the difference is *mithyā*, meaning that it is entirely dependent upon *satya*. The problem is the difference because, being dependent upon *satya*, *mithyā* is not another thing. The whole *jagat* is *mithyā*, depending upon the *satya-vastu* for its existence, and the *satya-vastu* is what is referred to by everyone as 'I,' *aham*. Therefore, anyone who says 'I,' including a mosquito, is *paraṁ-brahma* alone. You are not 'I' and *paraṁ-brahma*, you are only *paraṁ-brahma*.

Even the person who does not know is *paraṁ-brahma*. The statement, *tat tvam asi*, means you are *paraṁ-brahma* right now; it is not something that you become later. Śruti does not say, 'Ye shall become.' It says, '*tat tvam asi*, that thou art.' This sentence is possible only when the self is already Brahman, which is the vision unfolded in the previous verse and re-stated in the first line of the present verse; the one who sees me in all beings and all beings in me – *yaḥ māṁ paśyati sarvatra, sarvaṁ ca mayi paśyati*. This person is one who has the vision of the oneness of *ātmā*. Seeing *ātmā* in all beings and all beings in *ātmā* is the vision.

The result of the vision

What is the result of this vision? Here, Kṛṣṇa uses the first person, indicating that Kṛṣṇa is talking as Īśvara. He says, 'For the person having this vision, I will not become remote, *tasya ahaṁ na praṇaśyāmi*,' meaning that, 'I will no longer be something known only indirectly to the person.' Why? Because Īśvara is *ātmā*. I do not become an indirect object of worship that is sitting somewhere. I do not become someone who is away from the person, because, Īśvara is oneself, *ātmā*.

And not only that, the person also does not go away from me, *sa ca me na praṇaśyati*. I do not become remote for the person and the person does not go away from me. This fact was already there, but previously the person did not know it. Now one knows. This is not something that just happened because of some interference on the part of the Lord. It was true before and it is true now. All that has happened is that the person did not know it before and now he or she knows. The person now sees himself or herself in all beings and all beings in the self. A person of this vision never goes away from me, meaning there is no distance between me and the person. Neither the person goes away from me nor I go away from the person. I do not become remote for the person, and he or she does not become remote for me.

This means that previously there was some remoteness and Īśvara, *paramātmā,* was someone who was sought after, whose grace was invoked. Now all the prayers and rituals have paid off. The payoff is the vision that between *jīva* and Īśvara there is no difference. The difference is resolved. This is what is meant here by the statement, *tasya ahaṁ na praṇaśyāmi.* I do not become something that is away for this person nor is the person away from me.

The Lord is usually presented as though he is behind a veil, and that, he can see you but you cannot see him. Therefore, the Lord is someone who always seems to be looking into your private affairs. But in this verse, Kṛṣṇa is saying that the Lord has no veil or cover that prevents you from seeing him. Ignorance is the only veil there is and that covering has already been removed. So, there is no obstacle; there is only one vision, the vision of the *para-ātmā,* the whole. Everything resolves into this one *ātmā* alone.

Elsewhere, Śaṅkara says, '*ardha ślokena pravakṣyāmi yaduktaṁ grantha koṭibhiḥ,* in half-a-verse I shall explain what has been said before by millions of words and texts.' And, having already used one half of a verse to say this much, he completes the verse by saying, '*brahma satyaṁ jagan mithyā jīvaḥ brahmaiva na aparaḥ,* Brahman is *satya* and the whole world, *jagat,* is *mithyā,* and *jīva* is non-separate from Brahman.' This means that the body, mind, and senses are also *mithyā.* And the *jīva* that is other than the physical body, mind, and senses, that is *ātmā,* is Brahman. It means, I am everything, *idaṁ sarvam aham asmi.*

This is the vision that resolves the difference between the *jīva* and Īśvara, which is why Īśvara is never remote from you nor are you ever away from him. There is no difference other than what is caused by ignorance. Ignorance being removed, all that is there is one flame of consciousness in which everything exists – everything that is enquired into, everything that is not enquired into, the known and the unknown, all exist in *ātmā,* alone. The *ātmā* of Īśvara and the *ātmā* of *jīva* is one and the same *ātmā* whose *svarūpa* is consciousness. This consciousness, *ātmā,* alone is self-existent, the whole, which is Īśvara, which is the *jīva.*

Verse 31

The yogī – recognising me in all beings – abides in me

सर्वभूतस्थितं यो मां भजत्येकत्वमास्थितः ।
सर्वथा वर्तमानोऽपि स योगी मयि वर्तते ॥ ३१ ॥

sarvabhūtasthitaṁ yo māṁ bhajatyekatvam āsthitaḥ
sarvathā vartamāno'pi sa yogī mayi vartate (31)

yaḥ – the one who; *ekatvam* – oneness; *āsthitaḥ* (*san*) – having recognised; *sarvabhūtasthitam* – abiding in all beings; *mām* – me; *bhajati* – gains (the vision); *saḥ yogī* – that *yogī; sarvathā* – in whatever way; *vartamānaḥ* – remaining; *api* – even; *mayi* – in me; *vartate* – abides

The one who gains (the vision), having recognised the oneness of me abiding in all beings, that *yogī* abides in me whatever he (or she) does.

This verse continues to discuss the person who has the vision of the oneness of *ātmā* in all beings, who knows that *ātmā* is oneself alone, and is therefore, not separate from Īśvara. All this is restated here.

Māṁ sarva-bhūta-sthitaṁ yo bhajati, refers to the one who gains the vision of Īśvara as that, which abides in all beings. Therefore, the self is non-separate from Parameśvara. The vision that is gained is in terms of the oneness of *ātmā,* the oneness of *ātmā* that is never divided, that is the undivided whole. And the one who recognises Īśvara in this undivided form, *ekatvam āsthitaḥ,* the one who gains this vision of Īśvara – however he or she may live – remains with Īśvara, *sarvathā vartamānaḥ api saḥ yogī mayi vartate.* Thus Kṛṣṇa says, 'The person remains in me alone.'

This verse answers the question of whether, having gained the vision, it can ever be lost. I am often asked, 'Swamiji, suppose a person gains this vision, is it not possible that living in the day-to-day world of duality, the person can lose the *ātmā*? 'No!' Kṛṣṇa says here. Whatever the person does, whatever happens to the person, seeing, hearing, talking, walking, in whichever way he or she happens to live, whether as a *brahmacārī,* a *gṛhastha,* or a *sannyāsī,* as a man or a woman, young or old – *sarvathā vartamānaḥ api,* the vision remains. The stage of life the person is in or the profession he or she happens to be pursuing is all because of the person's *prārabdha*. In fact, there is nothing wrong for the person and there is nothing right either.

Whatever the *śāstra* says with reference to *dharma* and *adharma* no longer applies to the person who is above *dharma* and *adharma*. This must be clearly understood. The person is free and is called *mukta, nitya-mukta,* one who is always free. This free person never goes away from me. Never again do I become remote for the person because one can never be away from oneself.

Even now, I am not away from the truth of myself, *sat-cit-ānanda ātmā*. Only ignorance can keep me away and, for the person being discussed here, ignorance is gone. Therefore, wherever the person is, whatever one is doing, *sarvathā vartamānaḥ api*, the person remains in me, oneself, *mayi vartate*. There is no moving away from me for the *jīvan-mukta* that is, living, the person is liberated. This liberation, *mokṣa*, is the *phala*, the result of this vision, the knowledge of *ātmā*.

Īśvara is not remote from oneself

The conclusion here is that, Īśvara is not remote from oneself, *Īśvaraḥ na parokṣaḥ*. *Parokṣa* is what is inferred, believed, or presumed. You have a presumption that there is an Īśvara, which amounts to a belief because there is no verifiable proof. And, as long as existence of Īśvara is simply a belief, Īśvara is remote, who exists for you indirectly, *parokṣa*.

Similarly, if you say that a tree exists, but you do not directly see it, it is *parokṣa*. For example, by seeing smoke, you can assume there is fire, even though the fire is not directly seen by you. Any object whose existence you arrive at through inference is called *parokṣa,* indirectly known.

Whereas anything that is sensorily perceived, anything you see, hear, smell, taste, or touch, is called *pratyakṣa*. When I hold up a piece of crystal, knowing it is crystal it is *pratyakṣa* for me, but for you it will be *parokṣa* if you do not know whether it is crystal or glass. You can infer it is crystal until you feel the weight of it and then you will know. The point to be understood here is what is directly perceived is called *pratyakṣa* and what is indirectly arrived at is called *parokṣa.*

Īśvara cannot be *pratyakṣa.* If Īśvara could be directly perceived, it would mean that he is other than you, *anātmā.* Īśvara cannot be *anātmā* because he can never be an object for you. *Anātmā* is entirely dependent upon *caitanya, ātmā.* If Īśvara were to become *anātmā,* he would be *mithyā* and you, being *ātmā,* would become *satya*! Because Īśvara cannot be *anātmā,* he can never become *pratyakṣa,* an object of your perception. Nor can he be inferred, inference being based on perception. Still, you believe that Īśvara exists, which means Īśvara is *parokṣa.*

The person who believes that Īśvara exists is an *āstika.* And, for the *āstika,* there is a *pramāṇa,* a *śāstra,* through which he or she comes to understand, comes to believe that Īśvara exists. And because you believe, you give validity to the means of knowledge, the *śāstra,* even though what is said is not verifiable. Because some supporting logic is available, you accept that Īśvara exists. And this belief, acceptance, is *parokṣa-jñāna,* indirect knowledge.

Self-knowledge is immediate knowledge

But the knowledge being discussed in this verse is not *parokṣa-jñāna*. The one who has gained the knowledge of *ātmā* is the one who has gained the knowledge of oneself. Such a person concludes, 'I am everything. There is nothing separate from me.' Here, when the Lord says, 'me,' what is implied is pure consciousness, *caitanya*, which is *paraṁ-brahma, satya-jñāna-ananta-brahma*, and everything else is dependent upon that. And this *satya-jñāna-ananta-brahma*, is *ātmā*, oneself. Because there is no difference between Īśvara, Brahman, and myself, I never become *parokṣa* to him; nor does he become *parokṣa* to me. This is what we call *advaita*, the non-difference, *abheda*, between Īśvara and the *jīva*. The identity between *jīva* and Īśvara, *jīva-īśvara-aikya*, was pointed out in the previous verse also.

Śaṅkara too points out in his commentary of the previous verse that *ātmā* never becomes *parokṣa*. *Ātmā* is always free, *nitya-mukta*. There is no bondage for *ātmā* because there is nothing other than oneself; therefore, Kṛṣṇa says, 'The person remains in me alone, *mayi eva vartate*. It means that once ignorance is no longer there, there is no question of the knowledge being lost.

Knowledge of oneself, *ātmā-jñāna*, is not memory based. Only knowledge that is memory based can be forgotten. Whatever I have, I can always lose. Memory is for me, *ātmā*. Because memory is something I have, I can lose it. But, here, what is known is myself alone. The self-ignorance I had before is gone in the wake of knowledge wherein the self is equated with Brahman. Once gained, this knowledge is never lost.

Unless *ātmā* becomes *parokṣa,* there is no question of the wise person being away from me and *ātmā* can never become *parokṣa* because it is *nitya-aparokṣa,* it is always directly known by me. Whether I am a confused person, a discriminating person, or a *jñānī, ātmā,* is never *parokṣa. Saṁsāra* is directly known by the person; it is not something that is inferred. It is an experience for the person and, therefore *aparokṣa*. As a *saṁsārī, ajñānī,* 'I am' is *aparokṣa;* and as a *vivekī, jñānī,* also 'I am' is *aparokṣa*. Therefore, *ātmā* is *nitya-aparokṣa,* always self-evident.

Being *nitya-aparokṣa ātmā* is *nitya-mukta,* always liberated. Knowledge makes the person recognise the fact of being ever liberated, which is why the person is called *jīvan-mukta,* living, the person gains the knowledge that is liberation. Once this knowledge has been gained, one can do what one wants, perform *vaidika-karma,* teach or not teach. Let the person be in any stage of life and perform any action, he or she is still with me alone. Even, for the sake of argument, if such a person were to commit murder, the person would not be away from me because he or she is not a doer.

The next question, of course, is: 'Could such a person commit such actions?' 'No!' says Kṛṣṇa in the next verse.

Verse 32

Wrong action is not possible for the wise person

आत्मौपम्येन सर्वत्र समं पश्यति योऽर्जुन ।
सुखं वा यदि वा दुःखं स योगी परमो मतः ॥ ३२ ॥

ātmaupamyena sarvatra samaṁ paśyati yo'rjuna
sukhaṁ vā yadi vā duḥkhaṁ sa yogī paramo mataḥ (32)

arjuna – O Arjuna!; *yaḥ* – the one who; *sarvatra* – everywhere; *sukhaṁ vā* – either pleasure; *yadi vā duḥkham* – or pain; *ātma-aupamyena* – taking oneself as an example (basis); *samam* – the same; *paśyati* – sees; *saḥ* – that; *yogī* – *yogī*; *paramaḥ* – the most exalted; *mataḥ* – is regarded

> One who, taking oneself as an example (basis) in all situations, sees either pleasure or pain as the same, that *yogī*, Arjuna! is regarded as the most exalted.

Here, Kṛṣṇa obviates the problem of whether the wise person can perform any action of *adharma*, by showing that there is no way of his doing that. For such a person, *ātmā*, oneself, is the *upamā*, the example. The self itself becomes the example, *ātma aupamyam*.

One who is oneself as an example sees that which is equal in all beings, *sarvatra samaṁ paśyati*, as being equal to oneself alone. The person does not look upon others from any other matrix except oneself alone. With reference to all beings, the vision is equal, the same. One looks upon others as oneself alone on the basis of the example of oneself. This is one meaning. There is also another meaning, which we shall see later.

In the second line of the verse, the vision of sameness is pointed out in terms of happiness and pain, *sukhaṁ vā duḥkhaṁ vā*. My happiness, *sukha*, my welfare, is highly desirable to me, and therefore, I go for it, which is the same for everyone. Every being is equally interested in its own *sukha*. So, 'I' become the matrix, the basis, for my interaction with other beings. Similarly, *duḥkha* is what is not desirable for me or for anyone else either.

The basis of dharma

Here you can see how *dharma* itself is born. The very basis of *dharma* is the universal mutual expectation of people. What I expect of others is what others expect of me. If what is desirable, *sukha*, for me is desirable for others and what is undesirable, *duḥkha*, for me is undesirable for others also, then there is a common basis, which is what is meant by *dharma*.

Having the vision of sameness in all beings, then, the person discussed here does not do what is not desirable. So, what Kṛṣṇa said in the previous verse, 'Whatever the person does, he (or she) remains in me, *sarvathā vartamānaḥ api mayi vartate*,' is further explained here. What was said there could be misunderstood to mean that a *jñānī* could do things that are *adharma* and yet he remains in Īśvara. Therefore, answering the question, 'Will such a person do actions that are considered to be wrong, *adharma*?' Kṛṣṇa says 'No!' It is not possible because what is good for the *jñānī* is good for others too. And what is bad for the *jñānī* is bad for others also. If the *jñānī* does not like getting hurt, then he or she is not going to hurt anyone else. In this way, non-injury, *ahiṁsā*, becomes natural to the *jñānī*.

Even for a *vivekī*, a simple, mature person, *ahiṁsā* is a very common *dharma*. And, for a *jñānī*, who has lived a life of *dharma* and who has deliberately pursued and gained the knowledge, *dharma* becomes spontaneous, very natural.

If you look at any crime, like hurting another person, or any kind of action considered to be *adharma*, behind it there is always a small ego. Every ego is small, in fact. A big ego is also small, any ego being just a bubble filled with air. Whether the bubble is big or small, it is nothing but air. That is all there is to this ego business, just so much air. Ego itself is a false entity and this false entity is behind every crime, large or small.

Ego is ignorance-based

And what kind of ego is this? The ego of an insecure person, an insecure ego that has fear and greed. Because it has fear and greed, it is insecure; because it is insecure, it is frightened. A frightened person or a greedy person can perform actions that are not very committed to *dharma*. In fact, all unbecoming actions stem from the insecure ego and no ego is secure. Because the nature of ego is isolation, there is duality, *dvaita*.

In the *Bṛhadāraṇyakopaniṣad,* it is said that wherever there is duality, there will be fear – *dvitīyād vai bhayaṁ bhavati*[19] A similar statement is found in the *Taittirīyopaniṣad* conveying the same sense – *udaram antaraṁ kurute atha tasya bhayaṁ bhavati.*[20] The original duality is the duality between the individual, *jīva,* and Īśvara, the Lord, *jīveśvara-dvaita,* meaning that Īśvara is something other than you. This *dvaita* makes you small. If Īśvara is everything else, you become whatever is left out. Naturally, then, you become small. Everything else is infinitely large and you are small. And, once this original *dvaita* is there, there is the *dvaita* between one individual and another, *jīva-jīva-dvaita* and between the *jīva* and the world, *jīva-jagat-dvaita.*

---

19 *Bṛhadāraṇyakopaniṣad* 1.4.2

20 *Taittirīyopaniṣad* 2.7.1

Now, if the duality between *jīva* and *jīva* and between *jīva* and *jagat* is real, then the duality between *jīva* and Īśvara is also real. Why? Because, if the *jīva-jīva dvaita* and the *jīva-jagat dvaita* are real, there must be an Īśvara other than this *jagat*. Then that Īśvara is just another person, like any other *jīva*, and between him and the other *jīva*s, including myself, there will be a difference. Also, between all these *anātma*s and myself there will be difference. All the way there is difference, there being *dvaita* between the *jīva*s, the *jagat*, and Īśvara. If there is *dvaita* between these three – *dvaita* between the *jīva*s, between the *jīva* and the *jagat*, and between *jagat* and Īśvara – then your isolation is established. Mortality is established, imperfection is established, inadequacy is established all of which are accompanied by fear, greed, pain, sorrow and so on.

Since ego implies isolation, behind every crime there is ego. But Kṛṣṇa is talking about the *yogī* who has pricked the bubble of this ego. The bubble, ego, is no longer there; one ocean alone is there. Ego is ignorance based, ignorance of *ātmā*. Once the ignorance of *ātmā* is gone, all that remains is one *ātmā*, which is *paraṁ-brahma*. There is no ego anymore. And, when the ego is not there, where is the question of the person doing anything improper? The person abides in Īśvara alone, *mayi eva vartate*. But for the sake of argument, you can say that the person can do anything he or she likes. Even though the person still does various things, whatever these may be or however they are done, the person remains in me alone. This is *śāstra*.

When the Lord says, 'remaining in me alone,' it means that the person is never separate from him. In other words, the person and the Lord are one and the same. A person who has this equal vision everywhere has no necessity to do things that are not in keeping with *dharma*. The person naturally sees that what is *sukha* for him or her is also *sukha* for others and what is *duḥkha* for him or her is *duḥkha* for other people as well.

However, will the person who has this vision not compromise it in any way? After all, most people understand that what makes them happy or unhappy affects others in the same way, yet, they do not always behave according to *dharma*. Suppose something becomes so important to this person, is it not possible that the vision will be set aside, temporarily at least? In fact, this problem will not arise because, for the person who has this vision, there is no notion that 'I am limited.' There is knowledge that the same *ātmā* is in all beings and all beings are in oneself, *ātmā*, alone. The ego for this person is *bādhita*, sublated. It is no more taken as real.

Therefore, this person is one for whom *ahiṁsā* is natural, which is, in fact, the spirit of *sannyāsa*. A person who has this clear vision of *ātmā*, who is naturally, spontaneously, given to *ahiṁsā*, who no longer needs to practice *ahiṁsā* deliberately because it is his or her very nature, is described here as the most exalted, *parama* among *yogī*s.

A second interpretation of the verse

We can look at this verse in another way using the option offered by the word '*vā*' as 'or,' by adding this *vā*, or, to *sukha* and *duḥkha* – *sukhaṁ yadi vā duḥkham*. Here, situations are categorised in a two-fold way, those producing *sukha* and those producing *duḥkha*, both of which the wise person looks at equally, *samaṁ paśyati*. It means that, for the person, *sukha* and *duḥkha* are the same. Why, because one looks at them both with the example of oneself alone. *Ātmā* being the example, the basis of measurement, the matrix of judgement, the person sees that which is equal in both *sukha* and *duḥkha*.

How is this possible? Because the person understands the nature of *ātmā* as fullness, wholeness, and from this basis, one looks at *sukha* and *duḥkha*. Both are within that fullness alone. This does not mean that the person does not meet with situations producing *sukha* and *duḥkha*. The point being made here is that the person looks at all situations, even the *duḥkha* of death, from the basis of *ātmā* alone. Because the person knows oneself, *ātmā* as fullness there is no ripple of reaction whatever is the situation. To put it another way, when *sukha* comes, the person's fullness does not increase and when *duḥkha* comes, the fullness does not decrease, meaning that the person is always with Īśvara, *mayi eva vartate*. There is no situation which is going to take the person away from Īśvara.

This is the connection with the previous verse where it was said, 'Whatever the person does, *sarvathā vartamānaḥ api*.' There is no question of the person 'being away from me, Īśvara' or 'forgetting me,' because of any situation involving *duḥkha* or *sukha*. Why? Because *ātmā* is the example, *upamā*, the basis for the person, the *ātmā* that is *aham*, 'I.'

Previously, it was pointed out that *ātmā* is Parameśvara, *paramātmā*. Therefore, *paramātmā* is the *upamā*, the example, for the person who comes to bear upon all situations with the fullness that is the nature of *ātmā*. This particular interpretation is in keeping with the example of the river and the ocean in the second chapter of the *Gītā*, which says:

आपूर्यमाणमचलप्रतिष्ठं समुद्रमापः प्रविशन्ति यद्वत् ।
तद्वत्कामा यं प्रविशन्ति सर्वे स शान्तिमाप्नोति न कामकामी ॥७० ॥

āpūryamāṇam acalapratiṣṭhaṁ
samudram āpaḥ praviśanti yadvat
tadvatkāmā yaṁ praviśanti sarve
sa śāntim āpnoti na kāmakāmī (2.70)[21]

Apūryamāṇa means fullness, that which is completely filled from all sides, like the ocean, *samudra*. *Acala* means that the ocean remains in its own glory and does not move around. *Pratiṣṭha* is that which is well- rooted, meaning the ocean is well-rooted in its own glory.

Into this ocean, waters enter, *āpaḥ praviṣanti*, from different directions. Is the ocean affected in any way by this event? Does the oceanness increase? No. And if no waters enter for a time, because of drought, etc., the oceanness also does not decrease. Oceans do not dry up; nor do they overflow. Such situations simply do not occur.

Fullness depends on nothing

This example is a good one in terms of the fullness that is the nature of *ātmā*; the example holds water in other words! Whether the waters enter or do not enter, the ocean always remains the same. The oceanness does not depend upon any other source of water to be ocean. Similarly here, the *yogī*, a wise person, who is *ananta*, does not depend for his or her fullness upon a given situation. Whatever happens, *sukha* or

---

[21] Refer to Volume 2 - page 399

duḥkha, the person sees them both equally; therefore he or she remains tranquil, *sa śāntim āpnoti.* Whatever objects, *kāma*s enter, from whatever direction, through the gates of the five sense organs, they do not disturb the person at all, just as the ocean is not disturbed by the waters.

Whereas, the person who is a desirer of various objects, *kāmakāmī,* who is dependent upon their presence or absence for his or her happiness, is likened to a pond. If too much water comes in the form of rain or floods, you do not see the pond at all, and if there is no rain, it dries up altogether. Similarly, the *kāmakāmī* is like a yo-yo; if something desirable comes along, he or she goes up and if it is something undesirable, the person goes down. However, for the *yogī* discussed here, there is no yo-yo because he or she remains with me, the self, alone. Whatever the tragedy, even if it meets the classical orthodox definition of a genuine tragedy, the person remains the same. This is the *yogī* Kṛṣṇa is discussing here in keeping with the previous verse.

So, two interpretations are possible here – the *yogī* remains the same in any situation, whether it be *sukha* or *duḥkha* and the *yogī* looks upon others as one looks upon oneself. This being so, the person will not perform a wrong action. To treat others as you would have them treat you is applicable to everyone, in fact. Every human being is supposed to live this way, what to talk of a *yogī* !

No one can hurt another without getting hurt in the process, even though it may sometimes seem to be otherwise. We see this even in tennis matches. You begin with 'love' and then you fight to win. And, when you do win, you are ecstatic.

On the way to the net to shake hands with your opponent, you jump up and down and throw your racket into the air. You are very happy, until you see the other person's sadness in having lost. Then, all your joy goes. Do you know why? Because no human heart was ever made that cannot empathise with a person who is sad.

You know what it is to be on the other side of the net because you, too, have had days like that. Therefore, you cannot but pick up the other person's sadness immediately. Why, because you can never hurt another without getting hurt in the process. It is just not possible. We think that people given to crime have such hardened hearts that they can automatically do harm to others, but this is not true. Even psychopaths have their spells of empathy because of how the human heart is.

All human beings must follow the order of dharma

That you cannot hurt another without being hurt in the process is a fact for which there is a very simple rule – all human beings must follow what we call the order of *dharma*. This is the common basis for everyone, although it is not commonly pursued because of a fundamental insecurity. This fundamental insecurity is the human problem. The insecure person acts in unbecoming ways because there are priorities for the person, based on likes and dislikes. Wherever these priorities are, there will be confusion in terms of values, unless the person frees oneself from the sense of being small. The person who does this sees the sameness in all beings always, *sarvatra samaṁ paśyati* It is very clear to such a person that whatever is good for oneself, is good for others also. This is the *yogī* whom Kṛṣṇa praises here.

Even a mature person who tries to follow *dharma* will breach it now and again because some priority or other will always be there. Thus, you find that there is legitimate criticism, legitimate hurting. Because you cannot always take the hurt, sometimes you will hurt back, and this is considered to be legitimate in human interaction. Only a *jñānī* is able to view *sukha* and *duḥkha* in the same manner. Therefore, only a *jñānī* can be free, which is why with reference to all people, he or she is considered to be the most exalted, *sa yogī paramo mataḥ*.

So, we have these two ways of looking at the verse – the first in keeping with the *śāstra* and the other in terms of behaviour. One refers to the vision of the person and the other is expression in one's interaction.

Having said this much, the topic of *dhyāna-yoga*, meditation, contemplation, is complete. In fact, Kṛṣṇa has actually covered the topic twice, in two different ways. Thinking that he had done a good job Kṛṣṇa may have sat back a bit. Seeing that Kṛṣṇa had finished, Arjuna thinks it is a good time to ask a question, and does so in the next two verses.

Verses 33&34

The nature of Arjuna's problem is very clear

अर्जुन उवाच ।
योऽयं योगस्त्वया प्रोक्तः साम्येन मधुसूदन ।
एतस्याहं न पश्यामि चञ्चलत्वात् स्तिथिं स्थिराम् ॥ ३३ ॥

arjuna uvāca
yo'yaṁ yogastvayā proktaḥ sāmyena madhusūdana
etasyāhaṁ na paśyāmi cañcalatvāt stithiṁ sthirām (33)

arjunaḥ – Arjuna; *uvāca* – said; *madhusūdana* – O slayer of Madhu (Kṛṣṇa)!; *tvayā* – by you; *sāmyena* – as sameness; *yaḥ ayaṁ yogaḥ* – this *yoga*; *proktaḥ* – which was talked about; *etasya* – of this; *sthirām* – steady; *sthitim* – state (vision); *cañcalatvāt* – due to agitation; *aham* – I; *na paśyāmi* – do not see

Arjuna said:

Madhusūdana (Kṛṣṇa)! This *yoga* that you have talked about as sameness, I do not see its steady vision due to agitation (of the mind).

Here, Arjuna presents his problem, saying that this vision of sameness that Kṛṣṇa had just talked about was not as simple as it seemed, given the condition of his own mind. He describes his mind as agitated, *cañcala*. In fact later he is going to say, 'agitation is mind.' Because of this agitation, Arjuna does not think that there is any such thing as a steady vision of sameness and, even if there were, it would be very difficult to deal with his mind in order to gain such a vision.

Arjuna presents a problem that everyone can identify with, one that is very common for anyone who has a mind. What Kṛṣṇa had taught thus far seemed to have gone into Arjuna's head, but still he has a very valid doubt. For him, the whole teaching seems to boil down to two things – the mind that is composed and steady is the proper receptacle for this knowledge, and the knowledge had to be clear. This clarity could perhaps be gained easily by proper enquiry, and so on, if the mind were composed and steady. Therefore, Arjuna's question relates to the means for making the mind steady.

He finds his mind very turbulent. He also says that, it has its own roots. This proves that what is considered to be modern psychology can also be found in the *Gītā*. The mind does not seem to follow any rational way of operating. One may reason very clearly about how silly the mind can be, but still it has its own roots and its own modes of thinking. Therefore, Arjuna is asking, in a sense, whether there is a means, *upāya,* for making this mind steady enough to gain the knowledge.

How does one gain the mind that can gain the vision?

Introducing Arjuna's question, Śaṅkara indicates that the *yoga* Kṛṣṇa has been discussing thus far, that is, seeing the sameness in everything, has the status of being difficult to gain. Seeing that it is difficult to gain – *yathoktasya samyag-darśana-lakṣaṇasya yogasya duḥkha sampādyatām ālakṣya* – Arjuna wants to know the ways and means of gaining a mind that will easily assimilate this knowledge. That which is common in everything, the truth of everything, is called *samyag-darśana* or *ātma-darśana,* the vision of the sameness that is Brahman, that is *ātmā*. Because this vision is gained through the mind, Arjuna wants to know how to gain that particular frame of mind through which the knowledge could be gained.

Arjuna addresses Kṛṣṇa as Madhusūdana, meaning the destroyer of Madhu, the name of a demon Kṛṣṇa had slain. Madhu also means honey and is another name for the ego, *ahaṅkāra,* in Sanskrit. Everyone loves his or her own ego and wants to fatten it up, it seems. As a teacher, Kṛṣṇa was capable of destroying the *ahaṅkāra,* the false ego, with right knowledge and which is why Arjuna addresses him as Madhusūdana here.

Arjuna wants Kṛṣṇa to know that he does not think he could have this abiding vision of sameness. Occasionally, he might gain a little insight, but he knows that his mind does not remain steady for very long. Not only does Arjuna not see how this vision could remain steady, but he also knows the reason. It is because his mind is always in a state of agitation, *cañcalatvāt*. Because his mind is always in this state, he does not see the possibility of an abiding vision. The mind seems to have its own logic, its own roots, and even though he might gain some knowledge, that knowledge seems to have its own quarters, with no connection between the two. Naturally, then, Arjuna wants to know what could be done about this.

Arjuna says – mind is agitation

चञ्चलं हि मनः कृष्ण प्रमाथि बलवद्दृढम् ।
तस्याहं निग्रहं मन्ये वायोरिव सुदुष्करम् ॥ ३४ ॥

cañcalaṁ hi manaḥ Kṛṣṇa pramāthi balavad dṛḍham
tasyāhaṁ nigrahaṁ manye vāyoriva suduṣkaram (34)

Kṛṣṇa – O Kṛṣṇa !; *hi* – in fact; *manaḥ* – mind; *cañcalam* – is agitation; *pramāthi* – tyrant; *balavat* – strong; *dṛḍham* – well rooted; *aham* – I; *tasya* – of it; *nigraham* – control; *vāyoḥ iva* – as the wind; *suduṣkaram* – too difficult (impossible) to do; *manye* – think

> In fact, Kṛṣṇa! The mind is 'agitation,' a strong, well-rooted tyrant. I think of it as impossible to control as the wind.

Using a rather long compound, Saṅkara defines Kṛṣṇa here as *bhakta-jana-pāpādi-doṣa-ākarṣaṇaḥ*, one who removes, *ākarṣati,* all the limitations, *doṣa,* such as sins, etc., *pāpādi,* of people who are his devotees, *bhakta-jana*s. This is why the Lord is called Kṛṣṇa in the *Gītā.*

The words *pramāthi, balavat,* and *dṛḍha* are attributes of the mind that Arjuna talks about. Not only is the mind *cañcala,* it is also a tyrant, *pramāthi,* that which shakes one up. To say that the mind is agitated is not enough. In fact, mind is agitation.

The mind has the capacity to bring one's senses, body, reason, everything, under its control; it just takes charge of everything. One's reason does not seem to have any say over this mind. For instance, no one volitionally wants to become sad, but one is sad. No one wants to be angry, but one is angry. Emotions like sorrow and anger are conditions of the mind and seem to have a hold over the person. One's culture, upbringing, status, and knowledge do not seem to have any say when one is angry.

In fact, one's culture seems to be totally forgotten and an entirely new language emerges, one that is not found in any dictionary. This language, although generally understood by everyone, since everyone uses it occasionally, is usually kept suppressed. Culture implies language, but when a person becomes angry and uses such unbecoming, unexpected language, the person's culture is gone. No matter how refined and cultured, no matter how manicured and pedicured, all the culture the person has ever cultivated is nowhere to be seen in moments of anger.

The person's knowledge also is not available at such times. Everyone knows very well that sadness does not produce a desirable result. The sadder one is the more problems one has. No one has solved any problem through sorrow. This is all very clear, very rational, as Kṛṣṇa himself had said when he first began his dialogue with Arjuna saying, 'You grieve for those who should not be grieved for and yet you speak words of wisdom – *aśocyān anvaśocastvaṁ prajñāvādān ca bhāṣase.*'

Everyone knows this and other people also tell you. But sadness seems to be something that does not take your permission. If it did, you would definitely not give it. Who wants to be sad? Only when permission is sought is there a question of you granting it or not.

Sadness means there is a particular type of thinking going on; without thinking, you cannot be sad. Sadness is not like hunger, thirst, or sleep. Without thinking you become hungry, without thinking you go to sleep, especially after a big meal. And, in the morning, without thinking you are as hungry as a wolf. So, to be hungry you do not have to think, whereas to be sad you do. In fact, to be sad, angry, hateful, agitated, depressed, frustrated, you need to think a lot.

The mind is dṛḍha – it keeps one under its control

The mind is very much present, at the same time, it does not take your permission. This implies two people here, one who is highly cultured, educated, sophisticated, and very considerate, and whose language, style, demeanour and decorum are quite different from the other person, the angry person.

This person seems to have a parallel life, occupying the same mind and the same place, but this person seems to have his or her own roots and definitely seems to be in charge. And when this person takes charge, everything is gone. This is what is called *pramāthin* here, a tyrant that can disturb and take control of the body, mind, senses, everything.

One may now ask, 'If it takes charge like this, why not take control of it with some other greater force? After all, if someone wants to control me, I can also control that person. All I require is to reinforce myself properly with enough weapons, enough strength. Then I can regain control. But this kind of reinforcement does not work here. Whatever strength I manage to muster for myself to control this *pramāthin* is not adequate. The other always seems to be stronger. It controls me and it is strong, *balavat*. Its hold is so strong that I cannot wrench myself away from its control. I cannot even wriggle out of it. Nor can anyone else get out from under it either.

Arjuna describes the mind as *dṛḍha* here, meaning that it keeps one under its control, just like the silk that winds around the worm, keeping it inside the cocoon until it grows adequately to come out. *Dṛḍha* also can be translated as well-rooted. The mind has its own roots that seem to be so deep that nothing is strong enough to uproot it. Storms generally uproot things, but this mind cannot be uprooted by any storm. No amount of brainstorming can do it.

The mind has its roots in childhood and has picked up all kinds of problems from childhood onwards. As a child, one's perceptions are limited. And, to those perceptions, others are added along the way. Thus, there is a core personality with a lot of added embellishments. Together, they seem to be a person, someone, who is altogether different, whom we call the mind, the psychological mind. It is this psychological mind, the emotional mind, that Arjuna is talking about here, the mind that is *dṛḍha*, the well-rooted mind that controls everything. To control such a mind, Arjuna says, is something he considers to be very difficult to do, *tasya ahaṁ nigrahaṁ manye suduṣkaram*.

Duṣkara means 'difficult' and *suduṣkara* means 'very difficult.' Arjuna compares any attempt to control the mind with trying to catch the air in one's hand, *vāyoh iva suduṣkaram*. The air is not available for catching; therefore, to control it is impossible. Even if you try to trap the mind somewhere, like you can trap air, you cannot do it because the mind would always be outside of the trap you set for it. It would just look at you, almost teasing you.

Is this not what happens? You think you have given the mind a job to do, like chanting a *mantra*, 'Come on, turbulent mind, chant, okay?' Then you think that the mind is doing it, until you find that it is outside somewhere! The mind may have taken you so far away that you do not know how long you were there or remember what you were doing before. Somewhere, the mind trips you up and then takes you for a ride. It is so elusive that you cannot even set a trap for it, which is why the mind is compared to a monkey.

Therefore, to have to do something with this mind is no small job, Arjunja said. And he lived in an era where stress was not the concern it is today, since the society was not under so much pressure as it is today. Arjuna had a lot of leisure and did not have all the hurry that you have today. Yet, he had a mind, albeit a very cultured mind, that was *cañcala*. And if Arjuna's mind was *cañcala*, you can imagine what the mind of his cousin Duryodhana must have been like. Arjuna, at least, had no conflicts because he did not live a life of *adharma*. He lived a clean life, an unquestionable life, which meant that he slept well because he did not nurse any guilt inside. Whereas, Duryodhana was a guilty person from head to foot, with all the conflicts that goes with a life of *adharma*.

Arjuna was a man given to a life of *dharma*, right conduct, right values, and great achievements too. Thus, there was nothing for him to smart or feel spiteful about. He was successful in all his pursuits and had a lot of titles showered upon him. In other words, he was a master of his age, a man who, on any given day, could be proud of his life and his achievements. Everyone in the society looked up to Arjuna, even before the great war of *Mahābhārata* took place. He was a versatile person, a man of music, dance, archery, and other disciplines of knowledge. He was a great warrior and also a prince. But, even with all these qualifications, Arjuna's mind was *cañcala*.

Arjuna's problem is universal

If Arjuna's mind was nothing but agitation, what about those minds given to the modern phenomenon called stress? Something happens in Iran and, having read about it in the morning paper, you are already upset before you even have your shower! Anyone living in today's world, where the input is so much, can identify with Arjuna's problem and ask the same question. The problem is very well-known, as Saṅkara also confirms. In Arjuna's time the question was relevant. In Saṅkara's time it was relevant. And today it is relevant. In fact, the nature of the mind being what it is, it will always be relevant. Therefore, you have to know the ways of the mind by paying attention to it and gain certain mastery.

In the next verse, Kṛṣṇa answers Arjuna's question about how to manage the mind.

Verses 35&36

The mind is mastered by practice and objectivity

श्रीभगवानुवाच ।
असंशयं महाबाहो मनो दुर्निग्रहं चलम् ।
अभ्यासेन तु कौन्तेय वैराग्येण च गृह्यते ॥ ३५ ॥

śrībhagavān uvāca
asaṁśayaṁ mahābāho mano durnigrahaṁ calam
abhyāsena tu kaunteya vairāgyeṇa ca gṛhyate (35)

śrībhagavān – Lord Kṛṣṇa; *uvāca* – said;
mahābāho – O mighty armed (Arjuna)!; *asaṁśayam* – no doubt; *manaḥ* – mind; *durnigraham* – difficult to master; *calam* – is agitated; *tu* – but; *kaunteya* – O son of Kunti (Arjuna)!; *abhyāsena* – by practice; *ca* – and; *vairāgyeṇa* – by objectivity; *gṛhyate* – is mastered

Śrī Bhagavān said:

No doubt, Arjuna, the mighty armed! the mind is agitated and difficult to master. But, Kaunteya (Arjuna)! it is mastered by practice and objectivity.

Here, Kṛṣṇa first addresses Arjuna as '*mahābāho*, O Mighty armed!' Being a great warrior, Arjuna was of course considered to be mighty. But his might, his strength, should include his mastery over his mind. One's strength may be useful for knocking the heads of others, but it is not enough to take care of one's own silly mind. Kṛṣṇa confirms this here by saying, *asaṁśayaṁ*, 'no doubt,' indicating that there was no doubt that the mind is restless and difficult to master.

Who says the mind is not restless? To recognise that the mind is restless is to have won half the battle. Suppose someone tells me that his or her mind is agitated and I say that getting agitated is not good at all, that it does not solve anything and therefore do not get agitated. All that will happen is that the person will become more agitated! What use is such advice? It is not as though the person wants to get agitated. Therefore, this particular advice is useless. Telling someone not to get agitated does not help at all. Whereas, if I accept agitation as the nature of the mind, half the battle is won.

Acceptance is the first step

In the programme of recovery sponsored by Alcoholics Anonymous, the first step is for the person to say that he or she has no power over alcohol. This has to be accepted first; otherwise, there is no hope of recovery. The same thing is true with everything, not just alcohol. I have no power over anger. I have no power over this restless mind. When I accept this, then half the battle is won.

Kṛṣṇa accepts this one great psychological fact, that the nature of the mind is agitation. You do not try to remove the agitation; you simply accept that it is agitation. Do not get agitated over agitation, thinking that it is something you are going to solve. Also, do not think that your mind is something peculiar, because, it is not. Any mind is agitation. Agitation is the nature of the mind because the mind has to change, it is meant to change. Try to imagine a mind that has a constant thought. A constant thought means that you cannot see anything else. Ten miles ago, you saw one tree, and still the tree is right in front of you! Nothing else is there, no car, no person, nothing. You would not even survive with such a mind.

The mind must necessarily change. Just as in a movie, the frame must always be changing at a certain speed for you to be able to see objects, movement, etc., here too, the mind has to keep changing all the time so that you can see. This is why the mind is called *kṣaṇika*. One particular thought is always *kṣaṇika*, meaning that it does not even last for a second. Just to say the word 'second,' involves so many parts, so many frames, so many changes, all of which are *kṣaṇika*. This is the nature of the *vṛtti*, the thought. Even to recognise this fact, the mind has to be *kṣaṇika*.

Since the nature of the mind is *kṣaṇika*, naturally it is going to change. Therefore, Kṛṣṇa says, 'There is no doubt about it, Arjuna, the mind is *cala, cañcala*, restless.' *Cala* also means agitation. 'And, being *cala*, it is very difficult to control, *manaḥ durnigrahaṁ calam*,' he said. In other words, he agrees with what Arjuna has said about the mind, that it is as difficult to have mastery over the mind as over the wind. By repeating what Arjuna has said, he is saying that the nature of the mind should be accepted as such. Accept the fact that the mind is agitation, that it has its own roots, its own logic, and therefore it is never illogical.

We always think the mind is illogical, but that is not correct. The mind does have its own logic. If we suddenly think of something, we think that the thought has come from nowhere. But it has not come from nowhere; it has come from somewhere, meaning there is some logic for it. But why, when nothing has happened outside, when everything is calm, do I suddenly have this thought? It simply means that outside situations are not required for a thought to occur. I have enough going on inside for this to happen! Why, for example, in the midst of meditation, do I suddenly think of okras?[22] And why, when I am talking and wanting to come up with some funny word, did this word 'okra' come to me? There must be some logic for it. The point here is that whatever suddenly occurs in my head has its own logic.

There is nothing illogical in this world; there is always some logic. What is illogical, we find there is logic, that is,when something occurs, there is some reason for it. We must understand, then, that the mind is like this; it is its nature.

Does it mean that I should leave the mind as it is? I could say, 'Yes; the mind is agitation. Forget about it. Do not worry about it.' The problem, however, is that when the mind is agitation, I am agitation. Therefore, I have to learn to discover the distance between the mind and 'I.' This is the whole trick

---

[22] Okras, also known as lady's finger, is a flowering plant in the Mallow family.

here, which is why Kṛṣṇa tells Arjuna that the mind can be mastered by practice and objectivity, *abhyāsena tu kaunteya vairāgyeṇa ca gṛhyate*

Caring for the child within

By addressing Arjuna here as Kaunteya, the son of Kunti, Kṛṣṇa is indicating that the child was still there in Arjuna, which is where the mind has its roots. This child needs to be taken care of by the adult. Therefore, there is double child care. When you were a child, someone else took care of you, but now you have to take care of your inner child. The first child care is done by your parents or other adults, whereas this inner child care must be done by the person. Everyone nurses a child inside and that child has to be taken care of; everyone needs to do it.

There is always a child who was disappointed in his or her perceptions, 'My mother does not like me. My father hates me.' These were the child's perceptions and, because of the behaviour of the people involved, they have some validity. This is why the child remains inside the person. There is always a crying child, a weeping child, down below, which is why the mind suddenly takes off, especially when you reach the age of 35 years and over. This is the time that all the disappointments of the child come out one by one. And when you begin to study Vedanta they all come out!

Studying Vedanta means that you look at yourself. Previously, you were doing other things. Looking at yourself is the first thing that must be done here, which is when the child comes out. When else will this child be taken care of? It has to be taken care of; it has to be addressed. Otherwise, you become 75 years old and are still a child. This is the point Kṛṣṇa is making here by calling Arjuna as Kaunteya. First, he refers to Arjuna as an adult, *mahābāho,* and then asks him to take care of the child by addressing him as Kaunteya. Kṛṣṇa then tells Arjuna how this is to be done, saying that by practice and objectivity the mind can be mastered, *abhyāsena vairāgyena ca gṛhyate.*

What is *abhyāsa,* practice? It is the practice of *yoga* just discussed by Kṛṣṇa through which a certain distance is gained between your mind and yourself. This distance enables you to look at yourself positively, to see yourself exactly as you are, to see what the nature of 'I' is. In this way, you come to understand that every thought is you, no doubt, but that you are free from thought. Seeing this particular fact more and more, seeing it inside very clearly, is what is meant by *abhyāsa,* practice. Seeing this particular situation, thought being 'I,' while 'I' is not any thought, is what is called *nididhyāsana.* And doing the same thing again and again is called *abhyāsa,* which enables you to gain mastery over your mind, *abhyāsena gṛhyate.*

Practice and usefulness of japa

Here the practice, *abhyāsa,* of *japa* can also be included. Because the mind's nature is not predictable, what your next thought will be is also not predictable. It can be anything. Since the next thought can be anything, which you cannot predict what it will be, you create a predictable situation. Only then can you understand how the mind moves, and so on. In this way, you get to have certain hold over the mind, over the thinking process itself. This is why the mental repetition of a given *mantra*, a meaningful name, word, or sentence, called *japa*, is a must and is never given up, even by a *sannyāsī*.

A *brahmacārī* has a *mantra*, a *gṛhastha* has a *mantra*, a *vānaprastha* has a *mantra*, and a *sannyāsī* also has a *mantra*. There is no one who is without a word that is meaningful, either chosen by the person or given to that person. A particular *mantra* is important because it gives you certain hold. That is why *japa* is common to all traditions; it gives you this particular capacity of knowing exactly what is going to happen next. It is the only situation where the mind is predictable.

Even when you find yourself dwelling upon a particular object, you do not know what your next thought is going to be. And when you decided to dwell upon a given object, to enquire into it, you are not very clear about how the enquiry is going to proceed. Whereas, here, repetition being what it is, you have a definite occupation. This gives you a handle over the mind so that when it moves away, you understand what is happening. Again and again, you bring it back to the object of meditation.

Here, *ātmā* is 'as though' the object of meditation in order to make the mind abide in the *ātmā*, to make the mind *ātma-saṁstha*. This *abhyāsa*, practice, is the meditation that is in keeping with the teaching.

The repetition itself is called *abhyāsa*. Even in Sanskrit grammar, *abhyāsa* means duplication. Because of this *abhyāsa*, you learn the ways of the mind; you come to have some insight about it. In this particular *abhyāsa*, even the object of distraction becomes an object of meditation, as discussed earlier. Wherever the mind goes, there I turn my attention, *yatra yatra mano yāti tatra tatra samādhayaḥ*. Turning the attention from one thing to another becomes contemplation in which the attention moves from the object to the very basis of the object, *ātmā*. Therefore, there is no real distraction.

In this way, the distance between the thought and the self becomes very clear – that the thought is not everything; thought is imbued with the self. And, if I turn my attention towards the self, it becomes contemplation. I appreciate the self as independent of the thought. The more I appreciate this fact, thought becomes purely a role; it is not taken as everything. This is the distance that I come to know, a distance that does not imply physical distance or a particular condition of the mind. It is insight, appreciation itself, and this appreciation becomes the reality. This is the practice that Kṛṣṇa says would enable one to master the mind.

Vairāgya – objectivity

The second means for making the mind abide in itself, mentioned here by Kṛṣṇa, is *vairāgya*, objectivity. Why does the mind go here and there in the first place? The mind goes elsewhere purely due to lack of interest. The nature of the mind is to go wherever there is some kick, wherever there is something more interesting. Some interest must be there and towards that it goes. So, without your trying to dwell upon anything in particular, the mind naturally goes towards the objects that it finds more interesting.

The mind goes towards an object of love and towards an object of pain also, since pain means that something requires attention. These are the two places towards which the mind goes without any effort on your part. Why? Because one is interesting and the other requires attention. In an object of love there is some joy, pleasantness to which the mind naturally goes. And, towards any object that hurts you or has hurt you, the mind also goes quite naturally. One is positive, whereas the other, being something that requires attention, is negative.

Objects of pain can be taken care of by *abhyāsa*, whereas *vairāgya* is with reference to objects of love. By *abhyāsa*, certain distance can be developed between you and the pain, although this may take some time. *Vairāgya* is mentioned here separately because the source of all desires for happiness and security is what we call *śobhanādhyāsa*, meaning that you superimpose certain attributes upon various objects in the world, and then think these will bring you happiness and security. That a particular object is going to make you more secure is one such attribute. Or, by achieving this or that, you are going to be different; you are going to become somebody. You are going to be acceptable to yourself and to others; first to others and thereby to yourself.

We seek acceptance from others because of superimposition

Seeking acceptability from others is nothing but self-acceptance through others. Why should anyone accept you? So that you can accept yourself. Therefore, seeking the acceptance of others can always be reduced to self-acceptance.

Whether you seek the acceptance of others or you seek self-acceptance, it amounts to self-acceptance alone. Thus, either you seek acceptance through others or you yourself understand that you do not accept yourself and try to find out whether the self is acceptable, which is the real way of dealing with the problem, in fact.

Seeking self-acceptance, then, we superimpose certain attributes upon objects, thinking that a particular object is capable of giving something more than it can really give. Superimposing attributes that do not belong to the objects is what we call *adhyāsa*. When what is superimposed, *adhyasta*, is something positive, according to our thinking, it is called *śobhanādhyāsa* meaning that which is very pleasing, for which there is certain enchantment and infatuation. This infatuation or obsession is nothing but a superimposition, *śobhanādhyāsa*.

The absence of *śobhanādhyāsa* is what is meant by *vairāgya*. *Vairāgya* enables you to separate the objective attributes of any object from the subjective superimpositions you may have placed upon it. When superimposed attributes are understood as attributes that are superimposed, the object is reduced to its own status.

For instance, to think that the absence of money makes you a nobody is not true. The absence of money makes you money-less, that's all. It is a fact, the absence of money makes you money-less. Money-less, you cannot buy things, is another fact, which can be followed yet by more facts. That you cannot buy is true and that you cannot buy on credit is also true, since you have no money to pay later. Even if you buy on credit and do not pay it back, the time will come when you cannot buy on credit either. Who is going to give you credit if you do not pay? Endlessly, then, you can talk about facts.

That I am a nobody is not a fact; it is a superimposition. The feeling of being a nobody is something very intimate because one has a stereotype of success, a conditioning that takes place by growing up in a society where money is respected with awe and wonder. In such a society, a person's success is talked about only in terms of money. To value money in this way is meaningless, really. Any mafia don, mercenary or hit man, may also have lot of money. Just because a person has money does not mean that the person is successful. Nevertheless, this is the orientation of some societies in the world.

There is also another orientation that to be money-less is something wonderful. This orientation holds that without money one should be able to live one's life. Therefore, the person who lives without money, even a beggar who lives in the streets, is highly praised. This orientation is equally silly. Both orientations place a value on money, which is a problem. The problem is not the money itself; money is just money. It is neither the problem, nor the solution, although money can solve some problems, like anything else. Even a toothpick can solve certain problems.

The superimposition is not deliberate

Therefore, to think that money is the source of the problem is not correct. There is a superimposition here, which is not deliberately done by a person, but is something innate in a psyche that is exposed to certain value structure obtaining in a given society, causing the person to place an attribute on money that is not really there. This superimposition, *śobhanādhyāsa*, has to be neutralised by looking at money as money is, and nothing more. To say that money has no value is just another *adhyāsa*. You are seeing something that is not true. Similarly, if you add something more to money than is really there, it is also *adhyāsa*. Reducing the objects to their own status is enough. By doing this, you will find in yourself certain dispassion, which is *vairāgya*.

A person is dispassionate in the sense one is objective in one's judgements. *Vairāgya* is understood more in terms of objectivity. Unless we understand its meaning clearly, there will be more problems. It does not mean that there are no desires. To think so means that every desire becomes a new source of problems! We are not creating ideals here, which would only further distance us from ourselves. Therefore, we must be careful not to pick up any further confusion here. *Vairāgya* means to be free of the longing that implies superimposition, *śobhanādhyāsa*. This is accomplished by neutralising the *śobhanādhyāsa*, thereby judging situations properly.

Neutralising the superimposition

Any object of liking can become an object of obsession, sooner or later, and therefore, a problem. There are books being written today about people who love too much, meaning they cannot love at all. Because they cannot keep an object of love in its proper perspective, it becomes a problem for them. The object of love can consume a person so completely that it becomes an obsession, leading to attempts to control, vying for position and so on.

To neutralise *śobhanādhyāsa,* you need to understand the difference between the objective value and the subjective imposition of values upon the object. How is it possible to see this difference? Śaṅkara defines *vairāgya* here as the capacity to repeatedly see the limitations in both the seen and unseen objects of enjoyment, meaning here and in the hereafter, *vairāgyaṁ nāma dṛṣṭa-adṛṣṭa-bhogeṣu doṣa-darśana-abhyāsāt vaitṛṣṇyam.*

Here, limitations refer to what a given object can and cannot give. Any object has some *guṇa*s, virtues, and *doṣa*s, defects or limitations. Therefore, you must see these limitations clearly. For example, money can buy, but it cannot make you enjoy. Seeing this is what makes you dispassionate. Once you are dispassionate, then your relationship with money is proper. It is an objective relationship, which is what we are talking about.

Seeing things as they are

The capacity to look at things as they are is called objectivity. There is no judgement involved here, just an understanding of things as they are. This objectivity is especially important in terms of our subjective values because we do not know the objects of these values as they really are. We are not concerned here with the physical structure of objects, only with the value we superimpose upon them.

When I look at a given object, I see that there are a lot of projections involved. Therefore, I see these projections for what they are and I deal with them. By separating them in this way, I can look more objectively at how the object is going to make my life any better than it is now. Doing this again and again is *abhyāsa* and seeing the limitations of the objects is *vairāgya*. Repetition is essential because the subjective value does not go away just like that. This is because the value is something that is not deliberately imposed upon the object by you.

Suppose you buy a piece of bronze, thinking it is an antique. In fact, it has been oxidised to make it look very old. An ear has been cut, the nose poked, and some scratches put on it to make it look as though it has fallen down a few times. All of this has been deliberately done to increase its value. And you buy it, thinking it is an ancient piece. And when you realise that it is not an antique, you are disappointed and experience a sense of loss. Now, what did you lose here? Only the subjective value that you had superimposed on it. The bronze does have a certain objective value. Thinking it is an antique, you had placed a subjective value on it. That subjective value has little or nothing to do with the objective value of the object. To think of a simple piece of bronze as something great is purely subjective, nothing more.

People do the same thing with blue jeans, buying new jeans that have been made to look old. These jeans may even come with patches! Why? To make it look as though you have been around, for which you are prepared to pay a higher price. Again, this is purely a subjective value. From this we can understand the difference between the objective and subjective value of an object.

Previously you looked at the piece of bronze as an antique and now, knowing it is not an antique, you look at it as bronze. The object itself is the same as when you bought it – it had no ear then and it has no ear now! Only in your look is there a change. For all you know, it may be an antique. Perhaps the person who told you that it is not, wants to take it off your hands and sell it for a fortune! If this were to happen, you would feel like a fool, if you find out, of course. In the realm of subjective value, anything is possible.

The point I am making here is that if the vision of the object as an antique goes away, then the attitude you will have is dispassion towards the object. If it is an antique, it is an antique; there is no problem. You simply look at it as an antique. That society has jacked up the price because of the subjective value placed upon it, need not concern you at all. Whereas, if you are an antique collector, everything about you becomes antique!

There are people who want to collect and own certain objects to the point that it becomes an obsession with them. They call it an investment, but they will not part with it. For something to be an investment, you have to be able to sell it, but they will not sell because they have developed such an attachment for the object. There is no investment here; there is only a new problem that has been created. Only when the antique *buddhi* goes away, when the person can look at the object objectively, can there be *vairāgya*.

Vairāgya is nothing but one's emotional growth

When a subjective value superimposed upon an object is gone, then the object is just the object. This holds for all objects. That there is *śobhanādhyāsa*, a superimposition that has taken place naturally, an extra attribute that does not really exist in the object, has to be recognised. Therefore, again and again, you see the object as it is. And, in the wake of this knowledge the superimpositions go.

This does not mean that you need to continually remind yourself, 'This is not an antique, this is not an antique.' Such a *japa* you need not do. But, with reference to money, power, and the acceptance of others, *abhyāsa* and *vairāgya* are both necessary. Seeing the limitations of objects and situations, over and over again, is very important if one is to master the mind. Repetition is necessary because the superimposition is not a deliberate thing; it is not a mistake that you have made by taking something to be more valuable than it is. If it were a mistake, a one-time correction is adequate. Then there is objectivity. But, here, it is not by a one-time mistake that there is superimposition. It is by your being what you are, a psychological being, very firmly rooted in terms of your concept of success.

All concepts of success and *vairāgya*, dispassion, are within the range of psychology alone. *Vairāgya* is nothing but the emotional growth of the person. Growth is strictly in terms of understanding the limitations of an object or situation, again and again, until the superimposition falls apart. Then the world does not have a hold over you. Otherwise, the mind runs towards certain objects naturally because they have been given such importance by the society.

There is some pain involved with reference to certain old objects – what you could not get before, what you have lost in the past – which can cause problems in the mind. Whereas, if *vairāgya* is there, the old failures, those things that were sources of some pain for you, fall apart and new objects also do not have any hold over you. This is what is meant by seeing the limitations, *doṣa-darśana*, again and again, thereby bringing about a cognitive change, which frees the mind to a greater extent.

This mind – that is always chattering, always preaching, that is in the form of agitation, being away from the *dhyeya*, object of meditation, *ātmā*–is difficult to master, can be mastered by *abhyāsa* and *vairāgya*. However, you cannot simply sit there and expect the mind to take care of itself. You have to pay some attention to it, as Kṛṣṇa says here.

असंयतात्मना योगो दुष्प्राप इति मे मतिः ।
वश्यात्मना तु यतता शक्योऽवाप्तुमुपायतः ॥ ३६ ॥

asaṁyatātmanā yogo duṣprāpa iti me matiḥ
vaśyātmanā tu yatatā śakyo'vāptum upāyataḥ (36)

asaṁyata-ātmanā – by the one for whom the mind is not mastered; *yogaḥ* – *yoga*; *duṣprāpaḥ* – difficult to gain; *iti* – thus; *me* – my; *matiḥ* – vision; *tu* – whereas; *vaśyātmanā* – by the one whose mind is mastered; *yatatā* – by the one who makes effort;

upāyataḥ – with proper means; (that is, practice and objectivity); *avāptuṁ śakyaḥ* – (it) can be gained

> *Yoga* is difficult to gain for the one by whom the mind is not mastered. This is my vision. Whereas it can be gained by the one whose mind is mastered, who makes effort with the proper means (that is, practice and objectivity).

One who does not practice meditation, *abhyāsa*, and who does not have objectivity, *vairāgya,* is called *asaṁyata-ātmā* in this verse, meaning that the mind is not brought under control. Can the mind be brought under control? Yes, Kṛṣṇa says, but with difficulty; it is *duṣprāpa*. Furthermore, unless the mind is mastered, it is not possible to gain the *yoga* being discussed here, the capacity to see the sameness that exists in all beings and in which all beings exist. What Kṛṣṇa says here is his vision, *mati*, which is not the same as an opinion since it is not something that can be contended and dismissed.

By the practice of *abhyāsa* and *vairāgya*, the mind is brought into one's own hands, which is why the person who can do this is also called *vaśya-ātmā* here. Such a person is always alert. Alertness is something that should always be with you, not something practised for a period of time. For example, you cannot say that you practised alertness for six years and it was very good, just as you cannot say you practised breathing for six years. It is not as though you give up breathing after having practised it for some time; it is your very life. Alertness is the same.

By such a person who continues to maintain this alertness, *yatatā*, by the one who has a mastery over his mind, *vaśyātmanā*, it is possible to gain the vision of sameness, *yogaḥ avāptum śakyaḥ*.

Kṛṣṇa mentions in this verse that this *yoga* is gained by a particular means, *upāyataḥ*. What is that means, *upāya*? *Abhyāsa* and *vairāgya* are the means for gaining this vision, as Kṛṣṇa had already told Arjuna. Because *abhyāsa* and *vairāgya* are the means, Arjuna's gaining the *yoga* was no longer in Kṛṣṇa's hands, because he has already covered the subject matter. Now, it is something that has to be done and it is up to Arjuna to do it. He has to pay attention to his mind. Kṛṣṇa had said everything he could say. There was nothing more to be taught, only something to be done. *Vairāgya* and *abhyāsa* would take care of any problems, any obstructions to gaining the knowledge. This is why Kṛṣṇa does not say very much about the doing of it.

When there is something to be discussed, like the *vastu, brahma-ātmā*, then one can talk indefinitely, which is what Kṛṣṇa does and which is why there are eighteen chapters of the *Gītā*. But here, there is something to be done now by Arjuna; therefore, Kṛṣṇa leaves it at that. You will find that Kṛṣṇa talks a lot about *ātmā*, about the wise person, about the vision, but when it comes to meditation, which is to be done, there are only a few verses because it is something to be done.

Wherever there is something to be done, Kṛṣṇa states it briefly and adequately, and then continues on. Whereas, wherever something is to be unfolded, he goes on and on because it is something that has to be understood, not something that has to be done.

Verses 37-39

Arjuna presents another problem that is purely imagined

अर्जुन उवाच ।
अयतिः श्रद्धयोपेतो योगाच्चलितमानसः ।
अप्राप्य योगसंसिद्धिं कां गतिं कृष्ण गच्छति ॥ ३७ ॥

arjuna uvāca
ayatiḥ śraddhāyopeto yogāccalitamānasaḥ
aprāpya yogasaṁsiddhiṁ kāṁ gatiṁ Kṛṣṇa gacchati (37)

arjunaḥ – Arjuna; *uvāca* – said;
Kṛṣṇa – O Kṛṣṇa!; *śraddhāyā* – with faith in the *śāstra*; *upetaḥ* – endowed; *ayatiḥ* – one of inadequate effort; *yogāt* – from *yoga*; *calitamānasaḥ* – one whose mind wanders away; *yoga-saṁsiddhim* – success in *yoga*; *aprāpya* – not gaining; *kāṁ gatiṁ gacchati* – to which end does he (or she) go

Arjuna said:
The one who is endowed with faith in the *śāstra* (but) whose effort is inadequate, and whose mind wanders away from *yoga*, having not gained success in *yoga*, Kṛṣṇa! to which end does he (or she) go?

Just look at Arjuna's question. Suppose there is a man who has renounced all *karmas*, meaning *vaidika-karmas* and *laukika-karmas*, all the spiritual, social, and family duties that he is allowed to give up if he takes to a life of renunciation, *sannyāsa*. Why does anyone give up all this? In the hope of what? In the hope of gaining this *yoga* – the vision of *ātmā* in all beings and all beings in *ātmā*, *sama darśana*, he gives up all types of *karma*. This particular vision was the end in view when the person, Arjuna was talking about, became a *sannyāsī*.

As a *sannyāsī*, the person denies himself the various pleasures that can be picked up by living in the society and becomes a *bhikṣu*, a person who lives on alms. He has no money and does not know from where his next meal will come – that is, he lives on whatever comes his way. But, although he does not have the pleasures that a life of *saṁsāra* would have given him, renunciation is a good investment because he is going to get the great vision, liberation, *mokṣa*. It was for the sake of *mokṣa* alone that he gave up the other three human pursuits, *dharma*, *artha* and *kāma*.

This person has great *śraddhā* in the vision of the *śāstra* and the possibility of his gaining the knowledge of Brahman, *ātmā*, is definitely there. He knows that this knowledge is the *mokṣa* that he seeks. In the hope of gaining this knowledge, he has taken to the life of *sannyāsa* and continues to be a *sannyāsī*. In time, however, having not yet gained the knowledge, he becomes frustrated. He may have started his pursuit when he was very young and now he is old. Something has prevented him from gaining the knowledge. The teaching may not have been proper or, perhaps, he did not have enough inspiration. Or the problem may have been from the past, some backlog, some obstacle, from the past. Having reached this point, although he still has *śraddhā*, he is now an *ayati*, meaning that he does not have adequate effort.

Yati means a person of effort, one who has the capacity to make right effort, which is why a *sannyāsī* is called a *yati*. The person has a direction and is committed to a life of renunciation in pursuit of self-knowledge. But the *sannyāsī* Arjuna was talking about cannot be called a *yati;* he has become an *ayati* because adequate effort is not there and he does not know what it is, and is incapable of that effort.

That the effort is not adequate is very clear. Why? Because the problems continue. Things are not very clear to the person and therefore, he is *ayati*. He may have studied and done a lot of meditation. But all that he has accomplished is to become more aged, tired, and frustrated, *calitamānasa*. Arjuna wanted to know what would become of this tired, frustrated *sannyāsī*? He has *śraddhā* and therefore, he wants this knowledge. But things are not clear to him at all. Now Arjuna's doubt is, 'What would be his lot if he dies away before gaining the knowledge?' Therefore, Arjuna asks, 'What does he gain Kṛṣṇa, *kāṁ gatiṁ Kṛṣṇa gacchati*?'

We know very well what his lot in this life is. He has neither the joys of *saṁsāra* nor the joy of *mokṣa*. The small pleasures of *saṁsāra* are denied to him and also the pleasures of heaven, since he gave up *karma*s that would earn him such pleasure in the hope of gaining *jñāna*. And he does not get *jñāna* either. What then? Is he just left hanging somewhere?

A person who performs no *karma* obviously cannot gain the results of *karma;* therefore, there is no *karma-phala* for him.

Instead of performing *karma,* he spent his time sitting with his eyes closed, but nothing happened inside, except sleep perhaps. And nothing can be accomplished by sleep. Dreaming or day dreaming at least gives a person some kick, but what does sleep give? Nothing. Therefore, the *ayati* has not picked up any of the simple joys of *saṁsāra.* Nor has he picked up any *puṇya* for the next life; much less has he gained the knowledge that is liberation.

Does the person, whose mind wanders away from *yoga,* just fizzle out?

Will he become like a cloudlet that has become separated from a body of clouds, will he just disappear, fizzle out? Is this kingdom lost and the promised kingdom as well? For the *sannyāsī* of inadequate effort who has died, *mokṣa* is gone and *saṁsāra* is also gone, there being no accrued *puṇya.* With both of them gone, what will happen to him? Where will he go?

Of course, this was an imagined situation on Arjuna's part. He was not himself a *sannyāsī,* but perhaps he planned to become a *sannyāsī.* This did seem to be on his mind, as we saw earlier in the *Gītā.* In any case, Arjuna wants to know exactly what would happen to the one who did not gain the vision. Although this was not Arjuna's immediate problem, his question was a relevant one in terms of understanding what the *śāstra* has to say about *sannyāsa* and *karma-yoga.* Arjuna knew Kṛṣṇa to be the all-knowledge Īśvara and therefore, qualified to remove this particular doubt. No one else was equal to Kṛṣṇa; only he could answer this question, which was not a simple one, dealing as it did with what happens after one's life, as we know it, comes to an end.

Arjuna says, 'Please tell me, Kṛṣṇa, where does such a person go who has not gained success in *yoga* (in the form of gain of knowledge), *aprāpya yoga saṁsiddhiṁ kāṁ gatiṁ Kṛṣṇa gacchati*?' When knowledge is gained, *mokṣa* is gained, which is why knowledge is called a means for *mokṣa*. Thus, between the knowledge and *mokṣa* there is a connection, a connection of means and end, *sādhana-sādhya-sambandha*.

Arjuna wants to know what happens to the person who, having *śraddhā* in the vision, renounces everything and lives a life of *yoga* but does not gain the knowledge that is *mokṣa*. Having denied himself the pleasures of *saṁsāra* and also those of the other world, the person has been performing this *yoga*, meditation, for a long time and now he is very old and is dying away. He has given up all hope of gaining anything more in this life, let alone the knowledge that he has pursued for so long. What will happen to him? Will he not be completely destroyed?

Arjuna puts this question to Kṛṣṇa in the next verse:

कच्चिन्नोभयविभ्रष्टश्छिन्नाभ्रमिव नश्यति ।
अप्रतिष्ठो महाबाहो विमूढो ब्रह्मणः पथि ॥ ३८ ॥

kaccinnobhayavibhraṣṭaśchinnābhramiva naśyati
apratiṣṭho mahābāho vimūḍho brahmaṇaḥ pathi (38)

mahābāho – O mighty armed (Kṛṣṇa)!; *brahmaṇaḥ pathi* – in the path (knowledge) of Brahman; *vimūḍhaḥ* – the one who is deluded; *apratiṣṭhaḥ* – one who is without any support; *ubhaya-vibhraṣṭaḥ* – one who has fallen from both; *chinna-abhram iva* – like a cloudlet torn asunder; *kaccit na naśyati* – is he not destroyed?

> Deluded in the path (knowledge) of Brahman, is one who has fallen from both, being without any support, not destroyed, Kṛṣṇa, the mightyarmed! like a cloudlet torn asunder?

The person being discussed here is the same *sannyāsī* described previously by Arjuna as *ayati* one whose effort has not been adequate to gain the knowledge that is *mokṣa*. *Ubhaya-vibhraṣṭa* refers to the one who has fallen away from both lifestyles, *karma-yoga* and *sannyāsa*. This person has given up, fallen away from the way of life called *karma-mārga* or *karma-yoga*. *Karma-yoga* is a life of activity in which one also pursues the knowledge. The purpose of this lifestyle is to make one ready eventually to pursue knowledge by taking to a life of *sannyāsa*. Because he has slipped away from *karma-mārga*, the person is called *vibhraṣṭa* with reference to the *karma-mārga*. And, the life of renunciation, *yoga-mārga*, *brahmaṇaḥ panthā*, for which he gave up *karma-mārga*, has also proved to be abortive, fruitless. Therefore, in both, he is the loser; from both he has fallen away; he is *ubhaya-vibhraṣṭa*.

Having fallen away from both, where will he go now? He cannot go back to *karma-mārga* because he is perhaps too old to do anything. Besides, it is not proper to go from *sannyāsa* to *karma-mārga*. Nor does he have any enthusiasm to do so because he knows the *anityatva* of it all. Any enthusiasm he may have had for a life of *saṁsāra* as an *avivekī*, one without discrimination, is all gone and he does not have the satisfaction of being a *jñānī*, a wise man, either. Therefore, he is *ubhaya-vibhraṣṭa,* hanging somewhere in the middle, with no place to go. He cannot identify with the wise *sannyāsī*s nor with the ordinary people.

Not only does he have no place, no group to identify with, he is also deluded *vimūḍha*. He either feels he has made a mistake or he feels confused about whether he is a *jīva*, an individual, or *paraṁ-brahma*. Since this doubt remains, he has not accomplished anything by having taken to this path, this pursuit of the knowledge of Brahman.

There is no path to Brahman.

Śaṅkara clarified the meaning of the word *pathi*, in the path, in his commentary of this verse by adding the word *mārga*, thereby indicating that the lifestyle of *sannyāsa* is what is implied here. There is no 'way,' no 'path,' to Brahman as such; you are Brahman. And to gain this knowledge of Brahman, there is a pursuit, the pursuit of knowledge. And in this pursuit, the *sannyāsī* under discussion is deluded, *vimūḍha*. Thus, 'deluded in the path of Brahman' means that in gaining the knowledge of Brahman, in the pursuit of that knowledge, he is still confused and deluded.

Does such a person not destroy himself, *naśyati na kim*? Asking this question, Arjuna compared the destruction to that of a cloudlet that has separated itself from a large body of clouds, *chinna-abhram iva*. Not wanting to wait for the big body of clouds perhaps, this cloudlet separates itself in its haste to reach the Himalayas where it can sit on top of the mountains and not be disturbed. Instead, somewhere in the middle of India, tossed about by the howling winds, it just disappears, fizzles out.

So too, this person had dropped out of conventional society in his attempt to reach *mokṣa* quickly. He may even have gone to sit in the rarefied air of the Himalayas, but instead of becoming a true *sannyāsī*, he became a drop-out, just like the cloudlet. Does he not destroy himself in the same way that the cloudlet does?

Just as a cloudlet that remains with the large body of clouds can travel along and enjoy the view, so too, you can be with the main body of society and have some of the joys that such a life has to offer. The cloudlet that is prepared to travel at the same slow speed as the big body of clouds can look down at the mountains, up at the stars, and be protected by the winds of destruction. Otherwise, it gets destroyed.

Similarly, when you hurry ahead, you can become completely lost in the process because you have left the structure behind. *Sannyāsa* means just that – no structure. You can become anything. Without a structure, without any particular mode of life, nothing to pressure you into doing anything, you can become lazy too. When you are hungry, you can go for *bhikṣā* and then lie down back again without doing anything. A life of *sannyāsa* gives you this kind of licence. No one is going to question you. Society is not going to question you. And, since there is no work for you to do, there is no employer or employee. There is also no father or mother to worry about you, which sometimes keeps people on track. If the *sannyāsī* once had a wife and children, he has also given them up. Therefore, none of the societal norms are there for the *sannyāsī*. Nor is there any religious norm because the person who takes *sannyāsa* is absolved from performing all the *karma*s enjoined by the Veda. Therefore, there is no problem; you can be anything you want, even a hippie!

Thinking that such a person destroys himself, Arjuna asks Kṛṣṇa to clear his doubt with reference to the fate of the *ubhaya-vibhraṣṭa*.

एतन्मे संशयं कृष्ण छेत्तुमर्हस्यशेषतः ।
त्वदन्यः संशयस्यास्य छेत्ता न ह्युपपद्यते ॥ ३९ ॥

etanme saṁśayaṁ Kṛṣṇa chettum arhasyaśeṣataḥ
tvadanyaḥ saṁśayasyāsya chettā na hyupapadyate (39)

Kṛṣṇa – O Kṛṣṇa !; *me* – of mine; *etat* – this; *saṁśayam* – doubt; *aśeṣataḥ* – totally; *chettum* – to eliminate; *arhasi* – you should; *hi* – for; *tvadanyaḥ* – other than you; *asya saṁśayasya* – of this doubt; *chettā* – the remover; *na upapadyate* – is not there

Kṛṣṇa! You should eliminate this doubt of mine totally. For, other than you, there is no one who can be the remover of this doubt.

Arjuna knows that there was no one else who could answer his question. Only the all-knowledge Kṛṣṇa, as Īśvara, could answer it because only Īśvara knows what will happen to the *sannyāsī* after he dies away from this life without gaining knowledge of the self.

Chettā means the one who cuts or removes. Here it refers to the one who removes the doubt. Kṛṣṇa , then, was the hit man for the doubt – in fact, the only possible hit man. He alone was capable of eliminating Arjuna's doubts totally. Anyone else would have to say, 'This is what the *śāstra* says.' Whereas, Kṛṣṇa is the one who initiated the *śāstra* itself, as he said at the beginning of the fourth chapter, verse 1, '*imāṁ vivasvate yogaṁ proktavān aham avyayaṁ vivasvān manave prāha manurikṣvākave'bravīt*, I gave this eternal knowledge to Vivasvān who gave it to Manu, who gave it to Ikṣvāku.'

Therefore, Kṛṣṇa as Īśvara knew what it was all about. He also told Arjuna earlier that they had a number of births before, but only he, Kṛṣṇa, knew these births while Arjuna did not – *bahūni me vyatītāni janmāni tava cārjuna tānyahaṁ veda sarvāṇi na tvaṁ vettha parantapa.*[23]

From this, Arjuna concludes that Kṛṣṇa knows what happens to a soul after death and, therefore, is the right person to talk about it. Arjuna is praising his *guru* here, saying that there was no one equal to Kṛṣṇa, no one who could eliminate his doubt totally. In other words, no one else is qualified to answer his question.

Had Arjuna not asked this question, the *Gītā* would have ended three verses before. But, because Arjuna asks the question, Kṛṣṇa begins talking again.

---

[23] *Gītā* 4.5

Verse 40

Kṛṣṇa answers – anyone who performs good actions never comes to a bad end

श्रीभगवानुवाच ।
पार्थ नैवेह नामुत्र विनाशस्तस्य विद्यते ।
न हि कल्याणकृत्कश्चिद्दुर्गतिं तात गच्छति ॥ ४० ॥

śrībhagavān uvāca
pārtha naiveha nāmutra vināśastasya vidyate
na hi kalyāṇakṛt kaścid durgatiṁ tāta gacchati (40)

śrībhagavān – Lord Kṛṣṇa; *uvāca* – said;
pārtha – O son of Pṛthā; *tasya* – for him (or her); *vināśaḥ* – destruction; *iha* – here; *na eva vidyate* – indeed is not; *na* – nor; *amutra* – in the hereafter; *tāta* – O my son (Arjuna)!; *hi* – because; *kaścit* – any one; *kalyāṇakṛt* – who performs good actions; *durgatim* – a bad end; *na gacchati* – never reaches

Śrī Bhagavān said:

Indeed, Pārtha (Arjuna)! there is no destruction for him (or her), neither here nor in the hereafter, because any one who performs good actions never reaches a bad end.

Again, the person being discussed in this verse is that *sannyāsī*, that *yogī*, who was referred to previously as *ubhaya-vibhraṣṭa*, one who had fallen from both *karma-mārga* and *yoga-mārga* for the reasons we have already seen. In fact, the person is not *ubhaya-vibhraṣṭa* because, here, Kṛṣṇa says that there is no falling as such.

For the *sannyāsī* who has not completed the job properly, destruction is not there, *vināśaḥ na vidyate*, either here in this world, *iha*, or in any other world, *amutra*. Why? Because this person, although an *ayati*, has *śraddhā* in the *śāstra*. Having *śraddhā*, there can be no loss for him in this life and, therefore, the life of *sannyāsa* is not a bad investment. He knows what it is all about. Because he has *śraddhā*, there is no question of his being frustrated or sad in this world. He will simply continue to pursue the knowledge, pleasantly, happily, until he gains it. And, if *śraddhā* were not to be there, the person would naturally think that he had made a mistake. Thinking so, he would always go back. In either case, then, the problem of his being sad for what he has undertaken would not be there for the person.

'Nor will there be a problem later, that is, after death, *amutra*,' Kṛṣṇa says. He will come back to a situation that is conducive to the continuation of his pursuit of the knowledge that will give him *mokṣa*. Thus, Kṛṣṇa assures Arjuna that destruction is definitely not there for him, *vināśaḥ tasya na vidyate*.

Destruction here can only mean that the person comes back to a life that is worse than before, meaning that he gains a lower birth, than the one he previously had. But this will not happen, Kṛṣṇa says. There will be a higher birth, a better birth, because the person has lived a good life, he is a *kalyāṇakṛt*. *Kalyāṇa* means *mokṣa* and this person has taken a step towards *mokṣa* by living the life of *sannyāsa*. The *kalyāṇakṛt* is not a drop out or a hippie. For the sake of *mokṣa*, which implies an understanding of Īśvara, the person has given up everything.

And, being a *kalyāṇakṛt,* the person does not come to a bad end, *durgatiṁ na gacchati.*

Anyone, *kaścit,* who has done good action, charitable action, does not gain an undesirable end. At the worst, such a person, just proceeds from birth to birth, depending on the accumulated *karma* that precipitates a new body. But, once a person makes a step for the sake of *mokṣa,* whatever he or she has done before has already paid off. The moment the person turns one's attention towards oneself, there is no going back.

Generally, a person only goes after *anātmā,* not *ātmā.* For example, the physical body being *anātmā,* how to take care of it is also *anātmā.* How to take care of my mind is with reference to *anātmā.* How to take care of my money, power, family, is all with reference to *anātmā.* How to take care of my future, meaning my next body, is also regarding *anātmā.* Like this, everyone is interested in taking care of *anātmā* alone, and struggles to do so constantly.

In fact, this taking care of *anātmā* is only for taking care of *ātmā.* Taking care is not for the sake of *anātmā.* You do not take care of the body for the body's sake; it is for your sake, *ātmā*'s sake. Therefore, you take care of the *anātmā* for the sake of *ātmā* and, in the process, you totally neglect the *ātmā.* This, indeed, is the wonder and we call it *māyā.*

The moment a person begins to question whether he or she is doing the right thing, *ātmā* is being taken care of. And this does not take place in everyone. To ask, 'What is this *ātmā* that is so anxious to take care of *anātmā,*' is to question *ātmā* itself and is for *ātmā*'s sake, for one's own sake, alone. The one who begins to pay attention to *ātmā,* whether successful or not, has already traced one's way back. To question what is considered to be normal is to discover that the normal is abnormal. Such a person has made a step towards *mokṣa* and therefore, one is *kalyāṇakṛt.*

Kalyāṇa means auspicious. Therefore, *mokṣa* is *kalyāṇa.* Marriage is also called *kalyāṇa* because it marks the end of the *brahmacarya* stage of life and the auspicious beginning of the *gṛhasthāśrama* which will finally prepare one for *mokṣa,* the most auspicious. *Mokṣa* is the ultimate *kalyāṇa* and marriage is a *sādhana,* a means, for gaining the grand finale called *mokṣa.*

Changing the course of karma

Anyone who has made a step towards *mokṣa* is called *kalyāṇakṛt,* whether the person is a *karma-yogī* or a *sannyāsī.* Both of them are *kalyāṇakṛt*s alone because some action has been taken for the sake of *mokṣa.* Thereafter, progress is assured. Any *karma* waiting to take the body of a frog, a celestial, or anything else is all subjugated and no longer has any chance to express itself. Once the person is *kalyāṇakṛt,* the entire order, the entire flow, changes. Whereas, if you are simply going along with the flow, then all the accumulated *karma*s have the same chance. But when a particular set of *karma*s exerts more pressure for expression, then it has a greater chance of getting fulfilled.

Once you have changed the course, the order has to change. So, for the person who has *śraddhā,* all other *karma*s have to wait and the one for pursuing the knowledge proceeds.

And how long will the others have to wait? Until the person gains *kalyāṇa, mokṣa.* And once *mokṣa* is gained, all *karma*s disappear. They are finished for good; they do not exist at all. Therefore, to question whether one is a *kartā* is no ordinary question. Assuming one is a *kartā,* one performs good and bad actions. But, here, the very *kartā* is questioned. One asks, 'Am I a *kartā*?' This is the question that makes one a *kalyāṇakṛt* and, having asked it, no one reaches a bad end.

Kṛṣṇa addresses Arjuna here as *tāta,* a name used affectionately for either a father or a son in recognition of the closeness between them. A father is one who protects himself in the form of his son, the son being as good as him. When the son is happy, the father is happy. When the son grows up nicely, the father feels that he too has grown nicely. If the son is successful, the father also feels successful. So, whatever happens to the son happens to the father in that, it very much affects him. Therefore, there is no distance between the son and the father. For this reason, they are both called *tāta.*

Here, Arjuna is not Kṛṣṇa's son. But he is a father in the sense that a creator can be called father, *janaka.* There is the father who creates a body for you, *deha-janaka,* and a father who creates wisdom in you, *vidyā-janaka.* Because the wise person who is a teacher, *ācārya,* is one who gives you a complete rebirth in the form of wisdom, he is called father. Therefore, the author of the body and the author of the knowledge are called *tāta,* father.

The word '*tāta*' is used for a son as well as for a disciple, *śiṣya.* Arjuna is not Kṛṣṇa's son, but he is his *śiṣya* and a *śiṣya* is like a son, equal to a son. Therefore, Kṛṣṇa affectionately addresses him here as *tāta*, telling him that the *sannyāsī* who has *śraddhā*, but who does not gain the knowledge, does not come to a bad end.

Verses 41-44

What happens to the yoga-bhraṣṭa

प्राप्य पुण्यकृतां लोकानुषित्वा शाश्वतीः समाः ।
शुचीनां श्रीमतां गेहे योगभ्रष्टोऽभिजायते ॥ ४१ ॥

prāpya puṇyakṛtāṁ lokān uṣitvā śāśvatīḥ samāḥ
śucīnāṁ śrīmatāṁ gehe yogabhraṣṭo'bhijāyate (41)

yogabhraṣṭaḥ – one who has fallen from (did not succeed in) *yoga*; *puṇyakṛtām* – belonging to those who do good actions; *lokān* – worlds; *prāpya* – having gained; *śāśvatīḥ samāḥ* – countless years; *uṣitvā* – having lived (there); *śucīnām* – of the people committed to *dharma*; *śrīmatām* – of the wealthy (and cultured); *gehe* – in the home; *abhijāyate* – is born

> Having gained the worlds belonging to those who do good actions (and) having lived (there) for countless years, the one who did not succeed in *yoga* is born in the home of the wealthy (and cultured) people who are committed to *dharma*.

Both *iha-loka*, the here, and *para-loka*, the hereafter, are covered in this verse. *Puṇya-kṛtāṁ loka* refers to the worlds, *lokas*, gained by *puṇyakṛts*, *puṇya-karmakṛts*, those who have lived a life of *dharma*, performing good actions that produce *puṇya*.

Having gained these worlds, *prāpya puṇya-kṛtāṁ lokān*, how long does this person live in these worlds? Kṛṣṇa says, for countless number of years, *śāśvatīḥ samāḥ*; that is, he will live there for a very long time.

It must be remembered that the person being discussed here is the same *yoga-bhraṣṭa* mentioned earlier, one whom Arjuna thought would lose both worlds by not having succeeded in the pursuit of *yoga*, meaning the knowledge that is *mokṣa*. In fact, the person is not a *bhraṣṭa* at all because there is no falling here, as was mentioned before. Kṛṣṇa uses the word *yoga-bhraṣṭa* here because, in Arjuna's mind the person had fallen somehow. Therefore, Kṛṣṇa wants to negate any kind of falling with reference to this person by telling Arjuna that the person he thought of as *yoga-bhraṣṭa* is born, *abhijāyate,* into surroundings that are conducive to the pursuit of this knowledge.

Kṛṣṇa describes these surroundings with the words, *śucīnāṁ śrīmatāṁ gehe,* meaning in the house of a person of wealth and culture who is also committed to *dharma*, therefore called a *śuci*. The word *śrīmat* suggests wealth and abundance of comforts and so on. By the word *śuci,* culture is emphasised here because there can be an abundance of wealth in a home where, for example, the father is a mafia don. Such a house is not conducive to the pursuit of knowledge; it is more like a prison than a home with its high spiked walls and sentries posted everywhere. In such circumstances, wealth itself becomes a prison. This kind of wealth is not referred to here, the point being made by the word *śuci*.

The words *śucīnāṁ gehe* implies a family that has a value for values, a value for living a life of *dharma*. This is the kind of family into which the *yoga-bhraṣṭa* is born, Kṛṣṇa says. In these conducive surroundings, the person will pick up certain values. To be born into such a family is not easy and is to be recognised as a great advantage since a person can also be born into a place with some handicap or other. To have a father or mother who is an alcoholic is considered to be a wrong start. A wrong start, however, does not mean that there is nothing to be gained. Perhaps the person can exhaust something, which makes it a good start since all's well that ends well.

What is to be appreciated here is that to get out of a wrong start is very difficult. Whereas, where the start is conducive, then the person's pursuit of *mokṣa* can proceed. In the very beginning of his life, he will show the signs of a *sannyāsī* because he has to fulfil what he has started. The conducive surroundings enable him to live a life of prayer and think constantly of Īśvara. Thinking always of Īśvara, he looks into what Īśvara is, questions what the truth of everything is, what the cause of everything is – all of which is thinking of Īśvara, *īśvara-smaraṇa*.

From this we can see that there is no such thing as a bad lot for the person either in terms of this life or in the hereafter. Even coming back to this life, he picks up the thread and continues. And to facilitate his pursuit, his birth will be in a better place, meaning that it will be more conducive for gaining the knowledge.

Kṛṣṇa then mentions another possibility for the person who had not yet gained the knowledge.

अथवा योगिनामेव कुले भवति धीमताम्।
एतद्धि दुर्लभतरं लोके जन्म यदीदृशम्॥ ४२॥

athavā yogināṁ eva kule bhavati dhīmatām
etaddhi durlabhataraṁ loke janma yadīdṛśam (42)

athavā – or; *dhīmatām* – of people who are wise; *yoginām* – of *yogī*s; *eva* – indeed; *kule* – into the family; *bhavati* – is born; *yat īdṛśaṁ janma* – a birth such as this; *hi* – indeed; *loke* – in this world; *etat durlabhataram* – this (is) very difficult to gain

Or he is indeed born into the family of wise *yogin*s. A birth such as this is indeed very difficult to gain in this world.

We have seen that there is no such thing as a bad lot, *durgati*, for a *yogī*, a *sannyāsī*, who has the desire to know the self. Anyone who has taken a step towards knowing oneself has already initiated a process of unwinding oneself from *saṁsāra*. One winds oneself in *saṁsāra* by *karma* without even questioning whether one is a *kartā*, a doer. Then, within the *saṁsāra*, retaining the doership centred on the self, one tries to accomplish various ends. And these ends are accomplished on the basis of the desire for something other than *ātmā*, all of which we saw earlier.

Here, you are questioning the very *svarūpa* of *ātmā*. You may not know whether you are a *kartā*, but at least you are questioning, you are enquiring into it. By asking, 'What is *ātmā*?' you are not taking whatever *ātmā* is for granted. Generally, people only try to avoid the *duḥkha* that results from the limitations and bondage experienced by the *kartā*, the subject, without ever questioning the subject itself. Therefore, all their activity is only to bring about something desirable. This kind of life is called *saṁsāra*.

Saṁsāra is a disease and no one goes for the cure. But, once you pay attention to the very subject and ask, who is this subject, what is this 'I,' and so on, then you have initiated an auspicious desire, *śubhecchā*, a desire for *ātmā*, *ātma-icchā*, that has to result in *mokṣa*. Thus, Kṛṣṇa's assurance that there is no way that the person will come to a bad end. He also gave Arjuna a little inside information, as it were – 'The one you call *yoga-bhraṣṭa*, Arjuna, just picks up the thread in his next birth and continues his pursuit of knowledge.' The person's prayerful life itself produces certain *puṇya*. And because of that *puṇya*, the person gains a pleasant stay in the hereafter followed by rebirth in a situation conducive to his pursuit of knowledge.

The idea being conveyed here is that if there is a life after death, a world other than this one, that world will be good for the person. All experiences there will be happy experiences. Therefore, even in the hereafter, there is no such thing as a bad lot for the person. And, having enjoyed the result, the *puṇya*, of his prayerful life in the hereafter, he then comes back to this earth with an *adhikāri-śarīra*, a body that is qualified to gain the knowledge, meaning that the person returns as a human being. He will not come back in a lower form but will definitely be born as a human being into a set-up that is conducive for his pursuit. Therefore, there is no question of a bad lot anywhere.

Any physical body is called *yoni*, *yoni*, meaning womb, of which there are three types – *deva-yoni*, a celestial body;

manuṣya-yoni, the body of a human being; and *adho-yoni*, the body assumed by lower life beings. *Manuṣya-yoni* is the incarnation in which a physical body enjoying a free will is assumed, meaning a human body or its equivalent, here or anywhere else. A person need not be born on this particular planet necessarily, but in some set-up or other he will be born.

The person can be born into a family of yogīs

Here, Kṛṣṇa describes the set-up into which the person under discussion will be born as the home of a person who is highly cultured and wealthy, and at the same time, righteous, *śucīnāṁ śrimatāṁ gehe*. There may be wealth, but there will also be culture. And, if there is no wealth, there will definitely be a lot of culture. The family will also be highly ethical and committed to living a life of values. In this way, the person does not have a false start, a start that is handicapped in any way, and therefore, can easily pick up the thread of his pursuit of knowledge.

Or, Kṛṣṇa goes on to say, that the person can be born into a family of *karma-yogī, mumukṣu*. A father can be a cultured person, a religious person, and perhaps a wealthy person, without being a *karma-yogī*. Even to be born into such a family gives a person a good chance to gain the knowledge that is *mokṣa*. But, if the person is born into the house of a *karma-yogī*, he has an even better chance, is the point Kṛṣṇa is making here.

In this verse, *yogī*s refer to *karma-yogī*s since *sannyāsī*s do not have families. And these *karma-yogī*s are also well-informed people, *dhīmat*s. Because the word '*dhīmatām*' is used here, the father can be either a *jñānī* or a *mumukṣu*. The very least he will be is a *mumukṣu*. In either case, from childhood onwards, the person picks up certain values and has no problem taking to his pursuit again without any hindrance whatsoever. In other words, he will not need to work through problems related to his past and so on, because there is no problem.

In his commentary of this verse, Śaṅkara took the family of *yogī*s to mean a family in which there is lack of wealth, and said '*dāridrāṇāṁ yogināṁ kule*,' but where the father is a *yogī*. A poor man can also be a beggar, and to be born into such a home implies all kinds of problems. Whereas, here, the father is a *karma-yogī* and also a well-informed person who has no wealth whatsoever. He is a *paṇḍita*, a *brāhmaṇa*. There is no such thing as a rich *brāhmaṇa* because, to be a true *brāhmaṇa*, the person must have no wealth. Therefore, Śaṅkara was actually praising poverty here.

To be born as a human being there has to have been some *puṇya* and *pāpa*. The poverty of the person will exhaust all his *pāpa*s and his *puṇya* will be available for *yoga*. In this way, the person can take up to a life of *yoga*, *jñāna*, without any let or hindrance. This is why Śaṅkara said that it is better to be born into a family of a *karma-yogī* who may not be rich than to be born into a rich family that has a lot of culture.

Riches have a way of getting into your head and creating certain complexes that become problems. Poverty can also create complexes; it is true. Both inferiority complex and superiority complex are problems that have to be dealt with. However, if you are born into a family where there may not be riches but where the parents are *yogīs*, there is no problem. Because they are *yogīs*, the value structure is sound and the person does not have a complex that 'I am poor.' Even though there is no money, he does not think of himself as a poor person. Instead, he thinks of himself as a blessed person. To have the parentage where both parents feel blessed to be what they are, even though they have no money, is the right parentage. The point being made here is that if there is money, that is fine, but if there is no money, it is better – provided, of course, the parentage is proper.

Why two different kinds of families?

Why does Kṛṣṇa mention two different kinds of families in these two verses? Should not every *yoga-bhraṣṭa* be born into the same kind of family? No, the family one is born into depends upon the person's *karma*, their accrued *puṇya* and *papa*; everyone's *puṇya*s and *pāpa*s differ. These *puṇya-pāpa*s determine where a person is born, who his parents are, whether there is money or no money, and so on. Wherever the person is born, however, he retains his *yoga-saṁskāra*s, those impressions, tendencies, that he had gathered before; in other words, he comes along with his previous impressions, in the form of potential tendencies, which often manifest very early in life. A baby who cries all the time may become a musician and the child who destroys everything in sight may become a civil engineer. Let us see!

These tendencies are what we call *saṁskāra*s and they manifest in your life without your cultivating them. This is why two children who are born to the same parents are so different.

One child has certain tendencies and the other child has other tendencies. One child goes for music and the other for art because of their *saṁskāras*. These *saṁskāra*s are what is meant by *prārabdha-karma*, the *karma* that results in a certain body being born into a given situation and having a particular set of experiences. The *saṁskāra*s have to manifest themselves and they do so through certain professions, etc. *Yoga-saṁskāra*s are the same; they will be there in the psyche of the child whether he is born into a cultured family committed to *dharma* or into the family of a *karma-yogi*.

Therefore, the criterion is not to be born into a particular kind of family. This does not come into the picture at all, and there is no necessity for it. Wherever the person is born is fine because one is born with the *yoga-saṁskāra*s. However, certain opportunities are necessary so that the *yoga-saṁskāra*s that manifest will not be overwhelmed by *adharma-saṁskāra*s, which is also possible. Because wrong tendencies can be gathered as a child, these can overpower the *yoga-saṁskāra*s you had previously gathered. In order for the *yoga-saṁskāra*s to manifest naturally in the form of a serious pursuit of knowledge on the part of a person who was previously a *yogī*, the 'born again' *yogī* should not be overpowered by a life of *adharma*, wrong values, false values, and so on. Therefore, it is important for this person to have the proper set-up to pick up the thread and continue from where he left.

A seeker can be born anywhere

These two verses do not imply that everyone who takes to this pursuit has to be born in one of these two places either in a rich, cultured family or in a family of *karma-yogīs*. That is not the point here. The point is that those who desire self-knowledge are born everywhere. But we are not talking about all seekers here; we are talking specifically about people who were *sannyāsīs* or seekers before and did not accomplish what they had set out to accomplish before they passed away. These are the people whom Arjuna thought of as fallen people because they seem to have lost both worlds, the world of *saṁsāra* and the worlds produced by performing *karma,* and they did not gain the *yoga,* the vision of sameness. Therefore, in response to Arjuna's concern, Kṛṣṇa tells him here that they are born in a set-up where there is no obstacle to their pursuit of knowledge.

The *yoga-saṁskāra* will always be there; once the person directs his or her attention there, the *yoga saṁskāra* never dies. But it can be overpowered by *adharma*. And, even if it is overpowered by *adharma,* provided the person realises it, the *adharma* can be exhausted, purified, by living prayerfully. In this way, whatever *adharma-saṁskāra* are there are all exhausted; one is rid of them for good. Then the *yoga-saṁskāra* comes up again and the person continues.

To pick up this thread without any obstacles whatsoever, the person has to be born into a certain environment. For example, an environment where the father is seriously studying *vedānta-śāstra* and the mother is always talking about it, is a wonderful start indeed. As a child, I used to hear such talk constantly. For instance, if I asked my mother for something before going to bed, she would never say, 'I will give it to you tomorrow.' Instead, she would say, 'If you get up tomorrow, then I will give it to you.' This is a wonderful thing, 'if you get up' means 'if you survive.' And my mother was not the only person saying this; every other mother in India did the same thing. It is the culture. There are no promises, only the attitude, 'If we survive, we shall see.' This means that, from childhood onward, you accept the fact that you do not have complete control over things.

Control is a problem. Because you want to control, all the problems come. Whereas, if you accept that there can be many a slip between the cup and the lip, that there are things that you have no control over, then there is an attitude towards life that is very healthy. You do what you can and you are ready to take what comes. To have this attitude from childhood is a very good start, whatever other problems there may be. If everything else is also conducive, if there is education, values, and communication, it is a very wonderful start indeed.

Such a start is what Kṛṣṇa is referring to in these two verses. First, he says that to be born into the highly cultured and ethical family of a rich man is great. And then he says that there is another birth that is even greater, more rare, more difficult to accomplish – a birth enjoying the parentage of well-informed *karma-yogī*s.

Well-informed *yogī*s are those who know they are *yogī*s, which means they are *mumukṣus*. They know they are seeking knowledge, that they have to gain knowledge to gain *mokṣa.* To be born to parents of such wisdom, to have a birth of this nature, *yat īdṛśaṁ janma,* is very difficult to gain in this world, *etat hi durlabhataraṁ loke,* Kṛṣṇa says here, definitely more difficult than being born in a rich man's family, which is also difficult. Having gained the parentage of *yogīs*, however, the situation is much better, much more conducive, than the other, there being absolutely nothing to stop the person from pursuing *yoga* further.

The saying that a rich man can pass through the gates of heaven as easily as a camel can pass through the eye of a needle is not directed at the riches themselves. However, along with riches, there is usually an ego; therefore, there is no humility. A rich man thinks he can buy anything, accomplish anything. This is the problem; the riches themselves are not the problem.

Further, Kṛṣṇa says:

तत्र तं बुद्धिसंयोगं लभते पौर्वदेहिकम् ।
यतते च ततो भूयः संसिद्धौ कुरुनन्दन ॥ ४३ ॥

tatra taṁ buddhisaṁyogaṁ labhate paurvadehikam
yatate ca tato bhūyaḥ saṁsiddhau kurunandana (43)

tatra – there; *paurva-dehikam* – which existed in his previous body; *tam* – that; *buddhi-saṁyogam* – connection through the intellect; *labhate* – gains; *kurunandana* – O joy of the Kuru family (Arjuna)!; *ca* – and; *tataḥ bhūyaḥ* – further than that (gained previously); *saṁsiddhau* – for success (in *yoga*); *yatate* – strives

There, he gains a connection through the intellect with that which existed in his previous body and strives for further success (in *yoga*) than that (gained previously), Arjuna, the joy of the Kuru family!

Tatra refers to either of the two families referred to in the previous two verses, the cultured, *dhārmika* family of the wealthy man committed to *dharma* or the family of *yogī*s. There, the person picks up the thread of what existed in his previous life when he was a *sannyāsī*.

Previously the person enjoyed a particular body and, in that body, he began a life of *yoga,* a pursuit of knowledge which he did not gain before he passed away. Now, in the present body, his *buddhi* connects itself to what existed before, *taṁ buddhi-saṁyogaṁ labhate paurva-dehikam*. What kind of a connection is this? Is it something like spaceships docking? No. The connection with what existed before means that the person picks up the thread from where he left behind in a previous birth and continues to gain greater success. Then what happens? The person again becomes a *sannyāsī,* a *yati,* and because of the previous *saṁskāra*s, makes an even greater effort to gain more than he gained before, *tataḥ bhūyaḥ*. Why? For success in *yoga, saṁsiddhau,* to gain the knowledge that is *mokṣa*.

Kṛṣṇa uses Arjuna's words again here. Arjuna had asked, '*aprāpya yoga-saṁsiddhiṁ kāṁ gatiṁ Kṛṣṇa gacchati,* Kṛṣṇa, having not gained success in *yoga*, what end does the person reach?' Answering Arjuna's question, Kṛṣṇa talks about the same *saṁsiddhi*, success in *yoga,* which is in the form of self-knowledge. For gaining that *saṁsiddhi*, the person can make further effort because he has the *buddhi-saṁyoga*, the connection with the *saṁskāra*s he had before.

The connection with the past is by means of the intellect

This is why, wherever there is a man studying the *śāstras*, generally at least one of his children will show an interest at a very young age. This child will go and sit with the father and will not be interested in things that children are usually interested in. Why? Because there is a connection with the previous tendencies, *pūrva-saṁskāras,* through the intellect.

Arjuna was addressed as Kurunandana here, Kuru being the name of the family into which Arjuna was born. Kurunandana means the joy of the Kuru family. Kṛṣṇa perhaps uses this name here to remind Arjuna of the advantages of this present birth.

Further, Kṛṣṇa says:

पूर्वाभ्यासेन तेनैव ह्रियते ह्यवशोऽपि सः ।
जिज्ञासुरपि योगस्य शब्दब्रह्मातिवर्तते ॥ ४४ ॥

pūrvābhyāsena tenaiva hriyate hyavaśo'pi saḥ
jijñāsurapi yogasya śabdabrahmātivartate (44)

tena pūrva-abhyāsena – by this previous practice; *eva* – alone; *saḥ* – he; *hriyate* – is led; *avaśaḥ hi* – necessarily; *api* – even; *yogasya* – of *yoga; jijñāsuḥ* – as one who is desirous of the knowledge; *śabda-brahma* – the Veda; *ativartate* – goes beyond

> By this previous practice alone, he is necessarily led (to *yoga*). Even as the one who is desirous of the knowledge of *yoga* he goes beyond the Veda (the *karma-kāṇḍa* of the Veda).

Here, Kṛṣṇa intends to remove any doubt about whether the person would gain the knowledge once he began the pursuit. 'Suppose, just suppose, he does not gain the knowledge.

What will happen to him?' is the question dealt with here. Suppose he gets caught up in Sesame Street[24] as a child and then later gets lost on the 42nd Street,[25] what then? After all, there is no end to the streets in life that one can get lost on. Suppose the person gets lost in this way, then, how do the *yoga-saṁskāra*s stand a chance?

These hypothetical situations have no chance of occurring, Kṛṣṇa says here. Even if the person is not interested in this *yoga,* even if he wants to avoid it, it will keep popping up for him because the *saṁskāra* is there. No matter how hard he tries to avoid it, he will be taken away by it, helplessly, *avaśaḥ api hriyate.* Why? Because of his previous practice itself, by the pursuit of *yoga* that he had undertaken before, *tena pūrva abhyāsena eva.* He need not do anything now to become a seeker; the old pursuit is enough to carry him along. The word '*avaśa*' here implies that he has no control over the matter. He is absorbed by the *yoga,* taken away by it, pulled into it by the previous practice, even if he is not interested.

However, he is interested in it; in fact, he is interested in nothing else. He wants to know what it is all about. Even if he is not that interested, if he is only mildly curious, this *yoga* will keep popping into his head and he will want to know what self-knowledge is, what all the talk about enlightenment means, and so on. Kṛṣṇa says here that even a simple, curious desire is enough for him to be above the Veda, to transcend

---

[24] A popular TV serial in the United States

[25] A street in Manhattan, New York, famous for its night clubs, etc.

the Veda, that is, the *karma* portion of the Veda, *śabda brahma ativartate*. It will cause him to give up all the *karma*s again, become a *sannyāsī*, and continue his pursuit of knowledge. Nothing will interest him except the subject matter known as Vedanta. Nothing else, none of the means and ends discussed in the Veda, will interest him at all. In other words, in no time this person will discover *vairāgya*, dispassion, because it is natural for him.

There is no going back once self-enquiry has begun

Kṛṣṇa answers Arjuna's question by telling that once one has started enquiry into the self, there is no going back. Nor is there a bad end of any kind; there is only a continuous pursuit until what is to be gained, self-knowledge, is gained. Until then, the pursuit is never stopped, is never affected, in any way. This was an assurance. Kṛṣṇa's words are the *pramāṇa* here. Although there is some supporting logic, the words alone are the *pramāṇa*, there being no other way of proving them to be right or wrong.

Verse 45

The ultimate result of this pursuit

प्रयत्नाद्यतमानस्तु योगी संशुद्धकिल्बिषः ।
अनेकजन्मसंसिद्धस्ततो याति परां गतिम् ॥ ४५ ॥

prayatnād yatamānastu yogī saṁśuddhakilbiṣaḥ
anekajanmasaṁsiddhastato yāti parāṁ gatim (45)

tu – whereas; *prayatnāt* – by means of the will; *yatamānaḥ* – one who makes an effort; *yogī* – the *yogī*; *saṁśuddha-kilbiṣaḥ* – (is) cleansed of all impurities; *aneka-janma-saṁsiddhaḥ* – gathered in many births; *tataḥ* – then; *parām* – ultimate; *gatim* – end; *yāti* – gains

> Whereas the *yogī* who makes an effort by means of the will is cleansed of all impurities gathered in many births (in the past). Then, he (or she) gains the ultimate end.

In this verse, Kṛṣṇa picks up from where he left off when he had been talking about *yoga* and the *yogī* before Arjuna asked his question. Having defined *yoga* as the vision of sameness in all beings, he now talks about the *yogī* who has this vision, first referring to him as *yatamāna,* a person who is making effort. The word '*prayatna*' also means effort. Śaṅkara clarifies the use of these two words here, saying that *prayatna* refers to the will of the person, meaning that there is great will on the person's part because what is to be gained is very difficult to accomplish. It is against all odds, so to speak. Thus, *prayatnāt yatamānaḥ* refers to the one who is making effort with his or her will.

The *yogī* discussed here is also the one for whom all the impurities have been removed, cleansed, *saṁśuddha-kilbiṣa*. These impurities are the *rāga-dveṣa*s, the *pāpa*s and their psychological outcome like guilt, etc. The one who has cleansed himself or herself from all of them, by living a life of *karma-yoga* is *saṁśuddha-kilbiṣa*. This purification is not something that is accomplished in one lifetime, Kṛṣṇa says. It has taken many births to remove these impurities.

To be a seeker is no ordinary accomplishment

Even to have gained the *upādhi,* the body, of a seeker, a *mumukṣu,* to have the desire for *mokṣa,* is itself not an ordinary accomplishment. It has taken many births to come to this pursuit. The many births, *aneka-janma,* is only with reference to the past because now the person is studying the *Gītā*. Therefore, the person being addressed here is called *aneka-janma-saṁsiddha,* one who has taken many births to come to the point of wanting to enquire.

The desire for liberation itself is something born out of *aneka-janma*. The proper *antaḥ-karaṇa,* the mind, and the proper *upādhi* has to be gained for gaining this knowledge – all of which has now been accomplished by this person after many births. In each *janma* the person gathered a little bit of *yoga-saṁskāra,* the *saṁskāra* that is conducive to the pursuit of knowledge.

Gathering adequate *yoga-saṁskāra* over many births is a little like becoming a millionaire after you have gathered coupons for a long period of time. Even at the cost of money, you gather this kind of *saṁskāra,* which is an entirely different type of wealth. The person under discussion here has amassed *yoga-saṁskāra;* he went on gathering it and accumulating it like some great miser until, finally, the *puṇya* gathered makes him an *aneka-janma-saṁsiddha*. Therefore, *tataḥ,* having prepared himself in this way, the person is qualified for the knowledge.

We can also take *saṁsiddha* here to mean one who has clear knowledge, since the person is said to be a *saṁśuddha-kilbiṣa,* one whose mind is pure and who has gained *saṁsiddhi,* the vision of sameness. This clear knowledge is the result of a number of *janma*s in which the *yoga-saṁskāra* was gathered. Having this clear knowledge, then, the person is called *aneka-janma-saṁsiddha*.

An end that never ends

Knowledge being *mokṣa*, the person is also said to have gained the most exalted end, *parā-gati*. Every end comes to an end, but *mokṣa* is an end that does not come to an end. It is the one end from which you do not return. After all, any end that comes to an end is not really an end; it is only a lap, a circular lap. You keep moving around in the circle of *saṁsāra*, not getting out. All that happens is that you keep coming back to the same point. To distinguish *mokṣa* as an end from which, there is no coming back, the word 'end,' has an adjective here, *parā,* the most exalted end. *Mokṣa* is the end that is gained by one who pursues self-knowledge and it is an end from which there is no return.

Verse 46

Kṛṣṇa tells Arjuna to be a yogī

तपस्विभ्योऽधिको योगी ज्ञानिभ्योऽपि मतोऽधिकः ।
कर्मिभ्यश्चाधिको योगी तस्माद्योगी भवार्जुन ॥ ४६ ॥

tapasvibhyo'dhiko yogī jñānībhyo'pi mato'dhikaḥ
karmibhyaścādhiko yogī tasmād yogī bhavārjuna (46)

yogī – a *yogī; tapasvibhyaḥ* – to those who live a life of meditation; *adhikaḥ* – superior; *jñānībhyaḥ* – to the scholars; *api* – even; *adhikaḥ* – superior; *yogī* – a *yogī; karmibhyaḥ ca* – and to those who perform action; *adhikaḥ* – superior; *mataḥ* – is considered; *tasmāt* – therefore; Arjuna – O Arjuna; *yogī bhava* – be a *yogī*

> A *yogī* is considered superior to those who live a life of meditation, superior even to the scholars, and superior to those who perform action. Therefore, Arjuna! be a *yogī*.

Here, *adhika* means *utkṛṣṭa*, the best, the most exalted, in terms of what a person has to be. Kṛṣṇa has already defined the most exalted person as a *yogī*, a definition that he repeats in the next verse, as we shall see. In the present verse, this *yogī* is described as one who is superior to all the *tapasvī*s, those who perform various kinds of meditation, and to all the *karmī*s, meaning those who perform the enjoined *vaidika* rituals.

Both types of people, *tapasvī*s and *karmī*s, are *mumukṣu*s and are in no way being condemned here. In fact, they are people who engage in their respective activities for the sole purpose of becoming the *yogī* who is the most exalted of them all, the one who either pursues *dhyāna-yoga*, contemplation on *ātmā* as Brahman, or who has already accomplished it, having gained this knowledge. Such a *yogī* is definitely superior to these two types of people said here.

Scholarship alone does not give one the vision

The *tapasvī* is not one who has to find a particular end; rather, the very *tapas* has to resolve into this *yogī* alone. Thus, it can be said that the *yogī* is superior to the *tapasvī* – *tapasvibhyaḥ adhikaḥ yogī*. In the same way, the *yogī* is superior to the scholars, *jñānībhyaḥ adhikaḥ yogī*. Here *jñānī* refers to the one who knows the Veda. They can recite it and they may even know the meaning of the words. However, one does not gain the knowledge, the vision of the Veda, by mere scholarship alone. There has to be a commitment to this knowledge and its pursuit for there to be any possibility of gaining the vision of sameness in all beings.

Since this verse is about a *yogī* who already has the knowledge, scholarship that is talked about here must necessarily exclude Vedanta. Therefore, *jñānī* has to be taken as someone other than the *yogī* under discussion. Śaṅkara clarifies this point in his commentary to this verse by referring to *jñānī*s as those who have scholarship, *pāṇḍitya,* with reference to the meaning of the Veda, *śāstrārtha* specifically the first portion of the Veda, the *pūrva-mīmāṁsā śāstra*. We can also include the *vedānta-śāstra* here since scholars can know the meaning of the words without understanding that it is the meaning of themselves. However, *vedānta-śāstra* would usually not be included here because the verse itself is *vedānta-śāstra*. These scholars, then, are those who have scholarship in all the other *śāstra*s, but the *vedānta-śāstra* and their scholarship has to pay off in the form of this *yoga,* a *yoga* characterised by clear vision of the *vastu*, the truth of everything. Already having this vision, the *yogī* is said to be superior to the scholars, *jñānibhyaḥ adhikaḥ yogī*.

Therefore – be a *yogī*.

The *yogī* who is understood to be superior to the scholars and to the *tapasvī*s is also thought to be superior to those who perform rituals, the *karmīs* – *karmibhyaḥ adhikaḥ yogī*. So, what does Kṛṣṇa tell Arjuna to become? '*Tasmād yogī bhavārjuna*, therefore be a *yogī*, Arjuna!' Having been given this advice, what was Arjuna to do? Based on everything Kṛṣṇa has just said, this *yogī* is a *sannyāsī*, one who gives up everything and sits in meditation. Does this not mean that Arjuna has to do the same?

Originally, Kṛṣṇa had asked Arjuna to get up and fight, explaining that *karma* was better for him than *sannyāsa*. Whereas, now Kṛṣṇa is telling him to become a *yogī*, a *sannyāsī*. What does Kṛṣṇa mean by all of this? Again, Arjuna was confused.

The point Kṛṣṇa is making here is that first one lives a life of *karma-yoga* in order to gain a mind that is prepared for the knowledge. Then one becomes a *yogī*, a *sannyāsī*. In otherwords, you have to become a *yogī* after being a *karma-yogī*. This is what Kṛṣṇa means when he says, '*yogī bhavārjuna*, be a *yogī*, Arjuna!'

Yogī here means one who is firmly established in the clear vision, *saṁyag-darśana-niṣṭhā*, which means a *sannyāsī*. 'Become that *sannyāsī*, Arjuna,' Kṛṣṇa is saying. 'You need not give up your *karma* or anything. Running away is not going to help you in anyway. You must work towards becoming that *yogī* who has the clear vision. Therefore, become that *yogī*.'

Why does Kṛṣṇa compare this *yogī* to other *yogī*s here? Once the word *yogī* is mentioned, all kinds of ideas come to mind. Therefore, which should I become, becomes the question. Because everyone wants to become the best person, the most exalted person, *śreṣṭa-puruṣa*, Kṛṣṇa compares the *yogī* with the *tapasvī*s, the *pāṇḍitas*, and the *karmīs*. Having said that the *yogī* is superior to all of them, he urged Arjuna to become that most exalted *yogī*.

Kṛṣṇa defines *yoga* here in the sixth chapter of the *Gītā* as *duḥkha saṁyoga viyoga*, dissociation from association with sorrow. The verse presently under study has to be understood in the context of this definition and in terms of everything Kṛṣṇa has said previously. The sameness of vision, seeing oneself in all beings and all beings in oneself, is all part of what he has said.

Verse 47

The exalted yogī is one who has the sameness of vision

योगिनामपि सर्वेषां मद्गतेनान्तरात्मना ।
श्रद्धावान्भजते यो मां स मे युक्ततमो मतः ॥ ४७ ॥

yoginām api sarveṣāṁ madgatenāntarātmanā
śraddhāvānbhajate yo māṁ sa me yuktatamo mataḥ (47)

yaḥ – the one who; *śraddhāvān* – has *śraddhā; madgatena antarātmanā* – with a mind absorbed in me; *māṁ bhajate* – contemplates upon me; *saḥ* – he; *sarveṣāṁ yoginām* – among the *yogī*s; *api* – even; *yuktatamaḥ* – the most exalted; *me mataḥ* – (this is) my vision

> The one who has *śraddhā,* who with a mind absorbed in me, contemplates upon me, he is the most exalted among all *yogī*s (This is) my vision.

Kṛṣṇa knows that there were many kinds of *yogī*s, but he is not talking about any of them here. For *yogī*s who meditate on various deities, there is a certain duality in that they take themselves to be different from that upon which they are meditating. Therefore, they retain their sense of *kartā*, doership, and, as doers, they do various types of *yoga*. Although these meditators are all laudable, they are not the *yogī*. Kṛṣṇa is pointing out here the most exalted among *yogī*s – *yoginām api sarveṣāṁ yuktatamaḥ*.

The *yogī* being discussed is the one who contemplates upon Kṛṣṇa as Īśvara – *yaḥ māṁ bhajate* – not on a particular deity. Such a person meditates on the one who is everything, the one who is the cause of the world, *jagat-kāraṇa* and who is not separate from the *jīva-ātmā*. The mind of this *yogī* is totally absorbed in Parameśvara. Therefore Kṛṣṇa says, '*madgatena antarātmanā māṁ bhajate*.' In effect he was saying, 'I am he; he is I.' It means that, for this person, there is no separation between him and Īśvara. For this reason, then, the person is considered to be the most exalted among *yogī*s.

There are not two yogīs here

Here Kṛṣṇa is not comparing the *yogī* with the *yogī* in the previous verse; he is simply describing that same *yogī* further. If this point is missed, as it sometimes is, certain problems in understanding can arise. The *yogī* under discussion is the one who was said to be superior to those who meditate, superior to the scholars who know the Veda, and superior also to those who perform rituals. And why is this *yogī* superior? Because, contemplating on Parameśvara, the *para-ātmā* alone, the mind of the person is completely resolved. Having gained this identity, the person is said to be accomplished in *yoga*.

The previous verse actually completed this chapter on meditation, but Kṛṣṇa wants to briefly restate exactly what *yoga* is. The identity between Parameśvara and the *jīva* is *yoga*. Who gains this *yoga*? The one who has *śraddhā*, *śraddhāvān*, gains this *yoga*. *Śraddhā* is the attitude born out of the appreciation that *śāstra* is the means for gaining the knowledge that is *mokṣa*. Such a person gains the knowledge by meditating on Parameśvara until the identity between the *jīva* and Parameśvara, as revealed by the *śāstra*, is clear. Having gained this knowledge, the person is a *yogī*, the most exalted of human beings, there being no one superior to this *yogī*.

With this verse the sixth chapter comes to an end.

ॐ तत्सत् ।

इति श्रीमद्भगवद्गीतासूपनिषत्सु ब्रह्मविद्यायां योगशास्त्रे श्रीकृष्णार्जुन-
संवादे ध्यान-योगो नाम षष्ठोऽध्यायः ॥ ६ ॥

oṁ tat sat.

*iti śrīmadbhagavadgītāsūpaniṣatsu brahma-vidyāyāṁ yoga-
śāstre śrīkṛṣṇārjuna-saṁvāde dhyāna-yogo nāma
ṣaṣṭho'dhyāyaḥ (6)*

Om, Brahman, is the only reality. Thus ends the sixth chapter called *dhyāna-yoga* – having the topic meditation – in the *Bhagavadgītā* which is in the form of a dialogue between Śrī Kṛṣṇa and Arjuna, which is the essence of the *Upaniṣads*, whose subject matter is both the knowledge of Brahman and *yoga*.

Summary of chapters 1-6

With the completion of the sixth chapter, the first *ṣaṭka* – a group of six chapters – of the *Gītā* is over. Although the same topic, '*tat tvam asi*,' runs through all eighteen chapters, there is a marked difference between each of the three groups, as you will see when we take up the seventh chapter. '*Tat tvam asi*' is an equation that can be looked at in terms of these three groups of six chapters, each group called a *ṣaṭka* in Sanskrit. In the first *ṣaṭka*, the meaning of the word '*tvam*' is analysed. In the second, the meaning of the word '*tat*' is analysed. And in the third *ṣaṭka*, the meaning of the word '*asi*' that equates *tvam* and *tat*, is analysed. Thus, the three groups of six chapters deal predominantly with *tvam-pada-artha*, *tat-pada-artha* and *asi-pada-artha* respectively.

The six chapters that we have seen so far talk about *tvam*, you, as a person with *dharma-adharma* conflict. In the first chapter, Arjuna was presented in a tight situation, wherein his affections conflicted with the call of duty. One's duty is one thing and one's affections are quite another. And Arjuna found himself more moved by the love and affection he had for the elders of his family than by his duty.

As long as your duty does not come into conflict with your affection, it is easy to perform your duties. And, if your call of duty is so pronounced that your affection does not overpower it, you can still heed to the call and do your duty, meaning that you make your affection subserve the duty. However, there are also occasions where the affection gets the better of the duties, resulting in a conflict. This happens because you cannot dismiss duty just like that; it is something that you know is to be done; nor can you dismiss your affections just like that. The very fact that you sometimes go by your feelings prove that they are equally powerful and are capable of completely overpowering you occasionally, which is what happened to Arjuna.

Arjuna's predicament

Arjuna had a legitimate argument for wanting to get out of this particular situation because it was one in which a lot of blood would be shed. Since killing was involved, Arjuna's problem definitely had a valid basis. His entire predicament, leading to an action on his part, was presented in the first chapter by Arjuna himself. And, after he had finished, he sat back in the chariot, prepared to give up the battle. This was the action.

He had come to the battlefield armed and ready to fight. He had even asked Kṛṣṇa to take him to a spot where he could see those against whom he would be fighting. Until then, there was no problem. But, when he saw the people involved, he became different; only then did the problem arise. Only when one faces a situation can one understand the implications, and Arjuna saw the implications of this particular situation immediately. He saw that he had to fight against Droṇa and Bhīṣma, and he tried to tell Kṛṣṇa that this was not proper.

This was Arjuna's predicament, the predicament of 'you, *tvam*,' the *jīva*, the individual, who is subject to emotions, to right and wrong, *dharma* and *adharma*, and also to sorrow, *śoka*. Arjuna represented anyone who gets into a conflict and ends up in a state of sadness. Because Arjuna wanted to be free of this sadness, he talked to Kṛṣṇa. And this talking helped him not to get out of sorrow but to discover, in the process of talking, a problem that is more chronic to the human condition than the acute problem that was right there in front of him.

In front of Arjuna was the problem of having to fight this particular battle, whereas the more chronic problem was the human problem, 'I am subject to sorrow,' which is also a 'you, *tvam*,' problem. This is discerning the problem, discovering in oneself a desire for freedom from the original problem of sorrow. Kṛṣṇa had the knowledge that could make one free. Arjuna knew this fact, but he had not drawn upon it earlier because he had no interest in it before.

The first few years of Arjuna's life had been spent gathering valour, marrying, and so on. Later, of course, he got involved in all the problems that resulted in his going to the forest, where he spent thirteen years with no time for anything but survival and thinking about how to settle accounts with Duryodhana. With every thorn he removed from his foot, while walking in the forest, Arjuna was reminded of the hurt rendered by Duryodhana, whose scheming ways were responsible for his having to suffer in the forest in the first place. Therefore, Duryodhana was a much bigger thorn for Arjuna than any of the thorns he had to remove from his feet.

Arjuna had been born with a golden spoon in his mouth, yet he had to suffer this period of exile. The presence of his wife Draupadī in the forest was also a reminder of the account to be settled with Duryodhana, especially since she had decided not to tie her hair until the insult she had suffered had been avenged. Thus, her flowing hair would definitely have been a constant reminder to Arjuna about the need to get even with Duryodhana. Naturally, Arjuna had no time, no chance, to think about *ātmā*, Brahman, or anything.

Arjuna's lot is everyone's lot

What is to be understood here is that Arjuna's lot is the lot of any human being whose mind is possessed, seized by certain situations. This is all the meaning of *jīva,* individual, the meaning of the word 'you'– *tvam-pada-artha*. That I am hurt is 'you.' That I am subject to sorrow is 'you.' That I am called upon to do certain duties, having been born as a person into certain situations, is also 'you.' And that I am not able to fulfil these duties is 'you,' as well. Why am I not able to fulfil them? Because my affections are different from my duties, which is also 'you.' Therefore, all problems are 'you-problems' alone.

Arjuna recognised this problem in the battlefield when he saw all the implications of the impending war. He knew that no one really wins a war, that both sides are always losers. Even if there is victory, the loss is very big. That Arjuna saw this very well was clearly demonstrated when he said in so many words, 'Even though, I may get back the kingdom and have all kinds of comforts and enjoyments at my command, they would all be stained with the blood of such great people as Bhīṣma and Droṇa – *rudhira-pradigdha-bhoga*s. If, in order to buy this pleasure, I have to kill all these people, what a cost it is!'[1] This clearly shows that Arjuna thought that the battle was not a worthwhile activity on any grounds.

Having concluded that the battle was not worthwhile, his next thought was, 'What, then, is worthwhile?' If you cannot see anything worthwhile, you get frustrated and become a drop out. Dropping out itself is due to frustration, the frustration that comes from realising that what is commonly pursued is not worthwhile. Nothing else being very clear, the person may just drop out of everything altogether and, taking a guitar in hand, live the nomadic life of a wandering musician. A drop out can become a simple hobo also, all because of frustration.

Here, Arjuna's frustration was not due to a psychological problem. The problem was much more than that. Arjuna was a man of valour, a man of courage, culture, and education, a man who was highly worshipped by everyone. Because he was already known as a great man, he no longer needed to prove himself on the battlefield or elsewhere. He did not come from a dysfunctional family to have psychological problems. He was a normal person whose life was functional all the way. In fact, since he was a prince and a worthy person as well, he had grown into much more than an average person. Even so, Arjuna was a person, which is what people tend to forget.

Regaining the kingdom was no longer important

Arjuna was a human being with affections and, because of these affections, he could not see anything worthwhile about fighting. Therefore, he could not avoid the question, what is it

---

[1] *Gītā* 2.5

that is worthwhile? Arjuna knew the answer to this question because he was born into a culture that had a value for self-knowledge, which was why his father had gone to the forest, in fact. Arjuna also had known other people who pursued this knowledge. But, even though he knew such knowledge existed, he had not been drawn to it previously for the reasons we have already seen. Now, however, he found that he had no reason to fight, that regaining the kingdom and all that went with it would not solve the problem.

If Arjuna had not known about the knowledge, he would have had no place to go and nothing worthwhile to pursue. But he did know there was a direction. He knew the problem could be solved by gaining *śreyas*, *mokṣa*, and that there was no other way of solving it. He also knew that, to gain the knowledge, he had to become a *śiṣya*, disciple, which meant he had to have a teacher. Knowing Kṛṣṇa as he did, Arjuna knew that he would find no better teacher anywhere. Therefore, he said to Kṛṣṇa straightaway, 'I am your disciple. Please teach me all that is to be taught, so that, I may gain *śreyas* – *yat śreyaḥ syāt niścitaṁ brūhi tanme śiṣyaḥ te ahaṁ śādhi māṁ tvāṁ prapannam.*'[2]

Arjuna's problem is to be understood within the meaning of the word 'you,' *tvam-pada-artha*, because the conflict belongs to 'you, *tvam*,' alone. There is no problem whatsoever for Brahman, Īśvara, as we shall see in the second *ṣaṭka* of the *Gītā*, which talks of the *tat-pada-artha*. Īśvara has no problem; the

---

[2] *Gītā* 2.7

individual, *jīva*, has the problem and the individual has the *jijñāsa*, the desire for knowledge.

Until now, Arjuna's life had been worthwhile; even though it required a battlefield, it had helped him. Here, on the battlefield he had a desire for the knowledge. No one else on the battlefield had this desire, it seems, least of all Duryodhana. Fortunately, for Arjuna, Kṛṣṇa was also on the battlefield. Arjuna could talk to Kṛṣṇa , and, because he was ready for this knowledge, Arjuna found a teacher in Kṛṣṇa. How do we know Kṛṣṇa was a teacher? Because he taught Arjuna; he did not say, 'Shut up and fight!' and leave it at that. Although, Kṛṣṇa did say something similar to Arjuna in order to encourage him to do his duty, he taught him. If he had not, there would be no *Gītā*. Instead, Kṛṣṇa could have responded to Arjuna's request to teach him by giving Arjuna whatever psychological pep talk it would take to get him to fight. But Kṛṣṇa did not do this; with utmost seriousness, he began teaching Arjuna.

First, Kṛṣṇa told Arjuna that there was no reason for sorrow, *aśocyān anvaśocaḥ tvam*, and then proceeded to prove it in the remaining chapters of the *Gītā*. He told Arjuna that the wise people do not subject themselves to sorrow, whereas he, Arjuna, is subject to sorrow, in spite of talking words that smacked of wisdom. Kṛṣṇa was as much as telling Arjuna here that he was not as wise as his words would indicate. He did this so that Arjuna would listen to what he had to say. From the second chapter onwards, Kṛṣṇa taught what the nature of *tvam* and *tat* is, and then talked about the connection between the two.

'Tat Tvam Asi' is Vedanta

Tvam means 'you,' which means 'I' for each person. Therefore, the nature of 'I' is the meaning of the word *tvam* in the *mahā-vākya, tat tvam asi.* Vedanta, is nothing else but '*tat tvam asi,*' the statement that reveals the identity between the *jīva* and Brahman. In the first six chapters of the *Gītā,* Kṛṣṇa analysed this *tvam-pada,* the word 'you' meaning 'I,' and all that is connected to it. And how did he begin? By saying that *ātmā* is neither the subject, *kartā,* nor an object, *karma.*

To subject oneself to sorrow, one should be either a *kartā,* the subject, or *karma* an object. But, Kṛṣṇa said, *ātmā* is not subject to objectification; therefore, it can never be destroyed. Since *ātmā* is not even available for anyone to look at, where is the question of doing something to it? Time, *kāla* itself cannot approach the *ātmā* and no other means of destruction can make *ātmā* the subject of its destructive measures. *Ātmā* is therefore, definitely not an object, *karma.*

Here, it might be said that *ātmā* is not an object, perhaps it is the *kartā,* the subject. No, Kṛṣṇa said, it is neither a direct doer nor an indirect doer of any action. Therefore, it is free from *kartṛtva,* doership. It has neither doership nor enjoyership, nor does it have the status of being an object to anything else. All that is there is *ātmā* Kṛṣṇa said, *ātmā* that is free from everything and therefore, free from sorrow.

When Arjuna asked him to describe a wise person, Kṛṣṇa told him that a person of wisdom is one who is happy without there being any reason. Knowing the nature of *ātmā,* the *svarūpa* of *ātmā,* such a person is free from any limitation, being identical with Brahman, Īśvara. Here, the topic being *tvam-pada artha,* Kṛṣṇa mentioned the identity of *tvam* with Brahman, the *tat* of the *mahā-vākya, tat tvam asi,* but did not go into the meaning of *tat* at length, as he did in the second group of six chapters dealing with Īśvara. Because *tvam-pada-artha* is equated to *tat-pada,* a proper analysis of the meaning of *tat* is also necessary to complete the unfoldment of the equation, *tat tvam asi.*

If the individual is indeed Brahman, this knowledge has to be gained. Therefore, Arjuna had a doubt about what he should do. Should he just go with *karma* or take to a life of *sannyāsa*? Since knowledge would deliver the goods, he naturally thought he should go for the knowledge, but in the process of discussing this with Kṛṣṇa, he was advised to do what was to be done. Kṛṣṇa supported his advice with a number of arguments, saying that from any standpoint–from the power standpoint, the pain standpoint, or the duty standpoint–there was nothing that really barred Arjuna from doing what was to be done here and now. All this was discussed in the body of the second chapter. And, because Arjuna had a natural doubt, there is a third chapter, again covering *tvam-pada* alone.

If knowledge liberates – why do *karma* at all?

In the third chapter, Arjuna asked why he should not take to knowledge, which for him amounted to taking to the life of *sannyāsa,* if knowledge is what liberates? For him, *sannyāsa* and knowledge were identical. He acknowledged that if he were interested in anything other than knowledge, then of course he should do *karma.* But he was not interested in anything else. Therefore, he thought that he should take *sannyāsa* and pursue knowledge.

Arjuna knew that taking *sannyāsa* was the only way to be absolved from performing his various duties, that it was a ritual to release one from all rituals and all other duties as well. In other words, it is the final ritual. Once this ritual is over, there are no more roles to play and one is free to pursue knowledge alone. To Arjuna, this seemed to be the most desirable thing to do because he was no longer interested in the kingdom; he was only interested in *mokṣa*. It seemed to be the only course open to him and, therefore, he thought it correct.

While telling Arjuna that he should do his duty, Kṛṣṇa also made sure that Arjuna understood that knowledge alone liberates, that only the one who knows is free, and so on. Naturally, then, Arjuna wanted to know and to know thoroughly. From his question, however, it was very clear that he had some insight, but that his understanding of *karma* and *sannyāsa* was not at all clear. This was why he kept asking Kṛṣṇa to tell him which was better, *karma* or the pursuit of knowledge.

It seemed to Arjuna that Kṛṣṇa was contradicting himself, praising knowledge as the means for liberation and, at the same time, asking him to fight. Because Arjuna was confused, he asked Kṛṣṇa to decide which would be better for him. Would *karma* give him *mokṣa* or would *jñāna* give him *mokṣa*?

The two-fold lifestyle

In order to clear up Arjuna's confusion, Kṛṣṇa began again, saying that he himself had introduced this two-fold lifestyle in the beginning – *loke asmin dvividhā niṣṭhā purā proktā mayā anagha jñāna yogena sāṅkhyānāṁ karma yogena yoginām.*[3] One is called *jñāna-yoga* or *nivṛtti-mārga* and the other is called *karma-yoga* or *pravṛtti-mārga.* In *jñāna-yoga,* one withdraws, *nivṛtti,* from all activities to pursue knowledge and, in *karma-yoga,* one performs activities, *pravṛtti,* with the right attitude and pursues knowledge also. These two lifestyles are also found in the first two verses of the *Īśāvāsyopaniṣad.*

Having told Arjuna all this, Kṛṣṇa described *karma-yoga,* repeating what he had already said in the second chapter. He told Arjuna that *karma-yoga* is a means for *mokṣa,* that it is not something opposed to *mokṣa,* nor is it opposed to *sannyāsa.* Rather, it is another way of gaining *mokṣa,* a way that is available for those who are not prepared to live the life of a *sannyāsī.*

The lifestyle known as *sannyāsa* is not an easy one. Why? Because, in *sannyāsa,* you do not have a field wherein you can express yourself, and being able to express yourself is what helps you to mature. Therefore, it is preferable to be in the field, the world, and live a life of relationship within it. Relationship means playing various roles in the world whereby you get rid of your *rāga*s and *dveṣa*s. This is why Kṛṣṇa talked about *karma-yoga* predominantly in the third chapter. And for whom is this *karma-yoga*? Not for Īśvara. It is for the *jīva, tvam-pada-artha.*

---

[3] *Gītā* 3.3

Kṛṣṇa as Īśvara

Kṛṣṇa told Arjuna that what he had been telling him had been coming down throughout the ages. He had given this vision to humanity through the great sages, a few of whom Kṛṣṇa named at the beginning of the fourth chapter. Many kings knew it and all the *ṛṣi*s knew it. Even so, it is not easily available, which is why Duryodhanas are so many. On hearing this, Arjuna had a problem.

Kṛṣṇa had said that he had taught those who had lived at the beginning of the creation, like Vivasvān and others. How could this be? Kṛṣṇa was his contemporary. What was he talking about? Therefore, he wanted to know who this Kṛṣṇa really was? In reply, Kṛṣṇa told him that they both had had a number of births, and that he, Kṛṣṇa, knew all of his births, whereas Arjuna did not–*bahūni me vyatītāni janmāni tava ca arjuna tāni ahaṁ veda sarvāṇi na tvaṁ vettha parantapa*.[4] In other words, if Arjuna knew himself, he would be as free as Kṛṣṇa.

Kṛṣṇa then told Arjuna that he, Kṛṣṇa, was not an ordinary *jīva,* and that he was an incarnation of Īśvara; in other words, an *avatāra*. Even though he was available empirically in human form, he did not subject himself to the empirical rules of reality and therefore, he was not born of *karma*. He was born because of the prayers of the people. In fact, he was not even born. Knowing he is never born, he simply assumed a body.

---

[4] *Gītā* 4.5

Renouncing the doer

Kṛṣṇa also told Arjuna that this was not only true for him but that it was true for Arjuna as well. If Arjuna knew he was only assuming a body, that only a form is born, that he is never born, he would be the same as Kṛṣṇa. One has to know that 'I, *ātmā*,' is never born. This is what is meant by *jñāna-karma-sannyāsa*, the renunciation of *karma* through knowledge. Kṛṣṇa then defined *jñāna-karma-sannyāsa* as giving up *kartṛtva*, doership. And this giving up of *kartṛtva*, is not an action; it is a fact that has to be understood. *Ātmā* is already given up in the sense that *ātmā* is and always was free from doership. Knowing *ātmā* as being free from doership is *jñāna-karma-sannyāsa*, whereas in *karma-sannyāsa, karma*, is given up but the doer is still there giving up the *karma*.

You may tell everyone that you have given up all your *karma*s, that you are a *sannyāsī*, but it is the *kartā* that says this and this *kartā* has to be dealt with, even if you take to a life of *sannyāsa*. The person who says, 'I have done the last ritual,' is the *kartā* and that *kartā* is the one who has to be given up. Therefore, Kṛṣṇa told Arjuna that doership is what has to be given up.

Strictly speaking, only the person who is able to see actionlessness in the midst of all activities – *karmaṇi akarma yaḥ paśyet* – can be called a *sannyāsī*. This person is a *jñāna-karma-sannyāsī*, one who gives up all action by knowledge, by knowing that *ātmā* is not the doer. To make this even clearer, Kṛṣṇa said that the fire of knowledge, *jñāna-agni*, destroys all *karma*s.

Although Arjuna was getting the knowledge from Kṛṣṇa, still Kṛṣṇa told him, as part of the teaching, to gain the knowledge with the help of a teacher who knows. Approach such teachers, Kṛṣṇa said, and they will teach you. Having said all of this, again he told Arjuna to get up and take to *karma-yoga – yogam ātiṣṭha uttiṣṭha–*[5] Why? Because *karma* can only be given up in terms of knowledge and *karma-yoga* would prepare him for that knowledge. Therefore, it is not *karma-sannyāsa* that is important, but *jñāna-karma-sannyāsa*, and the difference between the two is to be clearly understood here.

Having again been told to take to *yoga*, Arjuna asked the same question, using different words, 'You praise *sannyāsa* and you also praise *yoga*, Kṛṣṇa. Of the two, please tell me, once and for all, which one is better – *sannyāsaṁ karmaṇāṁ kṛṣṇa punaryogaṁ ca saṁśasi yat śreyaḥ etayoḥ ekaṁ tat me brūhi suniścitam.*'[6] Here, Arjuna was saying that now he did not think that Kṛṣṇa was praising both *sannyāsa* and *karma*, but that he still had a problem. He still wanted to know which one would give him *śreyas*.

From this, we see that Arjuna was still beating the same drum, still harping on the same string of doubt. Therefore, once again, Kṛṣṇa told him that both lifestyles give *mokṣa*, but because *sannyāsa* is not as simple as giving up all of one's activities, the life of *sannyāsa* cannot be of any use to a person who is not prepared for it. Contemplativeness does not come by sheer will alone; in fact, the will does not come into it at all.

---

[5] *Gītā* 4.42

[6] *Gītā* 5.1

There is no choice really really speaking

Kṛṣṇa was telling Arjuna here that he could take to *sannyāsa* if he wanted to, that no one could stop him. But whether he would be a *sannyāsī* in temperament, in disposition, was anyone's guess. Whereas *karma-yoga* would in no way deny him the knowledge. In time, he would reach Brahman–*yoga-yuktaḥ muniḥ brahma na cireṇa adhigacchati.*[7]

Kṛṣṇa went on to say that the one who is endowed with *yoga* is one whose mind is purified and therefore, there is mastery over the sense organs. This is the preparation needed for knowledge to become very clear to the person. Then, the person knows that the self is the self of all beings and all beings are in the self. Once a person recognises this fact, then, even though he or she performs action, the person is not affected by the action, which is renunciation of action by knowledge.

Therefore, one is aiming to be a *tattvavit*, knower of the truth. And, to become a *tattvavit* there is a choice of lifestyle, but it is really not much of a choice. In other words, if one prefers to live a life of *sannyāsa,* thinking it will be more convenient than a life of *karma-yoga*, then one had better become a *karma-yogī*, Kṛṣṇa was saying. Whereas, the moment one thinks one does not require *sannyāsa*, then one can become a *sannyāsī*. That is how it is; *sannyāsa* will stick to the person if one is ready. If one is not ready taking to the lifestyle itself will not make one a *jñāna-karma-sannyāsī*. Because this

[7] *Gītā* 5.6

point has to be understood, Kṛṣṇa kept talking to Arjuna. Otherwise, he would simply have told him that he was unfit for *sannyāsa*.

Karma-yoga and then sannyāsa is the order

Kṛṣṇa was not saying there is no *sannyāsa*. He was saying there is, which is what Arjuna found so confusing. But Kṛṣṇa was not confusing Arjuna; he was educating him. He wanted Arjuna to see the difference between *karma-sannyāsa* and *jñāna-karma-sannyāsa,* because his question arose from confusion. He looked at *karma-yoga* and *sannyāsa* as black and white. In fact, there is no black and white here; nor is there any grey. Both *karma-yoga* and *sannyāsa* are equally efficacious, the only difference being that you have to be ready for a life of *sannyāsa*. This preparation is possible by living a life of *karma-yoga* before becoming a *sannyāsī*.

If you take to *sannyāsa* before you are ready, then, as a *sannyāsī,* you will still have to make yourself ready. It is a very difficult thing to do, like becoming a professor and then becoming qualified in your subject matter. It is not an easy situation, especially for your students! Similarly, if you take to *sannyāsa* before you are ready, you are a *sannyāsī* merely in name. To become a *sannyāsī* in the true sense of the word in such a situation is not impossible, but it is certainly very difficult.

Therefore, Kṛṣṇa wanted Arjuna to understand that the real meaning of *sannyāsa* is giving up action in terms of knowledge alone. There is no literal giving up here. By knowing you are not a doer, you give up doership, and then you are free.

In the meantime, Kṛṣṇa said, just do what is to be done, without being excited or restless about what you are doing or not doing, and in time, this knowledge, this *sannyāsa*, will be gained. For whom is the *sannyāsa*? Is it for Īśvara or for the *jīva*? Again, it is for the *jīva* alone.

Meditation

At the end of the fifth chapter, Kṛṣṇa introduced the topic of meditation, the predominant subject matter of the sixth chapter. The meditation discussed here can be taken as that which invokes the grace of the Īśvara, *saguṇa-brahma,* or contemplation on *ātmā* that is Brahman, *nirguṇa-brahma*. Both interpretations are possible because both are meant for *jñāna*.

Meditating on Īśvara is meant for grace and that grace is also necessary for *jñāna*. With that grace, you gain a teacher and thereby the knowledge that is *mokṣa*. If you already have a teacher and have done *śravaṇa* and *manana*, then you can live a life of contemplation, meditation, *nididhyāsana*. How you sit in meditation was also pointed out in this chapter. All this, the meditation and what precedes it, is for the *jīva* alone.

Thus, the first six chapters are about the *jīva,* the meaning of the word 'you,' *tvam-pada-artha,* and everything that concerns 'you.' What the individual has to do as a *karma-yogī*, *karma-yoga* is a way for this person to prepare the mind for gaining knowledge, that there is knowledge to be gained, that there is *sannyāsa* also – all these are relevant to the *tvam-pada-artha* alone. The nature of this *tvam*, *ātmā*, was revealed as being free from being either a subject, *kartā*, or an object, *karma,* and was equated to Īśvara, *tat-pada-artha*.

Because *tvam* and *tat* were equated in the analysis of the meaning of the word *tvam,* Īśvara, *tat,* also has to be analysed. Who is this Īśvara? How can I be Īśvara? Because there is a doubt about the validity of the equation, Īśvara is analysed in the next six chapters. Even though every chapter talks about the equation, the predominant topic of these next six chapters is Īśvara, the Lord.

The basis of Arjuna's fear

In the eleventh chapter, Arjuna gained a cosmic vision of the Lord with the grace of Kṛṣṇa. Although Arjuna gained this vision, it was not total because he did not include himself in it. And, because he makes this distinction between himself and the whole, there is fear.

Arjuna's fear was so great when faced with the cosmic vision of Īśvara that he begged Kṛṣṇa to revert to his human form. He found the old form, the one with the whip in hand, much easier and more pleasant to deal with, whereas in the cosmic form, the whole world was being devoured by Kṛṣṇa. All the beings that one could possibly imagine were between the molars of Īśvara. Hanging there, in the jaws of Īśvara, in the jaws of time, all the *jīva*s were being ground to powder, as it were. Arjuna saw all of this. Naturally, then, he was very frightened. Why? Because he excluded himself from the cosmic vision, meaning that he excluded himself from the whole! And because of that he was overwhelmed by that whole.

Concluding the second *ṣaṭka,* called *īśvara-ṣaṭka,* Kṛṣṇa talked about devotion to Īśvara, *īśvara-bhakti,* the topic of the twelfth chapter. The third *ṣaṭka,* the remaining six chapters of the *Gītā*, begins with Kṛṣṇa telling Arjuna that between him, Arjuna and Īśvara there is an identity. This identity is represented in the *mahā-vākya*, '*tat tvam asi*,' by the word *asi*, and is analysed in the last six chapters – what is this identity, what brings it about, and so on, are analysed. Again, Kṛṣṇa went into the means for this knowledge, the values, and a variety of other topics. This is because, although the identity between the *jīva* and Īśvara exists, it is not recognised. Therefore, the means that are to be used to bring this identity about, in terms of knowledge, is discussed from the thirteenth chapter onwards.

In this way, the three words, *tat, tvam* and *asi*, are each analysed in the three *ṣaṭka*s. We have already seen the first six chapters dealing with the *tvam-pada*. Now, from the first verse of the seventh chapter onwards, we will see the second group of six chapters, the topic of which is *tat*, Īśvara.

Chapter 7

ज्ञान-विज्ञान-योगः

Jñāna-vijñāna-yogaḥ

Topic of indirect and immediate knowledge

Introduction

The last verse of some chapters of the *Gītā* can seem out of context and therefore an interpolation. However, if you look at the verse from the standpoint of what is going to come, it proves to be a building block, a connecting link. In the fifth chapter, for instance, there are a couple of verses introducing meditation, which is the topic of the next chapter. In the sixth chapter, Kṛṣṇa says in the second last verse, '*tasmād yogī bhava,* therefore be a *yogī*.' The statement sums up the *yoga* of meditation. But in the verse that follows there is a building block. It contains a *praśna-bīja,* a seed of a question. It is not an explicit question. Let us look into the verse.

योगिनामपि सर्वेषां मद्गतेनान्तरात्मना ।
श्रद्धावान्भजते यो मां स मे युक्ततमो मतः ॥ ६. ४७ ॥

yoginām api sarveṣāṁ madgatenāntarātmanā
śraddhāvānbhajate yo māṁ sa me yuktatamo mataḥ (6.47)

Here Kṛṣṇa says, 'The one who has *śraddhā,* who with a mind absorbed in me, *madgatena antarātmanā,* contemplates upon me, he is the most exalted among the *yogī*s. (This is) my vision.' This is the seed for two obvious questions:

How does the *yogī* become one whose mind is absorbed in Īśvara?

What is the nature of Kṛṣṇa, the Lord?

Such a doubt is possible because this has not been explained in detail so far. Bhagavān detects the questions and he answers them in the chapters that follow – '*īdṛśaṁ madīyaṁ tattvam*, this is the nature of myself, this is how one is absorbed in me.'

Verse 1

Unfoldment to tat pada begins

In the first six chapters of the *Gītā*, the meaning of '*tvam*,' you, the *jīva*, in the *mahā-vākya*, '*tat tvam asi*,' was unfolded in detail. Now in the following six chapters, the word '*tat*,' Īśvara, the cause of everything, is the predominant topic.

With a desire to unfold this, Śrī Bhagavān says:

श्रीभगवानुवाच ।
मय्यासक्तमनाः पार्थ योगं युञ्जन्मदाश्रयः ।
असंशयं समग्रं मां यथा ज्ञास्यसि तच्छृणु ॥ १ ॥

śrībhagavān uvāca
mayyāsaktamanāḥ pārtha yogaṁ yuñjan madāśrayaḥ
asaṁśayaṁ samagraṁ māṁ yathā jñāsyasi tacchṛṇu (1)

śrībhagavān – Lord Kṛṣṇa; *uvāca* – said;
pārtha – O Pārtha!; *mayi* – in me; *āsaktamanāḥ* – the one whose mind is committed; *madāśrayaḥ* – having surrendered to me; *yogaṁ yuñjan* – taking to *yoga* (*karma-yoga*); *yathā* – in which way; *asaṁśayam* – without any doubt; *samagram* – totally; *mām* – me, Īśvara; *jñāsyasi* – you will know; *tat* – that way; *śṛṇu* – please listen

Śrī Bhagavān said:

Pārtha (Arjuna)! With a mind committed to me by taking to *yoga*, and having surrendered to me, Please listen to the way in which you will know me totally, without any doubt.

With the word '*mayi*' in the verse, Bhagavān introduces himself as the topic of this and the subsequent chapters. *Mayyāsaktamanāḥ*, *mayi*, in me, *āsaktamanāḥ*, a person whose mind is committed. *Madāśrayaḥ* is one for whom Parameśvara is the only *āśraya*, basis.

In his commentary, Śaṅkara explains the meaning of *madāśraya* as follows. A person becomes a desirer with reference to a desired end. To accomplish it he adopts a means appropriate to that end and that means is called *āśraya*. A ritual, like daily *agnihotra* is an *āśraya* for gaining *puṇya* to go to heaven. So, the person is called *agnihotrāśraya*. To accomplish *mokṣa* which *āśraya* should you have? The Lord says you should be *madāśraya*, *īśvarāśraya*, one whose *āśraya* is Īśvara. Generally you seek Īśvara for some end or the other. Here, the end you are committed to is Īśvara himself which is expressed in the word *mayyāsaktamanas*. The *īśvarāśraya* wants Īśvara, that is, he wants to be free from being a *jīva*. This is *mokṣa*. Parameśvara becomes the very end and also the means. Śaṅkara further says that the one who seeks only Parameśvara as the *āśraya*, giving up all other means becomes a *mayyāsaktamanas*. The Lord says, 'Such a person's mind is committed only to me because for him I am the means and I am the end.' These words are to be explainedin the chapter.

In seeking Parameśvara - the end and the means are the same

Here you are seeking knowledge, knowledge of the whole. This seeking is very peculiar because you can gain the whole by a means that is other than the whole. The only means of gaining the whole is to know that 'I am the whole.' There is no other way. Therefore, the end and the means, in the final analysis, become one and the same.

If the means is separate from the end, the end is going to be a limited one, appropriate to the means. If the whole is the end, the only means will be the whole; it cannot be less than that. Therefore, there are no means and end here, which is why it is said that the wise man's track leaves no footprints. We want to follow the track of a wise man, a man who has followed a path and reached the end, wisdom. It is said that following the track of a wise man is like following the footprints of a bird in the sky. What footprints does the bird leave behind as it flies? Such are the footprints left behind by the wise man. The idea is that the means and the end are one and the same. There is no track between time and the timeless, between finite and infinite, between the part and the whole, between *jīva* and Īśvara.

Having defined the seeker as one who is totally committed to the pursuit of Parameśvara, Kṛṣṇa continues. *Asaṁśayaṁ samagraṁ māṁ yathā jñāsyasi tacchṛṇu. Yathā*, in which way; *jñāsyasi*, you will know; *mām*, me, Īśvara; *samagram*, in totality; *asaṁśayam*, without any doubt; as a whole, as the one who is everything, endowed with all glories such as strength, power, overlordship and so on. *Tat*, that, *śṛṇu*, please listen. By what means, following which trail of thinking you will recognise me in totality, to that means, please listen.

This verse introduces what is going to come, not only in this chapter but in those to follow. The following six chapters deal primarily with Parameśvara. And there is one more verse of introduction here.

Verse 2

Vijñāna is distinguished from jñāna

ज्ञानं तेऽहं सविज्ञानमिदं वक्ष्याम्यशेषतः ।
यज्ज्ञात्वा नेह भूयोऽन्यज्ज्ञातव्यमवशिष्यते ॥ २ ॥

jñānaṁ te'haṁ savijñānam idaṁ vakṣyāmyaśeṣataḥ
yajjñātvā neha bhūyo'nyajjñātavyam avaśiṣyate (2)

idaṁ jñānam – this knowledge; *savijñānam* – along with immediate knowledge; *te* – to you; *ahaṁ vakṣyāmi* – I will teach; *aśeṣataḥ* – without any omission; *yat jñātvā* – knowing which; *iha* – here; *bhūyaḥ anyat* – any other thing that is more than this; *jñātavyam* – to be known; *na avaśiṣyate* – does not remain

> I will teach you without any omission, this knowledge, along with immediate knowledge, knowing which there remains nothing else to be known here.

Idaṁ savijñānam, this immediate knowledge, for which the subject matter is me, Parameśvara, the cause of everything, and who is everything, *te*, to you, *vakṣyāmi*, I will tell, *aśeṣataḥ*, without anything being omitted.

What kind of knowledge is this? When *jñāna* and *vijñāna* are mentioned together, it means that *vijñāna* is something different from *jñāna*. *Jñāna* can mean immediate knowledge but because he says *jñāna* with *vijñāna*, the *jñāna* is little less than *vijñāna*. Here, *vi* means *viśeṣa*, distinctive. Therefore, *vijñāna* is immediate knowledge and *jñāna* is indirect knowledge.

Kṛṣṇa says, 'I will give you this *jñāna* with *vijñāna*. For me it is a reality and therefore, what I teach you is something that I see. It is not merely what I have heard. This is what I see and what I see I am teaching you.' So, these words have *prāmāṇya*, the capacity to produce the same knowledge, the same vision in you. Once you see, you have *vijñāna* and you are left with no doubt, no vagueness. This is one meaning.

Another meaning would be, 'I will teach you this knowledge in a manner that will make it immediate for you, not indirect.' Again you understand that this knowledge is to be gained only as immediate, direct, knowledge, not as indirect knowledge. Generally, knowledge of Parameśvara is understood to be indirect. You tend to think of Parameśvara as someone unknown. One devotee said, '*yādṛśosi mahādeva tādṛśāya namo namaḥ*, O Bhagavan! I do not know how you are, what you are, where you are. So, in whichever form you are, I salute you again and again.' This person has a feeling, a sense, that there is a God. But how he is, what he is, he does not want to conclude. It is a prayer which has some faith but at the same time with certain vagueness and doubt. Perhaps it is the right prayer. We tend to make conclusions about Īśvara. He plays it safe. In effect he asks Īśvara, 'Please fill in all the qualifications you require to define yourself.' It is like addressing a letter,

'To whomsoever it may concern.' The one who receives the letter has to think, 'It is addressed to me.'

Here, however, it is just the opposite. Kṛṣṇa says, *īśvara-jñāna* need not be *parokṣa*, indirect. It can be *aparokṣa*. Only *aparokṣa-jñāna* of Īśvara is *mokṣa*. *Parokṣa-jñāna* is useful for offering prayers etc. But the final result of prayer is *aparokṣa-jñāna*, immediate knowledge of Parameśvara. With any other understanding you will be omitting yourself from Parameśvara and thereby editing him. Minus you, Parameśvara is only another *anātmā*, not *ātmā*. And if he is other than you, he becomes located somewhere. So, there is someone called *jīva* in the heart and another person called Īśvara out there somewhere in the vast space. This is duality. Anything other than you is *anātmā* and since only *ātmā* is conscious, *anātmā* is inert. It cannot reveal itself to you, the conscious being. If Īśvara is other than you, he is inert, and still you say he is *sarvajña*. It is merely lip service. But here Kṛṣṇa says, 'I will teach this immediate knowledge in its entirety without anything being left out.'

Praise of knowledge – knowing one thing everything is as well-known

To draw your attention, and to complete the thought, Kṛṣṇa praises this knowledge. *Yajjñātvā*, knowing which, *iha*, in this world or in the *śāstra*, *bhūyaḥ anyat*, anything else which is more than this, *jñātavyam*, to be known, *na avaśiṣyate*, is not there at all. Generally, when you know one thing, even though you know that one thing, there is always something else to know. In fact, even within that one thing there are lot of areas to be known. But here he says knowing that one thing, which is me, everything will be known, because I am everything.

However, you may ask, 'How can I know everything? I am capable of knowing only a few things.' Kṛṣṇa says that there is no *jñātavya vastu,* that is, something that really deserves to be known. After knowing this, nothing remains that deserves to be known. In this entire world only one thing is *satya,* and once you know *satya, mithyā* becomes naturally evident. What is *mithyā* is *satya* but *satya* is not *mithyā*. We discussed this in detail while dealing with the verse, *nāsato vidyate bhāvaḥ.*[1]

What is reckoned here as something to be known makes the difference in life. To know the *svarūpa* of me, Īśvara is to know everything. And *satya* happens to be the *svarūpa* of Īśvara which is you, which is why it is possible to shed your ignorance about the fact. You are a self-evident being whose *svarūpa* is *satya*. The knowledge of *satya,* the *ātmā,* is knowledge of everything. When you know this, you know that everything is me while I am independent of everything.

When you take the self as something different from everything, you find that everything else keeps colliding with you. The whole world becomes an impediment that you have to surmount, for it is how you look upon the world. *Aham,* opposed to the world, is to be understood as *sarva-ātmā,* the self of everything; it is Parameśvara. Kṛṣṇa is going to prove that *aham* is *paramātmā,* that 'I' is everything. Later he says,

---

[1] *Gītā* 2.16

'I am Brahman, the cause of the whole creation, the *tat-pada-artha,* and you are that Brahman.' And then he will say, 'The one who knows me as the self is the one who is not separate from me. He knows everything.'

Śaṅkara says here, knowing this there is no longer anything to be known in order to achieve something. The end that is to be achieved for a human being is achieved; nothing remains. He says further that the one who knows the truth of Īśvara becomes all knowing. There is no other knowledge that can make this claim. Every other form of knowledge is only of a given thing which is *mithyā*. Here, the knowledge is of that *satya* which is everything. Therefore, all you have to know is that *satya*. This is the secret of this knowledge.

Lord Gaṇeśa knew this secret. Lord Śiva had a partiality for Gaṇeśa. His younger son, Subrahmaṇya, was always complaining, 'Why are you so fond of Gaṇeśa?' So, Lord Śiva gave them both a test. He asked each of them to go around this entire world and come back. Now Subrahmaṇya thought, 'This is a wonderful chance for me to prove how great I am.' He was confident because he had a fine vehicle, a peacock. And he knew that Gaṇeśa was slow moving with a huge stomach and had only a mouse as a vehicle. If he gets on this vehicle when is he going to return? The poor mouse cannot even move. And so, Subrahmaṇya knew that he was going to win and set off on his peacock. But when he returned after his big trip, he found that Gaṇeśa already had the prize in his hand.

Surprised, he asked, 'How could you finish before me on your mouse? Where did you go?' Then Lord Śiva said,

'Do you know what he did? He went around me and Pārvatī.' Subrahmaṇya went all over the universe and Gaṇeśa just went round the Lord. And when Lord Śiva asked Gaṇeśa what he was doing, he said, 'You asked me to go around every place. You are everything. Therefore, I go around you.' Here it is the same thing; knowing this, there is nothing left out.

This simple story tells us that the Lord is everything and knowing his *svarūpa*, which is oneself, upon which the whole world exists and by whom the whole world is sustained is knowing everything.

Praising the knowledge of the one that is to be known, Kṛṣṇa presents its rarity.

Verse 3

This knowledge is rare in terms of its result

मनुष्याणां सहस्रेषु कश्चिद्यतति सिद्धये ।
यततामपि सिद्धानां कश्चिन्मां वेत्ति तत्त्वतः ॥ ३ ॥

manuṣyāṇāṁ sahasreṣu kaścidyatati siddhaye
yatatām api siddhānāṁ kaścinmāṁ vetti tattvataḥ (3)

sahasreṣu – among thousands; *manuṣyāṇām* – of people; *kaścit* – a rare person; *yatati* – makes effort; *siddhaye* – for *mokṣa*; *yatatām api siddhānām* – even among those seekers who are making effort; *kaścit* – (only) a rare person; *māṁ vetti* – comes to know me; *tattvataḥ* – in reality

Among thousands of people, a rare person makes effort for *mokṣa*. Even among those seekers making effort, (only) a rare person comes to know me in reality.

Śaṅkara says that since this knowledge has an extraordinary result, *mokṣa,* it is difficult to gain. The difficulty lies in the very uniqueness of this knowledge and it is this that accounts for its rarity.

Generally, knowledge itself is not an end. It is made use of for an end to be gained later. But here, upon knowing this there is nothing more for you to know, to gain, meaning you no longer have any *puruṣārtha*. In the choice of *mokṣa,* the results of the other three *puruṣārtha*s, *dharma, artha,* and *kāma,* are included because in choosing *mokṣa,* you choose the whole. *Mokṣa* means freedom – freedom from the pursuits of *dharma-artha-kāma* since it includes what is essentially achieved by any one of them. But *mokṣa* is not included in any one of them, or in all three of them put together. This result, *mokṣa,* is identical with knowledge. The *jñāna* itself is the end. Because of this unique nature of the result, this knowledge becomes a rarity.

This knowledge is rare in terms of its difficulty to gain

This particular knowledge is also rare because it is difficult to gain. Any knowledge is difficult when you are not prepared, and easy when you are. The nature of knowledge is such that it can be either difficult or easy. Easy is not even the word. You open your eyes and see a flower; it is neither easy nor difficult. All you require is eyesight and immediately the knowledge is gained. So, if a person is prepared, knowledge is simple; if not, it is not that simple. And the preparation for this knowledge is difficult. Therefore, the knowledge is called *durlabhatara*, most difficult.

How difficult it is, Kṛṣṇa points out by saying, '*manuṣyāṇāṁ sahasreṣu kaścit yatati siddhaye.*' '*Sahasreṣu manuṣyāṇāṁ kaścit*' is a typical Sanskrit expression. In English we have an equivalent expression, 'one in a million.' *Sahasreṣu* means among thousands, among thousands of people. A qualified recipient, *adhikārī*, is required for any knowledge to take place. The *adhikārī*s, those who are qualified to gain this knowledge are human beings, *manuṣya*s. This is the general qualification. Then, among these thousands of human beings who are capable of this knowledge, *manuṣyāṇām*, only one of them *kaścit*, the rare one, makes effort, *yatati*. He makes effort for the purpose of *siddhi*, *mokṣa*. In general, *siddhi* means success. But success in a human life is *mokṣa*, so, he says *siddhaye* for *mokṣa*.

Among thousands – one given person seeks ātmā

Why does he say, *kaścit yatati*, one person makes effort when all human beings are active? Because everyone makes effort, but for things other than oneself, for *anātmā*. When you are not happy with yourself, you have to keep yourself in good humour. To do this you have to pursue some desirable things.

However, here it is different because you question why you are unhappy with yourself, 'Am I unhappy by nature or am I just taking myself to be so?' Seeking an answer to this question is *ātma-icchā*, a desire to know yourself. If you want to know the *ātmā*, you are not seeking anything else for the sake of *ātmā*. For the sake of *ātmā*, *ātmārtha* alone, you seek *ātmā;* for the sake of you, you seek yourself. This is the difference.

Self-knowledge is for self-freedom. This is something you have to know and yet it does not strike you as a possibility. Therefore, Kṛṣṇa says, *kaścit yatati siddhaye*. Among all the human beings, there is a given person, a rare person, *kaścit*,who makes an effort for the purpose of *mokṣa, yatati siddhaye.*

Among the seekers – one given person knows the reality

Further, he says, *yatatām api siddhānām*, among the people who are making effort; *kaścit*, here is a rare person; *mām vetti*, who knows me; *tattvataḥ*, in reality.

*Siddha*s are people who have become successful. Here he says among the successful people, only one person knows me. Then what about the others who are also called successful by you? Do they not know you? If not, how can you call them successful? Therefore, *siddha* here is only a seeker. Being an adjective to *yatatām, siddhānām* means among the people who make effort for *siddhi*. The one who does so is considered a *siddha* already. Why? Because once he makes an effort, he will reach his end. Kṛṣṇa has already said anyone who makes effort for *mokṣa* does not come to a bad end, *na hi kalyāṇakṛt kaścit durgatiṁ tāta gacchati.*[2] So, keeping *mokṣa* in view as the result of their efforts, he calls a seeker *siddha* here. We also use words in this way. For example, a medical student is called

---

[2] *Gītā* 6.40

a doctor even though he has only completed two years of college. And it is accepted because he is going to become a doctor later.

Therefore, Śaṅkara considers those who are making effort for *mokṣa* to be *siddhas*, because they are going to become *siddhas*, if not in this life, later. Among them there is one who, at this time, knows me, *kaścit mām vetti*. Here Kṛṣṇa uses the present tense. One person knows me; others are in the process of knowing me.

Spiritual seekers are of many varieties. But you cannot call them as *siddhas*. Only those who engage themselves in the pursuit of the knowledge of the *svarūpa* of Parameśvara, are *siddhas*. And they are very few. Why is this so? *Adhikāritva*, qualification is necessary. It is like marathon running. A lot of people start but finally one person reaches the destination.

Kṛṣṇa says all this, not to frighten Arjuna but to enthuse him. If someone tells you that among thousands, one person really chooses to know and among those people who choose to know, one person knows, then even before you start you will think, 'I have no chance!' But Śaṅkara looks at the whole thing as something that is meant to create interest in Arjuna's mind. Why? Because the knowledge that Kṛṣṇa is going to unfold is something that is very important. So, this verse is to draw Arjuna's attention, and not to discourage him.

Having drawn Arjuna's attention by these three introductory verses which only mention the topic, Bhagavān now starts the description of Īśvara. We will see the verses later; now let us just see the meaning.

The two-fold cause of creation

There are two *prakṛtis*. The word '*prakṛti*' means that which has the essential capacity to create. *Prakṛti* is also called *kāraṇa*, the cause. Kṛṣṇa says, 'I have two *prakṛtis*; one is *svarūpa-prakṛti*, and the other is *svabhāva-prakṛti*.

Svarūpa-prakṛti

One *prakṛti* is the cause of everything, the truth of everything, without which nothing is possible. This is called *svarūpa* or *parā-prakṛti*. *Svarūpa* is that which makes something what it is. For example, ice is cold and that coldness is its *svarūpa*. You cannot remove it and still have ice. Similarly, here *ātmā* cannot give up its nature, consciousness. Consciousness is the *svarūpa* of *ātmā*; it is not a quality, an attribute of *ātmā*. There is no other person there for whom consciousness is an attribute. In fact, the 'I' itself is in the form of a conscious being alone. Therefore, consciousness is the *svarūpa* of *ātmā*. It is not an attribute of *ātmā*.

If consciousness is the *svarūpa* of *ātmā*, there are a few other facts we recognise about consciousness. It is *satya*, it is *ananta*, etc. From the various standpoints of our knowledge about the world, we say this consciousness is *satya*. It means everything else is not *satya;* this consciousness alone is *satya*. It is not that we are refusing to accept another *satya*. There is only one *satya;* that is *ātmā*. Generally, we think that what exists is *satya*. Here, we take that existence itself to be consciousness. And because it is *satya* it is *ananta*, without limit. *Satyaṁ jñānam anantaṁ brahma* is *ātmā*. This is the *prakṛti* of everything. Here you must understand *prakṛti* as the cause of everything, *sarvasya kāraṇam*. Therefore, it is called the *svarūpa-prakṛti*.

Svabhāva-prakṛti

There is another *prakṛti* which we call *svabhāva-prakṛti* or *aparā-prakṛti* consisting of the five elements, both subtle and gross. It is divided into *kāraṇa*, cause, and *kārya*, effect. Because the *kārya* is not separate from the *kāraṇa*, the *kārya* is also called *prakṛti*. Therefore, we have the expression *kārya-prakṛti*. A physical body consisting of the five elements is also *kārya-prakṛti* as are the sense organs, the mind, and *prāṇa*s. In other words, anything created, anything put together is a *kārya-prakṛti*. *Kārya* here is anything that is produced, anything put together. If we look at this *prakṛti*, this is also called *māyā*, *avyakta*, or *mūla-prakṛti*. This *prakṛti* is the *upādhi* from which the whole creation has come. And the *upādhi* is for *paramātmā*. Therefore, *sat-cit-ānanda-ātmā* becomes the real cause, *svarūpa-prakṛti*, for this entire world and *māyā* is the *svabhāva-prakṛti* or *kārya-prakṛti*.

Now, where does this *māyā* have its being? Is it in the product or in Brahman? It is in Brahman. It cannot be elsewhere because the product itself is *mithyā*. So, this *māyā* has its being in Brahman, *brahma-āśrayā hi māyā*. Brahman is *satyaṁ jñānam anantam* which is *ātmā*. That Brahman is the *āśrayā* for *māyā* and its products.

In this chapter, Lord Kṛṣṇa first talks about *kārya* or *aparā-prakṛti*. Then he says there is another *prakṛti*, *parā-prakṛti*. That is the real cause, without which there cannot be any creation. The real cause means that which supplies the existence, and without which there is no creation possible. He says, 'The truth of the whole creation, the real cause, is my *svarūpa*. And you are that *svarūpa*. That is the real *prakṛti* and therefore, what you have to know is that real *prakṛti* which is Īśvara in reality. You have to know these two types of *prakṛti*s, and know that the *svarūpa* or *parā-prakṛti* without which there is no creation at all, is yourself. I am you. In fact, I am the cause of everything and I am you.' This means you are the cause of everything as *satyaṁ jñānam anantaṁ brahma*.

The next question you will ask, will be, 'How can I be the cause? How can I be Īśvara?' If you say you are a *jīva*, you will continue to be a *jīva*. You will never become Īśvara. An individual is an individual; he is not going to become Īśvara. If you say, 'I am Īśvara,' then the problem is, where is this 'I' placed? That has to be understood. Therefore, in the verses that follow, Kṛṣṇa unfolds the two types of *prakṛti* to prove that Īśvara is everything and his *svarūpa* is you.

Verse 4

Prakṛti is divided in an eight-fold way

भूमिरापोऽनलो वायुः खं मनो बुद्धिरेव च ।
अहङ्कार इतीयं मे भिन्ना प्रकृतिरष्टधा ॥ ४ ॥

bhūmirāpo'nalo vāyuḥ khaṁ mano buddhireva ca
ahaṅkāra itīyaṁ me bhinnā prakṛtiraṣṭadhā (4)

bhūmiḥ – earth; *āpaḥ* – water; *analaḥ* – fire; *vāyuḥ* – air; *kham* – space; *manaḥ* – mind; *buddhiḥ* – intellect; *ahaṅkāra eva ca* – and indeed the sense of doership; *iti* – thus; *iyaṁ me prakṛtiḥ* – this *prakṛti* of mine; *aṣṭadhā* – in an eight-fold way; *bhinnā* – is divided

> Earth, water, fire, air, space, mind, intellect and indeed the sense of doership – thus this *prakṛti* of mine is divided in an eight-fold way.

The two-fold *prakṛti* mentioned in the introduction to this chapter is the cause of this entire world. In this chapter they are called *parā* and *aparā-prakṛti*s. *Parā-prakṛti* is the ultimate cause without which there is no effect possible. Then the immediate cause is called *aparā-prakṛti,* in other words, *māyā* and all that is immediately born of *māyā*. Because subtle elements are the causes for the gross elements which come later, they are mentioned first here as *aparā-prakṛti.*

Iyam, this entire world, is my *prakṛti, me prakṛti,* divided in an eight-fold way, *aṣṭadhā bhinnā. Aṣṭa* is eight; *aṣṭadhā* is eight-fold. Here he tells us what are the eight-fold subtle constituents beginning with the earth, *bhūmi,* as a *tanmātra,* a subtle element. *Tanmātra* means *tat mātra,* that alone is there. In grossification, each element combines with the other four elements. But in the subtle form, such a combination has not taken place; so, they are called *tanmātra*s. Each element has its own *guṇa* which we experience sensorily. For instance, the earth has its own *guṇa,* smell, and so, the smell *tanmātra* is what is referred to here as *bhūmi.* Similarly, the taste, *rasa tanmātra* is water, *āpaḥ;* form *tanmātra* is fire, *agni;* touch *tanmātra* is air, *vāyu,* sound *tanmātra* is space, *kham.*

Prakriyā – a teaching model

Using a particular model like this to teach the nature of the creation is using a *sṛṣṭi-prakriyā.* A *prakriyā* is a particular discussion which is useful for understanding the vision. The intention of using any *prakriyā* is only to point out that there is nothing other than *paraṁ-brahma*. So, the intention of a *prakriyā* dealing with creation, *sṛṣṭi*, is not to reveal the creation but to establish that there is nothing other than Brahman.

Like the *sṛṣṭi-prakriyā*, there are many other *prakriyās*, teachings models, such as *avasthā-traya-prakriyā*, an analysis of the three states of experience; *pañca-kośa-prakriyā*, an analysis of the five levels of one's experience of oneself; and *dṛk-dṛśya-prakriyā*, subject object analysis to distinguish *ātmā* from *anātmā* and later prove that *anātmā* is not separate from *ātmā* because it is *mithyā*. The five elemental model of this universe is a part of the creation or cause effect *prakriyā*, *sṛṣṭi-prakriyā*, or *kāraṇa-kārya-prakriyā*. We find this *sṛṣṭi-prakriyā* in many *Upaniṣads*.

Sṛṣṭi-prakriyā – analysis of creation in Chāndogyopaniṣad

In the sixth chapter of the *Chāndogyopaniṣad*, sage Uddālaka tells his son, Śvetaketu, that before the creation of this world there was only one thing. It was *sat*, existence, *advitīya*, non-dual, and there was nothing except that. *Advitīya* because there was no other *sat-vastu* like itself nor was there any *vastu* unlike itself, and in itself there were no parts. It was one, non-dual. Since there was no difference within itself nor was there any differentiating factor, it is a part-less whole.

Mentioning this *sat-vastu* in his opening statement, Uddālaka talks about the creation of the elemental world from this *sat-vastu*. He mentions only three elements, the elements that have form, *mūrta-bhūtas*. They are *agni*, fire; *āpaḥ*, water;

and *pṛthivī*, earth. The two elements without a form, *ākāśa* and *vāyu*, are not mentioned. The purpose was only to show that having come from *sat-vastu*, they do not have a being of their own apart from the *sat-vastu*. In fact, the creation is non-separate from its cause like the pot is non-separate from the clay.

Finally he says, 'O Śvetaketu, that *sat-vastu* is *ātmā*.' Everything else is created. The body is created, the mind is created, the senses are created. But what is not created is *ātmā*. And that is *sat-vastu* which was existent even before creation. Even now it is *sat-vastu*, uncreated *ātmā*. And therefore, '*tat tvam asi*, you are that.' From nine standpoints he points out that the *vastu* is always the same. Before and after the creation it is the same; that *ātma-vastu* did not undergo any change. Now, even though it is *upādāna-kāraṇa*, material cause, it is *upādāna-kāraṇa* in terms of *māyā*. Without undergoing any change itself, the *sat-vastu* manifests in the form of this world with the *śakti* of *māyā*. And the creation, being purely *nāma-rūpa*, is *mithyā*. The truth of the creation, the *sat-vastu* is you, *ātmā*. So, to create this vision that you are the *sat-vastu* and the world is non-separate from the *sat-vastu*, we have a *sṛṣṭi-prakriyā*.

Avasthā-traya prakriyā – analysis of the three states of experience in the Māṇḍūkyopaniṣad

Similarly, we find the *avasthā-traya-prakriyā* in the *Māṇḍūkya-Upaniṣad*. The first verse says all that is, all that was, and all that will be is but *oṁ-kāra*. Each individual letter of *om* was made to stand for something. *A-kāra* represents waking, the waker and the waking world, *u-kāra*, the dreamer and the dream world, *ma-kāra* the sleeper and the sleep experience.

All three of them are shown to be non-separate from the same *ātmā*, which itself is neither the waker consciousness, nor dreamer consciousness, nor sleeper consciousness. And it is not the consciousness inbetween waking and dream consciousness, nor is it all consciousness, or unconsciousness. Naturally, what remains after negating all this is consciousness as such. All other things qualify that consciousness. And this is the nature of yourself; that is called *caturtha*. It is neither waker, dreamer, nor sleeper. Therefore, *caturthaṁ manyante sa ātmā sa vijñeyaḥ*[3] – what is looked upon as *caturtha*, the fourth, that is the real *ātmā*. It is all three and is itself independent of all three. It does not undergo any change and is the *ātmā* in all three states. It has got to be known. This is the *avasthā-traya-prakriyā* discussed in the *Māṇḍūkyopaniṣad*, which is discussed in other *Upaniṣads* as well.

Pañca-kośa-prakriyā – analysis of the five levels of experience of oneself in the Taittirīyopaniṣad

In the *Taittirīyopaniṣad* there is a *pañcakośa-prakriyā*. It begins with the physical body, *anna-rasa-maya*, which is like a cover, *kośa*, because everyone mistakes it for *ātmā*. It is born out of the essence of the food that is eaten, *anna-rasa*. The assimilated form of food is *anna-rasa-maya*. The affix '*mayaṭ*' means modification, *vikāra*, so, *anna-rasa-maya* is a modification of the essence of food. We generally conclude that the body is *ātmā*. Therefore, *śruti* points out that there is another *ātmā*, which is more interior, subtler.

---

[3] *Māṇḍūkyopaniṣad* - 7

This is *prāṇa*. *Śruti* then describes the physiological function, *prāṇa-maya*. If you think this is *ātmā*, *śruti* leads you further to another *ātmā*, *mano-maya*, and from *mano-maya* to *vijñāna-maya*, the doer, then from *vijñāna-maya* to *ānanda-maya*.

Sukha, happiness is also experienced in different degrees because of shades of difference in *vṛttis*. So, within that *ānanda-maya*, *priya* is the first stage of happiness. Something that is pleasing or desirable to you is sighted; that is *priya*. Then what is desired is possessed by you; this is *moda*. The third stage in which it is experienced by you is *pramoda*. These are degrees of *ānanda*, all of which are particular modes of thought, *vṛtti-viśeṣas*. But in all the three, *priya*, *moda*, and *pramoda*, what is present is *ānanda*. That *ānanda* is myself, and that is Brahman.

Tanmātra-prakriyā – a type of sṛṣṭi-prakriyā

Here, Kṛṣṇa uses the *tanmātra-prakriyā*. *Tanmātra*, as we have seen, means the five subtle elements. These five subtle elements undergo a process of grossification whereby each element shares half of itself with the other four. Therefore, each gross element is five-fold and has one-eighth of each of the other elements. For example, *sthūla-ākāśa* is one-half *sūkṣma ākāśa*, one-eighth *sūkṣma vāyu*, one-eighth *sūkṣma agni*, one-eighth *sūkṣma āpaḥ*, and one-eighth *sūkṣma pṛthivī*. Thus every gross element is five-fold and because it is formed of these five-fold elements, the world itself is called *prapañca*, five-fold, in Sanskrit. This *prapañca* was originally *tanmātra*. Only that alone, *tat-mātra*, was there. In other words, in *ākāśa*, *ākāśa* alone was there; in *vāyu, vāyu,* alone; in *agni, agni,* alone; in *āpaḥ, āpaḥ* alone; in *pṛthivī, pṛthivī* alone. In the *sūkṣma* form they do not have these five-fold combinations; therefore they are called *tanmātras*.

These *tanmātras, ākāśa, vāyu, agni, āpaḥ, pṛthivī,* have been listed in the reverse order in this verse. If they are listed as space, air, fire, water, earth, it is in the order in which they were created, *sṛṣṭi-krama.* But because Arjuna is now looking at the already created, the *sṛṣṭi* that is there, the elements are listed beginning with *bhūmi.* These five elements have many synonyms. Here *pṛthivī,* the earth, is called *bhūmi; agni,* the fire, is called *anala;*[4] *ākāśa* is called *kham.* All the five of these elements are to be understood here as subtle, *sūkṣma,* because they are mentioned as the cause here.

Then *manas, buddhi, ahaṅkāra,* are also added to these elements. Since they are all products, they have to be looked at from the causal level. The five subtle elements with these three are the eight-fold cause for this entire *jagat.*

The cause of the mind is *ahaṅkāra.* So, in this verse, the word *manas* stands for *ahaṅkāra;* the word *buddhi* stands for *mahat-tattva;* the word *ahaṅkāra* stands for the unmanifest, *avyakta.* Kṛṣṇa wants to point out all the causes and he arranges them in the order that is generally discussed elsewhere. *Ahaṅkāra* is mentioned last because *avyakta,* the unmanifest, is the primary cause with reference to the creation.

---

[4] *Alaṁ na vidyate yasya* – the one who never says enough (in terms of fuel).

It is *upādāna-kāraṇa,* the material cause for the creation. While Brahman does not undergo any change, the *upādāna-kāraṇa* undergoes all the change and is therefore, looked at as *pariṇāmi,* that which undergoes modification.

Then there is a new problem. If you say Brahman is the cause, then Brahman must undergo some change in order to become the creation. Yes. As *pariṇāmi-kāraṇa* it does and that change takes place only in the *māyā-upādhi.* Only from the standpoint of *māyā* it is *pariṇāmi-kāraṇa;* from the standpoint of itself it is *vivarta-upādāna-kāraṇa;* it does not undergo any change. The material cause itself is analysed as a cause that undergoes change and as that which does not undergo any change. *Satyaṁ jñānam anantaṁ brahma* cannot undergo change. The *avyakta,* the *māyā,* alone undergoes changes.

Lord Kṛṣṇa says that, *māyā-śakti* itself has become this eight fold cause for the entire creation. So, in an eight-fold way this *māyā-śakti,* which is non-separate from me, is the cause for everything. *Māyā* is not a parallel reality; it is the Lord's own *śakti.* And in an eight-fold way, it becomes the *prakṛti* for the creation. This is called *aparā-prakṛti.* The other *prakṛti, parā-prakṛti,* is the *svarūpa,* the *svarūpa* of *ātmā.*

Verse 5

What has been described so far is aparā (svabhāva) prakṛti

अपरेयमितस्त्वन्यां प्रकृतिं विद्धि मे पराम् ।
जीवभूतां महाबाहो ययेदं धार्यते जगत् ॥ ५ ॥

apareyam itastvanyāṁ prakṛtiṁ viddhi me parām
jīvabhūtāṁ mahābāho yayedaṁ dhāryate jagat (5)

mahābāho – O mighty armed (Arjuna)!; *iyam aparā* – this (*prakṛti*) is lower; *tu* – whereas; *itaḥ anyām* – the one other than this; *me parāṁ prakṛtim* – my higher *prakṛti* (my very nature); *jīva-bhūtām* – that which is the essential nature of the individual; *viddhi* – please understand; *yayā* – by which; *idaṁ jagat* – this world; *dhāryate* – is sustained

> Arjuna, the mighty armed! This is (my) lower (*prakṛti*). Whereas, please understand the one other than this, my higher *prakṛti* (my very nature), which is the essential nature of the individual, by which this world is sustained.

Iyam, this *aparā-prakṛti* is the *prakṛti* which is the cause for everything created. This should not be taken as myself. It is *aparā-prakṛti*, a lower *prakṛti*. Therefore, Śaṅkara says, it is indeed *anarthaka*, something that brings about the undesirable. This is the *prakṛti* that creates all the problems. It is the one that causes you *duḥkha* by giving you a *jīva-śarīra* and so on. Out of this *prakṛti*, your body, mind, and senses are produced. And because of this alone, you have all the *duḥkha* associated with them in the form of all their limitations. All these are caused by *aparā-prakṛti*. Its very form is the bondage of *saṁsāra*. For this reason it is the lower *prakṛti*.

My real nature – parā-prakṛti – sustains everything

Then what is the higher *prakṛti*? *Tu*, whereas; *itaḥ anyām*, other than this; *me parāṁ prakṛtiṁ viddhi*, please understand my higher *prakṛti*. Other than this, please understand the *svarūpa* of myself, my very nature as the *parā-prakṛti*. Śankara says, this *parā-prakṛti* is *viśuddha*, pure, not touched by anything. *Parā* means *utkṛṣṭā*, the most exalted *prakṛti*. With reference to the other one, it is *utkṛṣṭā*, because if you know this *prakṛti*, you are liberated. The other *prakṛti* will bind you.

Here Kṛṣṇa, speaking as Īśvara, says, please understand my real nature and that is *jīvabhūta*, in the form of the *jīva*. And that is you. In this *prakṛti*, *ātmā* always remains the same. That *ātmā*, *sat-cit ātmā*, is the *kṣetrajña*, the one who knows the entire *kṣetra*. The *kṣetra* is the mind, intellect, doership, memory, body, senses, sensory world, etc. The *ātmā* that illumines all of them is *kṣetrajña*. That is the real meaning of the word *jīva*, the one who is in every *kṣetra*. Later Kṛṣṇa is going to say that in every body-mind-sense complex, *sarva-kṣetreṣu*, the one who remains there is *ātmā*, *kṣetrajña*.[5] This is not included in the *aparā-prakṛti*.

In *aparā-prakṛti* only the elements, the *ahaṅkāra*, *buddhi*, and *manas* are included. *Ātmā* is omitted. That is *parā-prakṛti* which is the one by which this entire world is sustained. *Yayā*, by this *parā-prakṛti* alone, *idaṁ jagat*, this entire world, *dhāryate*, is sustained.

Therefore, please understand that *parā-prakṛti*, which is other than this, *itaḥ anyāṁ parāṁ prakṛtiṁ viddhi*. Although both must be understood, Kṛṣṇa is going to say, this is the real *prakṛti*. This is my real nature, the cause for everything, and therefore, it is called *prakṛti*. It is this *prakṛti* from which everything

---

5 *Gītā* 13.2

has come, which remains always the same, which is indeed the *jīva*, the *ātmā*. Therefore, understand that *prakṛti* to be *parā*, *utkṛṣṭā*. The other one is *aparā-prakṛti*, the five elements, and so on. Having set this up, he is now going to reveal that there is nothing other than this *parā-prakṛti*.

Verse 6

Kṛṣṇa says, I am the cause for the projection and resolution of creation

एतद्योनीनि भूतानि सर्वाणीत्युपधारय ।
अहं कृत्स्नस्य जगतः प्रभवः प्रलयस्तथा ॥ ६ ॥

etadyonīni bhūtāni sarvāṇītyupadhāraya
ahaṁ kṛtsnasya jagataḥ prabhavaḥ pralayastathā (6)

sarvāṇi bhūtāni – all beings and elements; *etad-yonīni* – are those that have this (two-fold *prakṛti*) as their cause; *iti upadhāraya* – thus please understand; *aham* – I; *kṛtsnasya jagataḥ* – of this entire world; *prabhavaḥ* – am the cause; *tathā* – so too; *pralayaḥ* – (I am) the one into whom everything resolves

> Understand that all beings and elements have their cause in this two-fold *prakṛti*. (Therefore,) I am the one from whom this entire world comes; so too, I am the one into whom everything resolves.

Everything has its being in this two-fold *prakṛti*. *Etad* means this two-fold *prakṛti*. It includes all beings beginning from Brahmāji right down to a worm. In other words, all living beings, from A to Z, and all non living things also, from the space to the earth. All of them are included. Nothing is left out. Everything known and unknown, everything that may be there in the cosmos, and whatever is there sustaining it, the forces, laws, phenomena, then varieties of lower *loka*s like *atala*, and so on, and all the beings therein, and the higher *loka*s with their celestials – *yakṣa*s, *gandharva*s, *deva*s, Indra, right up to Brahmaji. With that everything is covered, all fourteen *lokas*, seven up and seven below. All this together is called one *brahmāṇḍa*. That *brahmāṇḍa* and everything that is there in it is *sarvāṇi bhūtāni*. *Etad*, this is the two-fold *prakṛti*. One is *ātmā*, *sat-cit-ānanda-ātmā*, *kṣetrajña-svarūpa-ātmā*, the *parā-prakṛti* of Īśvara. The other is the *māyā-upādhi*, and because of that all the elements and so on, is the *aparā-prakṛti*. Kṛṣṇa says, please understand this, *upadhāraya*.

So, *etad-yonīni* means those that have these (the two *prakṛti*s) as their causes. *Yoni* means cause. These two *prakṛti*s are the cause for everything in this *jagat*. Therefore, all the things in this *jagat* are called *etad-yonīni*.[6] The *aparā-prakṛti* is everything that is there and *parā-prakṛti* is the real cause, *satyaṁ jñānam anantaṁ brahma*. That alone is the cause for everything. Please understand that *prakṛti*. It is *jīvabhūta*, in the form of *jīva*, *ātmā*, *pratyagātmā*. That is the real *svarūpa*, the real cause for everything. All the *bhūtāni*, space, air, mind and so on, have their being only in this, in *paramātmā*. All beings have their basis only in *sat-cit-ātmā*. Therefore, *etad-yonīni sarvāṇi bhūtāni iti upadhāraya*, please ascertain, come to understand that all the things in this *jagat* have these two *prakṛti*s as their cause.

---

[6] *ete yoni yeṣāṁ te – etad-yonīni*

The Lord says, '*ahaṁ kṛtsnasya jagataḥ prabhavaḥ*, I am the cause for the projection of this entire world.' Which 'I'? This 'I' who has the two-fold *prakṛti*. The one that is in the form of this entire *jagat*, *aparā-prakṛti*, and the other one which is the real 'I' – *satyaṁ jñānam anantaṁ brahma, the parā-prakṛti*. And therefore, I am indeed the cause for the entire creation. Not only that. I am also the one into which this entire creation resolves, *pralayaḥ tathā*. *Tathā*, so too, *kṛtsnasya jagataḥ pralayaḥ*, I am the source into which everything resolves. I am the one from whom everything comes. I am the one into whom everything goes back. Therefore, there is nothing other than myself. When the creation is there, it is me because from me it has come. As I told you, this *aparā-prakṛti* which is the *pariṇāmi-upādāna-kāraṇa* is also nothing but me alone.

Bhagavān has already said that all the five elements and so on, are not other than myself; but as *sat-cit-ātmā*, as *kṣetrajña*, I have undergone no change whatsoever to become all this. So, now, when he says here, 'I am the one who is the *jīva*, *kṣetrajña*, and I am the one from whom the entire world has come, and unto whom it returns,' in effect he is saying, 'like me, you are also the cause of this entire world.' From the standpoint of *paramātmā*, you are the one who is *parā-prakṛti*, the cause for everything.

Then what is Īśvara? If you look at the *jagat* as an individual, then naturally you have a physical body, mind, and senses. The world is there. For all this you require a cause which is what we call *māyā-upādhi*. *Satyaṁ jñānam anantaṁ brahma* with *māyā* in the form of this entire world is Parameśvara.

From the standpoint of *parā-prakṛti*, all that is there is one, without which there is no *jagat* at all. It alone gives *sattā*, existence, to every aspect of the creation and it also gives *sphūrti*, that by which you come to know each and every thing. *Sattā, sat* and *sphūrti, cit*, by which this entire *jagat* is sustained, is *ātmā*. That is *parā-prakṛti*.

Definition of the cause – the maker and the material

In the previous verse, Kṛṣṇa said, 'I am the cause of the entire creation and also its point of dissolution.' When the Lord says he is the cause, how does he mean this? As a conscious being, the *nimitta-kāraṇa*, he is the cause in a three-fold way, as the creator, as the one into whom everything dissolves, and as the one who sustains everything.

Taittirīyopaniṣad also says the cause is the one from whom, *yataḥ* all these beings come, by whom, *yena*, they are sustained and into whom, *yat*, (here it means *yasmin)* they resolve.[7] This is the definition of the cause. The word '*yataḥ*' represents the fifth case used in the sense of that from which something is born. This indicates the *upādāna-kāraṇa*, the material cause. Then he says *yena*, by whom they are sustained, then *yasmin*, unto whom they go back, *yatprayantyabhisaṁviśanti*. Apart from this pronoun *yat*, there is no mention of any other cause. From this we understand that this *kāraṇa*, the cause is both *nimitta-kāraṇa* and *upādāna-kāraṇa*.

---

[7] *yato vā imāni bhūtāni jāyante, yena jātāni jīvanti, yatprayantyabhisaṁ viśanti* (*Taittirīyopaniṣad* 3.1)

Earlier in the *Taittirīyopaniṣad*, it is said, '*so'kāmayata*, He desired.' This clearly indicates the *nimitta-kāraṇa*. The one referred to later by the pronoun, *yat*, from which everything has come, *upādāna-kāraṇa*, is the same one who desired to become many and then created everything, *nimitta-kāraṇa*. From this it is clear that according to the *śruti*, the cause for this world is Parameśvara, both in the sense of the maker and the material.

When the *śāstra* analyses the cause, it unfolds what we call the *svarūpa*, the nature of that very cause. For that it has a different definition altogether – *satyaṁ jñānam anantaṁ brahma*. You will find that none of these words, even though they are defining words, has a particular quality. In fact, these words negate all qualities. So, Brahman, the cause, is revealed as *nirviśeṣa*, free from attributes, by words which negate all the attributes we know. Thus, the cause is presented as *nirvikalpa*, free from any form of duality.

The definition is that it is *satya*. And it is *anantaṁ satyam*. Therefore, it is not existent, as we usually understand, that is, its existence is not in terms of time. Similarly, *jñāna* is not the knowledge of any given thing. It is *anantaṁ jñānam*, unlimited *jñāna*, that is limitless consciousness. This definition, *satyaṁ jñānam anantaṁ brahma*, is *svarūpa-lakṣaṇa*.

Two types of lakṣaṇas:

Svarūpa-lakṣaṇa

There are two types of *lakṣaṇa*s, *svarūpa-lakṣaṇa* and *taṭastha-lakṣaṇa*. *Svarūpa-lakṣaṇa* reveals the essential nature of something.

For example, if you describe water as H_2O, this is *svarūpa-lakṣaṇa.* Water is nothing but these atoms. So if you describe water as H_2O, you are explaining the *svarūpa* of water. Here, the definition of Brahman as *satyaṁ jñānam anantaṁ brahma,* reveals the nature of Brahman, the *vastu*. It negates all attributes and then points out by implication that the *vastu* is the existence of anything that is existent and is the content of any form of knowledge.

Taṭastha-lakṣaṇa

Suppose, you want to indicate a particular house and you do so by saying it is the house on which the crow is sitting; that is *taṭastha-lakṣaṇa.* The crow is not a part of the house even though it helps you recognise the house. The next time you have to identify that house you need not wait for the crow to come and sit on it. Once you recognise the house, the crow is not a part of the understanding of the house. It is called *taṭastha-lakṣaṇa.*

Whenever creation is discussed in the *śāstra,* Brahman is presented as the cause from which everything has come, by which everything is sustained and into which everything resolves. Therefore, everything is Brahman. This is *taṭastha-lakṣaṇa.*

It is important to understand that Brahman itself has not undergone any change whatsoever to be this world, because the world is *mithyā.* Anything you analyse reveals itself to be only a name and form which is reducible to another name and form which again has its being in something else.

Satya must be understood to understand mithyā

A Buddhist will claim that, if you continue analysing like this, you will end up in non-existence. The conclusion will be that the world has its cause in the non-existent and the discovery that I am that non-existent is *nirvāṇa*. *Nirvāṇa* means extinguishing everything. This is the Buddhistic approach.

However, we do not mean that. The discovery here is that, I am the only *satya*, the only reality. Even though the Buddhistic analysis of *mithyā* looks the same, it is not, because *mithyā* is truly *mithyā* only when *satya* is appreciated. Otherwise *mithyā* becomes *satya*, a reality. *Mithyā* is defined as anything that has no independent existence, no basis of its own. So, by the very definition there is no such thing as *mithyā* without *satya*. Even though one may say the world is *mithyā*, he cannot appreciate it as such unless he appreciates *satya*. When the clay is appreciated as the truth of the pot, the pot is appreciated as *mithyā*. So, only in the wake of the appreciation of *satya* does *mithyā* become clear.

Two types of material cause:

Satyaṁ jñānam anantaṁ brahma is the *svarūpa* of *ātmā* and at the same time is the cause of everything. A question now arises whether as the cause of everything it undergoes any type of change in becoming the world? Further, does it have any other material apart from itself with which it creates the world? The *śāstra* makes it very clear that Brahman is *satya* and the *jagat*, the world, is *mithyā*. This being so, the world is non-separate from Brahman and so Brahman is the material cause. Here a problem arises. Īśvara, Brahman, with reference to the creation, is both *nimitta-kāraṇa*, the efficient cause and *upādāna-kāraṇa*, the material cause. We can understand that there is an Īśvara who is all-knowledge and so on, who is the efficient cause. But how can he be the material cause? Any material cause undergoes a change to become the effect. If the Lord himself is the material cause then he too must undergo a total change to become space, air and so on.

Vivarta-upādāna-kāraṇa

Here we have to make a very careful note. When we say Brahman is the *upādāna-kāraṇa* of this *jagat*, we mean it as *vivarta-upādāna-kāraṇa*. This is one particular word I have not unfolded so far. *Vivarta-upādāna-kāraṇa* is different from simple *upādāna-kāraṇa*. *Upādāna* is the material and as a material, generally we would expect that it undergoes a change to become the effect. This is what we commonly understand as *upādāna-kāraṇa*. This is called *pariṇāmi-upādāna-kāraṇa*. It undergoes a change. The example generally given to illustrate this is of the milk turning into yoghurt. Milk was sweet and liquid; now it is sour and semi-solid. It has undergone some change. No doubt milk is the *upādāna-kāraṇa* for the yoghurt, but the yoghurt is definitely not in the form of milk. The milk, which is the *upādāna-kāraṇa*, has undergone a change to become yoghurt.

Similarly if the Lord is understood to be the *upādāna-kāraṇa*, you may think that perhaps he also undergoes some change to become this *jagat*. Perhaps as *pariṇāmi-upādāna-kāraṇa*, he has indeed become the world, and as the material cause, must have undergone a change. If he has undergone a change, he is no longer in his original form. Therefore, all that is here now is the world. Where is the Lord? There is no Lord at all. This is an argument raised by some people to negate the Lord being the *upādāna-kāraṇa*.

This is too simplistic. The Lord, no doubt, is the material cause, *upādāna-kāraṇa*. But he is not the *pariṇāmi-upādāna-kāraṇa*. He is the *vivarta-upādāna-kāraṇa*. That is, without undergoing any change he is the *upādāna-kāraṇa*. This kind of *upādāna-kāraṇa* is called *vivarta-upādāna-kāraṇa*.

The definition of *vivarta* is, *sva-svarūpa-aparityāgena-rūpa-antara-āpattiḥ*, assuming another form without giving up one's own nature. An example is your own dream world. There you are the *nimitta-kāraṇa* and you are the *upādāna-kāraṇa*. Without undergoing any intrinsic change, without giving up its *svarūpa*, *ātmā* has become the world in the dream. There is the subject, there is an object, there is an action. All the *kāraka*s are involved. A *kāraka* is anything connected to an action. Relationships are also included like, this is my house, this is my son and so on. All these take place there without bringing about any intrinsic change in the *ātmā*. *Ātmā*, pure consciousness, alone is in the form of this dream. As in the dream, so it is in this waking state.

When we say the Lord is the *upādāna-kāraṇa* for the creation, we mean it as *vivarta-upādāna-kāraṇa*. It is like the rope, which, without undergoing any change, becomes the basis for the snake that is seen. Rope is *vivarta-upādāna-kāraṇa* for the snake.

Pariṇāmi-upādāna-kāraṇa – māyā

Since Brahman itself cannot undergo any change in order to be the cause of this creation it must have some *upādhi* which is as good as the creation. If the creation is *mithyā*, there must be an *upādhi* which is equally *mithyā*. That *upādhi* we call *māyā*, the *upādhi* for Brahman to be Īśvara, the creator. We can now say, from this standpoint, that Īśvara has undergone a change to become this *jagat*. From the standpoint of *māyā-upādhi* we call Īśvara the *pariṇāmi-upādāna-kāraṇa*.

When we look at Īśvara, Brahman, as the cause of everything, we look at it as the *vivarta-upādāna-kāraṇa*. That Īśvara you are. When I say that you are that Īśvara, I mean Īśvara as *vivarta-upādāna-kāraṇa*. When we talk about the world as non-separate from Īśvara, it is Īśvara that has become space, air and so on. Here we look at Īśvara from the standpoint of the *māyā-upādhi* which has undergone all the changes. When we say Brahman, besides being the *nimitta-kāraṇa*, the efficient cause, he is *upādāna-kāraṇa*, the material cause, what we mean is that, Brahman is the *vivarta-upādāna-kāraṇa*. And because of this *vivarta-upādāna-kāraṇatva* alone, it is possible to appreciate *ātmā* as *sat-cit-ānandaṁ brahma*.

Once, one high school teacher told me that Śaṅkara has said that God became the world. In the beginning there was God and then he created the world out of himself. So, God became the world. And now there is no God. It is exactly like making idli out of rice. The rice is gone; only idli is there. Later, I repeated this as Śaṅkara's philosophy to someone and he laughed so hard that I knew that there was some mistake in what I had said. But I did not know what the mistake was and he did not correct me either.

It is obvious. The mistake is that God is taken as *pariṇāmi-upādāna-kāraṇa*, and a material cause that undergoes a change. We require the technical term '*vivarta*' to understand this. Once we say Brahman is *vivarta-upādāna-kāraṇa*, Brahman remains as Brahman. That alone will work. *Satyaṁ jñānam anantaṁ brahma* always remains the same. Its *svarūpa* being what it is, it cannot undergo any change.

To understand the non-dual nature of Brahman, that there is nothing beyond Brahman and that the creation is not different from Brahman, this *kāraṇa-kārya-vāda*, discussion of cause effect is the set-up. Through this, one understands that all that is here is Brahman and I am none other than that Brahman.

Verse 7

Everything has its being in me – like the beads in a string

मत्तः परतरं नान्यत्किञ्चिदस्ति धनञ्जय ।
मयि सर्वमिदं प्रोतं सूत्रे मणिगणा इव ॥ ७ ॥

mattaḥ parataraṁ nānyat kiñcidasti dhanañjaya
mayi sarvam idaṁ protaṁ sūtre maṇigaṇā iva (7)

dhanañjaya – O Arjuna!; *mattaḥ parataram* – superior to me; *anyat kiñcit* – any other cause; *na asti* – there is not; *sūtre* – in a string; *maṇigaṇāḥ iva* – like the group of beads; *mayi* – in me; *idaṁ sarvam* – all this; *protam* – is woven

Dhanañjaya (Arjuna)! There is no other cause superior to me. All this is woven (has its being) in me, like the beads in a string.

In this verse, Kṛṣṇa says, 'O Dhanañjaya, (Arjuna), there is no other cause which is superior to me.' Previously he had said, 'I am the creator of this entire world and I am the place to which it returns.' There, he definitely talks about himself as *vivarta-upādāna-kāraṇa*. He says, 'Out of me everything has come; unto me everything returns.'

A pot maker cannot say, 'From out of me came this pot,' because it does come out of his efforts. But when the pot is destroyed, it does not go back to the pot maker. If something goes back to its cause, we understand the cause to be the *upādāna-kāraṇa*. The pot came out of clay, unto clay it will return. Therefore, when we say the effect goes unto the cause, it is always the *upādāna-kāraṇa*, the material cause.

In saying that the Lord is the one from whom the creation has come and to whom it goes back, we accept that the Lord is the *nimitta-kāraṇa*, the maker, as well as the *upādāna-kāraṇa*, the material. We have to understand this material cause to be the *vivarta-upādāna-kāraṇa*.

So, in this verse the Lord says, 'In this world, there is no cause other than me.' Here, *na kiñcit asti* can be either *kiñcit anyat nāsti*, there is no cause other than me, or *kiñcit parataraṁ nāsti*, there is no other cause superior to me. It indicates that the Lord is the uncaused cause of everything. If there were to be a cause for this cause, it in turn would require another cause and we would get into an infinite regression. Here we are talking of the cause, which is *satyaṁ jñānam anantaṁ brahma,* in which the whole world resolves. It is the point in which both the seer and the seen resolve and that is presented here as the cause of everything.

Then Kṛṣṇa says, '*mayi sarvamidaṁ protaṁ sutre maṇigaṇā iva,* into me alone all this is woven like a group of beads on a string.' Śaṅkara says that, this entire world is pervaded by Parameśvara like even a cloth that is pervaded by its threads. As a tapestry is not separate from its threads, the world is not separate from Parameśvara. Kṛṣṇa says it is *sutre maṇigaṇā iva,* like in one string a group of beads is strung together. By saying a group of beads he takes into account the variegated nature of the world. As beads of various shapes, sizes, colours and values are strung together in a single string, similarly, 'in me,' *paramātmā* alone, this world with its variety is strung. As *pratyagātmā,* I am the truth of everything that is here.

The limitation of this example is that the beads are different from the string. This is duality. The thread runs through the beads but is distinct from it. Parameśvara can also say, 'I am the thread of all the beings but I am distinct from all of them – being the basis of all of them and being *asaṅga* at the same time.' But here, there is no duality. Anything one experiences is non-separate from *ātmā,* the sustaining factor. Therefore, I am *ātmā,* the *pratyagātmā* of all beings experiencing different worlds. This is another meaning.

The word '*prota*' also suggests the expression *otaḥ protaḥ,* the warp and the woof. As in weaving, I am the warp and I am the woof. This variegated tapestry of the world is woven in *sat-cit-ātmā* alone. Existence, which is in the form of consciousness, is *sat-citātmā*, Brahman, and in this Brahman alone are the modifications of *māyā*. Wherever there is *māyā*, I am there because *māyā* has no existence apart from me, Brahman. This entire *jagat* which is *mithyā* is non-separate from me.

Now we can understand how this *jagat* is *īśvara-sṛṣṭi*, from Īśvara alone the *jagat* has come, *mattaḥ parataraṁ na anyat kiñcit asti*. In the previous verse the Lord says, 'I am the cause of the birth of this creation; I am the place where it resolves.' In this verse he adds, 'I am the sustaining factor. Not only does the creation come from me and go back to me, it is sustained by me. The essence of each and everything everywhere is me alone at different levels. I am the one who is in the form of the subtle elements. I am the sustaining factor of the gross elements. The gross elements can be reduced to the subtle, like matter can be reduced to energy. Similarly one can say matter is sustained by energy. If the *Gītā* were to be written today, Bhagavān could say, I am energy in the form of matter and therefore, all forms of matter are sustained by me, the energy. Then what is energy? That also can be reduced to *māyā*, which has no independent existence apart from Brahman. That Brahman which is *satyaṁ jñānam anantaṁ brahma* is *ātmā*.

Now he shows how each and every thing is non-separate from him because he is the essence of everything. That particular essence he points out here in order to reveal that the world is sustained by him. One can ask Bhagavān, 'What is the essence of each thing by which you sustain it? What are the characteristics you have with which you sustain everything?' A few more verses elaborate this.

Verses 8-12

Everything is non-separate from me

रसोऽहमप्सु कौन्तेय प्रभास्मि शशिसूर्ययोः ।
प्रणवः सर्ववेदेषु शब्दः खे पौरुषं नृषु ॥ ८ ॥

raso'ham apsu kaunteya prabhāsmi śaśisūryayoḥ
praṇavaḥ sarvavedeṣu śabdaḥ khe pauruṣaṁ nṛṣu (8)

kaunteya – O son of Kuntī (Arjuna)!; *aham asmi* – I am; *apsu* – in the water; *rasaḥ* – (basic) taste; *śaśi-sūryayoḥ* – in the moon and the sun; *prabhā* – the light; *sarva-vedeṣu* – in all the Vedas; *praṇavaḥ* – *om*; *khe* – in space; *śabdaḥ* – sound; *nṛṣu* – in human beings; *pauruṣam* – the strength

Kaunteya (Arjuna)! I am the taste (basic taste) in the water; I am the light in the moon and the sun; I am *om* in all the Vedas; I am sound in space; and I am the strength in human beings.

O Kaunteya (Arjuna) *raso'ham apsu*, I am the taste in the water. I am the essential characteristic of water which you experience in the form of taste. I am the subtle element of this gross element which you experience, the cause for water to be water. In other words, I am the essence of water. Essence here means taste because the taste of water is its unique property. If water has a quality of its own it is *rasa*, taste. Because of which water is water, that indeed I am. I am the truth of water. What makes the water distinguishable as an element from everything else? That is me, the taste in water.

Prabhā asmi śaśi-sūryayoḥ, I am the light in these famous luminaries, *śaśi,* the moon and *sūrya,* the sun,' says the Lord. There is no sun without light and without the sun's light the moon also would not be visible. I am the light in the sun; I am the light in the moon. Once I am the light in the sun then naturally I am the light in the moon because moonlight is nothing but the reflection of sunlight. That sunlight itself is me. I am the essence of the sun, the light because of which the sun is sun. And *prabhā aham asmi,* the reflected light, the light that shines because of which the moon is moon, that also is me.

Praṇavaḥ sarva-vedeṣu, in all the Vedas I am *praṇava.* The Vedas discuss varieties of things. And all those things can be reduced to one thing, *om.* In the *Kaṭhopaniṣad* it is said, 'I will tell you briefly that one thing that is talked about by all the Vedas desiring which people take to a life of *brahmacarya,* study, and so on–*om ityetat,* it is this *om.*'[8] *Praṇava, om,* is a well-known symbol for Brahman. Also the whole Veda can be reduced to *om.* I am that *om.*

Śabdaḥ khe means, I am the *śabda,* the sound, in space. Sound is not experienced by any other sense organ except the ears. To reach the ears, sound has to travel in space, so, the sound is manifest in space. Also, 'sound' stands for the

---

[8] *Kaṭhopaniṣad* 1.2.15

subtle element of space which sustains the gross element space as its cause.

Then again I am *pauruṣam nṛṣu*, in human beings I am *pauruṣa*, the strength. In the human physical body, whether male or female, there is certain strength. That strength I am. The body has got the capacity to do, to walk, to procreate; this is all *pauruṣa*. Whatever strength or capacity the body has, that *pauruṣam aham asmi*.

Two elements, water and space, are covered. The earth and fire that lends its heat are dealt with in the next verse. All the elements are not named here. Four are mentioned and the fifth, *vāyu*, we have to add. The idea here is not to enumerate everything but to mention a few things to prove that anything that is here is me. Anything that has a form, a particular quality is me. It does not gain its uniqueness by anything else. It is my creation, non-separate from me. In each and every thing, that which makes it distinct, different from everything else is all me. And therefore, everything is me.

पुण्यो गन्धः पृथिव्यां च तेजश्चास्मि विभावसौ ।
जीवनं सर्वभूतेषु तपश्चास्मि तपस्विषु ॥ ९ ॥

puṇyo gandhaḥ pṛthivyāṁ ca tejaścāsmi vibhāvasau
jīvanaṁ sarvabhūteṣu tapaścāsmi tapasviṣu (9)

pṛthivyāṁ ca – and in the earth; *puṇyaḥ gandhaḥ* – the sweet fragrance; *vibhāvasau ca* – and in the fire; *tejas* – the brilliance and the heat; *asmi* – I am; *sarva-bhūteṣu* – in all beings; *jīvanam* – the life itself; *ca* – and; *tapasviṣu* – in the ascetics; *tapas* – the ascetic disciplines and their results; *asmi* – I am

I am the sweet fragrance in the earth and the brilliance and heat in the fire. I am the very life in all beings and the ascetic disciplines and their results in the ascetics.

Kṛṣṇa continues to say that the essence of each object is he. 'All have come from me; they are non-separate from me; I am *puṇya gandhaḥ pṛthivyām*, the sweet fragrance in the earth.' All fragrance is from *pṛthivī*, earth because it has the special quality of smell. Kṛṣṇa mentions the sweet fragrance because it is the special fragrance that attracts people, like even the sweet fragrance in a flower. Even though the sweet fragrance is manifest in various things, it has its source only in *pṛthivī*. Therefore, in the *pṛthivī*, I am in the form of sweet fragrance; that is the *sūkṣma* aspect of *pṛthivī*.

Tejas ca asmi vibhāvasau. Vibhāvasau, in the fire, *tejaḥ asmi*, I am the brilliance. *Tejas* can also mean heat. Both the heat as well as the brilliance in the fire are me.

Jīvanaṁ sarva-bhūteṣu. Sarva-bhūteṣu, in all the beings, I am *jīvana*, the life that is there. *Jīvana* if taken as that which makes life possible will mean *anna*, the food because of which the growth and sustenance of the physical body is possible. That *anna*, *jīvana*, is I. Or, we can take *jīvana* as the life that is present in all living beings; that life, the very *prāṇa* is I. Both *prāṇa* and *anna* are *jīvana*; they make life possible.

So far Bhagavān has been speaking of the essence of things. Now he cites certain qualities. He says, '*tapasca asmi tapasviṣu*, I am the austerity in the ascetics.' *Tapasvin*s are the ascetics, who follow a life of prayerful disciplines. I am the very *tapas* in these *tapasvin*s who live a life of discipline, prayer and meditation.

I am that quality that makes them ascetics, *tapasvins*. It means any accomplishment, even in terms of *tapas*, is non-separate from Īśvara. The powers that one can accomplish, the power of concentration, absorption, purified heart, are called *tapas*. A *tapasvin*'s power is nothing but the manifestation of what is already possible in an unmanifest form because we can only tap what is available as a potential; we cannot create anything that is not there. These *tapasvins* only tap the potential which is Īśvara. Once a potential is tapped, it manifests. The discipline is born of the free will of the *jīva*, but when it manifests, the power enjoyed by the *tapasvin* is Īśvara. If that result were not there, nobody would do *tapas*. Like anything else, one does it for the *karma-phala*, the result. The *tapas* is the means for the result, which is already locked up as a potential in the *jīva*. It comes to manifestation which is me.

The power because of which a person becomes a *tapasvin* is also me. Unless the means is there, no end can be accomplished. And the means to become a *tapasvin*, like all means and ends, are according to the laws. Those laws are myself. Therefore, the *tapas* in every *tapasvin*, because of which he is a *tapasvin* is also myself. So, you cannot say you are a *tapasvin*, unless the 'I' is Parameśvara. And when you are borrowing the *tapas* from Īśvara, you cannot say you are the *tapasvin*.

Śaṅkara says here, 'In the *tapas* that is me all the *tapasvins* are woven.' We can keep extending these glories – I am the voice in the musician; I am the sound in the musical instruments; I am the very quality in the creation because of which a thing is a thing, a violin is violin, a guitar is guitar, a *vīṇā* is *vīṇā*. That because of which things are what they are, is myself.

बीजं मां सर्वभूतानां विद्धि पार्थ सनातनम् ।
बुद्धिर्बुद्धिमतामस्मि तेजस्तेजस्विनामहम् ॥ १० ॥

bījaṁ māṁ sarvabhūtānāṁ viddhi pārtha sanātanam
buddhirbuddhimatām asmi tejastejasvinām aham (10)

pārtha – O son of Pṛthā (Arjuna)!; *mām* – me, Parameśvara; *sarva-bhūtānām* – in all beings; *sanātanaṁ bījam* – as the eternal seed; *viddhi* – understand; *buddhimatām* – of those that have the capacity to discriminate, that is, the human beings; *buddhiḥ* – the intellect; *tejasvinām* – in the brilliant; *tejas* – the brilliance; *aham asmi* – I am

> Pārtha (Arjuna)! Understand me as the one who is the eternal seed in all beings. I am the intellect of those that have the capacity to discriminate; I am the brilliance in the brilliant.

Viddhi, understand, *mām*, me, Parameśvara, as the *bīja*, seed *sarva-bhūtānām,* in all living beings. The sense in which *bīja* is used here is different from the sense in which *yoni* was used previously when Bhagavān said, *etad-yonīni bhūtāni sarvāṇi,* this *prakṛti* of mine is the cause of everything. Here *bīja* is the seed form of any living being. Each tree has its own seed, which is the essence that makes it a given tree and not any other. Similarly, every animal and human being is so because of a particular seed. That biological source is me, Īśvara, and the laws that make it possible are also me. When a seed is planted, it sprouts within a given time. The biological law that causes the sprouting of the seed is myself. As pointed out earlier, here Kṛṣṇa is not talking about the general cause for the creation. Within the creation there is a further cause for creation. That final cause is also me.

Then he says, *sanātana*, eternal. *Sanātana* can go with *mām*, me, the one who is eternal, the seed of all beings. It can also be an adjective to *bīja* but that would make it the general cause which cannot be the meaning here. Though such a meaning is possible, it is not appropriate in the context. Therefore, the meaning is 'Please understand that the eternal me, Parameśvara, is indeed the *bīja*, the seed, of every living being.' This is in keeping with the flow of the unfoldment.

Similarly the statement, '*buddhiḥ buddhimatām asmi*.' This removes any *ahaṅkāra*. *Buddhimat*s are those who have the capacity to discriminate. Not all living beings have an intellect; so, *buddhimatām* means, 'among the human beings.' Each one has an intellect, a *buddhi* because of which he is called *buddhimat*. That *buddhi*, the rational capacity or the free will is the Lord. Therefore, if there is a person who can think properly, that accomplishment in terms of intellectual discipline is me. That capacity itself is me. Therefore, nobody can say that I am *buddhimat*. That *aham* can only be Parameśvara.

Tejas tejasvinām aham. *Tejas* means the shine of health or brilliance. 'Among the brilliant people, I am the brilliance.' He has already said 'I am the *buddhi*, intellectual capacity, in the human beings who are capable of thinking.' If so, why do only some become brilliant? It is true that everybody is *buddhimat* but the person who makes an effort is the one who becomes brilliant, who becomes educated. The brilliance that he is able to tap within himself is also me.

बलं बलवतां चाहं कामरागविवर्जितम् ।
धर्माविरुद्धो भूतेषु कामोऽस्मि भरतर्षभ ॥ ११ ॥

balaṁ balavatāṁ cāhaṁ kāmarāgavivarjitam
dharmāviruddho bhūteṣu kāmo'smi bharatarṣabha (11)

ca – and; *bharatarṣabha* – O foremost in the clan of Bharata (Arjuna)!; *balavatām* – of the strong people; *kāma-rāga-vivarjitam* – that which is free from desire and attachment; *balam* – the strength; *bhūteṣu* – in the beings; *dharma-aviruddhaḥ* – that which is not opposed to *dharma; kāmaḥ* – desire; *aham asmi* – I am

> Arjuna, the foremost in the clan of Bharata! In the strong I am the strength that is free from desire and attachment. In all beings, I am the desire that is not opposed to *dharma*.

'*Balaṁ balavatām asmi,* I am the strength of the strong people.' Developing physical strength requires dedication because strength is a potential which can be brought to manifestation. And what is potential is Īśvara. So, the strength that is developed is Bhagavān. People are not born with large biceps; they work for them. Even the free will required to accomplish this is Bhagavān. Therefore, that strength which is latent in people and is manifest in the *balavat*, the strong, the strength because of which he is called *balavat*, that strength I am. So, the person who is strong cannot say, I am strong, unless 'I am' is Īśvara.

Īśvara is not simply any *bala* but a *bala* that is devoid of *kāma* and *rāga* – *kāma-rāga-vivarjitaṁ balam aham asmi*. Generally, *kāma* is a word that covers *rāga-dveṣa*. But here *kāma* and *rāga* are mentioned separately. So, we need to look at the meaning differently. Here, *kāma* is a desire to accomplish what you do not have, and *rāga* is an attachment to what you have. In his commentary on this verse, Śaṅkara says that, *kāma* is a longing for objects which are not with you, which are away from you and therefore, to be accomplished by you. *Rāga* is attachment to objects which are already gained by you.

Here Bhagavān is saying, 'The strength in the strong that is without *kāma* and *rāga* is me.' This has to be mentioned with reference to strength. Earlier he said, I am the *buddhi* of the *buddhimat*, the *tejas* of the *tejasvin*, the *tapas* of the *tapasvin*.' There he did not qualify those with any adjective. But here when it comes to strength, a condition is mentioned because where there is strength, there can always be abuse. *Kāma* and *rāga* signify *ahaṅkāra*. Therefore, it is strength that is free from *ahaṅkāra*.

Even though it is not specifically mentioned, this can apply everywhere. If somebody has brilliance, it should also be *kāma-rāga vivarjitam*. *Kāma* and *rāga* are centred on *ahaṅkāra*, ego. So, what is there without the misappropriation of the *ahaṅkāra* is naturally Bhagavān. When ego is present, it sullies everything. If Bhagavān is not appreciated, the person with strength becomes a source of fear. If he has strength and also *kāma* and *rāga*, he is no longer Īśvara; he becomes a ruffian. If there is a strong man who does not have *kāma* and *rāga*, you will see only Īśvara. It is true even in music. If someone has a gift for music but has the sense that 'I am a musician,' then one cannot enjoy his music. The *ahaṅkāra* vitiates the beauty. And to the extent that he does not have *ahaṅkāra,* one can enjoy his music.

Here Bhagavān says, 'Understand me to be the very strength in the people who are strong and free from *ahaṅkāra.* Even in the people who have *ahaṅkāra* the strength is I, but it is not visible. A strong person can be a great support because if one has the protection of a strong man, one is fearless. But if he has *kāma* and *rāga,* he becomes a source of fear. Therefore, strength with *ahaṅkāra* is dangerous, which is why Kṛṣṇa tells this here. In fact, the whole thing is to remove *ahaṅkāra.*

'*Dharma-aviruddhaḥ bhūteṣu kāmo'smi bharatarṣabha,* O *Bharatarṣabha,* the foremost in the clan of *Bharata,* in the living beings I am the desire that is not against *dharma,*' said Kṛṣṇa. We always hear that desires should be removed. It is not possible. Kṛṣṇa says, '*ahaṁ kāmaḥ asmi,* I am the very desire.' *Kāma,* desire, is a *śakti,* a power without which there would be no creation. Therefore, *kāmo'smi,* I am that very form of desire. And what should this desire be like? It should be *dharma-aviruddha,* unopposed to *dharma.* There you can see Īśvara. Suppose a person is free from *ahaṅkāra* but has talents, skills, wisdom and so on, and no desire to do anything. They just remain inside. The person neither has a desire to talk, nor a desire to write much less a desire to share. Suppose the person does not have those desires, because he or she need not have desires, then Bhagavān has to say, I am the silence in the silent people. But the person can also have desires because desire itself does not bind. Therefore, Kṛṣṇa says that he is *dharma-aviruddha kāma. Dharma* is in keeping with the *śāstra* and in keeping with the universal order of ethics. The desire that is in keeping with *dharma* is the beauty of Bhagavān. It is the expression of Bhagavān. Anything beautiful has come out of such a desire. This is what we call *icchā-śakti,* the power of desiring which is part of *māyā-śakti.* So, in all beings, any desire that is unopposed to *dharma* is I.

Previously the Lord indicated the *jñāna-śakti* when he said he is *buddhi* in the *buddhimat* and *tejas* in the *tejasvī.* That *jñāna-śakti* is Bhagavān. He also said that he is *bala* in the *balavat.* This *bala* indicates *kriyā-śakti* which is also Bhagavān. Here, *icchā-śakti* is referred to and that also is Bhagavān.

Kṛṣṇa had said that, 'I am the desire which is not against *dharma.*' If a desire is against *dharma,* it belongs to the *jīva.* Even though the *jīva* is non-separate from Īśvara, for the time being we are giving the *jīva* a free will, since the desires and desire-prompted activities which are against *dharma* definitely belong to the *jīva.* They are not Īśvara.

Concluding this particular section using *ca* to connect, Kṛṣṇa says:

ये चैव सात्त्विका भावा राजसास्तामसाश्च ये ।
मत्त एवेति तान्विद्धि न त्वहं तेषु ते मयि ॥ १२ ॥

ye caiva sātvikā bhāvā rājasāstāmasāśca ye
matta eveti tān viddhi na tvahaṁ teṣu te mayi (12)

ye ca – and those; *eva* – indeed; *sāttvikāḥ* – born of *sattva; bhāvāḥ* – beings and things; *ye ca* – and those; *rājasāḥ* – born of *rajas*; (*ca* – and); *tāmasāḥ* – born of *tamas*; *tān* – them; *mattaḥ eva* – from me alone; *iti* – thus; *viddhi* – may you know; *te mayi* – they are in me; *tu* – but; *na aham* – I am not; *teṣu* – in them

> Those beings and things which are indeed born of *sattva*, *rajas*, and *tamas*, may you know them to be born from me alone. They are in me but I am not in them.

Ye ca eva sāttvikāḥ bhāvāḥ, those things which are born purely of *sattva*. Desires which are *sāttvika* in nature, like a desire to know, are born of *sattva*. If the *antaḥ-karaṇa* consists of three qualities, *sattva*, *rajas*, and *tamas*, *sattva* accounts for anything noble, anything in keeping with *dharma*. Even experiences like *sukha*, happiness, and *śānti*, tranquillity, are born of *sattva*. Right attitudes, devotion, prayer, are *sāttvikāḥ bhāvāḥ*. Those which are born of *rajas* like ambition, dislike, anger and so on, are *rājasa*. And those which are *tāmasa* in nature are born of *tamas*.

Or, we can take it this way. *Ye bhāvāḥ* can mean those living beings, and *sāttvika*s, can mean those who are born of *sattva*, like the *devatā*s. In this case it would mean predominantly *sattva*. The *rākṣasa*s and so on are born of predominantly *rajas*. Similarly, *tāmasa*s can mean those who are born of predominantly *tamas*, such as the animals. Then we have the human beings who are *sattva*, *rajas*, and *tamas* put together. This accounts for all types of beings.

Or we can take '*ye bhāvāḥ*' as those who are predominantly *sāttvika* or *rājasa* or *tāmasa*. People and the various beings are born out of their own *karma*. It being so, they are born of me because the very *karma* is me, the law of *karma* also is me. And further, the cause for everything is me; so, nothing is separate from me.

To be born, you require a physical body and for that you require the five gross elements. These are also me. You require subtle elements because without them there would be no subtle body nor would there be any gross elements. And the subtle elements are also born of Īśvara. To be born with a given body, all these are required. Therefore, there is nothing that is away from me. All of them are me. I provide the *upādāna*, material for all of them. So, according to your own *karma*, whatever form you take, whether it is *tāmasa* or *sāttvika* form, that form is non-separate from me.

Even though they are born of me, *na tu ahaṁ teṣu*, I, however, am not in them. It means I am not under their control. Since they are born of me, I do not depend upon their existence. It is similar to how the existence of clay does not depend on the existence of pot. So, *sāttvika*, *rājasa* and *tāmasa* are in me, all depend entirely upon me, upon my laws. They are born according to my laws, and the laws are me. Since everything is me they entirely depend upon me to exist – to breathe they require air which is me, they require water which is me, they require fire which is me, they require earth, food that is me. So, they all depend entirely upon me, but I am not in their hands.

Here, Śaṅkara gives an introduction to the next verse. Even though this is how it is – I am the taste in water, the strength in the strong, the desire itself, one from whom the *sāttvika*, *rājasa* and *tāmasa* are born, even though nothing is separate from me, the world of people does not recognise me, Parameśvara. Who is that Parameśvara? Śaṅkara tells here that he is *parama* as well as Īśvara. *Parama* indicates the *svarūpa* of Īśvara.

Whenever we use the word Parameśvara, it covers both the *svarūpa* of the Lord as well as his status of being *sarva-kāraṇa*, the cause of everything.

Why do we say *sarva-kāraṇa*? In the world we draw a line and delineate different causes. Physical bodies are born of physical elements. Therefore, the physical elements are the cause for the physical bodies. The physical elements themselves are products of subtle elements, and the subtle elements become the causes. In this way, we keep on tracing the cause. From the standpoint of a product we can trace the cause elsewhere, and that cause again is a product for which the *kāraṇa*, cause, is elsewhere. Since there are many *kāraṇa*s in this world we have to use the word *sarva-kāraṇa* for the cause of all. *Sarva-kāraṇa* is Īśvara.

Īśvara's *svarūpa* is ever pure, eternal, enlightened and limitless.

Then what is *parama*, Īśvara's *svarūpa*? It is to be understood here. Śaṅkara says that Īśvara's *svarūpa is nitya-śuddha-buddha-mukta-svabhāva*. It is an expression often used by Śaṅkara when he wants to reveal the *svarūpa* of *ātmā* which is *para*. The word '*para*' always qualifies either *ātmā* or Brahman.

Nitya is an important word to be understood properly. That which always is, is called *nitya*. If it always is, it is outside the scope of time. This is what we mean by eternal. *Ātmā* is *nitya*, eternal. The word *nitya* alone points out the nature of *ātmā* and also accompanies all the other words here. *Nitya* also serves as an adjective to *śuddha*, pure. And *śuddha* is the *svarūpa* of *ātmā*, which is *nitya*. Because it is *nitya*, it does not become pure nor is it subject to becoming impure. Therefore, he says *nitya-śuddha*. *Śuddha* here means that which is free from bondage, free from *saṁsāra*, free from *puṇya-pāpa-karma*.

Then he says *nitya-buddha*, always enlightened. In fact, *nitya-buddha* means never bound at all. *Buddha* means the one who is enlightened. If we say he is enlightened, it implies that there was a time when he was not enlightened. If he got enlightened, it was an event that took place at a given time. But here, *ātmā* is *nitya-buddha*. When a person says he is enlightened he only recognises the fact that he is always enlightened. Therefore, *nitya-buddha* expresses the fact that *ātmā* is always enlightened. Since the source of bondage is ignorance one who is *nitya-buddha* is naturally *nitya-mukta*, always free.

Are these *svarūpa*s, qualites?

If we look upon *nityatva*, *śuddhatva*, *muktatva*, as qualities, then the enlightened person may be considered to have these qualities. Any object has its own qualities because of which we call it an apple or by some other name. Unlike *ātmā*, an object does not have *nityatva*, *śuddhatva*, and *muktatva*. If these were qualities, then *ātmā* would be another object which has attributes of *nityatva*, *śuddhatva*, and *muktatva*. It would become another substantive enjoying its own qualities. It is not the case. *Ātmā* is not a locus in which qualities reside. When you identify an apple as sweet or red, you recognise those qualities in the particular object, which you call apple. If you identify a green leaf, then the leaf is seen and its colour green is seen abiding in or qualifying that leaf. Similarly, when you realise *ātmā*, will you see in the *ātmā nityatva* and so on, like you see the green in the leaf? No, you will not see these qualities. A word like *nitya* is not a quality; it is a *lakṣaṇa*.

Lakṣaṇa – a word that negates and retains part of its own meaning.

Nitya is used to reveal that the nature of *ātmā* is not time bound, *anitya*. Everything that we know is *anitya;* therefore, the word *nitya* becomes a *lakṣaṇa* to reveal the *svarūpa* of *ātmā*. *Ātmā* being self-evident and self-effulgent we only have to negate the erroneously superimposed attributes like *anityatva*, etc. And this is done by the word *nitya* which becomes a *lakṣaṇa*. The meaning of the word is retained. Any attribute which is time bound is negated by the word *nitya*. Similarly, *śuddha* negates impurities such as *rāga-dveṣa*s and *puṇya-pāpa-karma*s, while the word *buddha* negates ignorance as well as inertness. *Ātmā* is not inert; it is consciousness. And bondage is negated by saying *ātmā* is *mukta*.

Each word negates and also retains a part of its own meaning. It negates the status of being a quality but retains the root meaning. This is what we call *lakṣaṇa*, and the words are given a context to reveal the nature of *ātmā* which is free from attributes. It is our own *svarūpa* and it is the *svarūpa*, the *ātmā* of all beings, *sarvabhūta-ātmā*.

Śaṅkara says that the seed of *saṁsāra* is nothing but *ajñāna*, ignorance. Therefore, knowledge of this *nitya-śuddha-buddha-mukta-svabhāva-ātmā* is the cause for the burning of all *saṁsāra*. Any knowledge is not going to be different from the *svarūpa* of the object. So, here knowledge of *ātmā* is not separate from its *svarūpa*. Naturally then, the very knowledge of *ātmā* becomes the cause for burning of *saṁsāra*.

Śaṅkara continues to say that people do not know this 'I,' Parameśvara, who is the cause for burning the seed of the defect of the entire *saṁsāra*. They know me in some form but they do not know me properly. They have some appreciation that there is a cause. Though I am not separate from them, they do not know me. In the following verse Bhagavān shows the cause of the ignorance of the world.

Verse 13

People get deluded by modifications of the three guṇas

त्रिभिर्गुणमयैर्भावैरेभिः सर्वमिदं जगत् ।
मोहितं नाभिजानाति मामेभ्यः परमव्ययम् ॥ १३ ॥

tribhirguṇamayairbhāvairebhiḥ sarvam idaṁ jagat
mohitaṁ nābhijānāti mām ebhyaḥ param avyayam (13)

ebhiḥ – by these; *bhāvaiḥ* – things; *tribhiḥ guṇamayaiḥ* – that are the modifications of the three qualities; *sarvam* – entire; *idam* – this; *jagat* – world; *mohitam* – being deluded; *mām* – me; *ebhyaḥ param* – who is distinct from these (modifications of the *guṇas*); *avyayam* – who is changeless; *na abhijānāti* – does not know

> This entire world deluded by these things, which are the modifications of the three qualities, does not know me who is changeless and distinct from these (modifications of the *guṇas*).

Mayaṭ is a suffix, which has two meanings, *vikāra*, modification and *prācurya*, predominance or saturation. Here it is used in the sense of modification. What is modified is *guṇa*. *Ebhiḥ tribhiḥ guṇamayaiḥ* means by the modifications of these three qualities, *sattva*, *rajas*, and *tamas*. The modifications of these *guṇa*s Śaṅkara, says, produce varieties of likes, dislikes, delusions and so on.

Rāga is born of both *sattva* and *rajas*. There is a *sāttvika-rāga*, a desire born of *sattva* and a *rājasika-rāga*, a desire born of *rajas*. Suppose you want to study *Gītā*. It is a *sāttvika* desire. Any desire for knowledge is *sāttvika*. Desires born of *rajas*, such as ambition, name, fame, power and so on are *rājasika-rāga*s.

Dveṣa, dislike, is always born of *rajas*. *Moha*, delusion, is born of *tamas*. *Tamas* is ignorance and *moha* is its product. It is responsible for the false values. False values are born of delusion which in turn is born of *tamas*, ignorance. So, the root of the non-thinking and false values is ignorance. Later, in chapter 14, we will discuss the three *guṇa*s, *sattva*, *rajas* and *tamas* in detail.

Sarvam idaṁ jagat, this entire world, is *mohita*, deluded, by the modifications of these three *guṇa*s. When Śaṅkara talks of the whole world here, he does not mean the various objects. They do not have these problems. Even though *jagat* means the world, it has a restricted meaning here. Therefore, Śaṅkara immediately brings in the word *prāṇi-jāta*, the living beings, the human beings.

Mohita means deluded, but here it means lacking in discrimination between what is eternal and what is non-eternal.

This is the basis of a lack of understanding about what I am seeking, *puruṣārtha*. There is also a lack of discrimination with reference to *ātmā* and *anātmā*. So, at every stage it is a problem of discrimination.

Kṛṣṇa says here, '*māṁ na abhijānāti*, nobody understands me.' Being carried away by all this, they do not recognise me, even though I am not different from them. Then what is the nature of that 'I'? Kṛṣṇa says further, I am *param avyayam*. *Para* means the one who is distinct from the *guṇa*s and in whom the *guṇa*s exist. He is the one because of whom *guṇa*s have their status of being *guṇa*s. People do not recognise me, the one who is free from the three *guṇa*s.

Avyaya means that which does not die. Here it also includes what is not born. Therefore, Śaṅkara says it is free from the *ṣaḍ-bhāva-vikāra*s, six-fold modifications[9] beginning with birth and ending with death. If it does not die, it means that it is not born. It means further that it is not a particular object existing now. And if it does not undergo growth, then there is no metamorphosis and death. *Vyaya*, therefore, includes death and all those things that take place between birth and death – greying, ageing, wrinkling, and so on. *Avyaya* means the absence of these six-fold modifications.

Deluded by these three modifications of the *guṇa*s, people do not recognise Īśvara as the one who does not undergo any

---

[9] The the six-fold modifications are – *jāyate*, born; *asti*, is; *vardhate*, grows; *vipriṇamate*, undergoes changes; *apakśīyate*, decays; *vinaśyati*, is destroyed. Every object has these six-fold modifications.

of these changes. In their delusion they are busy trying to fulfil their desires all the while complaining about their inadequacy. In fact, they recognise Īśvara only as a cause of complaint. They keep complaining, 'You did not give me what I want. Why did you do this? Why you did not do this?' So, the Lord becomes an altar of complaint. He is like the supreme court, the last place of appeal. But he is not recognised as he is. He has pointed out the reason for this. And in the next verse he will tell who is going to cross *māyā* made up of these three *guṇa*s.

In the previous verse Kṛṣṇa said, 'This entire world, deluded by the modifications of the three *guṇa*s does not know me. Overcome by whatever happens in the mind, one identifies totally with it and therefore, does not recognise me, even though I am there as the very *ātmā* of all beings, independent of the *guṇa*s and their modifications.'

Then how is one to be released from this delusion and recognise the Lord? How do people cross this *māyā* which belongs to the Lord, if at all they can cross it? This is answered here.

Verse 14

Māyā is difficult to overcome but those who seek me cross this māyā

दैवी ह्येषा गुणमयी मम माया दुरत्यया ।
मामेव ये प्रपद्यन्ते मायामेतां तरन्ति ते ॥ १४ ॥

daivī hyeṣā guṇamayī mama māyā duratyayā
māmeva ye prapadyante māyām etāṁ taranti te (14)

hi – indeed; *eṣā* – this; *mama māyā* – my *māyā*; *guṇamayī* – which is the modification of the (three) *guṇas*; *daivī* – that which belongs to me; *duratyayā* – is difficult to cross; *ye* – those; *mām eva* – only me; *prapadyante* – who seek; *te* – they; *māyām etām* – this *māyā*; *taranti* – cross

> Indeed this *māyā*, which belongs to me, (the Lord), which is the modification of the three *guṇas*, is difficult to cross. Those who seek only me, they cross this *māyā*.

Right in the beginning Lord Kṛṣṇa says, '*eṣā mama māyā duratyayā hi*, indeed this *māyā* of mine is difficult to cross.' Deluded by the modifications of the mind we are not able to recognise our identity with Īśvara.

Further, he says that this *māyā* is *daivī*, belongs to the Lord and is *guṇamayī*, endowed with the three *guṇas*. As we have seen, the conditions of the mind are products of the qualities of *māyā*, that is, products of *sattva*, *rajas*, and *tamas*. Thus, *māyā* is *guṇamayī*, endowed with the three *guṇas*. It is this *māyā* manifesting as the mental modifications that seemingly obstructs the recognition of Īśvara. That has to be overcome; the reality has to be seen as it is.

Māyā is *daivī*, it belongs to Īśvara; it is the very basis of Parameśvara. So, it does not affect him; it becomes a power for him. Pervading everything Parameśvara is called Viṣṇu and this *māyā* is his *svabhāva*, his nature. His *svarūpa* is different as we have seen, but his *svabhāva* is omniscient, almighty and so on – these qualities are due to *māyā*. And it is the product of this *māyā* that we are not able to easily overcome.

Even though it is not impossible to cross this *māyā*, Lord Kṛṣṇa acknowledges here that it is difficult. The difficulty is that when you are overwhelmed by or under the spell of the *guṇa*s, there is no possibility of overcoming them. Unless you are able to see yourself as distinct from them, you cannot recognise them as the causes for the activities of the mind. The difficulty is that you see this only when you are not under the spell of the *guṇa*s, in other words, to get out of the spell, you have to be out of the spell. This is a problem. You cannot get out of the spell unless you are out of the spell and as long as you are under the spell, you cannot get out of the spell. And you want to get out of the spell. It is a very difficult situation.

Having said how difficult it is, Kṛṣṇa does not leave it there. He says here that there is one way out, *ye mām eva prapadyante etāṁ māyāṁ taranti te,* those who seek only me, cross this *māyā*. Those who pursue only me, *mām eva prapadyante,* they cross over, *te taranti,* this *māyā, etāṁ māyām.* If they are under the spell of *māyā,* searching for a way to overcome it within the very *māyā* they cannot cross it. In the name of searching for a solution, they will remain under the spell of *māyā*. They have to seek me alone. Only then can they get out of the spell of *māyā*.

Later Kṛṣṇa is going to say, having totally surrendered all *dharma*s and *adharma*s unto me, may you approach me as the only refuge, *sarva dharmān parityajya mām ekaṁ śaraṇaṁ vraja.*[10] Keeping that fact in view, he says here, '*mām eva ye prapadyante,*

---

[10] *Gītā* 18.66

those who seek me alone.' Śaṅkara, immediately follows this *mām* with the adjective, *svātma-bhūtam*, the one who is of the nature of oneself, the one who is *sarva-ātmā*, the self of everything. Me, who is of the nature of oneself, they seek as the self of everything, the basis of this *māyā* which is non-separate from oneself, the seeker's *ātmā*. At the same time it is totally free from *māyā* and its products, the *guṇa* modifications. Those who seek refuge only in this *ātmā* will cross *māyā*.

Śaṅkara's expression, *sarva-ātmā*, can also mean those who seek *paramātmā* with their whole hearts and souls. For the enquiry and the *vastu* itself, there is love, and the commitment is total. So, *sarva-ātmā* can mean a person who is emotionally committed to this pursuit. Such a person and such people alone, cross this *māyā* which, Śaṅkara says, is *mohinī*.

Māyā is mohinī – the one who deludes

Mohinī means the one who deludes by fascinating you and luring you away from your purpose. Lord Viṣṇu assumed the form of a *mohinī*, an enchanting girl. In one instance, he appeared in this form to an *asura* who had invoked Lord Śiva, who is a reckless giver. He is easily satisfied, therefore, he is called *āśutoṣa*, *āśu* means quickly and *toṣa* is one who is satisfied – the one who is satisfied quickly. So he does not think of the consequences of his giving. When the *asura* performed *tapas*, austerities, and prayed, Lord Śiva appeared and asked him what he wanted. Being an *asura*, he did not ask for anything we would consider very desirable. He asked that whomsoever he happened to touch should be reduced to ashes. Because of this, he was called Bhasmāsura. Bhasma means ashes.

And Lord Śiva said, '*tathāstu*, so be it.' Once Lord Śiva says *tathāstu* he does not think about it. He is so satisfied with the devotee and his devotion that he grants whatever he or she wants. So Lord Śiva said, '*tathāstu*, let it be so, as you have asked, you will have. Whomsoever you touch, you will find to be a heap of ashes.' When this was granted to Bhasmāsura, he wanted to know if it worked. He said to Lord Śiva, 'You may be deceiving me, so please give me your head. Let me try it on you first.' Lord Śiva ran for his life. He ran from one place to another and finally went to Lord Viṣṇu who is generally the rescuer. Lord Viṣṇu then appeared to the *asura* in the form of a *mohinī*, a highly fascinating girl. When Lord Viṣṇu assumes this form, he manifests every charm wrapped up in one physical frame. With all his wiles and charms, Lord Viṣṇu came in the form of this *mohinī* whom he created out of his *māyā*. And when Bhasmāsura saw her, he forgot that he had been running after Lord Śiva. Lord Śiva disappeared and the *mohinī* entered Bhasmāsura's head. And wherever the *mohinī* went, he went after her.

The *mohinī* then said, 'You are an *asura* and without chanting the *gāyatrī-mantra*, you cannot touch me because I am a celestial damsel.' Bhasmāsura said he would touch her after chanting the *gāyatrī*. Now, before one chants the *gāyatrī-mantra*, one has to touch one's head and say, '*praṇavasya*.' When the *asura* put his hand on his head, he became a heap of ashes. Because of this, he was known as Bhasmāsura.

Lord Viṣṇu appeared as a *mohinī* in many such instances. *Māyā* therefore, is *sarva-bhūta-mohinī*, the deluder of all creatures.

No one is an exception to this. *Māyā* lures a person and keeps him or her fascinated; therefore, one forgets everything. This is *mohinī* and it comes in a variety of forms – power, money, fame and so on. This *māyā*, the one who enchants everyone, keeps everybody under its spell until they cross over.

How do they overcome *māyā*? Kṛṣṇa says, 'Because I am the one who has crossed over, by seeking me alone they overcome *māyā*. In fact, I am the one who has always been free. I remain as the *ātmā* of everyone. Therefore, there is no real difficulty if they seek me. Those who seek me alone cross over this *māyā* – *mām eva ye prapadyante māyām atitaranti te*.'

Some erroneous interpretations of such verses

Such verses are celebrated by devotees. Devotion itself is not a problem. The problem arises when, out of that devotion, a philosophy is created. In commenting on a verse like this some devotees will say that the statement means, by worshipping Kṛṣṇa alone, one can cross this *māyā*. If anyone worships any other god, that person cannot cross this *māyā*. There is a small *Upaniṣad* known as *Kalisantaraṇopaniṣad* that presents the *mantra*, '*hare rāma hare kṛṣṇa*.' Based on this there is a popular verse[11] that says that to overcome impurities in this *kaliyuga* chanting the name of Hari alone is enough. Whether this *Upaniṣad* was added later, we do not know, but it is counted as one of the *Upaniṣad* in the Hundred and eight *Upaniṣad*s.

---

[11] कलौ कल्मष चित्तानां पापद्रव्योपजीविनाम् । विधिक्रियाविहीनानां हरेर्नामैव केवलम् ॥

In it, there is the *mantra* – *hare rāma hare rāma, rāma rāma hare hare; hare kṛṣṇa hare kṛṣṇa, kṛṣṇa kṛṣṇa hare hare*. In this *mantra*, Rāma is called first, Kṛṣṇa second. Now a devotee in the *Hare-kṛṣṇa* sect will not say Rāma first. He will start with *hare kṛṣṇa* and then say *hare rāma* because he considers Kṛṣṇa superior. The belief is that you must worship only Kṛṣṇa because Lord Kṛṣṇa said here, *mām eva, kṛṣṇam eva*. Therefore, he alone should be worshipped who will take you away from *māyā*, to his abode in *Vaikuṇṭha*. The problem is, *Vaikuṇṭha* is also within *māyā*.

Prapatti

Another religious sect claims that in this verse Bhagavān is saying that the only way to cross *māyā* is to totally surrender to Viṣṇu. They ritualise it and call it *prapatti*. As a part of the ritual they tattoo a *śaṅkha*, conch, on one hand and *cakra*, disc, on the other symbolising total surrender to Lord Viṣṇu who carries *śaṅkha* and *cakra*. It is symbolic and there is no problem with this. The *śaṅkha* symbolises a call, a message, and *cakra* stands for the destruction of ignorance. Perhaps the idea is that apparently Kṛṣṇa is saying, 'If you respond to my call of the Veda, then my *cakra* will take care of your *saṁsāra*. It will destroy your ignorance, your sorrow.'

However, in the Vedic tradition, you are not supposed to injure your body or anyone else's. It is *hiṁsā*, injury, especially burning is considered to be a very sinful action. In any case, some devotees do this with the thought, 'You are the only refuge for me. With my body, mind, senses, and so on, I surrender to you.' This surrender is very beautiful. But the difficulty is, how do you surrender? How are you going to surrender the body, mind, and senses to the Lord when they are the Lord? Further, you yourself, your physical body, your mind, and all the created products are born of *māyā*. If your *ātmā*, the one that is surrendering, is also a product, how are you going to cross *māyā* by surrendering in this way? You can only remain within it.

The religion of *prapatti* advocates surrender alone and claims that Bhagavān teaches this here when he says, *ye mām eva prapadyante*. It says that the word *mām* in this statement indicates Viṣṇu because Kṛṣṇa is Viṣṇu. The word *eva* indicates that Viṣṇu alone is to be worshipped, not any other *devatā* such as Śiva, Allah, or the Father in heaven. And a simple act of devotion, he says, is not enough. *Prapatti*, total surrender, is required. *Ye prapadyante* means those people, who are doing this *prapatti*, surrender.

A further difficulty is that since Kṛṣṇa says *ye mām prapadyante*, we now have *mām*, indicating Īśvara and *ye*, indicating the *jīvas*, individuals. The devotees are doing the act of *prapatti* and the object of their surrender is Lord Viṣṇu. Therefore, there is duality – *kartṛ-karma-bheda* and *jīva-īśvara-bheda*. To consider that Īśvara and *jīva* are different is to dismiss *mokṣa* because there is no possibility of *mokṣa* when there is duality.

The intention here is not to discredit *prapatti* or any other form of worship. It is just to show some of the endless distortions that are possible and how necessary proper understanding is for *mokṣa*.

Resolution of the seeming duality

When Lord Kṛṣṇa says, *ye māṁ prapadyante,* there is a seeming duality. So, we have to understand what he means by looking into the context. In the beginning of this chapter he said, 'I am going to teach you exactly what is knowledge along with immediate understanding without anything being left out, *jñānaṁ te ahaṁ savijñānam idaṁ vakṣyāmi aśeṣataḥ*. I will give you, not merely knowledge, but immediate knowledge.'

Later he is going to say, 'There are many people who are devoted to me. The distressed raise their prayers to me, as do those who want to accomplish things. And the people who want to know about me, of course, are devoted to me as are the ones who do know me, the *jñānī*s. All of them are devotees. But understand that the *jñānī* is no longer separate from me. He is me, *jñānī tu ātmaiva me mataṁ*.'[12] So, the knowledge, that Bhagavān has promised to teach, resolves the duality between *jīva* and Īśvara.

The Lord will also say very clearly that, he is the one who has entered into all beings as 'I' and that he is the *ātmā* of all beings, *sarvasya cāhaṁ hṛdi sanniviṣṭaḥ*.[13] As the space seemingly enters the pot as it is created, *ātmā* having created everything seemingly enters everything, remaining the same, as the uncreated basis of everything. Throughout the *śāstra*, the *jīva* is never said to have been created; it is very important to understand this. The physical body, the mind, the senses are

---

[12] *Gītā* 7.18

[13] *Gītā* 15.15

created because they are assembled. But the *jīva* is never created. It is the changeless *ātmā*, the very *ātmā* of every being. After the entire process of creation, *ātmā* remains the same as the 'I' of everything. And that 'I' is independent of all the three *guṇas*.

These three *guṇas* are to be overcome. How? Since Lord Viṣṇu has already overcome them, has them under his control, Kṛṣṇa says here, *mām eva prapadyante*, they seek only me, the one who is everything. Then they are released.

Introducing the next verse Śaṅkara says, if this is so, why does not everyone seek you? Kṛṣṇa answers this here.

Verse 15

The people who do not seek Īśvara at all

न मां दुष्कृतिनो मूढाः प्रपद्यन्ते नराधमाः ।
माययापहृतज्ञाना आसुरं भावमाश्रिताः ॥ १५ ॥

na māṁ duṣkṛtino mūḍhāḥ prapadyante narādhamāḥ
māyayāpahṛtajñānā āsuraṁ bhāvam āśritāḥ (15)

duṣkṛtinaḥ - those who do wrong actions; *mūḍhāḥ* - those who are deluded; *narādhamāḥ* - the lowest among men; *na māṁ prapadyante* - do not seek me; *māyayā* - by *māyā*; *apahṛtajñānāḥ* - robbed of their discrimination; *āsuraṁ bhāvam* - condition of those who revel in sense pursuits (doing things not good for them); *āśritāḥ* - they have resorted to

Those who do wrong actions, who are deluded, who are the lowest among men, do not seek me. Robbed of their discrimination by *māyā*, they have resorted to the condition of those who revel in sense pursuits.

These are those who, even though they can cross over this *māyā* by seeking me, do not seek me, *mām na prapadyante*. Why? Because they are *mūḍhas*, *duṣkṛtins*, *narādhamas*, and *māyayā apahṛta-jñānāḥ*. You cannot say more. Kṛṣṇa simply piled up these characteristics which, in short, make them *āsuraṁ bhāvam āśritāḥ*, people who have resorted to the condition of indulging in what is not good for them. Let us see the meaning of the individual words.

Duṣkṛtinaḥ means those who, either in this life or in the previous ones, have done *papa-karmas*, wrong actions. And *duṣkṛtins* can also be taken as those who continue to do so.

Mūḍhāḥ means those who are deluded. Why do they do these wrong actions? Because they are *mūḍhāḥ*, deluded. To put it in a simple form they have confusion with regard to priorities. What exactly is important and what is not is not very clear. As a result, sometimes the end becomes so important, the propriety of the means is not considered. Even for religious fanatics, the end becomes so important that they compromise with reference to the means. It is unfortunate. These people are *mūḍhās*, deluded as they are about *kārya* and *akārya*, what is to be done and what is not to be done. As a result, they become *duṣkṛtins*, people who did wrong actions previously and continue to do so under the spell of *māyā*.

Śaṅkara says *narādhamāḥ*, among the human beings, there are people who are *utkṛṣṭa*, exalted; *adhama*, lowly and *madhyama*, in between, average. Being lowly in terms of behaviour is entirely due to thinking. Essentially there is no sinner. But due to ignorance and lack of discrimination, people do behave improperly. They can gain a good discriminative faculty through doing good *karma* at least in this life. But even for this, a change in thinking has to occur, which is why grace is required and therefore, prayer.

Why are they like this?

Māyayā apahṛta-jñānāḥ, these are people whose discrimination is robbed away by *māyā*. *Apahṛta-jñāna*s are those who have lost their *viveka* because of the very *māyā* that they have to cross. *Māyā*, we have seen, means ignorance and its products, likes and dislikes and so on. It becomes a decoy. Robbed by this *māyā* one is bereft of his treasure, *jñāna*, which here means *viveka*. That rational discriminative faculty is one's treasure. And if the treasure, given only to a human being, is taken away by *māyā*, these people become totally given to the condition of an *asura*, *āsuraṁ bhāvam āśritāḥ*.

Who is an *asura*?

Āsuraṁ bhāvam āśritāḥ refers to people who have resorted to the qualities of an *asura*. *Sura* means the one who revels in himself or in things that are good. *Asura* means the opposite, that is, the one who revels in things that are not good. It can also mean *asuṣu ramate*, the one who revels only in the sense organs meaning the sense enjoyments such as wine, woman, horse-race, discos and so on. Or, as Śaṅkara takes it, *hiṁsā anṛtādi lakṣaṇam āsuraṁ bhāvam* – *āsura-bhāva* is nothing but a tendency to hurt others, to tell lies, and so on. *Hiṁsā* means hurting another for the sake of personal gain like money or pleasure. *Anṛta* is falsehood and *ādi* can be taken to mean other false values like stealing and so on. *Lakṣaṇa* means characteristic. So, these are the characteristics of the state of mind and lifestyle of an *asura*. Given to this, naturally, they do not seek Īśvara. Carried away by fancies and wrong values, they will be totally given to the life of an *asura*, and they do not come to Īśvara at all. They do not even think of Īśvara. The Lord just does not come into their lives.

Kṛṣṇa himself tells us in the next verse that to overcome this seemingly hopeless situation one need not even know Īśvara as oneself. Just the understanding that there is Īśvara is good enough. Then certain attitude and prayer will develop and one will find that changes begin to take place. These changes occur only with a prayerful attitude and recognition of Īśvara in one form or another. This really paves the way for an inner conversion to take place.

Therefore, it is not totally hopeless; there is a chance. Kṛṣṇa is going to explain that in the next verse. From here till the end of the chapter he will be talking about *sukṛtins*, people given to good works and attitudes. Even for those who are prayerful only in distress, there is hope. They may not think of Īśvara at all until they get into trouble; but at least they think of Īśvara at that time. There are some who, even in trouble will not think of him. But even if they think of him only in distress, there is a change. It is what we call conversion. Once Īśvara is accommodated in one's life, the change takes place thereafter.

Verse 16

Four types of devotees:

चतुर्विधा भजन्ते मां जनाः सुकृतिनोऽर्जुन ।
आर्तो जिज्ञासुरर्थार्थी ज्ञानी च भरतर्षभ ॥ १६ ॥

caturvidhā bhajante māṁ janāḥ sukṛtino'rjuna
ārto jijñāsurarthārthī jñānī ca bharatarṣabha (16)

caturvidhāḥ – four-fold; *janāḥ* – people; *sukṛtinaḥ* – who do good actions; *mām* – me; *bhajante* – worship; *arjuna* – O Arjuna!; *ārtaḥ* – the one in distress; *arthārthī* – the one who seeks security and pleasure; *jijñāsuḥ* – the one who desires to know; *ca* – and; *jñānī* – the one who knows; *bharatarṣabha* – O the foremost in the clan of Bharata!

> Arjuna, the foremost in the clan of Bharata! People given to good actions, who worship me are four-fold– the distressed, the seeker of security and pleasure, the one who desires to know (me), and the one who knows (me).

Sukṛtinaḥ janāḥ, the people who do good deeds. As a contrast to the *duṣkṛtins* who do not seek the Lord, in this verse Kṛṣṇa tells us of the *sukṛtinaḥ janāḥ*, those people who do good actions now, or did them in previous lives. He says, '*bhajante mām*, they seek me. It is because of the *puṇya* earned through their good actions that they seek me.'

There are two types of *puṇya*. One gives wealth, pleasures, comfort, parentage and so on. For this one does not require any culture or inner growth. There is another *puṇya* which is purely spiritual, and that *puṇya-karma* expresses itself no matter where one is born. Even if a person has a difficult beginning, it does not in any way deter him or her in his seeking. Those who have this type of *puṇya-karma*, those *sukṛtin*s, worship me, Īśvara, *māṁ bhajante.* They recognise Īśvara.

Among those *sukṛtin*s who recognise and worship me, Īśvara, there are four types, *caturvidhāḥ – caturvidhāḥ bhajante mām. Vidhā* means variety. Therefore, there are four varieties of devotees. All of them have sufficient recognition of Īśvara to be devotees but among them there is a gradation. The degree of recognition, their attitude, approach, prayers, and so on, determine the four types. Kṛṣṇa says they are, '*ārtaḥ jijñāsuḥ arthārthī jñānī ca bharatarṣabha.*'

Ārtaḥ

Ārti means any sorrow, grief, sadness, distress, discomfort, trouble and so on. Śaṅkara defines *ārta* as one who is seized by distress, caused by a thief, tiger, or disease. Tigers were common in those days when India was full of forests; so, Śaṅkara commonly uses the tiger as an example. When a person is seized by some distress, whom will he call as a last resort? If he has some *puṇya-karma*s there is Īśvara in his life and he will call upon him, but only when he is in distress. Till then he does not think of him. But at least during that spell of distress he does think of Īśvara because he does not see anyone else who can help him. This kind of devotee is called *ārta,* a devotee in distress.

Arthārthī

Artha means that which is desired. In this context it means wealth and things similar to it – power, progeny and so on. One wants these and to get them, the *arthārthī* invokes the grace of Bhagavān. He thinks that he cannot live happily without them and so he makes use of the various means to get them. He uses local influence, money, and so on, along with Bhagavān, because he recognises that there is always a factor over which he has no control. As a devotee, he is mature enough to recognise the chance element, which he recognises as *daiva*. And there is no way of having any control over it without some grace.

So, whenever he wants to accomplish something, he invokes the grace of Īśvara to control certain factors that he cannot control or even know. He will perform rituals in order to invoke Īśvara's grace to help him gain whatever he wants. This is *kāmya-karma, karma* done with a desire to accomplish a given end within *saṁsāra*. The one who does *kāmya-karma* is an *arthārthī*. But he is also an *ārta,* a devotee in trouble. When he is in trouble, he will of course, invoke the Lord. An *ārta,* however, is not an *arthārthī*. Because only in distress can he think of God.

Jijñāsuḥ

The third one is *jijñāsuḥ*. The order in the verse, *ārta jijñāsu, arthārthī,* is for the sake of metre. But in order of their understanding the *ārta* and the *arthārthī* belong to one group, the *jijñāsu* and the *jñānī* to another. *Jijñāsu* is the one who desires to know. What does he want to know is also important because even the *duṣkṛtin*, one who does wrong actions, wants to know a lot of things such as how to open locks, and so on. But here, the subject matter is Īśvara, the truth of Īśvara, *bhagavat-tattva*. The *jijñāsu* is not invoking Īśvara's grace for simple accomplishments. He wants to know the truth of Īśvara, the ultimate cause of everything. And this *jijñāsu* is a great devotee. He does not use Bhagavān as an accomplice for his small pursuits. He wants to know who is Īśvara and as a *bhakta* he invokes Īśvara's grace for this. He offers his prayers and also performs his daily and occasional duties, *nitya-naimittika-karma*. He does all this to gain *antaḥ-karaṇa-śuddhi*, a clear mind, and knowledge of Īśvara.

Knowledge of Īśvara is nothing but knowledge of *ātmā*. Īśvara, the cause of everything, happens to be in essence, oneself. If Īśvara were other than *ātmā*, he would be *anātmā*, and therefore, inert. The only conscious being is *ātmā*, and Īśvara is not separate from it.

This seeming difference between Īśvara and the individual is due to *upādhi*, as we have seen. There is only one reality which the *jijñāsu* wants to know. He is a devotee because he seeks the help of Īśvara and performs prayerful actions to earn this help. His actions are not for limited ends within *saṁsāra*, *kāmya-karma*s. The *ārta* and *arthārthī* are *kāmī*s because their *karma*s are *kāmya-karma*s. The *jijñāsu*, however, is a *karma-yogī*; so, his is a different type of devotion. Because of his extra *puṇya*, he has *viveka*, discrimination, and because of that he is a *jijñāsu*.

Jñānī

Then there is a fourth *bhakta*. Kṛṣṇa says, all four recognise me and to the degree they recognise me they are in union with me. The fourth one's recognition is complete; his identification is total. When one is a *jijñāsu* one necessarily becomes a *jñānī*, the one who knows the truth of Lord Viṣṇu, Parameśvara, as oneself. Such a person is a real *bhakta*.

The *jñānī*'s devotion is what we call *sādhya-bhakti*. There are two types of *bhakti*. One is *sādhana-bhakti*, a devotion to Īśvara as a means. This is the devotion of a *jijñāsu*. But the *bhakti* of one who understands Īśvara, who recognises the truth of Īśvara as *ātmā*, is *sādhya-bhakti*. It is a *bhakti* that has fulfilled itself in the form of *parama-prema-svarūpa-bhakti*, absolute love.

What is this absolute love? Between the object of love and the person who loves, there is no difference at all. Love consumes all the differences. That is what we call absolute love and it is only in the form of knowledge. The non-difference is already accomplished because Īśvara is *ātmā*. It is a fact that only needs to be recognised.

When there is already non-difference, its recognition is called *ananya-bhakti*. *Ananya* means there is no other. The altar of *bhakti* and the seeker, the devotee, are one and the same self. That *bhakti* is not time bound or comparable because it is a fact. This is the devotion of a *jñānī*. For him, the *bhakti* has fulfilled itself. So, how can we call him a *bhakta*? He is still a *bhakta* if we consider a *bhakta* as someone who is in union with Īśvara. The other three are also in union with Īśvara, but, for them, Īśvara is other than themselves and therefore *parokṣa*, remote.

For a *jñānī*, Īśvara is *aparokṣa*, immediate. It is the only difference, and it is a great difference. Again among the three, Īśvara is always *parokṣa* for the *ārta* and the *arthārthī* but for a *jijñāsu* he is *parokṣa* only for the time being.

Parokṣa means indirectly known, as omniscient, almighty and so on. The difficulty is with the little knowledge I have, how can I appreciate omniscience? With my limited power, how can I appreciate what is all-powerful? By no stretch of the imagination is that possible. For an *ārta* and an *arthārthī* then, Īśvara is always *nitya-parokṣa,* indirectly known.

For a *jijñāsu,* however, there is a possibility of Īśvara becoming *aparokṣa* and for the *jñānī,* he is *aparokṣa* because Īśvara, the cause of everything, is non-separate from *ātmā*. Even though Īśvara is the *ātmā* of everyone, it is only the *jñānī* who appreciates it. Only he has an intellect subtle enough to recognise what is true for everyone. And the *jñānī* is distinguished here among the *bhakta*s as a fulfilled *bhakta*. The *jijñāsu* is going to be fulfilled and even the others will be fulfilled in time. Eventually they will come to Īśvara. The *ārta,* the devotee in distress, will become an *arthārthī* and then a *jijñāsu* because he has devotion. His recognition of Īśvara paves the way for his progress.

Bhakti, devotion, is any type of union between *jīva* and Īśvara. By a proper action or even a thought you are uniting yourself to Īśvara. But *jñānī* does not try to make a bridge between *jīva* and Īśvara. Gaining the knowledge, he finds that he is always united. There is only one thing–Īśvara, that is *ātmā*. There is no second thing at all to unite with. So, he is *nitya-yukta,* always united. This is told in this next verse.

Verse 17

The jñānī is eka-bhakta – always united to Īśvara

तेषां ज्ञानी नित्ययुक्त एकभक्तिर्विशिष्यते ।
प्रियो हि ज्ञानिनोऽत्यर्थमहं स च मम प्रियः ॥ १७ ॥

teṣāṁ jñānī nityayukta ekabhaktirviśiṣyate
priyo hi jñānino'tyartham ahaṁ sa ca mama priyaḥ (17)

teṣām – among these; *jñānī* – the one who knows (me); *ekabhaktiḥ* – whose devotion is resolved in oneness; *nityayuktaḥ* – always united (to me); *viśiṣyate* – is distinguished; *hi* – because; *aham* – I am; *jñāninaḥ* – to the *jñānī*; *atyartham* – very much; *priyaḥ* – dear; *sa ca* – and he; *mama priyaḥ* – is dear to me

Among these, the *jñānī*, always united (to me), his devotion resolved in oneness, is distinguished because I am very much dear to him and he is also dear to me.

Teṣāṁ jñānī nitya-yuktaḥ, among these four devotees, the *jñānī* is always united to Īśvara. *Jñānī* means the one who has immediate knowledge of the truth of Īśvara. He is a *tattvavit*, knower of the truth. Because of this knowledge, he is always united to Īśvara, *nitya-yukta*. This is a very important word here.

As long as Īśvara is *parokṣa*, remote, one has to make a connection with him. If one has certain recognition of Īśvara, one connects oneself by some prayer, thought, a *mantra*, meditation, or some act like a ritual. If the connection is for redemption from some distress, it is the connection of an *ārta-bhakta*, but it is not *nitya*, permanent. An *ārta-bhakta* is united for now; later he or she will not be. It is the same for the *arthārthī*. When one undertakes something important, one thinks about Īśvara and then begins that action. At this time one is united to Īśvara. The *jijñāsu* is more or less always united because his or her whole mind is consumed by the desire to know the truth. And the truth is Īśvara. Therefore, the *jijñāsu*'s mind is more often than not connected. As a *mumukṣu*, he or she is a *karma-yogī* and therefore, has *prasāda-buddhi*. The attitude is, '*yat yat karma karomi tat tat tava ārādhanam*, whatever action I do, is offered to you.' A *jijñāsu* conforms to *dharma* because that is Īśvara for him or her. Therefore, the *jijñāsu* is more or less *nitya-yukta*. More or less because he or she does not yet know the *tattva*, Īśvara's truth. So too, a *sannyāsī*, renunciate, seeking *mokṣa* is more or less a *nitya-yukta*.

The *jñānī*, however is *nitya-yukta*. There is identity between Īśvara and *jīva* and he recognises that. This fact is revealed by the *śāstra* which he exposed himself to as a *jijñāsu*. Because of his desire to know, he enquired into the meaning of the *mahā-vākyas* like *tat tvam asi*. And in these, the identity is revealed. The one who understands that revelation is a *tattvavit*, the knower of the truth. And he is always *nitya-yukta*, united to Īśvara.

Further, he is *eka-bhakti*. For him there is only *ātmā*. Previously he was also a devotee, but now his very devotion resolves into one *ātmā*. The difference between *jīva* and Īśvara is resolved and in his understanding of the identity between *jīva* and Īśvara, there is resolution of his devotion. His devotion to enquiry, and so on resolves into that. Therefore, he is called *eka-bhakti*. And he is *viśiṣyate*, distinguished as the most exalted among the four.

The jñānī is distinguished

All of them are devotees but the *jñānī* has a special feature that makes him stand out. This is told here not to set the *jñānī* apart as someone extraordinary. What is pointed out is the extent to which one's devotion has to mature. It has to mature in a knowledge by which one becomes *nitya-yukta*, always united to Īśvara. The devotion should resolve in that knowledge. Therefore, the one who knows is *jñānī viśiṣyate*, distinguished.

Bhagavān started off this chapter saying, *jñānaṁ savijñānaṁ vakṣyāmi*, I will tell you about knowledge along with *vijñāna*. Here he says that the one who has that knowledge is a *jñānī*, the most exalted among the four types of devotees.

Kṛṣṇa says, when someone is in distress, he calls upon me and for the time being he is one with me. At that time he considers me to be his only refuge. But it is only when he is in distress. So, what is he really interested in? Is he interested in me or is he interested in getting relief from his distress? He is not interested in me, really. He wants to make use of me like any other commodity. Because there is no other commodity that will release him, he resorts to me. For him I am another source of help that he makes use of, only for release from his plight. Being a *saṁsārī* he is subject to getting into one difficulty after another, and then he has to make use of the help available, local as well as non-local. The non-local help is me, Īśvara.

Bhagavān continues, it is not exactly that I am a value for him. The value is to get out of trouble. My value is that I am useful for that. I am a common tender, like money. For the devotees for whom I am *parokṣa*, I am not truly beloved, *priya*. Even a *jijñāsu* has not understood me; so, I am not totally *priya* for him either. For him what is *priya* is *mokṣa*. He wants release from bondage and therefore, he invokes me.

Only for the *jñānī*, I am the most beloved, *priyaḥ hi jñāninaḥ atyartham aham*, because only he knows me as *ātmā*, the object of all love. *Ātmā* is *ānanda*, the only value in the whole creation. It therefore, becomes the object of all love. Here Kṛṣṇa uses the word *atyartha*, absolutely. So, for the *jñānī*, I am totally beloved. *Ātmā* is known to him as *sat-cit-ānanda-ātmā* and love resolves into that *ātmā*. *Ānanda*, fullness which is the nature of *ātmā*, becomes love whenever there is a relationship. If the object to which he is related happens to seek redress, then the love becomes service or compassion. The same love keeps on changing into various forms. Emotionally, *ātmā*, being *ānanda* and I being known to him as *ātmā*, I am the most beloved for the *jñānī*.

The *jñānī* is the most beloved to me, *atyarthaṁ sa ca mama priyaḥ*. *Atyartha* is used for both Īśvara and the *jñānī*. Therefore, the Lord says that he, the *jñānī*, is the most beloved for me because he is me. In the next verse he says, *jñānī tu ātmaiva me matam*. He is my most beloved because he is me, *sat-cit-ānanda-ātmā*. *Priya* is *ātmā*. Why? Because *ātmā* is the most beloved. So, *saḥ*, he, is *mama*, my *priyaḥ*, that is, *ātmā*.

In these two verses, Kṛṣṇa has shown that four types of people worship him. They are, *ārta*, a devotee in distress, *arthārthī*, one who invokes him not only in distress but also when he wants to accomplish something, *jijñāsu* who wants to know the *svarūpa* of Bhagavān, and *jñānī* who knows the *svarūpa* of Bhagavān and also knows that essentially he is not different from Bhagavān. Among these four, *jñānī* is the most exalted. Even though they are all devotees, the Lord singles out the *jñānī* as the one who has accomplished what devotion can accomplish. The others are united to him whenever they pray, but a *jñānī* is always united to him because he is a *tattvavit;* he knows the truth of Īśvara as not separate from him. Naturally he is always united. Because he has the knowledge that he is *ātmā* which is *ānanda-svarūpa,* the object of absolute love, the Lord says, 'I am the most beloved to him and he the most beloved to me.'

Now if this is so, what about the other three devotees? Are they not beloved to Bhagavān?

Verse 18

All devotees are exalted but the wise person is myself alone

उदाराः सर्व एवैते ज्ञानी त्वात्मैव मे मतम् ।
आस्थितः स हि युक्तात्मा मामेवानुत्तमां गतिम् ॥ १८ ॥

udārāḥ sarva evaite jñānī tvātmaiva me matam
āsthitaḥ sa hi yuktātmā mām evānuttamāṁ gatim (18)

sarve eva ete – all these indeed; *udārāḥ* – are exalted; *jñānī tu* – but the wise person; *ātmā eva* – myself alone; (*iti*) *me matam* – this is my vision; *hi* – because; *saḥ* – he; *yukta-ātmā* – the one whose mind is absorbed in me; *mām eva* – me indeed; *anuttamāṁ gatim* – the end beyond which there is no other end; *āsthitaḥ* – has reached

> All these are indeed exalted, but the *jñānī*, the wise person, is myself alone. This is my vision. Because he, the one whose mind is absorbed in me, has indeed reached me, the end beyond which there is no other end.

Sarve ete udārāḥ, all of these devotees are exalted. All of them recognise me. So, from the standpoint of those who do not recognise me at all, they are exalted. They are mature people because they recognise me. This is what Kṛṣṇa says. But Śaṅkara takes it a little differently. He takes the word '*ete*, these,' to mean the other three devotees because Bhagavān has already singled out the *jñānī* as the most beloved.

The Lord said, 'I consider the *jñānī* as me, *jñānī tu ātmaiva (iti) me matam*.' If they are exalted, why is the *jñānī* distinguished as the most beloved? Śaṅkara says that there is no devotee of Īśvara who is not beloved to him. Each one becomes the recipient of his grace. But the *jñānī* is the most beloved, because, the Lord says, 'He is myself alone. He is not separate from me. Therefore, he is definitely different. The others are also not different from me. But they have not recognised the fact. I have no partiality because I am already everyone. It is not that only the *jñānī*'s *ātmā* is my *ātmā*. The fact remains the same for all. But because of the *jñānī*'s recognition that *ātmā* is Parameśvara, he becomes me and I become him. *Me matam* means 'that is my vision.' The word *mata* is used in the sense of 'an opinion.' It is a very clear vision for Kṛṣṇa.

What he means by this is that the *jñānī*'s *ātmā* is not different from that of Kṛṣṇa, the Lord. Therefore, the *jñānī* is the most beloved for the Lord. Why is this so?

The jñānī is not different from Bhagavān

In answering this he defines the *jñānī* – *sa hi yuktātmā mām eva anuttamāṁ gatim āsthitaḥ*. He is the one whose mind is absorbed in me, *sa hi yukta-ātmā*. For that *jñānī*, the most exalted end is me. *Anuttamā gati* means an end beyond which there is nothing greater. In other words, there is no other end. And the *jñānī*, who accomplishes that end, who reaches me, is indeed the most exalted because he is myself. We can also take *anuttamāṁ gatim āsthitaḥ* as the one who remains in this end of all ends, the one who is established in this knowledge, who has *jñāna-niṣṭhā*. That *jñānī* is indeed the most exalted because he is not other than Īśvara.

The praise of a *jñānī* here is to point out that devotion is meant only for this knowledge. There is a claim that *jñāna* is for devotion. The thinking is that you must know Īśvara, so that you can have devotion for him. But if I know *ātmā* as Īśvara, the devotion resolves. Till then it is devotion; its culmination is knowledge. So, it is clear that devotion is not after knowledge; it is before. Devotion is for the sake of knowledge and knowledge itself is devotion.

The definition of *bhakti* is, *parama-prema-svarūpa*. *Prema* means love. *Parama-prema-svarūpa* is absolute love. Between the object of love and the one who loves there is no difference whatsoever. When there is love then there is no other, *ananya*; the devotee and the altar of devotion are one and the same.

That devotion is nothing but *jñāna*, knowledge. Expressing the same thing another way, it is *sādhya-bhakti*, an end in itself, the fulfilled devotion of the *jñānī*.

Verse 19

The jñānī is again praised

बहूनां जन्मनामन्ते ज्ञानवान्मां प्रपद्यते ।
वासुदेवः सर्वमिति स महात्मा सुदुर्लभः ॥ १९ ॥

bahūnāṁ janmanām ante jñānavān māṁ prapadyate
vāsudevaḥ sarvam iti sa mahātmā sudurlabhaḥ (19)

bahūnāṁ janmanām – of many births; *ante* – at the end; *jñānavān* – the one who has knowledge; *vāsudevaḥ-sarvam iti* – 'Vāsudeva is everything' thus; *māṁ prapadyate* – reaches me; *saḥ mahātmā* – that wise person; *sudurlabhaḥ* – is very rare

At the end of many births, the one who has gained the knowledge 'Vāsudeva is everything,' reaches me. That wise person is very rare.

Bahūnāṁ janmanām ante, at the end of many births, *jñānavān*, the wise man, *māṁ prapadyate*, seeks me. Does it mean that if one begins in this life, one will become a *jñānī* only after a number of births? No. Śaṅkara says that, the word *bahūnām* indicates a number of births wherein one had gathered enough *puṇya* conducive to knowledge. One has any number of births before one begins to recognise the fundamental problem and seek a solution.

The word '*jñānavān*' can be taken in two ways. He can be the one whose mind, at the end of many births, is mature enough to gain this knowledge. Because of his maturity, he seeks me, *māṁ prapadyate*. Such a person alone becomes a *jñānī*. Or *jñānavān* is the one who has the knowledge. He reaches me. How does he reach Bhagavān?

Everything is Vāsudeva

Because of his knowledge, the *jñānavān* understands Vāsudeva alone is everything, as himself, *vāsudevaḥ-sarvam*. Vāsudeva is non-separate from *ātmā*. So the gain is recognition of the identity between the 'I' of the *jīva* and the 'I' of Īśvara and seeing all that is here is Vāsudeva. Everything is non-separate from that cause. And the product, the creation is *mithyā*. It has no existence apart from its cause which he recognises as *satya*. And he sees very clearly that the only *satya* is *ātmā*, which is Brahman and recognises therefore, that everything is Vāsudeva. Kṛṣṇa says, in this knowledge he reaches me.

This makes it very clear that devotion after knowledge is not what is meant here. If Vāsudeva is everything, he cannot be separate from you. If he is minus you, he is not everything. And he would also be *anātmā*, which, as you have seen, would mean he is *jaḍa*, inert. If Īśvara is inert, he depends entirely upon you to be known, like any other inert object. But it is not so. Everything depends on *ātmā*, the only thing that is real, the *satya-vastu*. And *ātmā* happens to be Īśvara. Therefore, you can say, '*aham idaṁ sarvam*, I am all this.'

This is what the *śāstra* says throughout in various ways. Everything is Brahman alone; there is no multiplicity here at all, *sarvaṁ khalu idaṁ brahma neha nānā asti kiñcana*. Further, without the world, *ātmā* is *pūrṇa*, whole, and with the world, it is whole, *pūrṇamadaḥ pūrṇamidam*. Wholeness is not going to be improved upon. Therefore, the world being *mithyā* is not an addition to Brahman; it is dependent on and non-separate from Brahman. And Brahman itself has not undergone any change whatsoever to become the world. Without Brahman there is no world either. Without a reality, there is no *mithyā*.

The *śāstra* reveals the identity using the method called *bādhāyāṁ sāmānādhikaraṇyam.*

To reveal this, *śāstra* uses a linguistic method called *bādhāyāṁ sāmānādhikaraṇyam. Samāna* means 'the same' and *adhikaraṇa* means 'locus.' When two things have the same locus, then one is said to be a *samāna-adhikaraṇa* with reference to the other. The condition in which two objects enjoy the same locus is called *sāmānādhikaraṇya.*[14] There are two types of *sāmānādhikaraṇya.* In a blue pot, both the blue colour and the pot are in the same locus; they have the same *adhikaraṇa.* Similarly, when you say, 'Rāma is a musician,' both Rāma and the musician reside in the same locus. Rāma is the musician and the musician is Rāma. A is B and B is A. Therefore, there is *sāmānādhikaraṇya* between A and B.

However, when we say the world is Brahman, the situation is different. The world is Brahman alright but Brahman is not the world. A is B but B is not A. This kind of *sāmānādhikaraṇya* is called *bādhāyāṁ sāmānādhikaraṇyam.* To illustrate, let us consider the following situation. Suppose a stump of a tree is

---

[14] समानम् अधिकरणं ययोः तयोः भावः सामानाधिकरण्यम् ।

mistaken for a person. Then the one who knows that it is not a person, points out that it is but a stump of a tree and not a person. He says, '*sthāṇuḥ ayaṁ puruṣaḥ*, this person is a stump of a tree.' It means, what one sees as the person is a stump of a tree. In Sanskrit, both *puruṣa*, the 'person,' and *sthāṇu*, the 'stump,' have the same case ending. This indicates that they have the same locus. But are there two things here? No. What is referred to as *puruṣa*, a person, is *sthāṇu*, the stump of a tree. First one sees it as a person and then the person resolves into the stump. The person does not qualify the stump, like blue qualifies the pot; the person resolves into the stump. This kind of *sāmānādhikaraṇya* in which one is negated, that is, one resolves into the other is called *bādhāyāṁ sāmānādhikaraṇyam*. The *śāstra* uses this technique of *bādhāyāṁ sāmānādhikaraṇyam* to explain the fact that what we perceive as the pluralistic world is in fact one non-dual Brahman.

This is what is said here by the statement, *vāsudevaḥ-sarvam*. The word Vāsudeva we have seen is the one in whom everything has its being and who is in the form of consciousness, *caitanya*. Vasu is the one in whom everything exists, by whom everything is sustained. It causes everything to exist in itself and is the basis of every existence. And Vasu is *deva*. Its own nature is pure consciousness, *deva*. From the standpoint of the world, it is *vasu*, the cause of everything and from its own standpoint it is consciousness, *deva*. This Vasudeva itself is Vāsudeva, which is why it is oneself, the conscious being, *pratyagātmā*. Therefore, his knowledge is, '*aham idaṁ sarvam*, I am everything or *vāsudevaḥ-sarvam*, Vāsudeva is everything. In this way he reaches me.

It is difficult to find a mahātmā who has this knowledge

Kṛṣṇa says, *sa mahātmā sudurlabhaḥ*. Such a *jñānī* is *sudurlabha*, very hard to come by. He recognises me as *ātmā* of all beings. So, his *ātmā* is *mahān*, great, limitless. One who has this knowledge is a *mahātmā*. Generally the word *mahātmā*, is used for any *sādhu*, saint. In that case, the word *ātmā* refers to the *antaḥ-karaṇa* and the word *mahātmā* indicates a person whose mind or heart is very big. But here, because of the context, *mahātmā* is the one whose *ātmā* is Brahman. There is no one equal to a *mahātmā* because one cannot improve upon limitlessness. Such a *mahātmā* is very difficult to find which is why, even though all are beloved to the Lord, the *jñānī* is distinguished.

In this verse Kṛṣṇa says that it is very difficult to find a *mahātmā*, who knows everything is Vāsudeva. Even though only devotees are being discussed here, all of them are not able to recognise Vāsudeva as *ātmā*. Why is it so difficult to recognise that the Lord is everything? This is the reason.

Verse 20

Desires rob one's discrimination

कामैस्तैस्तैर्हृतज्ञानाः प्रपद्यन्तेऽन्यदेवताः ।
तं तं नियममास्थाय प्रकृत्या नियताः स्वया ॥ २० ॥

kāmaistaistairhṛtajñānāḥ prapadyante'nyadevatāḥ
taṁ taṁ niyamam āsthāya prakṛtyā niyatāḥ svayā (20)

taiḥ taiḥ kāmaiḥ – by their own particular desires; *hṛta-jñānāḥ* – whose discrimination is robbed away; *taṁ taṁ niyamam* – whatever are the stipulations for that; *āsthāya* – following; *prakṛtyā svayā* – by their own dispositions; *niyatāh* – driven; *anya-devatāh* – other (lesser) deities; *prapadyante* – they worship

> Those people whose discrimination is robbed away by their own particular desires, driven by their own dispositions, worship other deities following what is stipulated.

Hṛta-jñānāḥ are those whose discrimination is robbed away. *Hṛta* means robbed, taken away, and what is robbed is *jñāna*, discrimination. If they do not have discrimination between *ātmā* and *anātmā*, what they want will not be very clear to them.

How have they been robbed of their discrimination? *Kāmaiḥ taiḥ taiḥ*, by those desires. Because desires differ from person to person, the plural is used here. Each person has his or her own unique desires, and by those, one is robbed of one's discrimination. Without an object you cannot have a desire. So, Śaṅkara says here that your discrimination is robbed away by objects like son, wealth, heaven and so on – *putra-paśu-svargādi viṣayaiḥ*. *Putra* is son. If you have money, you want a heir. Even if you have no money, and have nothing to give, you still want a son. Perhaps the hope is that the son will improve your lot. So you want to continue to live in the form of your son. You also want a son to continue the family name. And every woman has an inbuilt desire to have a child because there is a natural fulfilment in it. If she chooses not to, it is because of other problems. In Indian society there is also a religious reason to have a son. Only a son can perform the funerary rites of a parent. *Putra* also stands for *kāma,* different forms of pleasure. The desire for progeny is one of the most powerful desires and is therefore, mentioned separately. *Paśu,* cattle, is the symbol for forms of wealth. In an agricultural society, the number of cattle a person had indicated the amount of land he owned. *Svarga* is heaven. The word *ādi* meaning etcetera indicates power, fame, and so on.

By these various objects of desire, people are *hṛta-jñāna*s, those who are robbed of their discrimination. Because of the predominance of the desires for various things, discrimination between *ātmā* and *anātmā*, or between *nitya* and *anitya* does not arise in such people. They are too busy fulfilling their desires.

They implore other *devatā*s impelled by their own disposition.

Anya-devatāḥ prapadyante, they propitiate other *devatā*s. In doing so, they meet with a number of obstructions. To ward these off and enhance the results of their efforts, they invoke Īśvara in the form of different *devatā*s. They implore, *prapadyante,* other gods, *anya-devatā*s. There are prayers to invoke a specific *devatā* for a specific result, and for certain results there are certain specified rituals. So, to fulfil their desires they invoke various other *devatā*s.

The *devatā*s they worship are looked upon as other than *ātmā,* which is Vāsudeva. They do not think about *ātmā,* being Vāsudeva and that they have to gain this knowledge. The *jijñāsa,* desire for knowledge, does not arise in them.

Driven by their own dispositions, *svayā prakṛtyā niyatāḥ,* they approach other *devatā*s for what they want or they go to *deva-loka* and become *devatā*s themselves as a result of their worship. When the same result can be achieved by worshipping any deity, why should one choose a given deity? It depends upon one's own *saṁskāra,* tendency. Perhaps one had worshipped that deity in his or her previous life, or in this life. Because of what was done before, certain things attract, certain things do not. Even though they may not have prejudices against other deities, still, one attracts. So, they follow that particular form of worship, all for the fulfilment of their own unique set of desires.

They worship according to stipulations.

How do they worship? Following a particular stipulation, *taṁ taṁ niyamam āsthāya,* they invoke a given *devatā.* The repetition, *taṁ tam,* indicates that according to each desire, there is a particular type of worship available. If one wants a son, one cannot perform a ritual which is meant to bring rain. The person will perform *putra-kāmeṣṭi,* the ritual meant for the birth of a son. There are rules for, how to perform this ritual, who are the *devatā*s involved, what are the oblations, what are the *mantra*s, and what are the gifts to be given. All these are called *niyama*s, rules. *Āsthāya* means 'following these rules or stipulations.'

Driven by their own disposition, following a particular set of rules, they worship *devatā*s other than *ātmā,* Vāsudeva. There is nothing wrong in this. The only problem is that they are only interested in *dharma-artha-kāma.* So, it becomes very difficult to see Vāsudeva as everything. To gain this vision they have to see the limitations of these desires and pursue the understanding of *ātmā*. And for that they must have *nitya-anitya-viveka*. The desire for *mokṣa* must be there. If it is not, the desire for *dharma-artha-kāma* loom large in their minds.

Even Arjuna, up to now, was only interested in *dharma-artha-kāma*. He became interested in *mokṣa* only a few chapters ago, since Kṛṣṇa started talking to him a few hours ago, perhaps. Before that Arjuna was interested in fighting and in establishing *dharma*.

Therefore, robbed of their discrimination by various desires, driven by their particular disposition, they propitiate different *devatā*s according to the stipulations. As a result, they do not come to Īśvara. It applies to all forms of religion where Īśvara is other than you.

Verse 21

In whichever form people worship me – in that form I bless them

यो यो यां यां तनुं भक्तः श्रद्धयार्चितुमिच्छति ।
तस्य तस्याचलां श्रद्धां तामेव विदधाम्यहम् ॥ २१ ॥

yo-yo yāṁ yāṁ tanuṁ bhaktaḥ śraddhayārcitum icchati
tasya tasyācalāṁ śraddhāṁ tāmeva vidadhāmyaham (21)

yaḥ yaḥ – whoever; *bhaktaḥ* – the devotee; *yāṁ yām* – whichever; *tanum* – particular form; *śraddhayā* – with faith; *arcitum* – to worship; *icchati* – wishes; *tasya tasya* – for each one of them; *tām eva śraddhām* – indeed that *śraddhā*; *acalām* – firm; *vidadhāmi aham* – I make

Whoever be the devotee and in whichever form (of a deity) he wishes to worship with faith, indeed, I make that faith firm for him.

Yaḥ yaḥ bhaktaḥ – whoever be the devotee, whether he or she be an *ārta*, devotee in distress, an *arthārthī*, someone who wants help for his or her accomplishments, *yāṁ yāṁ tanum*, whichever particular form, *śraddhayā arcitum icchati*, he desires to worship with faith, I make that faith unshakeable, so says Bhagavān. *Bhakta* here is a person whose primary concern is fulfilling his desires; but because he has *śraddhā*, he is a devotee rather than a simple *kāmī*. This restricts the meaning of *bhakta* to an *ārta* and an *arthārthī*. He will invoke the Lord in a particular form, *tanu*, according to his *śraddhā*; but because he does not see that Vāsudeva is everything, he propitiates a particular aspect of the Lord and performs a specific ritual invoking that form of *devatā*.

With *śraddhā* he desires to worship, or to praise a particular form of *devatā*. According to his understanding he may insist that this is the only form of the Lord or he may accommodate other forms of worship.

The Lord himself establishes a devotee's *śraddhā*.

The Lord says, '*tasya acalāṁ śraddhāṁ vidadhāmi aham.*' What is important here is *śraddhā*. Earlier Kṛṣṇa had said that, the one who has *śraddhā* gains knowledge of the identity of the individual and Īśvara, *śraddhāvān labhate jñānam.*[15]

---

[15] *Gītā* 4.39

In this verse he says whatever *śraddhā* he now has, that, I make it firm, unshakeable, for him –*tasya acalām śraddhāṁ vidadhāmi aham*. For the one whose *śraddhā* manifests as a worship of a particular *devatā* for a particular result, I make his *śraddhā* firm. How? By giving the results. Suppose someone performs a particular ritual and he does not get the promised result, then his *śraddhā* will quickly disappear. I make sure that it does not by giving the results. They are doing *karma*s for which results are to be given. That result I give. Even though they are worshipping only a fraction of me, even though they do not worship me totally, still I make firm whatever *śraddhā* they have. I am available in the particular form of *devatā* that they invoke. No *devatā* is separate from me but I am more than these *devatā*s. The difficulty is that these devotees think that this particular *devatā* is Īśvara. But I do not disturb that at all. I give them results only according to their *śraddhā*. If I were to interfere and tell them, 'I am you,' it would not help because they are not ready for it. Even if the Lord appears before such people, they will ask for a promotion. They already have certain firmness in their *śraddhā*.

Verse 22

I make their śraddhā more firm by giving the result

स तया श्रद्धया युक्तस्तस्याराधनमीहते ।
लभते च ततः कामान्मयैव विहितान्हि तान् ॥ २२ ॥

sa tayā śraddhayā yuktastasyārādhanam īhate
labhate ca tataḥ kāmān mayaiva vihitān hi tān (22)

saḥ – he; *tayā śraddhayā* – with that faith; *yuktaḥ* – being endowed; *tasya* – of that (deity); *ārādhanam* – worship; *īhate* – engages in; *ca* – and; *tataḥ* – from that (worshipped deity) *mayā eva* – by me alone; *vihitān* – ordained; *hi* – because/definetely; *tān kāmān* – those desired objects; *labhate* – he gains

> He who, endowed with that faith, engages in worship of that (deity), gains from that (deity he has worshipped) those objects of desire that are definitely ordained by me alone.

There are two different ways of reading the second line of this verse as given below:

1. मया एव विहितान् हि तान् कामान् लभते

   mayā eva vihitān hi tān kāmān labhate

2. मया एव विहितान् हितान् कामान् लभते

   mayā eva vihitān hitān kāmān labhate

Here in the second reading, *hitān kāmān* will mean very desirable objects.

1. He who, endowed with that faith, engages in worship of that (*devatā*), gains from that (*devatā* he has worshipped) those objects of desire that are definitely ordained by me alone.
2. He who, endowed with that faith, engages in worship of that (*devatā*), gains from that (*devatā* he has worshipped) the very desirable objects of desire that are ordained by me.

Saḥ yuktaḥ tayā śraddhayā, this is a person endowed with *śraddhā* in the Veda which promises a particular result for a given ritual. A given means is capable of producing a given result and the connection between them is permanent. This is the order, the law of *karma* which is Īśvara. How do you know these various means and ends are connected? When you perform a ritual, what is its connection to a son, or the rains? This connection is revealed in the *śāstra* which is given by Īśvara. *Śraddhā* means the acceptance of that connection. 'If I do this, this will happen. Therefore, I do this.' It is the *śraddhā* of the person that is spoken here. Then he engages in worship of that form of *devatā* with this *śraddhā–tasya ārādhanam īhate.*

Labhate ca tataḥ kāmān, from that *devatā* he gains those objects of his desire. *Kāma* can mean both desire and the object of desire. Here it means the desired objects. *Tataḥ,* from that, meaning from the *devatā* whom he has worshipped. And Kṛṣṇa says here that the *devatā* this person has worshipped is nothing but him.

The Lord says, '*mayā eva vihitān hi tān,* by me alone the results of their worship are ordained.' People perform rituals or offer prayers with *śraddhā* and obtain the results. I, the Lord, determine these results but they think they come from the *devatā* that they worshipped. They do not recognise Īśvara, but it does not matter. The prayer has given the result, and therefore, the *śraddhā* becomes more firm. Next time the prayer will be better in order to get a better result until there is maturity in the understanding.

The first reading is, *tān vihitān kāmān labhate hi,* they gain those ends because they are ordained by me. Here *hi* means 'because.' It is all arranged by Parameśvara, who is omniscient and therefore, knows that this *karma* has precisely this result.

Everything that is done is taken into account; so, we sometimes see different results for the apparently same action. Two people may perform a ritual, *putra-kāmeṣṭi*, for the gain of a son. One has a beautiful son who is very bright and healthy. The other has a son born with poor eyesight. It means that in the performance of the ritual by the second person, there was some problem. He did get a son, but there was some omission or commission in the ritual and the results have to be given only according to the *karma* performed. Both of them did the same ritual but one did it better than the other, so he gets a better result. Who is to decide all this? Śaṅkara says here that the one who is omniscient, the Lord, gives the result.

Hi can also mean definitely. A given means produces a given result and there are degrees of results because there are variations both in how the ritual is performed and the person's knowledge of what he is doing. How much one understands when performing a ritual also determines the nature of the result. All these conditions, including one's attitude when giving the gifts affect the result. If he had a sense of loss that affects the result because one is supposed to give with a full heart, with the feeling that one could not have given more. A person's *śraddhā,* knowledge, and the mode of performance are in different degrees, and these determine the result. So, each one gets exactly what he or she must. Here *hi* has the meaning of definitely, necessarily. These are the meanings if we read the words as follows, *vihitān hi tān*. Here the words *hi* and *tān* have been read separately as two words instead of *hitān* as one word.

In the second reading it is read together as one word, *hitān*. So, the statement would be *mayā eva vihitān hitān kāmān labhate*. Here these results are desirable ends that are *hita*, good for you, *hitān kāmān*. Śaṅkara cautions here that they are not totally desirable because *kāma* is never really *hita*, desirable. Desires and desired objects which are other than ourselves, are not what is good for us. They cause pain when they are unfulfilled and even when they are fulfilled, they ultimately come to an end and cause grief. They have limitations. So, they are not *hita*, the most desirable. Kṛṣṇa elaborates this in the next verse.

Verse 23

For those of limited discrimination – the result is limited

अन्तवत्तु फलं तेषां तद्भवत्यल्पमेधसाम् ।
देवान्देवयजो यान्ति मद्भक्ता यान्ति मामपि ॥ २३ ॥

antavat tu phalaṁ teṣāṁ tadbhavatyalpamedhasām
devān devayajo yānti madbhaktā yānti mām api (23)

tu – but; *alpa-medhasāṁ teṣām* – for those who have limited discrimination; *tat phalam* – that result; *antavat* – finite (having an end); *bhavati* – is; *devayajaḥ* – those who worship the deities; *devān* – the deities; *yānti* – go to; *madbhaktāḥ* – those who worship me; *api* – indeed; *māṁ yānti* – go to me

But, for those of limited discrimination, that result is finite. The worshippers of the deities go to the deities; the worshippers of me go to me indeed.

Teṣāṁ alpa-medhasām – *alpa* means a little, *medhas* means capacity to think; so, *alpa-medhas* is one who has a limited capacity to think, to enquire. Because they engage in such limited pursuits they are *alpa-medhasaḥ*. Here, it specifically means the one who has limited *viveka*. They do have some *viveka* because they are devotees. They have *dharma-adharma-viveka* and they recognise Īśvara in some form. But this is a limited *viveka*.

For those of *alpa-medhas, tad phalam antavad bhavati*, the result, of the *karma*s they do, is *antavat*. *Antavat* means that which has an end. In terms of time there is an end. Being a result it will definitely perish. In terms of place, it is finite. Any result that takes you to another place is limited because in going to one place, another is missed. If a person goes to heaven, he does not go to other *loka*s such as *brahma-loka*. Even in heaven, he will occupy a given position and enjoy only the benefits of that position; so, there is a limitation in terms of what is enjoyed. Some things are available for enjoyment while some are not. The degree of pleasure he will experience is again limited because of the limitation of the body he gets. And whatever be his enjoyment, it is only for a finite length of time. So, in every respect the result is *antavat*, limited. For such people of limited discrimination, the result of worship is only finite; it has an end.

Devān deva-yajaḥ yānti. Because they worship various *devatā*s or perform rituals invoking various deities, they are called *deva-yajaḥ*. As a result of such worship they go only to those *devas*, *devān yānti.* They go to the world where the particular deity resides and become *devatās*, denizens of the heavens etc. If one worships Indra he goes to *indra-loka* and becomes another *deva* in that world. But that *deva* is still a *jīva*.

Heaven is definitely a limited end. And this is the maximum one can get from *karma*. There they may find themselves employees in the palaces of the *devas*. But the *devas* themselves look up to Indra who looks up to Bṛhaspati who is his *guru*. These are the places, positions, and are therefore, *upādhis*. So, those who experience them are mere *jīvas*. They have better powers, better sense perception, and a better capacity to enjoy, but it is only for a given length of time. Later Kṛṣṇa is going to say that when the *puṇya* that got them there is exhausted, they will leave that particular *loka* and enter another, *kṣīṇe puṇye martya lokaṁ viśanti*.

Those who seek Īśvara directly gain him.

Mad-bhaktāḥ mām apiyanti, whereas those who seek me directly come to me; they become me. If they want to know what is Parameśvara, what is this *ātmā*, they become me because Parameśvara is *ātmā*. What was said before is confirmed here. They become *mahātmās*, who know that all this is Vāsudeva, *vāsudevaḥ-sarvam*. There is only one *ātmā*, which is me and that they come to recognise as themselves. Thus they come to me alone.

Both make effort but the result is vastly different.

Śaṅkara points out here that even though the effort is the same, there is great disparity in the result. Those who pursue the *devatās* make effort but they do not seek me for a result that has no end. Rituals are fraught with effort – *kāyika-karma*, physical; *vācika-karma*, oral; and *mānasa-karma*, mental. One has to gather the materials and then take great care to perform the ritual properly. Then he has to distribute wealth. Appropriate *mantra*s are to be chanted and they must also be done properly. Meditation upon the deity is prescribed and this too is not easy.

In seeking Parameśvara also there is effort. You have to dedicate yourself to the pursuit of this knowledge and deny yourself certain pleasures that you might have otherwise enjoyed. Then there is the study of language, and in earlier times, the study of logic. Today we assume that you have some logic from your general education because for Vedanta you require certain intellectual discipline. Previously it was acquired by the study of logic and grammar. In fact, just the study of Sanskrit grammar develops the capacity to think properly. All this requires effort. The study of logic, especially, is most tortuous. It requires a lot of effort. You have to keep track of everything that was said and learn its jargon; the whole language changes. To say a pot is filled with water they will say the object that is conditioned by the word called pot is filled with the thing which is conditioned by the word water. And filled is neither less nor more. By the time he completes the statement, it will be in the form of two paragraphs. This is Indian logic. It is very thorough.

For a ritual, you make a lot of effort and to conduct this enquiry you also make a lot of effort. But for the first, you get a limited result and for the other, the result is limitless; the very seeker is resolved. What kind of a bargain is this?

There is no bargain at all. And for the *vivekī*, there is no choice either. Only for the *avivekī* does there seem to be some choice.

Even the effort is disparate.

The effort, however, is not really equal. *Paramātmā* is not separate from *ātmā*, the seeker; it is already accomplished. It is oneself alone. And yet, without *viveka*, a person abandons it and pursues something else. One has nectar in one's hand and gives it up and extends the other hand for some gruel. *Ātmā* is already available without any effort. One has only to claim it, nothing else. Only a single effort is involved here, knowledge. But if one does not discern this, he or she has a lot of things to do.

If one has *vairāgya*, clarity about what produces what, and if one loves knowledge, all one has to do is only to enquire. What effort is there in that? Yet when one undertakes this pursuit, the whole society will sympathise with the person, thinking that he or she is making a great sacrifice and wondering what is wrong with the person. But one does not feel one has sacrificed anything. One has a commitment to the pursuit of knowledge; and so, there is no real giving up and no effort.

For a person with such a commitment this concept of giving up is sheer nonsense. When the fruit is ripe it detaches itself from the tree; it does not give up anything. It falls off the tree because otherwise it would hang and rot. It has to fall so that another tree will come out of it. Giving up is only from the standpoint of a person who has some difficulties, not for the person who has maturity. For such a person there is no giving up, there is simply growing out of.

Others consider that one has made a foolhardy step. But if the person is a *vivekī*, he or she will understand them. They have their own value system. If they ask this person what he or she will do for the next meal, he or she will say, 'When I am hungry I will think about it.' The future is not a problem for him or her. For such a person there is no effort at all in this pursuit.

The whole pursuit being in the form of enquiry, all one requires is one's mind. For rituals, a lot of ingredients are required but for knowledge, only the mind. And there is no sense of effort in the enquiry because all along one is discovering something. And that is all one wants. All along it is beneficial, not just at the end. It is one continuous pleasant affair. From the beginning it is an end in itself and therefore, it is entirely different from any other pursuit.

So, in fact, there is no equality of effort. And in terms of the result they are definitely different. One is *saṁsāra*; the other is *mokṣa*. They are opposites. Yet people do not come directly to Bhagavān, so, he shows them sympathy here in this verse.

Those who seek me directly attain me while those who look upon *artha* and *kāma* pursuits invoke various deities and gain only the limited results they seek. Kṛṣṇa has already explained the meaning of the word *mām*, me, as the one who is the self of everything, the one the *jñānī* knows as himself. He says that these people recognise his essential form and therefore, are non-separate from him, the Lord. The whole presentation here is from the standpoint of *paramātmā*. Either Vyāsa introduces Kṛṣṇa here as Īśvara or Kṛṣṇa introduces himself as Īśvara. Whether Kṛṣṇa was a historical figure or an *avatāra*, does not matter. The next verse he is introduced very clearly.

Verse 24

Lack of discrimination denies recognition of Īśvara

अव्यक्तं व्यक्तिमापन्नं मन्यन्ते मामबुद्धयः ।
परं भावमजानन्तो ममाव्ययमनुत्तमम् ॥ २४ ॥

avyaktaṁ vyaktim āpannaṁ manyante māmabuddhayaḥ
paraṁ bhāvam ajānanto mamāvyayam anuttamam (24)

abuddhayaḥ – those who lack discrimination; *avyayam* – changeless; *anuttamam* – beyond which there is nothing greater; *mama paraṁ bhāvam* – my limitless nature (as *ātmā*); *ajānantaḥ* – not knowing; *mām avyaktam* – me who is formless; *vyaktim āpannam* – as one endowed with a manifest form; *manyante* – look upon

> Those who lack discrimination, not knowing my limitless, changeless nature beyond which there is nothing greater, look upon me, who is formless, as one endowed with a manifest form.

Abuddhayaḥ means those who have insufficient *viveka*. The negative particle '*a*' here means inadequacy as used often in an expression such as, 'I have no money.' Everyone has *buddhi*, intellect, but if they lack *viveka*, they are called *abuddhis*, people of limited discrimination. In the context here they are devotees but because they are *abuddhis*, lacking in discrimination, they look upon me as Viṣṇu in this particular form of Kṛṣṇa.

Avyaktaṁ māṁ vyaktim āpannaṁ manyante, they look upon me who is *avyakta* as *vyakta*. *Avyakta* has two meanings. Śaṅkara takes it here as *aprakāśa*, not known as an object. It is not accessible to any means of knowledge we have and therefore, is not known directly.

The other meaning of *avyakta* is unmanifest. Because they lack discrimination they look upon me as now endowed with a particular manifest form, *manyante vyaktim āpannam*. I am considered to be Lord Viṣṇu who was in heaven, *Vaikuṇṭha*, and has now come here as Kṛṣṇa.

Īśvara's real nature is not known.

Why do they consider me as *vyaktim āpannam* when I am *avyakta?* Because *mama paraṁ bhāvam ajānantaḥ*, they do not know my limitless nature, the nature of *paramātmā*. So, it looks as though what is *avyakta* has become *vyakta*.

The word '*vyakta*' can be looked at in another way. The nature of *paramātmā*, Īśvara, is always *vyakta*, manifest. It is *nitya-aparokṣa*, always available, for the following reasons. Any experience is imbued with the very nature of *ātmā*. Whatever is the experience, there is the presence of consciousness, the nature of *ātmā*. A given experience is of an object that was previously away from you and has now come into the range of your experience. Since it was not there before, it will not be there in the same form the next minute. The object can also be a thought form without a corresponding external object. Whatever be the object, in the experience of every object, one thing is invariable, experience. The object is a qualifying factor to experience. Without a particular object there is only *anubūti svarūpa*, consciousness.

Just as all the beads of a necklace run through one thread, similarly in all forms of experience, what is always present is consciousness, the *svarūpa* of *ātmā*. Is it away from you, that is, is it *parokṣa*? Is it perceived by you as an object, *pratyakṣa*? If it is, it was not perceived previously and therefore, later it will not be perceived. This contradicts your experience of yourself. *Ātmā* is not an object of perception, much less an object of inference. Any inference is because of the presence of *ātmā*. Therefore, *ātmā* is neither something remote that is inferred, *parokṣa*, nor an object of perceptual experience, *pratyakṣa* which is why it is called *aparokṣa*. It is immediately known yet not perceived or inferred.

An orientation can persist after knowledge.

One who knows this contemplates upon the knowledge constantly recalling me, Parameśvara, to his mind. This recollection is always preceded by *śravaṇa*, listening to the *śāstra*. Unless you have already collected an experience you cannot recollect it. Parameśvara is understood through the *śāstra*. But even after exposure to the *śāstra* and analysis of it, you can still have the orientation that you are the body. This is called *deha-ātma-buddhi*.

There is a difference between orientation and confusion. A simple confusion requires clarification only once. Suppose you use the wrong key to unlock a door. You immediately understand the confusion because the door does not open.

Therefore, you choose the right key and confusion is resolved. There is no further problem. But suppose a door gets sealed off and a wall is erected behind it. Even though you know there is no longer a functional door there, out of habit you will try to open it for some time. Then you remember; this is orientation.

For me[16] this problem is very visible. When I travel by car, I always sit in the passenger seat. In India, I know the cars have right hand drive and that I am supposed to go to the left door, not to the right door. But when I go to India after being in America for some time, I go only to the right door. Why? There is no confusion. I know what is left and right. I know in America it is left hand drive and in India right hand drive. Yet I commit a mistake because there is an orientation.

When there is such an orientation you have to remember. It does not go away just because you have resolved the confusion. Nor does it go by a single recollection of what you know. The notion that *ātmā* is the body and the body is *ātmā*, is what we call *deha-ātma-buddhi*. This confusion is resolved by the *śāstra*. Once it is resolved you should not have any problem. But you see that the problem continues. Either the *śāstra* is not properly understood or the problem continues because of orientation. Even in one life so many years have been invested in this notion. How are you going to remove it just because somebody said '*tat tvam asi*?' The orientation has to go.

---

[16] Swamiji

How to correct the orientation?

To help remove this orientation, you need the exposure to the teaching, direct and indirect. Then there is *brahma-abhyāsa* which consists of dwelling upon that, *tat-cintanam*, talking about it, *tat-kathanam*, mutual discussion among seekers, *anyonyaṁ tat prabodhanam*. Contemplation is also included. Living with the knowledge in this way for a length of time is remembering, *smaraṇam*. And it is absolutely necessary.

This is to be done as long as necessary. Śaṅkara says elsewhere, *satataṁ smarati nityaśaḥ. Nityaśaḥ* means always and so does *satata*. Why does he use two words with the same meaning? *Satata* has the sense of without any interval, remembering Īśvara constantly. Remembering here is spending your time in contemplation, in dwelling on the truth of Īśvara as revealed by the words of the śāstra. The word *nityaśaḥ* also means 'always,' but it has the sense of a length of time. You can dwell constantly for one day, two days, one week or one year. So, constantly, for how long is this to be done? For this Bhagavān says, '*nityaśaḥ*, for a long time.' The affix '*śas*' on *nitya* gives the meaning of abundance. *Nitya* means always and adding '*śas*' to it extends it. It is not a one or two days or a three-year affair. It is to be done as long as you are alive.

However, it is not an unpleasant task. It is a very pleasant affair. Constantly remembering the fact that *aham* is Parameśvara is something that you love. It is the highest form of joy because you cannot be better than that. It is not simple self-hypnotism. It is knowledge born of *śāstra*, and again and again you dwell upon that. Somehow the mind will pose the question, 'How can you be Parameśvara? It may argue, 'How can you be Parameśvara in spite of a backache.' You now have a contemplative theme. This is how the contemplation continues. Anything that opposes the vision has to be met with. How long should this go on? Śaṅkara says, as long as one is alive. In the beginning perhaps it is something that has to be done consciously. Then later it becomes very natural. There is really nothing for you to think about.

If the fact, '*ahaṁ parameśvaraḥ*' is very clear to you, then, there is no problem. Your mind does not pose any objections. Neither a mental condition nor a condition of the physical body is taken to be the nature of *ātmā*. Things are viewed as they are. In this case you do not need to do anything.

However, when you require *smaraṇa*, for how long should it be done? As long as it has got to be done, it is done. The Lord says, 'The one who constantly dwells upon me through listening, answering objections, contemplation and even *satsaṅga*, as long as one is alive, for him or her I am *sulabha*, easily gained.'

Gaining Parameśvara is sulabha – easy

There are a number of reasons why Īśvara is easily gained. Any accomplishment requires some effort, even wearing your clothes. Suppose you have a shirt that is a little tight. When you are in a great hurry, you would rather not wear it because it takes a half a minute extra to put it on. You want to avoid that extra time and effort.

Now suppose you need some money. You have to put in effort. If you want power, you have to put in effort. If you want pleasure, it takes some effort on your part. To create a pleasurable situation you have to manipulate a lot of things. Only then can you relax and enjoy. And if you want to go to heaven, effort is involved – lot of things have to be avoided and many things have to be done.

However, the Lord says that the gain of Brahman is *sulabha*. While going to *brahma-loka* requires the maximum amount of effort, gaining Brahman is no effort. If it is argued that always dwelling upon Brahman is an effort, it is not. In fact, there is no effort in dwelling upon what you love.

Everybody loves to stand before the mirror. Even an old man who has cataract in his eyes and is not able to see well, stands before the mirror and tries to look at himself. Why, because of love for *ātmā*. Here, it is not an effort, because love is not an effort; it is very natural. For a *mumukṣu*, dwelling upon Parameśvara is a matter of love.

It is very natural because *ātmā* is of the nature of absolute love. Any form of love extended towards any object is, after all, for my own sake. That object makes me pleased and therefore, becomes an object of my love. What I really love is my pleased self, *ātmā*. Since *ātmā* is Parameśvara, whose nature is *ānanda*, there is nothing more to be desired. Being absolute fullness, *ātmā* becomes the object of absolute love. Because it is the most desirable, dwelling upon it becomes joyous; it is not a painful affair. It is what you love the utmost.

Nothing new is produced either because *ātmā* is already existent as Parameśvara. The result is not born of effort; it is born purely of recognition. There is no effort involved; nothing new is added; nothing old is removed. The accomplishment is of an already accomplished fact. Therefore, it is *sulabha*, easily gained.

Then you may argue that the removal of ignorance is an effort. In fact, you only recognise and in the recognition, ignorance gets removed. You do not do any action. It is purely an activity of the *pramāṇa*. Therefore, it is *sulabha*. The one who dwells upon me is endowed with a mind, which is tranquil, contented, and under control, in the sense that it does not have any problem with reference to reflection on Parameśvara.

Whenever the mind is free, it goes towards Bhagavān, like a person who loves someone. The mind very naturally goes towards the object of love. It does not require an appointment. Similarly here, the mind of a *mumukṣu*, a *jijñāsu*, will naturally go towards *paramātmā*, the *vastu*. You have understood the nature of *paramātmā* as something that is not different than yourself. So where else will the mind go?

Until that takes place, you continue to do *śravaṇa*. Will is used in the beginning and later the very subject matter takes over. Afterwards you do not require any will at all. It is something like going to a *kumbha-mela*. You do not require a road map. All you have to do is get into a crowd that is going. Soon the momentum of the crowd is so great that even if you want to go back, you cannot. It becomes like a moving ramp. People from behind push you and you keep moving. You are in the stream. You keep moving and you find yourself right in front of Gaṅgā! This is exactly what happens here. Certain will is required until you get into the stream of thinking of understanding. Once clarity is there, there is no effort at all.

In the previous verse, Kṛṣṇa said that these people who lack discrimination, not knowing my real nature, look upon me as someone who has a form. They think I am someone remote from them who has assumed a body and come here from another place. In fact, I am the whole world and I am the *ātmā* of everyone. This is my real nature, changeless and beyond which there is nothing greater. Not knowing me in this way, they regard me as having a given form.

Śaṅkara asks, what is the reason for this ignorance? Why do they worship other *devatā*s and pursue smaller ends? Why do people not directly seek the Lord? Kṛṣṇa points this out in the next verse.

Verse 25

Covered by māyā – not everyone recognises Bhagavān

नाहं प्रकाशः सर्वस्य योगमायासमावृतः ।
मूढोऽयं नाभिजानाति लोको मामजमव्ययम् ॥ २५ ॥

nāhaṁ prakāśaḥ sarvasya yoga-māyāsamāvṛtaḥ
mūḍho'yaṁ nābhijānāti loko mām ajam avyayam (25)

yoga-māyā-samāvṛtaḥ – completely covered by *yoga-māyā*; *sarvasya* – for everyone; *na ahaṁ prakāśaḥ* – I am not recognised; *ayaṁ lokaḥ* – this person; *mūḍhaḥ* – being deluded; *ajam* – one who is unborn; *avyayam* – one who is changeless; *mām* – me; *na abhijānāti* – does not clearly know

> Completely covered by *yoga-māyā,*[17] I am not recognised by everyone. This deluded person does not know me clearly as the one who is unborn and changeless.
>
> Alternate Reading:
>
> I, completely covered by *māyā*, united with the three *guṇa*s, am not recognised by everyone. A person is deluded and does not know me properly as the one who is unborn and changeless.

Na ahaṁ prakāśaḥ sarvasya, I am not known to all people. *Na ahaṁ prakāśaḥ* means I do not come to light. Even the people who see me now, see me as this boy from Brindāvan. They do not recognise me, Īśvara at all. The Lord says, 'I cannot be known by all people.' Śaṅkara adds here, that the Lord can be seen only by certain *bhakta*s, seekers. It means Īśvara comes to light only for those who seek him and are qualified to recognise him, not to everyone. Why?

People are covered by *māyā* – *lokaḥ yoga-māyā-samāvṛtaḥ.* Śaṅkara says *yoga* means the connection or tying together of the three *guṇa*s. It is *māyā*. By that *māyā*, united to the three *guṇa*s, they are covered. Previously it was said that people are deluded by the three *guṇa*s – *tribhiḥ guṇa mayaiḥbhāvaiḥ ebhiḥ sarvam idaṁ jagat mohitam.*[18] As we saw, it is the product of the *guṇa*s that delude. *Sattva* accounts for happiness, *rajas* for

---

[17] *Māyā* united with the three *guṇa*s.

[18] *Gītā* 7.13

sorrow, and *tamas* for dullness. By these, people are covered. *Āvṛta* means 'covered' and *samāvṛta* means 'totally covered.' By this *yoga-māyā*, the three *guṇa*s and their products, people are totally covered.

What is covered? Suppose consciousness, *ātmā*, is covered, then, you would not be able to know anything; there would be no world, that is, there will be *jagadāndhya-prasaṅga*.[19] You must know this expression, which is used often in the *śāstra*. How would there be no world? If the eyes are obstructed you cannot see; if the ears or any of the five sense organs are obstructed, they cannot perceive. Similarly, if consciousness is really obstructed by this *yoga-māyā*, then, you will not perceive anything. The mind will not be able to observe the world; there would be *jagadāndhya-prasaṅga*. *Jagadāndhya* means being blind to the world. It is contrary to your experience. You do experience the world. Consciousness is not covered by anything, which is why you are able to see, hear, think, even to say 'I am a *saṁsārī* and therefore, a *mumukṣu*.' All this is possible because consciousness is never covered.

Then what is covered? The verse says, '*lokaḥ*.' *Loka* is defined as *lokyate anena iti*, that by which something is known, experienced. If that is so, is it the unconditioned consciousness, *ātma-caitanya*, or is it *pramātṛ caitanya*, consciousness conditioned as a knower, that is indicated by the word *loka*? Consciousness is never covered. We have seen that. Therefore, *loka* here means

---

[19] The possibility of the world being absent for a person.

the knower, *pramātṛ caitanya*, the one who recognises an object. It is only from the *pramātṛ*'s standpoint that there is covering,

What is covered for the knower is the nature of *ātmā*. It is not understood. Any understanding is for the knower. Therefore, it is from the *pramātṛ*'s standpoint that we say the nature of *ātmā* is covered by *māyā*, ignorance.

It is mistaken for a doer, an enjoyer, and therefore, someone subject to birth, death and so on. It is an error on the part of the knower who is consciousness essentially. That very consciousness obtaining as the knower is covered by ignorance.

Mūḍhaḥ na abhijānāti mām, being deluded the person does not recognise me. Naturally when the mind is totally covered by *māyā*, a person is deluded and does not recognise me. The external world, the physical body, and so on, are not deluded, nor is consciousness, *ātmā*. There is only one thing in this world that can be deluded, the mind, *antaḥ-karaṇa*; delusions reside only there. *Loka*, the consciousness conditioned by the mind, called the knower, does not know me. That knower alone is deluded, nothing else. Therefore, he or she does not know me, *māṁ na abhijānāti*.

Abhijānāti is a very good word here. *Jānāti* means 'he knows.' *Abhijānāti* means 'he knows properly.' *Na abhijānāti* means 'he does not know properly.' All devotees know Īśvara in some form other than themselves, as another individual located somewhere in the world, as *parokṣa*. The Lord says, 'The whole world is me but a devotee looks upon it as something different from me. Even though I am his very *ātmā*, he does not recognise that. On the contrary, all that he recognises about me, I am not.' Only one thing is there, Brahman; no history, no biography, no problems, only *satyaṁ jñānam anantaṁ brahma.* It was like that before, it is like that now and it will always be like that. But that he does not know. And not knowing me like this, he also does not know himself. He knows only what he is not. After saying, 'I am,' he will relate an elaborate history and will add psychology to it by bringing in the subconscious or the unconscious. Therefore, he has a variety of histories. And they are all valid, because he does not know me, *māṁ na abhijānāti.* He knows me, but only well enough to commit a mistake about me.

The original mistake is not corrected

Even to mistake something you must have some knowledge of it. You must see the rope; only then can you mistake it for a snake. Similarly *ātmā* has to be known in some way before you can commit any mistake about it. And it is always available for one to commit a mistake. *Ātmā* is always *nitya-aparokṣa,* self-evident, evident enough for the *buddhi* to commit a mistake uniformly. Then we keep compounding it. Through experiences, the mistake gets more and more complicated. It is what we call living.

There is one fundamental error followed by a variety of others. These entrench the original mistake. It is buried under the other mistakes you are now busy correcting. But it is always there. Therefore, no matter how much you keep correcting the secondary mistakes, you do not arrive at the right solution. It is like solving an arithmetic problem. You commit a mistake in the first step of simple addition, then you commit a mistake in multiplication, then in division. Afterwards you correct the mistakes in multiplication and division. But you do not think you can commit a mistake in addition because it is such a simple thing. Therefore, you get the wrong answer. The same is true with *saṁsāra*. The original mistake is not corrected. Before continuing the seeking, the first step is to find out, if am I a seeker. Do I have to seek? If that is not answered properly and you keep on correcting every subsequent step, it is meaningless.

Uniqueness of ignorance of ātmā

Ignorance of *ātmā* is different from ignorance of an object like a pot. There are many things in this world, like a pot, which you do not know and are therefore, objects of your ignorance. *Ātmā*, however, unlike a pot, is not an object of ignorance or knowledge. It does not have its basis in *yoga-māyā* and therefore, like a pot, it cannot be an object of *yoga-māyā*, ignorance. It is self-evident and is the basis of both ignorance and knowledge.

Being covered by *yoga-māyā* amounts to this. The knowledge that has to take place in the *buddhi* is now covered or obstructed by the products of the three *guṇa*s. The obstruction is not for *ātmā*; it is for the mind where the knowledge has to take place. Therefore, we say that there is ignorance of *ātmā* until the knowledge takes place. In other words, it is there until it goes away for good.

Uniqueness of knowledge of ātmā

When we say knowledge is obstructed by *yoga-māyā*, what do we mean by *jñāna*, knowledge? Two meanings are possible.

One is *jñapti-svarūpa-jñānam*, pure consciousness. The other is, *jñāyate anena iti jñānam*, that by which a given object is known, that is, the instrument of knowledge. This is *vṛtti-jñāna*.

Now, consciousness is not obstructed by *yoga-māyā*. As we have seen, it would mean that there would be *jagadāndhya-prasaṅga*. That is, the world would not be recognised. Therefore, the only other thing that can be obstructed is *vṛtti-jñāna*, that by which something is known. This knowledge, which removes ignorance and error, takes place only where a *vṛtti* can take place, that is, in the *buddhi*. There is no other place where it can occur. *Ātmā* has to be understood only by the mind, *manasā eva anudraṣṭavyaḥ*.

Not understanding the *śāstra*, people interpret statements like, '*yato vāco nivartante aprāpya manasā saha*,'[20] to mean, 'You must transcend the mind, etc.' What is said there is that, along with the mind the words come back having not accomplished *ātmā*, that is, having not objectified *ātmā*. *Ātmā* is not available for objectification by a *vṛtti*. You cannot relate to it as you would to an object like a pot or a tree.

You relate to the object of a *vṛtti* as, 'This is the object, I am the knower of this object.' Can you relate this way to a *vṛtti* for which the 'object'[21] is *ātmā*? Can you say, 'This is *ātmā*' like how you can say, 'this is pot?' If you can, then, who are you? This knower-known difference, which is always present

---

20 *Taittirīyopaniṣad* 2.4.1

21 The word object is put within quotes to indicate that *ātmā* can never be an object of our perception.

between the object and the knower does not exist with reference to the nature of the knower. Then how do you ever recognise it?

A special *pramāṇa*, a special *vṛtti* – *akhaṇḍa-ākāra-vṛtti.*

Any *vṛtti* leading to knowledge can be produced only by a *pramāṇa*, means of knowledge. To generate a *vṛtti* that will remove self-ignorance, your known means of knowledge, perception and inference, will not work because they reveal only objects. Only *śabda-pramāṇa* can create the *vṛtti* that destroys ignorance of the subject, *ātmā*. *Ātmā* is not created by the *pramāṇa*; it is because of *ātmā* that the *pramāṇa*s can even be operated. It is the *vṛtti* that is created. And the *śāstra* is the *pramāṇa* which can create this new knowledge, *vṛtti-jñāna*, by a sentence that reveals the truth of the knower. This sentence, *mahā-vākya*, creates the *vṛtti* that removes the ignorance of the nature of the knower. This *vṛtti* is the *akhaṇḍa-ākāra-vṛtti.*

Akhaṇḍa-ākāra-vṛtti means that between the object of knowledge and the knower there is no difference. What is common between Īśvara and the *jīva* is *akhaṇḍa*, limitlessness. After negating the differences, the *śāstra* says, '*tat tvam asi*, that Īśvara is you.' This creates a *vṛtti* that brings about the understanding that the meaning of the word 'you' and the meaning of the word Īśvara are the same. What abides as the basis of everything, *jīva* and Īśvara, is one consciousness. This particular recognition, brought about by the *vṛtti*, takes place in the mind destroying ignorance of the fact that *ātmā* is *akhaṇḍa*, limitless.

Before that, the knower is covered by *yoga-māyā* and therefore, does not recognise his limitlessness. When the mind is under the spell of the *guṇa*s and their products, there is no possibility of this *vṛtti-jñāna*, '*ahaṁ brahma asmi*, I am Brahman.' Hence the Lord says, 'Being covered by *yoga-māyā* naturally, people are deluded and do not recognise me, *mūḍhāḥ ayaṁ māṁ na abhijānāti*.

What is not known?

Bhagavān says, 'One does not know me properly…' Who is that 'me'?

It is *aja*, the unborn self. Certain things are not born but they die, like ignorance. It cannot have a beginning. If it began, something must have been there before it came into existence; something that is opposed to ignorance must have been present before it. It can only be knowledge. Where there is no darkness, there is necessarily light. Similarly, where there is no ignorance there is necessarily knowledge. But if knowledge was there, how could ignorance come about? Therefore, we understand that ignorance has no beginning. Can we also say it has no end? No. Ignorance of *ātmā* or anything else has no beginning but it ends when we know what it is.

Ātmā also cannot have a beginning. If it came into existence at a given time, you must have been there to note it. Otherwise how do you know that it was born? If you were there to observe the birth of *ātmā* you had to be a conscious being. But that is *ātmā*. *Ātmā* cannot simultaneously exist and observe the termination of its own non-existence. And when *ātmā* does exist, there is no possibility of its having had a non-existence and subsequent birth. Therefore, *ātmā* has to be *aja,* unborn. *Ātmā* is thus beginningless, but unlike ignorance, it is endless. It is *avyaya,* it does not change, *na vyeti iti avyayam.* It has no decline, no destruction. Kṛṣṇa says, 'They do not know me as the one who is not born and is never destroyed, the one who is eternal.'

Is Bhagavān also covered by *yoga-māyā*?

Śaṅkara raises a question here. If Bhagavān cannot be known properly by all beings because he is covered by *yoga-māyā* then, is his nature also not covered to himself by *yoga-māyā*? After all, that *yoga-māyā* is his *māyā*. Without it, he cannot function. May be he is also covered by it and he does not know himself! Śaṅkara refutes this argument. He says that the difference lies in the fact that Īśvara is the *māyāvī,* the one who wields *māyā*. And *yoga-māyā* is his *upādhi*. All three *guṇa*s of *yoga-māyā* are glories for him; they do not bind or obstruct him in any way.

The ancient Indian *māyāvī,* as reported even in Śaṅkara's *bhāṣya,* is a type of magician who creates a spell. His magic is not simply a sleight of hand. He makes you see things that he apparently produces and then makes them disappear again. Everybody else is under the spell, but the *māyāvī* is not. If he were, there would be no magic. Similarly, Īśvara with his *māyā* is the greatest magician. He creates the entire names and forms, which, if analysed, do not exist at all. All that is there is consciousness. But still the names and forms appear. This is the magic.

Therefore, Īśvara is a magician alright, but he does not come under the spell of his magic. All the *jīva*s, however, are very much under the spell. To break it what should you do? Just as you go to the local *māyāvī* and ask him what the trick is, you must seek the *māyāvī*, Parameśvara, to find out what the truth of this *māyā* is, and who this *māyāvī* is. That is what the *śāstra* does. It tells us who this *māyāvī* is and what this *māyā* is. It is like a magic book that reveals the secret of what looked like a great trick. You expected to discover something miraculous and complicated. When it is explained, it looks so simple. You feel foolish. It is the same thing here. Once you know, every seeking seems foolish. That 'I was seeking' is itself foolish. To know this you go to the *māyāvī* and ask him to explain what it is all about. This is what the Lord explains in the *Gītā*.

Īśvara, the *māyāvī*, is not affected by his *māyā*. That is the difference between *jīva* and Īśvara, which the Lord explains in the next verse.

Verse 26

When Īśvara is not known

वेदाहं समतीतानि वर्तमानानि चार्जुन ।
भविष्याणि च भूतानि मां तु वेद न कश्चन ॥ २६ ॥

vedāhaṁ samatītāni vartamānāni cārjuna
bhaviṣyāṇi ca bhūtāni māṁ tu veda na kaścana (26)

arjuna – O Arjuna!; *samatītāni bhūtāni* – all things/beings that have gone before; *vartamānāni ca* – and all that exist now;

bhaviṣyāṇi ca – and those that will exist (in the future); *ahaṁ veda* – I know; *tu* – but; *na kaścana* – no one; *māṁ veda* – knows me

> Arjuna! I know all beings that have gone before, that exist now and that will exist in the future. But no one knows me.

The Lord says, 'I, however, know not only myself but also what had gone before, *samatītāni*.' *Atītāni* is what had gone before and the prefix '*sam*' makes it each and every thing that had gone before. *Bhūtāni* means all beings. And also Arjuna, things that are existent now, *vartamānāni ca*, and the beings that are going to be born in different forms, *bhaviṣyāṇi ca*, I know, *ahaṁ veda*.

Māṁ tu veda na kaścana, but there is no one who knows me,' says Bhagavān. To that Śaṅkara adds here, 'No one knows the Lord except that one person who has reached the Lord's refuge, who seeks the Lord as his most intimate self, *pratyagātmā*.' There has to be at least one such person, otherwise the *śāstra* would be useless.

In any theology, Īśvara is accepted as the efficient cause, the author of the entire world. And the creation, in most theologies, is looked upon as real. This is the problem. Certain theologies confound this further by claiming that Īśvara has created this world, which is real, out of nothing. That something has come out of nothing is not intelligible. A variation on this is that Īśvara has created the world out of his power.

Not only has he created the world, he has created each individual – every body, every mind and every soul. Among the theologies that hold this view, some contend that only human beings have a soul. Animals and other creatures do not, which is why even a very religious person will have no qualms about killing animals and eating meat. His theology tells him that they have no souls and are meant for food.

Thus each human being has a soul and each soul has to seek God, because God loves him. First he creates me, condemns me to this body with its problems, creates many difficulties for me, and then asks me to believe that he loves me, because he is my father. If he loves me why should he create all these irritants, some of which are not even visible? At least, if I can see them I can deal with them. But it is not so. I innocently breathe in, because I was made that way, and inhale all sorts of germs. Then when I breathe out, the germs remain inside and cause disease in me. And I am told he loves me! When this is so, every individual has to seek the mercy of Īśvara, through a mediator, of course, because he is a sinner. This is an erroneous conclusion, and as long as it is there, there is no way Īśvara can be known. He is, by the very definition, *nitya-parokṣa*, eternally remote.

If Īśvara is other than me, I have to assign a place for him somewhere in this creation. Suppose he is in heaven, and I go there and get very near to him. After all he must have a body of his own, his own *ātmā*, mind, senses and so on. No matter how near I am, I will only see that he has a body and he is right in front of me, yet *parokṣa*. I will not know the truth of Īśvara. Even though I am standing before Īśvara and saying that he is all-knowledge and so on, with my limited knowledge, how am I going to understand that? I will know only as much as my limited understanding will allow. How am I going to understand omniscience? It can never be understood by an *alpajña,* someone with limited knowledge. All-knowledge will remain only with the one who is all-knowing.

Every contention of this sort was covered by Bhagavān himself in the simple statement, '*avyaktaṁ māṁ vyaktim āpannaṁ manyante abuddhayaḥ,* those who lack discrimination consider me, the one who is unmanifest as one endowed with a particular form. So, they do not know me.'[22] This is what Śaṅkara is talking about here, the absence of knowledge of the truth of Īśvara. Because of that, all these beliefs arise.

The truth of Īśvara

The truth is, Īśvara is consciousness, Brahman, conditioned by *māyā – māyā-avacchinna-caitanya. Māyā* is the *upādhi* for Brahman. At this point, one may ask as to what is the difference between Īśvara, which is Brahman conditioned by *māyā-upādhi,* and Brahman? *Māyā* does not exist apart from Brahman. It depends upon it entirely. Being *mithyā, māyā*'s reality is Brahman, so, *māyā* is also Īśvara. And Īśvara is nothing but Brahman.

The *śruti* points out, and my own experience confirms the same. When I look at this world, I find any given thing is nothing but a name and a form. No matter what I analyse, I find it reduced to something else which is in turn reduced to

---

[22] *Gītā* 7.24

something else. I cannot say categorically of anything that it exists of its own accord. Everything is reduced to its constituent reality. The constituent reality of the table is nothing but its substance, wood, which itself is reduced to particles and so on. Everything is reducible. So, we have a world whose reality is *mithyā*; it exists but not independently.

To create this *mithyā* world, Īśvara requires some material, a *mithyā* cause. That is *māyā*, the factor responsible for making the same limitless consciousness appear as *sarvajñā*, all-knowledge; *sarva-śaktimān*, all-powerful, *sarva-sṛṣṭi-kartā*, the author of this whole world. The authorship, and so on, belong only to what is conditioned by *māyā*, Brahman. That Brahman, consciousness, *ātmā*, with reference to *māyā* becomes the author of the creation. Because he is *sarvajña*, he does not have doership. He knows himself. Omniscience, and so on, is with reference to *māyā-upādhi*. With reference to himself he is *satyaṁ jñānam anantaṁ brahma*, pure consciousness. He is not ignorant of this fact.

The material because of which he is called Īśvara, his *māyā-upādhi*, becomes the material cause for the whole world. As a material cause, *māyā* must undergo changes to become this variegated world and is therefore, as we have seen, *pariṇāmi-upādāna-kāraṇa*, a material cause that undergoes modification. *Māyā* changes to become space, air, fire, water, earth, plants, food, a physical body, etc. The whole world is *māyā*. And *māyā* is Īśvara. Therefore, the world is Īśvara who, in reality, is nothing but consciousness, Brahman. Brahman, however, does not undergo any change and is therefore, as we have seen, *vivarta-*

upādāna-kāraṇa, something that does not undergo any change, and yet makes all changes possible. From the standpoint of consciousness, Brahman is *vivarta-upādāna-kāraṇa,* whereas *māyā* is *pariṇāmi-upādāna-kāraṇa.* Thus, Brahman is the material and also the efficient cause for this entire world because Īśvara is nothing but Brahman.

Īśvara is aparokṣa

When you talk of the entire world, you generally exclude your own body. This is the whole problem. Everything that is created has to be included – your physical body, *prāṇa,* senses, mind, and the entire subtle and gross world. You can now say, everything is Īśvara and that Īśvara is nothing but Brahman. Now between Īśvara and the world what is the difference? There is none at all. And between Īśvara and Brahman there is no difference. Therefore, everything is nothing but Brahman, *sarvaṁ khalu idaṁ brahma,* there is nothing else here, *neha nānā asti kiñcana.*

Right now, I, as an individual, am discussing this about Īśvara. And my physical body as well as your physical body is included in the *īśvara-upādhi.* The *prāṇa,* sense organs, mind, intellect, memories are also included. Only *ātmā,* consciousness is left out. Now it is very clear how Īśvara is *aparokṣa.* When you say, 'I am,' that 'I' is Brahman, consciousness. There is no other 'I.' Consciousness is Brahman and Brahman is Īśvara. This entire world, including the body, mind, senses etc., is Īśvara. And what is behind all of them is consciousness, Brahman. So, everything is you. So, where is Īśvara? You, consciousness, are the only Īśvara; there is no other. Everything is Īśvara and therefore, everything is you. This is what we call *jīva-īśvara-abheda,* the non-difference between the individual and Īśvara. Īśvara is nothing but Brahman, consciousness, and that consciousness is you. This is *aparokṣa.*

There is no *parokṣa-īśvara* in reality. Only the person who does not have this knowledge looks upon Īśvara as parokṣa. Such a person is only interested in an Īśvara who is parokṣa. And this is because he or she has not understood that there is no such thing as *parokṣa-īśvara.*

Bhagavān has said however that even if they invoke me as *parokṣa-īśvara,* still I will establish their *śraddhā* by giving appropriate results for their actions.[23] The hope is that one day, because of their good *karma,* they will also come to know Īśvara. A devotee will never go to a bad lot, whatever be his or her religion. One day, the devotee will realise the truth because good *karma*s have their results.

However why do they worship other *devatā*s? Why do they seek not Īśvara directly? It is because they do not know; they do not even suspect the truth of Īśvara. In fact they establish a theology that is against it. The theology may draw out of them certain emotional commitment that does not allow them to analyse the theology objectively. They cannot even acknowledge the possibility of knowing the Lord. If that is so, how can they recognise him as *aparokṣa* that is, as oneself?

---

[23] *Gītā* 7.21-22

Obstructed by *yoga-māyā*, people do not understand the truth of the Lord and therefore, do not know him. What are these obstructions? The expression, *yoga-māyā*, indicates these very broadly. Now these are given in some detail in this verse.

Verse 27

People are totally deluded due to delusion of the opposites

इच्छाद्वेषसमुत्थेन द्वन्द्वमोहेन भारत ।
सर्वभूतानि सम्मोहं सर्गे यान्ति परन्तप ॥ २७ ॥

icchādveṣasamutthena dvandvamohena bhārata
sarvabhūtāni sammohaṁ sarge yānti parantapa (27)

bhārata – O the one who is born in the Bharata race (Arjuna)!; *parantapa* – O scorcher of the enemies! *sarge* – in this creation; *icchā-dveṣa-samutthena* – arising from desire and aversion; *dvandva-mohena* – due to delusion of the opposites; *sarva-bhūtāni* – all beings; *sammohaṁ yānti* – go into a state of total delusion

> Bhārata (Arjuna), the scorcher of the enemies! All beings, due to delusion of the opposites arising from desire and aversion, go into a state of total delusion in this creation.

Sarva-bhūtāni sammohaṁ sarge yānti, all beings in this creation, from the beginning of creation, go to a state of total delusion. *Sarge*, in creation, means they have this delusion even when they are born. What is that delusion and how is it caused? It is a delusion which is born of *dvandva*, the opposites, *dvandva-mohena*. What are those opposites and where do they come from? They arise from desire and aversion, *icchā-dveṣa-samutthena*. Likes and dislikes create opposites, committed opposites, out of which, *moha*, delusion, is born.

The problem with opposites.

The opposites themselves are not a problem. Heat is not a problem nor is cold. Similarly success or failure is not a problem. In fact, even labelling something as success indicates that there is already a problem. How do you label something as success? It is purely from the standpoint of your expectation. Suppose you are a cook and tasting the food you have prepared, you decide it is a failure. But the person for whom you have prepared it thinks it is wonderful. You think it is failure because it is over-cooked. But it is exactly the way he likes it. So, is it success or failure? There is no such thing as success and failure; it is your own creation. You set arbitrary goals for yourself and then judge yourself as a success or failure. The very word success has an element of subjective judgement. And so does the word failure.

These opposites are created by your own *icchā* and *dveṣa*. *Icchā* is *rāga*, what you want. *Dveṣa* is what you do not want. Some opposites are created by Īśvara, like hot and cold, night and day. What you do and do not want are created only by you. Suppose you want the day to be lengthened and the night to be shortened. It is a *dvandva* created by you. Īśvara only created day and night. It is your likes and dislikes that make it a set-up for you in terms of opposites. You want one; you do not want the other. This is what is called being caught between the horns of the opposites. You can only get caught if you have powerful likes and dislikes. Only then will you have delusion about success, failure, gain, loss and so on. These consume your attention, keeping you busy and worried either about the previous failure or the imminent failure.

It is because you want to control everything that you have all these problems. With two hands and legs and five senses, some of which do not function well, and a mind, which has very limited information, you want to control the whole world. You cannot even control the bugs. How are you going to control the entire world? In this attempt to control, you fall under a great spell of delusion.

Śaṅkara says that *icchā* and *dveṣa* themselves are the opposites, opposed to each other like heat and cold. One is the cause of pleasure, the other of sorrow. An *icchā* has something desirable as its object, capable of giving you pleasure. *Dveṣa* has something undesirable, capable of giving you pain. Śaṅkara adds, in their own time people had one set of likes and dislikes; later they may be different. They are connected to the individual. As they arise in one's mind, they create *moha*, delusion.

Strong likes and dislikes control the discriminative faculty causing a multifaceted delusion. This obstructs the rise of knowledge of the reality of Īśvara and *jīva*. In the *Gītā*, all of psychology is brought under *icchā* and *dveṣa*; and it is adequate to explain the problems. If one is able to manage one's likes and dislikes, one has the right mind for this knowledge. But this *moha*, born of the opposites, completely deludes people.

Delusion obstructs even the desire for knowledge

A delusion obstructs even the desire for self-knowledge, leave alone other knowledge. In a mind which is possessed by likes and dislikes, even correct knowledge of external objects is not possible. For instance, there was this man who was possessed by greed. To save money he always purchased the cheapest items. Once he bought a bag of coffee for only three rupees when its normal price would be ten rupees. When he got home, he discovered that only the top half inch was coffee; the rest was sawdust. Because of *icchā*, his greed, his vision was blinded.

*Icchā-dveṣa*s also include anxiety and fear. *Icchā* produces anxiety and *dveṣa*, produces fear. A person with fear will see a snake in every rope, a thief in every post. When the likes and dislikes are powerful, they cause a variety of mental conditions producing an inner torpor that does not allow you to see things as they are. This is *moha*. It is like a veil that partially blinds the intellect and as a result things are not seen properly. What has no value seems to have an overwhelming value. If even external objects are not very clear, you will not be able to discern between what is proper and improper. *Puruṣārtha* will definitely not be clear and priorities will be confused. Where is the question of knowledge of *ātmā*?

In verses 18 and 19 of this chapter, Bhagavān had talked about the *jñānī*, the one who knows him. Who are these people who come to know Bhagavān directly?

Verses 28-30

Released from the delusion of opposites – people of good actions reach me

येषां त्वन्तगतं पापं जनानां पुण्यकर्मणाम् ।
ते द्वन्द्वमोहनिर्मुक्ता भजन्ते मां दृढव्रताः ॥ २८ ॥

yeṣāṁ tvantagataṁ pāpaṁ janānāṁ puṇyakarmaṇām
te dvandvamohanirmuktā bhajante māṁ dṛḍhavratāḥ (28)

tu – but; *yeṣām* – for whom; *puṇya-karmaṇām janānām* – people of good actions; *pāpam antagatam* – *pāpa* has to come to an end; *te* – they; *dvandva-moha-nirmuktāḥ* – being released from the delusion of the opposites; *dṛḍha-vratāḥ* – being of firm commitment; *māṁ bhajante* – seek/reach me

> But people of good actions, for whom *pāpa* has come to an end, being released from the delusion of the opposites and firm in their commitment, they seek/reach me.

The word '*tu*' meaning 'however,' is to distinguish these people from those in the previous verses. *Yeṣāṁ janānāṁ puṇya-karmaṇām* means 'for those people who have done good *karmas*.' They refuse to be under the spell of their likes and dislikes and instead use their free will to do good *karma* and refrain from *pāpa-karma*. In doing good *karma* they neutralise the old *pāpas* by creating *adṛṣṭa*. And they insulate themselves against doing new *pāpa-karma* by daily prayers and adherence to *dharma*. These are *puṇya-karmās*, that is, these are people whose actions are good and are done with a proper attitude. Śaṅkara defines *puṇya-karma* as *karma* which causes purification of the mind. And the person who has done such actions is called a *puṇya-karmā*. And also these are those for whom the *pāpa-karma*s have reached their end, *yeṣāṁ pāpam antagatam*. This means the tendency to do wrong actions is no longer there. It is not necessary for them to use their will to avoid *pāpa-karma*. These are mature people. They are free from *pāpa-karma* because they no longer have even the tendency to do them.

How to free oneself from *pāpa karma*.

In the beginning you use your will against *pāpa-karma* and later it is not necessary. For example, in every culture there are swear words. Suppose a person has been brought up in an environment where it is common to use these words. One day he decides that he is not going to use them any more. In the beginning, especially when he gets angry, they will come to the tip of his tongue. But using his will he can curb them there. Very cautiously, very wilfully he will choose words that are more objective. He will have to do this for some time. Afterwards those words do not even come to his mind; they just disappear from his language. No will is required. They are out of his system.

This is how you change. Tendencies for *pāpa-karma* cannot remain in you when you keep doing *puṇya-karma*. There is a reason for this. When you do any type of action, it produces a *saṁskāra*. The more you do it, the more you reinforce a tendency for that type of *saṁskāra*, action. If water flowing down a mountain repeatedly follows the same track, the track becomes deeper and deeper. It is also true with reference to *saṁskāra*. *Karma* creates a *saṁskāra* and because of *saṁskāra*s we tend to repeat the *karma*, which is why criminals become habitual offenders. They are prone to a given type of offence and certain way of doing it. Some are burglars. Then among them, one always comes through the window, another through the door. That tendency, once it is formed, is like water running down a mountain creating deeper and deeper tracks and making it more and more impossible for the water to go anywhere else. Similarly, *saṁskāra*s create thought ravines that result in habitual actions. A tendency is formed to do the same thing and the more it is done, the stronger the tendency becomes.

To break out of it, you need to use your will. And to do this, you need to undergo a cognitive change. You have to look at your life differently and it is possible only by some grace, some help. Once you get it, the course of your life changes and the old tendencies start to fall away.

For the *puṇya-karmā*s, those who do *puṇya-karma*s, the *pāpa-saṁskāra*s themselves have been eliminated. And the *pāpa*s, which were done before are neutralised to a great extent. Such people have reached the end of their *pāpa-karma*s. That is, they have almost reached the end. It is not complete because both *pāpa* and *puṇya* will go away only with knowledge. These are people whose minds are more or less unaffected by *pāpa-karma*s. The mind abides. It is a pure mind.

Freed from delusion, one seeks Īśvara.

Te dvandva-moha-nirmuktāḥ, they become completely liberated from the delusion of the opposites, *rāga-dveṣa*. *Mukta* means 'liberated,' *nirmukta* means 'totally liberated.'

Because of powerful likes and dislikes, one can only think of what one wants. Right and wrong are not considered; naturally, one will do *pāpa-karma*. But if these likes and dislikes are taken care of, the mind will present one with what is proper and what is not. Then one is freed from the inner torpor, the delusion of the *dvandva*s.

Māṁ bhajante, they worship me. Such people are the ones who recognise what is really to be sought in life. Then they see the meaning of the words of the *śāstra*. Before, because of *rāga-dveṣa*s, they had no time even to look at the *śāstra*. Now all the words become alive and they seek Parameśvara, *paramātmā*. Who are they?

Dṛḍha-vratāḥ are people with firm vows and commitment

Dṛḍha-vratāḥ are people with a firm commitment. *Vrata* is a vow, a commitment; *dṛḍha* means firm. These are people of firm vows, of great commitment. Śaṅkara says that only in this way can one gain the truth, *paramārtha-tattva*. It requires a firm resolve. Because of that, they give up other pursuits. They are no longer under the spell of *rāga-dveṣa*s and pursue only those desires useful to their *puruṣārtha*, which is *mokṣa*. They become *sannyāsī*s either in spirit or take to the order itself.

A real *sannyāsī*'s mind is the most mature mind because it has no concern for tomorrow. Such a mind can be either careless or mature. A foolhardy, misadventurous person also does not think about tomorrow. He squanders everything today and tomorrow, he begs. Even though he has a lot of desires to fulfil, he does not plan for the future. This is foolish. Whereas a *sannyāsī* is a person who does not care about tomorrow because he knows tomorrow will take care of itself. And he is content with what he has. Such a person has the sanest mind. Just think about it; there is no saner mind. It is not born of carelessness but of certain contentment and a trust in oneself and in Īśvara.

The person understands that one's daily requirement is very little and he or she will always get it. That is *sannyāsa*. Such people of firm commitment, 'seek me and they gain me,' says the Lord. *Bhajante* can mean both the above; but 'they seek' is more appropriate in view of the following verse. Totally free from the delusion of the opposites they seek Īśvara. They give up everything else to recognise *paramātmā*.

For what purpose do they seek Īśvara? What do they gain?

Taking refuge in me one gains freedom from death

जरामरणमोक्षाय मामाश्रित्य यतन्ति ये ।
ते ब्रह्म तद्विदुः कृत्स्नमध्यात्मं कर्म चाखिलम् ॥ २९ ॥

jarāmaraṇamokṣāya mām āśritya yatanti ye
te brahma tadviduḥ kṛtsnam adhyātmaṁ karma cākhilam (29)

jarā-maraṇa-mokṣāya – for freedom from old age and death; *mam āśritya* – having taken refuge in me; *ye yatanti* – those who make effort; *te* – they; *tad brahma* – that Brahman (the cause of creation); *kṛtsnam adhyātmam* – wholly as themselves; *karma ca akhilam* – and *karma* in its entirety; *viduḥ* – know

> Having taken refuge in me, those who make effort for freedom from old age and death, they know that Brahman wholly as themselves and they also know *karma* in its entirety.

Bhagavān says, '*jarā maraṇa mokṣāya ye yatanti*, those who make effort for freedom from old age and death, *maṁ āśritya*, by taking refuge in me, *tad brahma adhyātmaṁ viduḥ*, they know that Brahman wholly as themselves. One always wants freedom from what is undesirable, never from the desirable. Old age is undesirable. No one wants to age because it means death is nearing. A human being is allotted only a finite number of years. Therefore, every year that goes by is a year closer to death. That is one problem with old age. The second problem is that one by one, the bodily functions begin leaving the person. The presiding deities of the sense organs, take their leave as though to say, 'This is enough. I supported you for so many years. What did you accomplish? Good bye.' When the presiding deities which make the eyes see, the ears hear, etc., leave, all that remains is a cavity, a *golaka*, where once there was sight, hearing etc. As these deities depart, one by one, one finds that the sense organs are no longer as efficient as they once were; everything becomes a nuisance. Nobody wants it.

The rest of the body also begins to disintegrate. The joints become stiff and it becomes difficult to take the body around.

Getting up is a chore; lying down is a chore. Then getting up from lying down is a chore. Sometimes the peristaltic movement stops functioning and even eating is a chore. Remembering becomes a very big task. This is *jarā*, old age. Who wants it? Everyone wants freedom from it. Certainly nobody wants *maraṇa*, death. There is always a love to be free, free from ageing, free from death and so on.

Ageing and death stand for the other changes a body goes through – birth, growth, metamorphosis, decline, as well as the mental modifications such as doership and enjoyership in the form of pleasure and pain. All our notions about ourselves are based on these and it is from these that we want to be free.

The intense desire for this freedom is born of the conclusion, 'I am subject to ageing; I am mortal.' As long as such a conclusion is there, there will be a desire for release. But it is not possible and we know that. So, there is always a desire to live a day more. And we know that it is not always going to be possible. So, there is helplessness and naturally, a fear. If we could help ourselves, there would be no fear. But we cannot stop ageing, much less death.

A person who is not under the spell of *rāga-dveṣas* has a mind that can discern this and seek a real solution. You understand what has value in this life and seek *paramātmā*, now, before old age and death come. You discern that you want to get out of this problem entirely, not just out of the ageing body. You want to get out of the notion, 'I am subject to old age and death.'

The body does not say, 'I am afraid of old age.' It just survives the years like a stone or any other inert object. It has no notion that it is getting older. You are the one who recognises yourself as someone subject to old age and death. So, *mokṣa* is not from physical old age or physical death. It is from the notion, 'I am subject to old age and death.' From that notion alone is freedom and it is the only freedom possible. It is also the only freedom required because 'I,' *aham*, alone is the problem. All the problems are centred on 'I.' The problem of self-identity is what causes fear. Therefore, for release from it, you seek *paramātmā*.

How does one seek freedom from death?

Taking refuge in Īśvara, they make effort, *mām āśritya yatanti*. *Mām* means me, Īśvara. So, pursuits based on their likes and dislikes are given up, and now they are seeking Īśvara. After analysing their experiences, they find that fulfilment of *rāga-dveṣa*s is not exactly what they are seeking. That 'I am subject to *rāga-dveṣa*s' is the problem. If that is very clear to a person, one's refuge is Īśvara and he or she becomes a *jijñāsu*.

Now that you are no longer under the spell of likes and dislikes, and the tendency for improper actions is also gone there is discrimination. You want only to know what Parameśvara is and seek his grace for that knowledge. To know Parameśvara is to know him as yourself. There is no other Īśvara. He is not separate from you nor is he separate from the world. If there is any sense of separation it is due to ignorance. Therefore, Bhagavān says, 'Taking refuge in me, invoking my grace, they seek to know me.' For this they make efforts, *yatanti*. How? With a mind absorbed in me through *śravaṇa, manana,* and *nididhyāsana* – these three keep you absorbed. Previously the mind was dwelling upon the objects of *rāga-dveṣa*s, and now it is led to dwell upon Parameśvara through enquiry into the *śāstra*.

To see the difference between this pursuit and all other, just observe your mind when you turn the pages of an attractively printed catalogue. Potential *rāga-dveṣa*s, even unheard of *rāga-dveṣa*s would surface. You see something you had never even thought about and suddenly it is a want. It is one type of mind.

Then see what happens when you read the pages of the *Upaniṣad*s or *Gītā*. The mind is entirely different. The words of the *śāstra* create a mind that is fulfilled, resolved, the opposite of a mind in pursuit, which is why they say that *paunaḥ puṇyena śravaṇaṁ kuryāt,* listening to the *śāstra* is to be done again and again. It creates an orientation. Even though what is to be understood is only one, *tat tvam asi,* the elaborate study of the *śāstra* is to keep the mind exposed for a good length of time to this thinking about realities. While doing *śravaṇa,* there is naturally *manana*. Doubts are raised and answered. Through this exposure you get an insight, and certain *vastu-jñāna* takes place. You contemplate upon that and gain increasing clarity. This is *nididhyāsana*.

Spending your time in these three, *śravaṇa, manana* and *nididhyāsana,* is reflecting on Parameśvara. This is the *brahma-abhyāsa* that we saw previously, *tat cintanaṁ tat kathanam anyonyaṁ tat prabodhanam*. Reflecting on the subject matter, talking about it to others and discussing with fellow students trying to understand and help each other is all part of *brahma-abhyāsa*. This is what is meant by taking refuge in Parameśvara. It is important to understand the meaning of these expressions.

I read one commentary long ago that interpreted taking refuge in Īśvara to mean going to him for protection as even you would go to a stronger person when you are in trouble. Such appeals will definitely bless you. Any good *karma* will give its result. But to think that Īśvara is just another person who is protecting you is simplistic. *Parameśvara-āśraya* is something that requires understanding. It is not that simple. It is an absorption, a committed thinking and dwelling upon, which is accomplished by *śravaṇa*, *manana*, and *nididhyāsana*. This is *parameśvara-āśraya*.

The wise know Brahman as not separate from themselves

Te brahma tad viduḥ, having resorted to Parameśvara, *te*, these people, *viduḥ*, come to know, *tad brahma*, that Brahman. From this it is clear that *āśraya* is in the form of enquiry and the result is that they come to know Parameśvara as not separate from themselves. *Tat* is *paraṁ-brahma*, who is *satyaṁ jñānam anantaṁ brahma* and the cause of the whole creation. Taking refuge in Īśvara, the cause of everything, coming to him, they naturally know everything.

Now look at this sentence, *mām āśritya yatanti*, taking refuge in me they make effort. What do they get? They get to know that Brahman, *te viduḥ tad brahma*, because I am *paramātmā*.

It makes the meaning of *yatanti* very clear; the effort is for the sake of knowledge.

That knowledge is for *jarā-maraṇa-mokṣāya,* freedom from old age and death. It means all you require for freedom is knowledge. But by knowing how can you escape from old age and death? All the *jñānī*s are dead and gone! That is, the bodies of the *jñānī*s are gone. A *jñānī* is never gone because he is *paraṁ-brahma;* he is not separate. Bhagavān had said earlier, '*jñānī tu ātmā eva me matam,* I consider the *jñānī* as myself.'[24]

From this we understand that they know Brahman not only as the cause of creation and therefore, *parokṣa,* remote, but as *aparokṣa,* not other than themselves. It is unlike what happens to Arjuna in the eleventh chapter, Kṛṣṇa gave Arjuna the capacity to see him in his cosmic form. As Arjuna looked, he saw the whole cosmos within Lord Kṛṣṇa. All the stars and heavens, the earth, the people, the Pāṇḍavas as well as Duryodhana and his group were within him. He saw everyone on the battlefield writhing within the mouth of time, sticking between the teeth of Lord Death as they were being consumed by time. He saw them all, not dead, but in the process of dying. Arjuna was frightened. He saw the whole cause of creation in a particular form. Everything was included in that form, both cause and effect, so, it was impossible to distinguish them. Seeing all this, he was frightened because he did not see himself there. It is enough for fear. Wherever you make even a small division, there you will have fear, *udaram antaraṁ kurute atha*

---

[24] *Gītā* 7.18

tasya bhayaṁ bhavati.[25] So, Arjuna asked Kṛṣṇa to return to his original form and experienced a great relief. The fear and the relief were because Arjuna did not include himself. So, Brahman has to be understood not just as the cause of creation but also as oneself.

They also know Brahman entirely as themselves, *kṛtsnam adhyātmam. Kṛtsna* means total, entire. *Adhyātma* means with reference to *ātmā*, yourself. You have to see Brahman as totally identical with yourself, *pratyagātmā*. The truth of *ātmā* happens to be identical with Brahman. The one who knows this understands everything connected to *ātmā* as identical with Brahman, *kṛtsnam adhyātmaṁ tad viduḥ*.

They also understand karma in its entirety

Because of that, they now understand *karma* also very well, *karma ca akhilaṁ te viduḥ*. One understands, 'I do not do any action nor do I cause anything to be done.' At the same time actions are done. One understands the truth of *karma* and the word *akhila*, which means entirely. Therefore, it indicates that now he understands *karma* in its entirety. The truth about *karma* is that the doer, the object of action, the means of doing the action, the purpose of doing the action, from where the action originates, anything connected to the action, and the locus of the action are all Brahman. We saw this in the fourth chapter. In a ritual, the means by which an oblation is offered, the oblation itself, the fire unto which it is offered and the one who

[25] *Taittirīyopaniṣad* 2.7

makes the offering are all Brahman.[26] This is the truth of *karma* and one also knows this. In one's vision, *karma* is neither opposed to Brahman nor is it something that has Brahman as its result. The one who knows this sees Brahman everywhere.

What is this Brahman that these people come to know so totally?

साधिभूताधिदैवं मां साधियज्ञं च ये विदुः ।
प्रयाणकालेऽपि च मां ते विदुर्युक्तचेतसः ॥ ३० ॥

sādhibhūtādhidaivaṁ māṁ sādhiyajñaṁ ca ye viduḥ
prayāṇakāle'pi ca māṁ te viduryuktacetasaḥ (30)

ye ca – and those; *mām* – me; *sādhibhūta-adhidaivam* – as centred on the physical world and as centred on the *devatā*; *sādhiyajñaṁ ca* – and as centred on the rituals; *viduḥ* – know; *te* – they; *yukta-cetasaḥ* – whose minds are absorbed in me; *prayāṇakāle'pi* – even at the end of their life; *māṁ viduḥ* – know me

> Those who know me as centered on the physical world, the *devatās* and the rituals, whose minds are absorbed in me, even at the end of their life, they know me.

The Lord says, 'Those who know me in this form they alone gain me.' Here *mokṣa* is the *phala*, result meaning, the *puruṣārtha* is *mokṣa*. It was said previously in verse 28, that these people are *dṛḍha-vratas*. And Śaṅkara had pointed out that these

---

[26] *Gītā* 4.24

people are *suniścita-vijñānāḥ*. These are people who have ascertained the *puruṣārtha* before they commit themselves to the pursuit of the knowledge of Parameśvara. So, it was said, in verse 29, that having taken refuge in me, those who make effort for freedom from old age and death, they know that Brahman wholly as themselves, *jarā-maraṇa-mokṣāya māṁ āśritya ye yatanti, te tad brahma viduḥ*. Up to verse 28, Bhagavān was talking in the first person. Now suddenly in verse 29, he put it in the third person and said, *te adhyātmaṁ brahma viduḥ*, they understand the *pratyagātmā* as *paraṁ-brahma* and also understand all that is connected to *pratyagātmā*. They understand that the *kartā, karma, karma-phala*, etc., are *mithyā*. Now in this verse Kṛṣṇa reverts back to the first person again and continues.

He says that, previously what was said as Brahman is myself. He says, those who know me, as *sādhibhūta, sādhidaiva* and *sādhiyajña*, know me as themselves, *adhyātmaṁ te viduḥ, ātmatvena te viduḥ*. Brahman as *jagat-kāraṇa* is *adhibhūta, adhidaiva* and *adhiyajña*. This Brahman they know as themselves. It is a particular style of talking which is called *rāśīkṛtya kathanam*, a collective mention, putting everything together and saying, 'All this is myself.' Otherwise it will be an endless process of saying, 'I am this, I am that, etc.' By saying, I am the one who obtains in the form of the *devas*, in the form of the factors related to *yajña* or *yajña-puruṣa*, in the form of the *bhūtas*, the five elements, or the *kārya-karaṇa-saṅghāta*, the body-mind-sense complex; it means *sarvaṁ-brahma*, all this. This is a way of saying that everything is Brahman. One often finds this particular expression in the *śāstra, adhibhūta, adhidaiva* and *adhiyajña*. It is very important to know what these words mean. Bhagavān will also talk about it in the next chapter because Arjuna is going to ask a question about these words.

The Lord says, '*sādhibhūta adhidaivam māṁ sādhiyajñaṁ ca ye viduḥ*, they know me, Īśvara, who is *sādhibhūta, sādhidaiva*, and *sādhiyajña*. The word '*sa*' that is compounded to the words *adhibhūta*, etc., is *saha* which means 'along with.' In these expressions, what is indicated is Īśvara, the one who exists in the form of the sun, moon, stars, etc., and all the *devatā*s thereof.

Adhibhūta is what is centred on the *bhūta*s, *bhūtāni adhikṛtya bhavati iti adhibhūta*. The *bhūta*s can be taken as the *kārya-karaṇa-saṅghāta*s. Therefore, Bhagavān says, 'What obtains in all the *kārya-karaṇa-saṅghāta*s is myself alone as *pratyagātmā*. The *bhūta*s can also be taken to mean the five elements. Similarly, *adhidaiva* is what is centred on the *devatā*s, *devān adhikṛtya vartate iti adhidaiva*. *Adhiyajña* is what is centred on the *yajña*s, the rituals etc. It means that Bhagavān is the one who is the form of the very ritual, *yajño vai viṣṇuḥ, yajñādhipati* because he is the real receiver of the offerings in the *yajña*. And he is the one who is in the form of *karmādhyakṣa* and *karma-phala-dātā*.

So, Bhagavān says, 'These people recognise me as the one who is in the form of this world, as *adhibhūta*, from whom nothing is separate and also as the *devatā*s, as *adhidaiva*, the one from whom no *devatā* is separate.' Further he says, 'They also recognise me as *adhiyajña*.' *Yajña* means a ritual. Thus he says, 'These people see that the *karma*, the result of *karma*, and the *devatā* invoked are me. They recognise me as the truth of *karma*.'

Adhyātma is what is centred on the individual. In the previous verse, Bhagavān talked only about *adhyātma*. He had said that they know Brahman as *adhyātma, pratyagātmā*. Now, he converts the whole thing into Īśvara again. That is, he says Īśvara is Brahman. This is how non-difference between Īśvara and the *jīva* is established.

Knowledge of Īśvara as both efficient and material cause

When a given phenomenon, like the sun, is looked upon as Īśvara, Īśvara is considered the *upādāna-kāraṇa*, material cause. This is the *adhibhūta* vision of Īśvara. When Īśvara is considered as the *nimitta-kāraṇa*, efficient cause, of the sun, etc., it is the *adhidaiva* vision. These are the two levels – Īśvara as *nimitta-kāraṇa* is *adhidaiva*, and as *upādāna-kāraṇa* is *adhibhūta*.

These people also know Īśvara as *adhyātma*, which was pointed out in the previous verse. *Adhyātma* is also Brahman. That is, they see themselves as Brahman. Then, what is left out? Nothing! Everything is Bhagavān. The world is Bhagavān, the *devatā*s are Bhagavān, your physical body, mind and senses together called *adhyātma* and *pratyagātmā* are all Bhagavān. This is one way of saying everything is Bhagavān. Nothing else is there here in this universe other than Bhagavān.

Therefore, the Lord says, 'Those who know me in this form are non-separate from myself.' First, you recognise Īśvara as *parokṣa*, that is, you understand that this entire *jagat* is Īśvara. Then, you internalise the whole thing and understand, 'my own body, mind, senses are Bhagavān. The *pratyagātmā*, consciousness, behind this body-mind-sense complex is the truth of Bhagavān.

Those who are *yukta-cetasaḥ – yuktaṁ ceteḥ yeṣāṁ te –* meaning those whose minds do not have any inhibiting factors, know me like this even at the time of travel, death. There is a belief, which cannot be supported with any great logic, that what kind of course the departing soul takes depends on what the final thought of the person was when he or she was dying. That is why in India, there is a custom of naming people with the names of the Lord. A person dying is likely to call out his son by name and if that is the name of the Lord he will be reminded of Bhagavān and it would give him a good *gati*.

However, it is not easy to remember the Lord at the time of death. Unless all one's lifetime one has lived a life keeping the Lord in mind, it is not possible. The thought of Nārāyaṇa will not come even if one has named his son as Nārāyaṇa. He will tend to use some diminutive of the name and never remember Bhagavān. Even a great *upāsaka* is not going to remember his *upāsya* at the time of death because his attachment to his own children and so on, is so much that he will remember only those things. Or he will think of his omissions and commissions and will be riddled with guilt and hurt. Unless a person is very mature, it is not easy to have the thought of the Lord at the time of death.

While this is so, the Lord says, 'If you know me there is no such problem. Whether it is at the time of death or not, there is no question of your losing sight of me, *vismaraṇaṁ nāsti*.

Without knowing the Lord, it is a question of Nārāyaṇa *nāma-smaraṇa*, remembering the name of Nārāyaṇa; but here it is *nārāyaṇasya-tattva-jñāna*, knowing the truth of Bhagavān as yourself. Here there is no ignorance of Bhagavān at all. The knowledge '*nārāyaṇaḥ-aham*, I am Nārāyaṇa,' is not subject to *vismaraṇa*, forgetfulness. Ignorance cannot come back. Even if a person goes into a coma, it does not really create ignorance. The mind may not function and may be incapable of responding to the external world but the ignorance gone is gone. It can never come back.

Therefore, Bhagavān says, '*prayāṇakāle'pi māṁ viduḥ*, even at the time of death they know me.' This is the meaning of the word *api* in this statement. At the time of death even though there is generally *vismaraṇa* for most people including the *upāsaka*s, the *jñānī*s do not have this *vismaraṇa*. When they are alive and well in the body and mind with strong commitment they put forth adequate and proper effort to know Bhagavān, *māṁ viduḥ*. How do they know? They know that all that is here is Bhagavān, *idaṁ sarvam aham asmi iti viduḥ sādhibhūta adhidaivaṁ sādhiyajñaṁ māṁ viduḥ*.

They also know that Bhagavān, Īśvara, who is in the form of all this, is not separate from themselves, *sādhibhūta adhidaivaṁ sādhiyajñaṁ māṁ ātmatvena viduḥ*. And they know this even at the time of death when generally there is *vismṛti*. It is because there is no *smṛti-apekṣā*, dependence on memory for this knowledge unlike the knowledge of other things in this world. Self-knowledge is not to be remembered; only self-ignorance has to go. This is because the self is always evident. Therefore, the Lord says these people who are *yukta-cetasaḥ*, and do not have any inhibiting factor that prevents the knowledge, know me even at the time of death.

Even at the time of death, their knowledge stands firm

Finally what the Lord says with reference to the final moment also means this, 'Even those who only know me at the time of death, who gain this knowledge then, or those who have been living with this knowledge and are not swayed from it right up to the time of death because it is so clear, they know, *prayāṇa kāle'pi māṁ te viduḥ yukta-cetasaḥ*. Those minds are united to me, know me, not just remember me, even at the time of death. There is no return for them.' They are Brahman.

When I am everything and everywhere, who is to return, and from where? I can go to some place and return, if I am not there already. If I am only here, then I can go to heaven and come back. But heaven also is me, the heavenly bodies are me, the *devatā*s are me, the angels are me, the celestials are me. The local world is me, the sun, the moon and stars, the physical body, mind and senses, are all me because I am Brahman. Tell me now, who is to go and where?

Thus those who know these five, that is, *adhyātma (pratyagātmā* their innermost self, and the body-mind-sense complex), *karma* in its entirety, *adhibhūta*, *adhidaiva*, and *adhiyajña* as Brahman, for them their knowledge of the identity between themselves and Īśvara stands firm and unaffected even at the time of death. They were free while living; they are free even after this body has fallen.

Thus ends chapter seven in which the *tat-pada-vācya*, the actual meaning of the word *tat* which is the *svarūpa* of Īśvara and the *tat-pada-lakṣya*, the implied meaning of the word *tat*, which is Brahman, was explained. We have already seen in the first *ṣaṭka* that the *tvaṁ-pada-lakṣya*, the implied meaning of the word *tvam* is also Brahman. This is how the *vākya*, '*tat tvam asi*' is unfolded.

ॐतत्सत् ।

इति श्रीमद्भगवद्गीतासूपनिषत्सु ब्रह्मविद्यायां योगशास्त्रे श्रीकृष्णार्जुन-संवादे ज्ञान-विज्ञान-योगो नाम सप्तमोऽध्यायः ॥ ७ ॥

oṁ tat sat.

iti śrīmadbhagavadgītāsūpaniṣatsu brahma-vidyāyāṁ yoga-śāstre śrīkṛṣṇārjuna-saṁvāde jñāna-vijñāna-yogo nāma saptamo'dhyāyaḥ (7)

Om, Brahman, is the only reality. Thus ends the seventh chapter called *jñāna-vijñāna-yoga* – having the topic of indirect and immediate knowledge – in the *Bhagavadgītā* which is in the form of a dialogue between Śrī Kṛṣṇa and Arjuna, which is the essence of the *Upaniṣads*, whose subject matter is both the knowledge of Brahman and *yoga*.

We have to see what this *oṁ tat sat* means. Later Bhagavān himself is going to say '*oṁ tat sat iti nirdeśaḥ*.'[27] Here in this

---

[27] *Gītā* 17.23

statement all the three words are in *sāmānādhikaraṇya*, that is, they are in apposition. It means, what is *om*, that, *tat* is *sat*. *Om* is the name for Parameśvara. Therefore, it is an invocation consisting of a single syllable. Thus it is a *bījākṣara*. *Bījākṣara*s are actually words consisting of a single syllable. In a *mantra*, *om* is considered to be the *bījākṣara* of all *bījākṣara*s – *bījākṣarāṇāṁ bījākṣaram om*. That is, from it originates all other *bījākṣara*s. This is because *om* is used to invoke Parameśvara who is everything, that is, all that was in the past, that is in the present, that will be in the future – *bhūtaṁ bhavat bhaviṣyat sarvaṁ omkāra eva, yat ca kālātītaṁ tadapi oṁkāra eva*.

Then there are other *bīja*s that invoke various aspects of Parameśvara. For example, the *bījākṣara* '*hrīm*' invokes the *śakti* of Īśvara. Since this *śakti* has the power to create or the power to destroy, either of them can be invoked by adding the appropriate *bījākṣara*. If you want to invoke Lakṣmī, you add *śrīm*, and the *mantra* now would be '*oṁ hrīm śrīm*.' *Om* stands for Parameśvara, *hrīm*, stands for the *śakti* of Parameśvara and *śrīm* stands for Lakṣmī. Similarly '*gam*' stands for Gaṇeśa. Thus we have a variety of these *bījākṣara*s and through these we invoke an aspect of Īśvara. *Om* is the source of all *bījākṣara*s. It invokes Parameśvara, which is why it is added before every *nāma* invoking Īśvara.

Oṁkāra thus is the *abhidhāna*, the name for the *abhidheya*, the named, Brahman. Therefore, *om tat sat* means Brahman alone is *sat*. *Om* is that Brahman which is *jagat-kāraṇa*, and *tat*, that, alone is *sat*, *satya*, the truth of everything. Lot of words have been said and all said and done, that Brahman alone is the *satya-vastu*, the truth of everything. Lot of things may or may not have been said properly; they may or may not be understood properly. Finally, what is to be understood is *om tat sat*. Thus it marks the conclusion.

This chapter is called *jñāna-vijñāna-yoga*, that is, it has the topic of *jñāna* and *vijñāna*. The word *jñāna* indicates that this chapter has the knowledge of Parameśvara. The knowledge of what the *tat-pada* stands for is the predominant topic of this chapter. The word *vijñāna* indicates that the knowledge is so complete that even at the time of death there is no possibility of *vismaraṇa*. Thus ends the seventh chapter.

Alphabetical index of verses

Text	Chapter	Verse	Vol	Page
akīrtiṁ cāpi bhūtāni	02	34	2	189
akṣaraṁ brahma paramam	08	03	6	23
akṣarāṇām akāro'smi	10	33	6	410
agnirjyotirahaḥ śuklaḥ	08	24	6	102
acchedyo'yam adāhyo'yam	02	24	2	151
ajo'pi sannavyayātmā	04	06	4	26
ajñaścāśraddadhānaśca	04	40	4	276
atha kena prayukto'yam	03	36	3	220
atra śūrā maheṣvāsā	01	04	1	180
atha cittaṁ samādhātum	12	09	7	177
atha cettvam imaṁ	02	33	2	187
atha cainaṁ nityajātam	02	26	2	157
athavā yoginām eva	06	42	5	251
athavā bahunaitena	10	42	6	437
atha vyavasthitān dṛṣṭvā	01	20	1	203
athaitadapyaśakto'si	12	11	7	188
adṛṣṭapūrvaṁ hṛṣito'smi	11	45	7	91
adeśakāle yaddānam	17	22	8	276
adveṣṭā sarvabhūtānām	12	13	7	204
adharmaṁ dharmam iti yā	18	32	9	123

Text	Chapter	Verse	Vol	Page
adharmābhibhavāt kṛṣṇa	*01*	*41*	*1*	*232*
adhaścordhvaṁ prasṛtāstasya	*15*	*02*	*8*	*72*
adhibhūtaṁ kṣaro bhāvaḥ	*08*	*04*	*6*	*23*
adhiyajñaḥ kathaṁ ko'tra	*08*	*02*	*6*	*21*
adhiṣṭhānaṁ tathā kartā	*18*	*14*	*9*	*62*
adhyātmajñānanityatvam	*13*	*11*	*7*	*399*
adhyeṣyate ca ya imam	*18*	*70*	*9*	*564*
anantavijayaṁ rājā	*01*	*16*	*1*	*200*
anantaścāsmi nāgānām	*10*	*29*	*6*	*402*
ananyacetāḥ satatam	*08*	*14*	*6*	*65*
ananyāścintayanto mām	*09*	*22*	*6*	*253*
anapekṣaḥ śucirdakṣaḥ	*12*	*16*	*7*	*234*
anāditvānnirguṇatvāt	*13*	*31*	*7*	*483*
anādimadhyāntam anantavīryam	*11*	*19*	*7*	*38*
anāśritaḥ karmaphalam	*06*	*01*	*5*	*5*
aniṣṭam iṣṭaṁ miśraṁ ca	*18*	*12*	*9*	*53*
anudvegakaraṁ vākyam	*17*	*15*	*8*	*255*
anubandhaṁ kṣayaṁ hiṁsām	*18*	*25*	*9*	*104*
anekacittavibhrāntāḥ	*16*	*16*	*8*	*202*
anekabāhūdaravaktranetram	*11*	*16*	*7*	*30*
anekavaktranayanam	*11*	*10*	*7*	*23*

Text	Chapter	Verse	Vol	Page
antakāle ca mām eva	*08*	*05*	*6*	*28*
antavat tu phalaṁ teṣām	*07*	*23*	*5*	*391*
antavanta ime dehāḥ	*02*	*18*	*2*	*97*
annādbhavanti bhūtāni	*03*	*14*	*3*	*89*
anye ca bahavaḥ śūrāḥ	*01*	*09*	*1*	*188*
anye tvevam ajānantaḥ	*13*	*25*	*7*	*465*
aparaṁ bhavato janma	*04*	*04*	*4*	*20*
apare niyatāhārāḥ	*04*	*30*	*4*	*224*
apareyamitastvanyām	*07*	*05*	*5*	*316*
aparyāptaṁ tadasmākam	*01*	*10*	*1*	*191*
apāne juhvati prāṇam	*04*	*29*	*4*	*220*
api cetsudurācāro	*09*	*30*	*6*	*295*
api ced asi pāpebhyaḥ	*04*	*36*	*4*	*258*
aprakāśo'pravṛttiśca	*14*	*13*	*8*	*28*
aphalākāṅkṣibhiryajño	*17*	*11*	*8*	*246*
abhayaṁ sattvasaṁśuddhiḥ	*16*	*01*	*8*	*147*
abhisandhāya tu phalam	*17*	*12*	*8*	*249*
abhyāsayogayuktena	*08*	*08*	*6*	*47*
abhyāse'pyasamartho'si	*12*	*10*	*7*	*180*
amānitvam adambhitvam	*13*	*07*	*7*	*359*
amī ca tvāṁ dhṛtarāṣṭrasya	*11*	*26*	*7*	*55*

Text	Chapter	Verse	Vol	Page
amī hi tvāṁ surasaṅghā viśanti	11	21	7	42
ayaneṣu ca sarveṣu	01	11	1	193
ayatiḥ śraddhayopeto	06	37	5	233
ayuktaḥ prākṛtaḥ stabdhaḥ	18	28	9	113
avajānanti māṁ mūḍhāḥ	09	11	6	203
avācyavādāṁśca bahūn	02	36	2	193
avināśi tu tadviddhi	02	17	2	93
avibhaktaṁ ca bhūteṣu	13	16	7	430
avyaktādīni bhūtāni	02	28	2	163
avyaktād vyaktayaḥ sarvāḥ	08	18	6	77
avyakto'kṣara ityuktastam	08	21	6	93
avyakto'yam acintyo'yam	02	25	2	154
avyaktaṁ vyaktim āpannam	07	24	5	397
aśāstravihitaṁ ghoram	17	05	8	234
aśocyān anvaśocastvam	02	11	2	42
aśraddadhānāḥ puruṣāḥ	09	03	6	143
aśraddhayā hutaṁ dattam	17	28	8	286
aśvatthaḥ sarvavṛkṣāṇām	10	26	6	397
asaktabuddhiḥ sarvatra	18	49	9	240
asaktiranabhiṣvaṅgaḥ	13	09	7	388
asatyam apratiṣṭhaṁ te	16	08	8	186
asau mayā hataḥ śatruḥ	16	14	8	197

Text	Chapter	Verse	Vol	Page
asaṁyatātmanā yogo	*06*	*36*	*5*	*230*
asaṁśayaṁ mahābāho	*06*	*35*	*5*	*214*
asmākaṁ tu viśiṣṭā ye	*01*	*07*	*1*	*186*
ahaṁ kraturahaṁ yajñaḥ	*09*	*16*	*5*	*231*
ahaṅkāraṁ balaṁ darpam	*16*	*18*	*8*	*205*
ahaṅkāraṁ balaṁ darpam	*18*	*53*	*9*	*304*
ahamātmā guḍākeśa	*10*	*20*	*6*	*383*
ahaṁ vaiśvānaro bhūtvā	*15*	*14*	*8*	*113*
ahaṁ sarvasya prabhavo	*10*	*08*	*6*	*350*
ahaṁ hi sarvayajñānām	*09*	*24*	*6*	*263*
ahiṁsā satyamakrodhaḥ	*16*	*02*	*8*	*148*
ahiṁsā samatā tuṣṭiḥ	*10*	*05*	*6*	*333*
aho bata mahatpāpam	*01*	*45*	*1*	*244*
ākhyāhi me ko bhavān	*11*	*31*	*7*	*61*
ācāryāḥ pitaraḥ putrāḥ	*01*	*34*	*1*	*221*
āḍhyo'bhijanavān asmi	*16*	*15*	*8*	*199*
ātmasambhāvitāḥ stabdhā	*16*	*17*	*8*	*203*
ātmaupamyena sarvatra	*06*	*32*	*5*	*195*
ādityānām ahaṁ viṣṇuḥ	*10*	*21*	*6*	*386*
āpūryamāṇam acalapratiṣṭham	*02*	*70*	*2*	*399*
ābrahmabhuvanāllokāḥ	*08*	*16*	*6*	*72*

Text	Chapter	Verse	Vol	Page
āyudhānām ahaṁ vajram	10	28	6	400
āyuḥsattvabalārogya	17	08	8	241
ārurukṣormuneryogam	06	03	5	13
āvṛtaṁ jñānam etena	03	39	3	231
āśāpāśaśatairbaddhāḥ	16	12	8	193
āścaryavat paśyati kaścidenam	02	29	2	167
āsurīṁ yonim āpannāḥ	16	20	8	209
āhārastvapi sarvasya	17	07	8	240
āhustvām ṛṣayaḥ sarve	10	13	6	371
icchādveṣasamutthena	07	27	5	422
icchā dveṣaḥ sukhaṁ duḥkham	13	06	7	352
iti guhyatamaṁ śāstram	15	20	8	135
iti te jñānam ākhyātam	18	63	9	356
iti kṣetraṁ tathā jñānam	13	18	7	435
ityarjunaṁ vāsudevastathoktvā	11	50	7	100
ityahaṁ vāsudevasya	18	74	9	575
idamadya mayā labdham	16	13	8	196
idaṁ tu te guhyatamam	09	01	6	114
idaṁ te nātapaskāya	18	67	9	554
idaṁ śarīraṁ kaunteya	13	01	7	260
idaṁ jñānam upāśritya	14	02	8	5

Text	Chapter	Verse	Vol	Page
indriyasyendriyasyārthe	*03*	*34*	*3*	*196*
indriyāṇāṁ hi caratām	*02*	*67*	*2*	*374*
indriyāṇi parāṇyāhuḥ	*03*	*42*	*3*	*241*
indriyāṇi mano buddiḥ	*03*	*40*	*3*	*234*
indriyārtheṣu vairāgyam	*13*	*08*	*7*	*383*
imaṁ vivasvate yogam	*04*	*01*	*4*	*3*
iṣṭān bhogān hi vo devā	*03*	*12*	*3*	*79*
ihaikasthaṁ jagat kṛtsnam	*11*	*07*	*7*	*19*
ihaiva tairjitaḥ sargaḥ	*05*	*19*	*4*	*364*
īśvaraḥ sarvabhūtānām	*18*	*61*	*9*	*348*
uccaiḥśravasam aśvānām	*10*	*27*	*6*	*399*
utkrāmantaṁ sthitaṁ vāpi	*15*	*10*	*8*	*101*
uttamaḥ puruṣastvanyaḥ	*15*	*17*	*8*	*123*
utsannakuladharmāṇām	*01*	*44*	*1*	*242*
utsīdeyurime lokā na	*03*	*24*	*3*	*137*
udārāḥ sarva evaite	*07*	*18*	*5*	*374*
udāsīnavadāsīnaḥ	*14*	*23*	*8*	*47*
uddhared ātmanātmānam	*06*	*05*	*5*	*20*
upadraṣṭānumantā ca	*13*	*22*	*7*	*448*
ūrdhvaṁ gacchanti sattvasthāḥ	*14*	*18*	*8*	*36*
ūrdhvamūlam adhaḥśākham	*15*	*01*	*8*	*66*

Text	Chapter	Verse	Vol	Page
ṛṣibhirbahudhā gītam	13	04	7	349
etacchrutvā vacanaṁ keśavasya	11	35	7	69
etadyonīni bhūtāni	07	06	5	318
etanme saṁśayaṁ kṛṣṇa	06	39	5	241
etān na hantum icchāmi	01	35	1	221
etānyapi tu karmāṇi	18	06	9	31
etāṁ dṛṣṭim avaṣṭabhya	16	09	8	189
etāṁ vibhūtiṁ yogaṁ ca	10	07	6	347
etairvimuktaḥ kaunteya	16	22	8	213
evamukto hṛṣīkeśaḥ	01	24	1	209
evam uktvārjunaḥ saṅkhye	01	47	1	246
evam uktvā tato rājan	11	09	7	22
evam uktvā hṛṣīkeśam	02	09	2	29
evam etad yathāttha tvam	11	03	7	12
evaṁ paramparāprāptam	04	02	4	3
evaṁ pravartitaṁ cakram	03	16	3	100
evaṁ bahuvidhā yajñāḥ	04	32	4	234
evaṁ buddheḥ paraṁ buddhvā	03	43	3	247
evaṁ satatayuktā ye	12	01	7	124
evaṁ jñātvā kṛtaṁ karma	04	15	4	97
eṣā te'bhihitā sāṅkhye	02	39	2	200
eṣā brāhmī sthitiḥ pārtha	02	72	2	408

Text	Chapter	Verse	Vol	Page
omityekākṣaraṁ brahma	*08*	*13*	*6*	*63*
oṁ tatsaditi nirdeśaḥ	*17*	*23*	*8*	*278*
kaccinnobhayavibhraṣṭaḥ	*06*	*38*	*5*	*237*
kaccid etacchrutaṁ pārtha	*18*	*72*	*9*	*568*
kaṭvamlalavaṇātyuṣṇa	*17*	*09*	*8*	*243*
kathaṁ na jñeyam asmābhiḥ	*01*	*39*	*1*	*228*
kathaṁ bhīṣmamahaṁ saṅkhye	*02*	*04*	*2*	*11*
kathaṁ vidyām ahaṁ yogin	*10*	*17*	*6*	*379*
karmajaṁ buddhiyuktā hi	*02*	*51*	*2*	*295*
karmaṇaḥ sukṛtasyāhuḥ	*14*	*16*	*8*	*33*
karmaṇaiva hi saṁsiddhim	*03*	*20*	*3*	*118*
karmaṇo hyapi boddhavyam	*04*	*17*	*4*	*104*
karmaṇyakarma yaḥ paśyed	*04*	*18*	*4*	*106*
karmaṇyevādhikāraste	*02*	*47*	*2*	*237*
karma brahmodbhavaṁ viddhi	*03*	*15*	*3*	*92*
karmendriyāṇi saṁyamya	*03*	*06*	*3*	*42*
karśayantaḥ śarīrastham	*17*	*06*	*8*	*235*
kaviṁ purāṇam anuśāsitāram	*08*	*09*	*6*	*50*
kasmācca te na nameran	*11*	*37*	*7*	*74*
kāṅkṣantaḥ karmaṇāṁ siddhim	*04*	*12*	*4*	*71*
kāma eṣa krodha eṣaḥ	*03*	*37*	*3*	*223*

Text	Chapter	Verse	Vol	Page
kāmakrodhaviyuktānām	05	26	4	406
kāmam āśritya duṣpūram	16	10	8	191
kāmātmānaḥ svargaparāḥ	02	43	2	220
kāmaistaistairhṛtajñānāḥ	07	20	5	381
kāmyānāṁ karmaṇāṁ nyāsam	18	02	9	16
kāyena manasā buddhyā	05	11	4	333
kārpaṇyadoṣopahatasvabhāvaḥ	02	07	2	21
kāryakaraṇakartṛtve	13	20	7	442
kāryam ityeva yatkarma	18	09	9	36
kālo'smi lokakṣayakṛt pravṛddho	11	32	7	62
kāśyaśca parameṣvāsaḥ	01	17	1	201
kirīṭinaṁ gadinaṁ cakrahastam	11	46	7	92
kirīṭinaṁ gadinaṁ cakriṇaṁ ca	11	17	7	32
kiṁ karma kim akarmeti	04	16	4	101
kiṁ tadbrahma kim adhyātmam	08	01	6	20
kiṁ punarbrāhmaṇāḥ puṇyāḥ	09	33	6	304
kutastvā kaśmalam idam	02	02	2	3
kulakṣaye praṇaśyanti	01	40	1	231
kṛpayā parayāviṣṭo	01	28	1	213
kṛṣigaurakṣyavāṇijyam	18	44	9	166
kairliṅgaistrīnguṇānetān	14	21	8	43

Text	Chapter	Verse	Vol	Page
krodhād bhavati sammohaḥ	02	63	2	355
kleśo'dhikatarasteṣām	12	05	7	149
klaibyaṁ mā sma gamaḥ pārtha	02	03	2	9
kṣipraṁ bhavati dharmātmā	09	31	6	299
kṣetrakṣetrajñayorevam	13	34	7	491
kṣetrajñaṁ cāpi māṁ viddhi	13	02	7	267
gatasaṅgasya muktasya	04	23	4	190
gatirbhartā prabhuḥ sākṣī	09	18	6	238
gāṇḍīvaṁ sraṁsate hastāt	01	30	1	216
gām āviśya ca bhūtāni	15	13	8	112
guṇān etānatītya trīn	14	20	8	41
gurūn ahatvā hi mahānubhāvān	02	05	2	17
cañcalaṁ hi manaḥ kṛṣṇa	06	34	5	208
caturvidhā bhajante mām	07	16	5	364
cāturvarṇyaṁ mayā sṛṣṭam	04	13	4	79
cintām aparimeyāṁ ca	16	11	8	193
cetasā sarvakarmāṇi	18	57	9	337
janma karma ca me divyam	04	09	4	51
jarāmaraṇamokṣāya	07	29	5	430
jātasya hi dhruvo mṛtyuḥ	02	27	2	159

Text	Chapter	Verse	Vol	Page
jitātmanaḥ praśāntasya	06	07	5	29
jñānayajñena cāpyanye	09	15	6	228
jñānavijñānatṛptātmā	06	08	5	34
jñānena tu tadajñānam	05	16	4	353
jñānaṁ karma ca kartā ca	18	19	9	88
jñānaṁ te'haṁ savijñānam	07	02	5	296
jñānaṁ jñeyaṁ parijñātā	18	18	9	84
jñeyaḥ sa nityasannyāsī	05	03	4	303
jñeyaṁ yattat pravakṣyāmi	13	12	7	405
jyāyasī cetkarmaṇaste	03	01	3	6
jyotiṣām api tajjyotiḥ	13	17	7	432
tacca saṁsṛtya saṁsṛtya	18	77	9	580
tataḥ padaṁ tat parimārgitavyam	15	04	8	75
tataḥ śaṅkhāśca bheryaśca	01	13	1	196
tataḥ śvetairhayairyukte	01	14	1	197
tataḥ sa vismayāviṣṭo	11	14	7	27
tattvavit tu mahābāho	03	28	3	155
tatra taṁ buddhisaṁyogam	06	43	5	259
tatra sattvaṁ nirmalatvāt	14	06	8	15
tatrāpaśyat sthitān pārthaḥ	01	26	1	211
tatraikasthaṁ jagat kṛtsnam	11	13	7	26

Text	Chapter	Verse	Vol	Page
tatraikāgraṁ manaḥ kṛtvā	*06*	*12*	*5*	*67*
tatraivaṁ sati kartāram	*18*	*16*	*9*	*68*
tat kṣetraṁ yacca yādṛk ca	*13*	*03*	*7*	*347*
tadityanabhisandhāya	*17*	*25*	*8*	*282*
tadbuddhayastadātmānaḥ	*05*	*17*	*4*	*355*
tadviddhi praṇipātena	*04*	*34*	*4*	*247*
tapasvibhyo'dhiko yogī	*06*	*46*	*5*	*266*
tapāmyaham ahaṁ varṣam	*09*	*19*	*6*	*242*
tamastvajñānajaṁ viddhi	*14*	*08*	*8*	*21*
tamuvāca hṛṣīkeśaḥ	*02*	*10*	*2*	*40*
tameva śaraṇaṁ gaccha	*18*	*62*	*9*	*351*
tasmācchāstraṁ pramāṇaṁ te	*16*	*24*	*8*	*219*
tasmāt praṇamya praṇidhāya	*11*	*44*	*7*	*89*
tasmāt tvam indriyāṇyādau	*03*	*41*	*3*	*239*
tasmāt tvam uttiṣṭha	*11*	*33*	*7*	*64*
tasmāt sarveṣu kāleṣu	*08*	*07*	*6*	*40*
tasmād asaktaḥ satatam	*03*	*19*	*3*	*115*
tasmādajñānasambhūtam	*04*	*42*	*4*	*284*
tasmād omityudāhṛtya	*17*	*24*	*8*	*280*
tasmād yasya mahābāho	*02*	*68*	*2*	*376*
tasmānnārhā vayaṁ hantum	*01*	*37*	*1*	*227*

Text	Chapter	Verse	Vol	Page
tasya sañjanayan harṣam	*01*	*12*	*1*	*195*
taṁ vidyād duḥkhasaṁyogam	*06*	*23*	*5*	*128*
taṁ tathā kṛpayāviṣṭam	*02*	*01*	*2*	*1*
tānahaṁ dviṣataḥ krūrān	*16*	*19*	*8*	*205*
tāni sarvāṇi saṁyamya	*02*	*61*	*2*	*352*
tulyanindāstutirmaunī	*12*	*19*	*7*	*244*
tejaḥ kṣamā dhṛtiḥ śaucam	*16*	*03*	*8*	*148*
te taṁ bhuktvā svargalokaṁ	*09*	*21*	*6*	*249*
teṣāmahaṁ samuddhartā	*12*	*07*	*7*	*155*
teṣāmevānukampārtham	*10*	*11*	*6*	*361*
teṣāṁ jñānī nityayuktaḥ	*07*	*17*	*5*	*370*
teṣāṁ satatayuktānām	*10*	*10*	*6*	*358*
tyaktvā karmaphalāsaṅgam	*04*	*20*	*4*	*168*
tyājyaṁ doṣavad ityeke	*18*	*03*	*9*	*24*
tribhirguṇamayairbhāvaiḥ	*07*	*13*	*5*	*348*
trividhā bhavati śraddhā	*17*	*02*	*8*	*228*
trividhaṁ narakasyedam	*16*	*21*	*8*	*211*
traiguṇyaviṣyā vedāḥ	*02*	*45*	*2*	*229*
traividyā māṁ somapāḥ	*09*	*20*	*6*	*245*
tvam akṣaraṁ paramaṁ	*11*	*18*	*7*	*34*
tvam ādidevaḥ puruṣaḥ	*11*	*38*	*7*	*76*

Text	Chapter	Verse	Vol	Page
daṇḍo damayatām asmi	*10*	*38*	*6*	*426*
dambho darpo'bhimānaśca	*16*	*04*	*8*	*176*
daṁṣṭrākarālāni ca te mukhāni	*11*	*25*	*7*	*53*
dātavyam iti yaddānam	*17*	*20*	*8*	*271*
divi sūryasahasrasya	*11*	*12*	*7*	*25*
divyamālyāmbaradharam	*11*	*11*	*7*	*24*
duḥkham ityeva yatkarma	*18*	*08*	*9*	*35*
duḥkheṣvanudvignamanāḥ	*02*	*56*	*2*	*324*
dūreṇa hyavaraṁ karma	*02*	*49*	*2*	*287*
dṛṣṭvā tu pāṇḍavānīkam	*01*	*02*	*1*	*176*
dṛṣṭvedaṁ mānuṣaṁ rūpam	*11*	*51*	*7*	*101*
devadvijaguruprājñapūjanaṁ	*17*	*14*	*8*	*252*
devān bhāvayatānena	*03*	*11*	*3*	*76*
dehī nityam avadhyo'yam	*02*	*30*	*2*	*178*
dehino'smin yathā dehe	*02*	*13*	*2*	*62*
daivam evāpare yajñam	*04*	*25*	*4*	*208*
daivī hyeṣā guṇamayī	*07*	*14*	*5*	*351*
daivī sampadvimokṣāya	*16*	*05*	*8*	*180*
doṣairetaiḥ kulaghnānām	*01*	*43*	*1*	*238*
dyāvāpṛthivyoridam antaraṁ hi	*11*	*20*	*7*	*40*
dyūtaṁ chalayatām asmi	*10*	*36*	*6*	*422*

Text	Chapter	Verse	Vol	Page
dravyayajñāstapoyajñāḥ	04	28	4	217
drupado draupadeyāśca	01	18	1	201
droṇaṁ ca bhīṣmaṁ	11	34	7	67
dvāvimau puruṣau loke	15	16	8	122
dvau bhūtasargau loke'smin	16	06	8	182
dharmakṣetre kurukṣetre	01	01	1	151
dhūmo rātristathā kṛṣṇaḥ	08	25	6	105
dhūmenāvriyate vahniḥ	03	38	3	228
dhṛtyā yayā dhārayate	18	33	9	125
dhṛṣṭaketuścekitānaḥ	01	05	1	180
dhyānenātmani paśyanti	13	24	7	457
dhyāyato viṣayān puṁsaḥ	02	62	2	355
na kartṛtvaṁ na karmāṇi	05	14	4	348
na karmaṇāmanārambhāt	03	04	3	28
na kāṅkṣe vijayaṁ kṛṣṇa	01	32	1	218
na ca tasmānmanuṣyeṣu	18	69	9	562
na ca matsthāni bhūtāni	09	05	6	156
na ca māṁ tāni karmāṇi	09	09	6	180
na caitadvidmaḥ kataranno	02	06	2	19
na jāyate mriyate vā kadācit	02	20	2	115
na tadasti pṛthivyāṁ vā	18	40	9	143

Text	Chapter	Verse	Vol	Page
na tad bhāsayate sūryo	*15*	*06*	*8*	*88*
na tu māṁ śakyase draṣṭum	*11*	*08*	*7*	*21*
na tvevāhaṁ jātu nāsam	*02*	*12*	*2*	*57*
na dveṣṭyakuśalaṁ karma	*18*	*10*	*9*	*41*
na prahṛṣyet priyaṁ prāpya	*05*	*20*	*4*	*374*
na buddhibhedaṁ janayed	*03*	*26*	*3*	*146*
nabhaḥspṛśaṁ dīptam	*11*	*24*	*7*	*50*
namaḥ purastād atha pṛṣṭhataste	*11*	*40*	*7*	*81*
na māṁ duṣkṛtino mūḍhāḥ	*07*	*15*	*5*	*360*
na māṁ karmāṇi limpanti	*04*	*14*	*4*	*94*
na me pārthāsti kartavyam	*03*	*22*	*3*	*131*
na me viduḥ suragaṇāḥ	*10*	*02*	*6*	*320*
na rūpamasyeha tathopalabhyate	*15*	*03*	*8*	*74*
na vedayajñādhyayanaiḥ	*11*	*48*	*7*	*96*
naṣṭo mohaḥ smṛtirlabdhā	*18*	*73*	*9*	*571*
na hi kaścit kṣaṇamapi	*03*	*05*	*3*	*37*
na hi dehabhṛtā śakyam	*18*	*11*	*9*	*48*
na hi prapaśyāmi	*02*	*08*	*2*	*22*
na hi jñānena sadṛśam	*04*	*38*	*4*	*267*
nātyaśnatastu yogo'sti	*06*	*16*	*5*	*97*
nādatte kasyacit pāpam	*05*	*15*	*4*	*351*

Text	Chapter	Verse	Vol	Page
nānto'sti mama divyānām	10	40	6	429
nānyaṁ guṇebhyaḥ kartāram	14	19	8	38
nāsato vidyate bhāvo	02	16	2	71
nāsti buddhirayuktasya	02	66	2	370
nāhaṁ prakāśaḥ sarvasya	07	25	5	405
nāhaṁ vedairna tapasā	11	53	7	103
nimittani ca paśyāmi	01	31	1	217
niyatasya tu sannyāsaḥ	18	07	9	34
niyataṁ kuru karma tvam	03	08	3	50
niyataṁ saṅgarahitam	18	23	9	100
nirāśīryatacittātmā	04	21	4	175
nirmānamohā jitasaṅgadoṣāḥ	15	05	8	84
niścayaṁ śṛṇu me tatra	18	04	9	27
nihatya dhārtarāṣṭrān naḥ	01	36	1	223
nehābhikramanāśo'sti	02	40	2	207
naite sṛtī pārtha jānan	08	27	6	108
nainaṁ chindanti śastrāṇi	02	23	2	144
naiva kiñcitkaromīti	05	08	4	326
naiva tasya kṛtenārtho	03	18	3	110
pañcaitāni mahābāho	18	13	9	59
patraṁ puṣpaṁ phalaṁ toyam	09	26	6	269

Text	Chapter	Verse	Vol	Page
parastasmāt tu bhāvo'nyo	*08*	*20*	*6*	*87*
paraṁ brahma paraṁ dhāma	*10*	*12*	*6*	*370*
paraṁ bhūyaḥ pravakṣyāmi	*14*	*01*	*8*	*2*
paritrāṇāya sādhūnām	*04*	*08*	*4*	*45*
pavanaḥ pavatām asmi	*10*	*31*	*6*	*406*
paśya me pārtha rūpāṇi	*11*	*05*	*7*	*17*
paśyādityān vasūn rudrān	*11*	*06*	*7*	*18*
paśyāmi devāṁstava deva dehe	*11*	*15*	*7*	*28*
paśyaitāṁ pāṇḍuputrāṇām	*01*	*03*	*1*	*178*
pāñcajanyaṁ hṛṣīkeśaḥ	*01*	*15*	*1*	*198*
pārtha naiveha nāmutra	*06*	*40*	*5*	*243*
pitāsi lokasya carācarasya	*11*	*43*	*7*	*86*
pitāham asya jagato	*09*	*17*	*6*	*235*
puṇyo gandhaḥ pṛthivyāṁ ca	*07*	*09*	*5*	*334*
puruṣaḥ prakṛtistho hi	*13*	*21*	*7*	*445*
puruṣaḥ sa paraḥ pārtha	*08*	*22*	*6*	*96*
purodhasāṁ ca mukhyaṁ mām	*10*	*24*	*6*	*393*
pūrvābhyāsena tenaiva	*06*	*44*	*5*	*261*
pṛthaktvena tu yajjñānam	*18*	*21*	*9*	*93*
prakāśaṁ ca pravṛtiṁ ca	*14*	*22*	*8*	*44*
prakṛtiṁ puruṣaṁ caiva	*13*	*19*	*7*	*438*

Text	Chapter	Verse	Vol	Page
prakṛtiṁ svām avaṣṭabhya	09	08	6	174
prakṛteḥ kriyamāṇāni	03	27	3	150
prakṛterguṇasammūḍhāḥ	03	29	3	163
prakṛtyaiva ca karmāṇi	13	29	7	478
prajahāti yadā kāmān	02	55	2	313
prayatnād yatamānastu	06	45	5	263
prayāṇakāle manasācalena	08	10	6	56
pralapan visṛjan gṛhṇan	05	09	4	326
pravṛttiṁ ca nivṛttiṁ ca	16	07	8	184
pravṛttiṁ ca nivṛttiṁ ca	18	30	9	117
praśāntamanasaṁ hyenam	06	27	5	161
praśāntātmā vigatabhīḥ	06	14	5	77
prasāde sarvaduḥkhānām	02	65	2	367
prahlādaścāsmi daityānām	10	30	6	403
prāpya puṇyakṛtāṁ lokān	06	41	5	248
bandhurātmātmanastasya	06	06	5	25
balaṁ balavatāṁ cāhaṁ	07	11	5	339
bahirantaśca bhūtānām	13	15	7	425
bahūnāṁ janmanām ante	07	19	5	377
bahūni me vyatītāni	04	05	4	23
bāhyasparśeṣvasaktātmā	05	21	4	379

Text	Chapter	Verse	Vol	Page
bījaṁ māṁ sarvabhūtānām	*07*	*10*	*5*	*337*
buddhiyukto jahātīha	*02*	*50*	*2*	*290*
buddhirjñānam asammohaḥ	*10*	*04*	*6*	*333*
buddherbhedaṁ dhṛteścaiva	*18*	*29*	*9*	*116*
buddhyā viśuddhayā yukto	*18*	*51*	*9*	*303*
bṛhatsāma tathā sāmnām	*10*	*35*	*6*	*419*
brahmaṇo hi pratiṣṭhāham	*14*	*27*	*8*	*58*
brahmaṇyādhāya karmāṇi	*05*	*10*	*4*	*329*
brahmabhūtaḥ prasannātmā	*18*	*54*	*9*	*313*
brahmārpaṇaṁ brahma haviḥ	*04*	*24*	*4*	*193*
brāhmaṇakṣatriyaviśām	*18*	*41*	*9*	*146*
bhaktyā tvananyayā śakyaḥ	*11*	*54*	*7*	*104*
bhaktyā mām abhijānāti	*18*	*55*	*9*	*316*
bhayādraṇāduparatam	*02*	*35*	*2*	*191*
bhavān bhīṣmaśca karṇaśca	*01*	*08*	*1*	*188*
bhavāpyayau hi bhūtānām	*11*	*02*	*7*	*10*
bhīṣmadroṇapramukhataḥ	*01*	*25*	*1*	*209*
bhūtagrāmaḥ sa evāyam	*08*	*19*	*6*	*83*
bhūmirāpo'nalo vāyuḥ	*07*	*04*	*5*	*308*
bhūya eva mahābāho	*10*	*01*	*6*	*315*

Text	Chapter	Verse	Vol	Page
bhoktāraṁ yajñatapasām	05	29	4	413
bhogaiśvaryaprasaktānām	02	44	2	225
maccittaḥ sarvadurgāṇi	18	58	9	342
maccittā madgataprāṇāḥ	10	09	6	352
matkarmakṛt matparamo	11	55	7	108
mattaḥ parataraṁ nānyat	07	07	5	328
madanugrahāya paramam	11	01	7	8
manaḥprasādaḥ saumyatvam	17	16	8	258
manuṣyāṇāṁ sahasreṣu	07	03	5	301
manmanā bhava madbhakto	09	34	6	307
manmanā bhava madbhakto	18	65	9	362
manyase yadi tacchakyam	11	04	7	14
mama yonirmahadbrahma	14	03	8	8
mamaivāṁśo jīvaloke	15	07	8	91
mayā tatam idaṁ sarvam	09	04	6	147
mayādhyakṣeṇa prakṛtiḥ	09	10	6	183
mayā prasannena tavārjunedam	11	47	7	94
mayi cānanyayogena	13	10	7	392
mayi sarvāṇi karmāṇi	03	30	3	167
mayyāveśya mano ye mām	12	02	7	129
mayyāsaktamanāḥ pārtha	07	01	5	293

Text	Chapter	Verse	Vol	Page
mayyeva mana ādhatsva	12	08	7	171
maharṣayaḥ sapta pūrve	10	06	6	345
maharṣīṇāṁ bhṛguraham	10	25	6	394
mahātmānastu māṁ pārtha	09	13	6	216
mahābhūtānyahaṅkāro	13	05	7	351
mā te vyathā mā ca vimūḍhabhāvo	11	49	7	98
mātrāsparśāstu kaunteya	02	14	2	65
mānāpamānayostulyastulyo	14	25	8	47
māmupetya punarjanma	08	15	6	69
māṁ ca yo'vyabhicāreṇa	14	26	8	56
māṁ hi pārtha vyapāśritya	09	32	6	302
muktasaṅgo'nahaṁvādī	18	26	9	106
mūḍhagrāheṇātmano yat	17	19	8	269
mṛtyuḥ sarvaharaścāham	10	34	6	415
moghāśā moghakarmāṇo	09	12	6	209
ya imaṁ paramaṁ guhyam	18	68	9	559
ya enaṁ vetti hantāram	02	19	2	110
ya evaṁ vetti puruṣam	13	23	7	451
yaccāpi sarvabhūtānām	10	39	6	428
yaccāvahāsārtham asatkṛto'si	11	42	7	83
yajante sāttvikā devān	17	04	8	232

Text	Chapter	Verse	Vol	Page
yajñadānatapaḥkarma	*18*	*05*	*9*	*30*
yajñaśiṣṭāmṛtabhujo	*04*	*31*	*4*	*227*
yajñaśiṣṭāśinaḥ santo	*03*	*13*	*3*	*83*
yajñārthāt karmaṇo'nyatra	*03*	*09*	*3*	*55*
yajñe tapasi dāne ca	*17*	*27*	*8*	*285*
yajjñātvā na punarmoham	*04*	*35*	*4*	*252*
yatato hyapi kaunteya	*02*	*60*	*2*	*349*
yatanto yoginaścainam	*15*	*11*	*8*	*104*
yataḥ pravṛttirbhūtānām	*18*	*46*	*9*	*173*
yatendriyamanobuddhiḥ	*05*	*28*	*4*	*409*
yato yato niścarati	*06*	*26*	*5*	*159*
yatkaroṣi yadaśnāsi	*09*	*27*	*6*	*279*
yattadagre viṣam iva	*18*	*37*	*9*	*133*
yattu kāmepsunā karma	*18*	*24*	*9*	*102*
yattu kṛtsnavad ekasmin	*18*	*22*	*9*	*95*
yattu pratyupakārārtham	*17*	*21*	*8*	*274*
yatra kāle tvanāvṛttim	*08*	*23*	*6*	*101*
yatra yogeśvaraḥ kṛṣṇo	*18*	*78*	*9*	*581*
yatroparamate cittam	*06*	*20*	*5*	*116*
yatsāṅkhyaiḥ prāpyate sthānam	*05*	*05*	*4*	*317*
yathākāśasthito nityam	*09*	*06*	*6*	*163*

Text	Chapter	Verse	Vol	Page
yathā dīpo nivātastho	*06*	*19*	*5*	*112*
yathā nadīnāṁ bahavo'mbuvegāḥ	*11*	*28*	*7*	*57*
yathā prakāśayatyekaḥ	*13*	*33*	*7*	*489*
yathā pradīptaṁ jvalanaṁ	*11*	*29*	*7*	*58*
yathā sarvagataṁ saukṣmyād	*13*	*32*	*7*	*488*
yathaidhāṁsi samiddho'gniḥ	*04*	*37*	*4*	*264*
yadagre cānubandhe ca	*18*	*39*	*9*	*141*
yadahaṅkāram āśritya	*18*	*59*	*9*	*344*
yadakṣaraṁ vedavido vadanti	*08*	*11*	*6*	*58*
yadā te mohakalilam	*02*	*52*	*2*	*299*
yadādityagataṁ tejo	*15*	*12*	*8*	*110*
yadā bhūtapṛthagbhāvam	*13*	*30*	*7*	*480*
yadā yadā hi dharmasya	*04*	*07*	*4*	*38*
yadā viniyataṁ cittam	*06*	*18*	*5*	*107*
yadā sattve pravṛddhe tu	*14*	*14*	*8*	*30*
yadā saṁharate cāyaṁ	*02*	*58*	*2*	*335*
yadā hi nendriyārtheṣu	*06*	*04*	*5*	*16*
yadi mām apratikāram	*01*	*46*	*1*	*245*
yadi hyahaṁ na varteyam	*03*	*23*	*3*	*135*
yadṛcchayā copapannam	*02*	*32*	*2*	*184*
yadṛcchālābhasantuṣṭo	*04*	*22*	*4*	*182*

Text	Chapter	Verse	Vol	Page
yadyad ācarati śreṣṭhaḥ	*03*	*21*	*3*	*128*
yadyadvibhūtimatsattvam	*10*	*41*	*6*	*432*
yadyapyete na paśyanti	*01*	*38*	*1*	*228*
yayā tu dharmakāmārthān	*18*	*34*	*9*	*128*
yayā dharmam adharmaṁ ca	*18*	*31*	*9*	*122*
yayā svapnaṁ bhayaṁ śokam	*18*	*35*	*9*	*130*
yastvātmaratireva syād	*03*	*17*	*3*	*104*
yastvindriyāṇi manasā	*03*	*07*	*3*	*44*
yasmāt kṣaram atīto'ham	*15*	*18*	*8*	*129*
yasmānnodvijate loko	*12*	*15*	*7*	*228*
yasya nāhaṅkṛto bhāvo	*18*	*17*	*9*	*71*
yasya sarve samārambhāḥ	*04*	*19*	*4*	*152*
yaṁ yaṁ vāpi smaran bhāvam	*08*	*06*	*6*	*38*
yaṁ labdhvā cāparaṁ lābham	*06*	*22*	*5*	*128*
yaṁ sannyāsam iti prāhuḥ	*06*	*02*	*5*	*11*
yaṁ hi na vyathayantyete	*02*	*15*	*2*	*69*
yaḥ śāstravidhim utsṛjya	*16*	*23*	*8*	*216*
yaḥ sarvatrānabhisnehastattat	*02*	*57*	*2*	*332*
yātayāmaṁ gatarasam	*17*	*10*	*8*	*244*
yā niśā sarvabhūtānām	*02*	*69*	*2*	*378*
yānti devavratā devān	*09*	*25*	*6*	*265*

Text	Chapter	Verse	Vol	Page
yāmimāṁ puṣpitāṁ vācam	*02*	*42*	*2*	*220*
yāvat sañjāyate kiñcit	*13*	*26*	*7*	*467*
yāvadetān nirīkṣe'ham	*01*	*22*	*1*	*206*
yāvānartha udapāne	*02*	*46*	*2*	*235*
yuktaḥ karmaphalaṁ tyaktvā	*05*	*12*	*4*	*336*
yuktāhāravihārasya	*06*	*17*	*5*	*100*
yuñjannevaṁ sadātmānam	*06*	*15*	*5*	*91*
yuñjannevaṁ sadātmānam	*06*	*28*	*5*	*164*
yudhāmanyuśca vikrāntaḥ	*01*	*06*	*1*	*180*
ye caiva sātvikā bhāvāḥ	*07*	*12*	*5*	*342*
ye tu dharmyāmṛtam idam	*12*	*20*	*7*	*249*
ye tu sarvāṇi karmāṇi	*12*	*06*	*7*	*155*
ye tvakṣaram anirdeśyam	*12*	*03*	*7*	*131*
ye tvetad abhyasūyanto	*03*	*32*	*3*	*186*
ye'pyanyadevatā bhaktāḥ	*09*	*23*	*6*	*262*
ye me matam idaṁ nityam	*03*	*31*	*3*	*172*
ye yathā māṁ prapadyante	*04*	*11*	*4*	*62*
ye śāstravidhim utsṛjya	*17*	*01*	*8*	*225*
yeṣām arthe kaṅkṣitaṁ no	*01*	*33*	*1*	*219*
yeṣāṁ tvantagataṁ pāpam	*07*	*28*	*5*	*426*
ye hi saṁsparśajā bhogāḥ	*05*	*22*	*4*	*385*

Text	Chapter	Verse	Vol	Page
yogayukto viśuddhātmā	*05*	*07*	*4*	*323*
yogasannyastakarmāṇam	*04*	*41*	*4*	*279*
yogasthaḥ kuru karmāṇi	*02*	*48*	*2*	*261*
yogīnām api sarveṣām	*06*	*47*	*5*	*270*
yogī yuñjīta satatam	*06*	*10*	*5*	*60*
yotsyamānān avekṣe'ham	*01*	*23*	*1*	*208*
yo na hṛṣyati na dveṣṭi	*12*	*17*	*7*	*239*
yo'ntaḥ sukho'ntarārāmaḥ	*05*	*24*	*4*	*399*
yo mām ajam anādiṁ ca	*10*	*03*	*6*	*329*
yo mām evam asammūḍho	*15*	*19*	*8*	*131*
yo māṁ paśyati sarvatra	*06*	*30*	*5*	*185*
yo yo yāṁ yāṁ tanuṁ bhaktaḥ	*07*	*21*	*5*	*385*
yo'yaṁ yogastvayā proktaḥ	*06*	*33*	*5*	*205*
rajastamaścābhibhūya	*04*	*10*	*8*	*25*
rajasi pralayaṁ gatvā	*04*	*15*	*8*	*31*
rajo rāgātmakaṁ viddhi	*04*	*07*	*8*	*19*
raso'ham apsu kaunteya	*07*	*08*	*5*	*332*
rāgadveṣaviyuktaistu	*02*	*64*	*2*	*363*
rāgī karmaphalaprepsuḥ	*18*	*27*	*9*	*111*
rājan saṁsṛtya saṁsṛtya	*18*	*76*	*9*	*579*
rājavidya rājaguhyaṁ	*09*	*02*	*6*	*122*

Text	Chapter	Verse	Vol	Page
rudrāṇāṁ śaṅkaraścāsmi	*10*	*23*	*6*	*391*
rudrādiyā vasavo ye ca sādhyāḥ	*11*	*22*	*7*	*45*
rūpaṁ mahatte bahuvaktranetram	*11*	*23*	*7*	*47*
labhante brahmanirvāṇam	*05*	*25*	*4*	*403*
lelihyase grasamānaḥ samantāt	*11*	*30*	*7*	*59*
loke'smin dvividhā niṣṭhā	*03*	*03*	*3*	*15*
lobhaḥ pravṛttirārambhaḥ	*14*	*12*	*8*	*27*
vaktum arhasyaśeṣeṇa	*10*	*16*	*6*	*376*
vaktrāṇi te tvaramāṇā viśanti	*11*	*27*	*7*	*54*
vāyuryamo'gnirvaruṇaḥ śaśāṅkaḥ	*11*	*39*	*7*	*79*
vāsāṁsi jīrṇāni yathā vihāya	*02*	*22*	*2*	*136*
vidyāvinayasampanne	*05*	*18*	*4*	*361*
vidhihīnam asṛṣṭānnam	*17*	*13*	*8*	*250*
viviktasevī laghvāśī	*18*	*52*	*9*	*303*
viṣayā vinivartante	*02*	*59*	*2*	*340*
viṣayendriyasaṁyogād	*18*	*38*	*9*	*138*
vistareṇātmano yogam	*10*	*18*	*6*	*380*
vihāya kāmānyaḥ sarvān	*02*	*71*	*2*	*404*
vītarāgabhayakrodhāḥ	*04*	*10*	*4*	*54*
vṛṣṇīnāṁ vāsudevo'smi	*10*	*37*	*6*	*424*
vedānāṁ sāmavedo'smi	*10*	*22*	*6*	*387*

Text	Chapter	Verse	Vol	Page
vedāvināśinaṁ nityam	02	21	2	124
vedāhaṁ samatītāni	07	26	5	415
vedeṣu yajñeṣu tapaḥsu caiva	08	08	6	109
vyavasāyātmikā buddhirekeha	02	41	2	211
vyāmiśreṇeva vākyena	03	02	3	8
vyāsaprasādācchrutavān	18	75	9	577
śaknotīhaiva yaḥ soḍhum	05	23	4	390
śanaiḥ śanairuparamet	06	25	5	146
śamo damastapaḥ śaucam	18	42	9	150
śarīraṁ yadavāpnoti	15	08	8	98
śarīravāṅmanobhiryat	18	15	9	66
śuklakṛṣṇe gatī hyete	08	06	6	107
śucau deśe pratiṣṭhāpya	06	11	5	67
śubhāśubhaphalairevam	09	28	6	284
śauryaṁ tejo dhṛtirdākṣyam	18	43	9	163
śraddhayā parayā taptam	07	17	8	265
śraddhāvanan asūyaśca	18	71	9	566
śraddhāvān labhate jñānam	04	39	4	270
śrutivipratipannā te	02	53	2	303
śreyān dravyamayād yajñāt	04	33	4	239
śreyān svadharmo viguṇaḥ	03	35	3	302

Text	Chapter	Verse	Vol	Page
śreyān svadharmo viguṇaḥ	*18*	*47*	*9*	*188*
śreyo hi jñānam abhyāsāt	*02*	*12*	*7*	*194*
śrotrādīnīndriyāṇyanye	*04*	*26*	*4*	*212*
śrotraṁ cakṣuḥ sparśanaṁ ca	*05*	*09*	*8*	*100*
śvaśurān suhṛdaścaiva	*01*	*27*	*1*	*211*
sa evāyaṁ mayā te'dya	*04*	*03*	*4*	*7*
saktāḥ karmaṇyavidvāṁso	*03*	*25*	*3*	*140*
sakheti matvā prasabhaṁ	*01*	*41*	*7*	*83*
sa ghoṣo dhārtarāṣṭrāṇām	*01*	*19*	*1*	*203*
satataṁ kīrtayanto mām	*09*	*14*	*6*	*220*
sa tayā śraddhayā yuktaḥ	*07*	*22*	*5*	*387*
satkāramānapūjārtham	*17*	*18*	*8*	*266*
sattvaṁ rajastama iti	*14*	*05*	*8*	*12*
sattvaṁ sukhe sañjayati	*14*	*09*	*8*	*23*
sattvāt sañjāyate jñānam	*14*	*17*	*8*	*34*
sattvānurūpā sarvasya	*17*	*03*	*8*	*230*
sadṛśaṁ ceṣṭate svasyāḥ	*03*	*33*	*3*	*193*
sadbhāve sādhubhāve	*17*	*26*	*8*	*284*
samaduḥkhasukhaḥ svasthaḥ	*14*	*24*	*8*	*47*
samaṁ kāyaśirogrīvam	*06*	*13*	*5*	*77*
samaṁ paśyanhi sarvatra	*13*	*28*	*7*	*475*

Text	Chapter	Verse	Vol	Page
samaṁ sarveṣu bhūteṣu	*13*	*27*	*7*	*472*
samaḥ śatrau ca mitre ca	*12*	*18*	*7*	*242*
samo'haṁ sarvabhūteṣu	*09*	*29*	*6*	*291*
sargāṇām ādirantaśca	*10*	*32*	*6*	*408*
sarvakarmāṇi manasā	*05*	*13*	*4*	*343*
sarvakarmāṇyapi sadā	*18*	*56*	*9*	*333*
sarvaguhyatamaṁ bhūyaḥ	*18*	*64*	*9*	*359*
sarvataḥ pāṇipādaṁ tat	*13*	*13*	*7*	*410*
sarvadvārāṇi saṁyamya	*08*	*12*	*6*	*63*
sarvadvāreṣu dehe'smin	*14*	*11*	*8*	*26*
sarvadharmān parityajya	*18*	*66*	*9*	*369*
sarvabhūtastham ātmānam	*06*	*29*	*5*	*174*
sarvabhūtasthitaṁ yo mām	*06*	*31*	*5*	*190*
sarvabhūtāni kaunteya	*09*	*07*	*6*	*165*
sarvabhūteṣu yenaikam	*18*	*20*	*9*	*90*
sarvam etad ṛtaṁ manye	*10*	*14*	*6*	*374*
sarvayoniṣu kaunteya	*14*	*04*	*8*	*11*
sarvasya cāhaṁ hṛdi	*15*	*15*	*8*	*115*
sarvāṇīndriyakarmāṇi	*04*	*27*	*4*	*216*
sarvendriyaguṇābhāsam	*13*	*14*	*7*	*417*
sahajaṁ karma kaunteya	*18*	*48*	*9*	*202*

Text	Chapter	Verse	Vol	Page
sahayajñāḥ prajāḥ sṛṣṭvā	*03*	*10*	*3*	*70*
sahasrayugaparyantam	*08*	*17*	*6*	*75*
saṅkaro narakāyaiva	*01*	*42*	*1*	*236*
saṅkalpaprabhavān kāmān	*06*	*24*	*5*	*146*
santuṣṭaḥ satataṁ yogī	*12*	*14*	*7*	*219*
sanniyamyendriyagrāmam	*12*	*04*	*7*	*131*
sannyāsastu mahābāho	*05*	*06*	*4*	*320*
sanyāsasya mahābāho	*18*	*01*	*9*	*9*
sannyāsaṁ karmaṇāṁ kṛṣṇa	*05*	*01*	*4*	*297*
sannyāsaḥ karmayogaśca	*05*	*02*	*4*	*300*
sādhibhūtādhidaivaṁ mām	*07*	*30*	*5*	*438*
sāṅkhyayogau pṛthagbālāḥ	*05*	*04*	*4*	*313*
siddhiṁ prāpto yathā brahma	*18*	*50*	*9*	*250*
sīdanti mama gātrāṇi	*01*	*29*	*1*	*214*
sukhaduḥkhe same kṛtvā	*02*	*38*	*2*	*197*
sukham ātyantikaṁ yattat	*06*	*21*	*5*	*117*
sukhaṁ tvidānīṁ trividham	*18*	*36*	*9*	*133*
sudurdarśam idaṁ rūpam	*11*	*52*	*7*	*102*
suhṛnmitrāryudāsīnamadhyastha	*06*	*09*	*5*	*47*
sthāne hṛṣīkeśa tava prakīrtyā	*11*	*36*	*7*	*72*
sthitaprajñasya kā bhāṣā	*02*	*54*	*2*	*308*

Text	Chapter	Verse	Vol	Page
sparśān kṛtvā bahirbāhyān	*05*	*27*	*4*	*409*
svadharmam api cāvekṣya	*02*	*31*	*2*	*181*
svabhāvajena kaunteya	*18*	*60*	*9*	*346*
svayam evātmanātmānam	*10*	*15*	*6*	*375*
sve sve karmaṇyabhirataḥ	*18*	*45*	*9*	*170*
hato vā prāpsyasi svargam	*02*	*37*	*2*	*195*
hanta te kathayiṣyāmi	*10*	*19*	*6*	*382*
hṛṣīkeśaṁ tadā vākyam	*01*	*21*	*1*	*204*

Books by Swami Dayananda Saraswati

Public Talk Series :

1. Living Intelligently
2. Successful Living
3. Need for Cognitive Change
4. Discovering Love
5. The Value of Values
6. Vedic View and Way of Life

Upaniṣad Series :

7. Muṇḍakopaniṣad
8. Kenopaniṣad

Prakaraṇa Series :

9. Tattvabodhaḥ

Text Translation Series :

10. Śrīmad Bhagavad Gītā
    (Text with roman transliteration and English translation)
11. Śrī Rudram
    (Text in Sanskrit with transliteration, word-to-word and verse meaning along with an elaborate commentary in English)

Stotra Series :

12. Dīpārādhanā
13. Prayer Guide
    (With explanations of several Mantras, Stotras, Kirtans and Religious Festivals)

Moments with Oneself Series :

14. Freedom from Helplessness
15. Living versus Getting On
16. Insights
17. Action and Reaction
18. Fundamental Problem
19. Problem is You, Solution is You
20. Purpose of Prayer
21. Vedanta 24x7
22. Freedom
23. Crisis Management
24. Surrender and Freedom
25. The Need for Personal Reorganisation
26. Freedom in Relationship
27. Stress-free Living
28. Om Namo Bhagavate Vāsudevāya
29. Yoga of Objectivity

Bhagavad Gītā

30. Bhagavad Gītā Home Study Course
    (Hardbound - 9 Volumes)

Meditation Series :

31. Morning Meditation Prayers
32. What is Meditation?

Essays :

33. Do all Religions have the same goal?
34. Conversion is Violence
35. Gurupūrṇimā
36. Dānam
37. Japa
38. Can We?
39. Moments with Krishna
40. Teaching Tradition of Advaita Vedanta
41. Compositions of Swami Dayananda Saraswati

Exploring Vedanta Series : (*vākyavicāra*)

42. śraddhā bhakti dhyāna yogād avaihi ātmānaṁ ced vijānīyāt

Books translated in other languages and in English based on Swami Dayananda Saraswati's Original Exposition

Tamil

43. Veeduthorum Gitopadesam (9 Volumes)
    (Bhagavad Gītā Home Study Course)
44. Dānam

Kannada

45. Mane maneyalli Adhyayana (7 Volumes)
    (Bhagavad Gītā Home Study Course)
46. Vedanta Pravesike

Malayalam

47. Muṇḍakopaniṣad

Hindi

48. Ghar baithe Gītā Vivecan (Vol 1)
    (Bhagavad Gītā Home Study Course)
49. Antardṛṣṭi (Insights)
50. Vedanta 24X7
51. Kriya aur Pratikriya (Action and Reaction)

English

52. The Jungian Myth and Advaita Vedanta
53. The Vedantic Self and the Jungian Psyche
54. Salutations to Rudra
55. Without a Second

Biography

56. Swami Dayananda Saraswati
    Contributions & Writings
    (Smt. Sheela Balalji)

Distributed in India & worldwide by
Motilal Banarsidass - New Delhi
Tel : 011 - 2385 8335 / 2385 1985 / 2385 2747

Also available at :

ARSHA VIDYA RESEARCH AND PUBLICATION TRUST 32 / 4 Sir Desika Road Mylapore Chennai 600 004 Telefax : 044 - 2499 7131 Email : avrandpt@gmail.com Website : www.avrpt.com	ARSHA VIDYA GURUKULAM Anaikatti P.O. Coimbatore 641 108 Ph : 0422 - 2657001 Fax : 0422 - 2657002 Email : office@arshavidya.in Website : www.arshavidya.in
ARSHA VIDYA GURUKULAM P.O.Box 1059. Pennsylvania PA 18353, USA Ph : 001-570-992-2339 Email : avp@epix.net Website : www.arshavidya.org	SWAMI DAYANANDA ASHRAM Purani Jhadi, P.B.No. 30 Rishikesh, Uttaranchal 249 201 Telefax : 0135 - 2430769 Email : ashrambookstore@yahoo.com Website : www.dayananda.org

Other leading Book Stores:

Chennai:	**044**
Motilal Banarsidass	24982315
Giri Trading	2495 1966
Higginbothams	2851 3519
Pustak Bharati	2461 1345
Theosophical Publishing House	2446 6613 / 2491 1338
The Odessey	43910300
Bengaluru:	**080**
Gangarams	2558 1617 / 2558 1618
Sapna Book House	4011 4455 / 4045 5999
Strand Bookstall	2558 2222, 25580000
Vedanta Book House	2650 7590
Coimbatore:	**0422**
Guru Smruti	948677 3793
Giri Trading	2541523

Trivandrum:	**0471**
Prabhus Bookhouse	2478 397 / 2473 496
Kozhikode:	**0495**
Ganga Bookhouse	6521262
Mumbai:	**022**
Chetana Bookhouse	2285 1243 / 2285 3412
Strand Bookstall	2266 1994 / 2266 1719/ 2261 4613
Giri Trading	2414 3140

Printed in France by Amazon
Brétigny-sur-Orge, FR

15412407R00286